D1715762

Population and Social Organization

World Anthropology

General Editor

SOL TAX

Patrons

CLAUDE LÉVI-STRAUSS
MARGARET MEAD
LAILA SHUKRY EL HAMAMSY
M. N. SRINIVAS

MOUTON PUBLISHERS · THE HAGUE · PARIS
DISTRIBUTED IN THE USA AND CANADA BY ALDINE, CHICAGO

Population and Social Organization

Editor

MONI NAG

MOUTON PUBLISHERS · THE HAGUE · PARIS

DISTRIBUTED IN THE USA AND CANADA BY ALDINE, CHICAGO

General Editor's Preface

Kinship and family studies are among the very oldest in the anthropological tradition; species fertility is usually considered subject matter related to human biology and evolution. But we have come only lately to questions which have put family and fertility studies together, while resisting treating fertility as a national or international "problem." This book, called forth in part by the World Population Conference in Bucharest in 1974, and especially for the IXth International Congress of Anthropological and Ethnological Sciences, treats the relationship between demographic and social organization variables cross-culturally. It suggests why anthropologists trust individual families — when circumstances permit them adequate freedom and opportunities — to make decisions on child-bearing which are advantageous to them and also turn out to suit the collective good. Here is certainly the richest body of data on these subjects to date, from which readers can draw their own conclusions.

Like most contemporary sciences, anthropology is a product of the European tradition. Some argue that it is a product of colonialism, with one small and self-interested part of the species dominating the study of the whole. If we are to understand the species, our science needs substantial input from scholars who represent a variety of the world's cultures. It was a deliberate purpose of the IXth International Congress of Anthropological and Ethnological Sciences to provide impetus in this direction. The *World Anthropology* volumes, therefore, offer a first glimpse of a human science in which members from all societies have played an active role. Each of the books is designed to be self-contained; each is an attempt to update its particular sector of scientific knowledge and is written by specialists from all parts of the world. Each volume should be read and reviewed individually as a separate volume on its own given subject. The set as a whole will indicate what changes are in store for anthropology as scholars from the developing countries join in studying the species of which we are all a part.

The IXth Congress was planned from the beginning not only to include as many of the scholars from every part of the world as possible, but also with a view toward the eventual publication of the papers in high-quality volumes. At previous Congresses scholars were invited to bring papers which were then read out loud. They were necessarily limited in length; many were only summarized; there was little time for discussion; and the sparse discussion could only be in one language. The IXth Congress was an experiment aimed at changing this. Papers were written with the intention of exchanging them before the Congress, particularly in extensive pre-Congress sessions; they were not intended to be read aloud at the Congress, that time being devoted to discussions — discussions which were simultaneously and professionally translated into five languages. The method for eliciting the papers was structured to make as representative a sample as was allowable when scholarly creativity — hence self-selection — was critically important. Scholars were asked both to propose papers of their own and to suggest topics for sessions of the Congress which they might edit into volumes. All were then informed of the suggestions and encouraged to re-think their own papers and the topics. The process, therefore, was a continuous one of feedback and exchange and it has continued to be so even after the Congress. The some two thousand papers comprising *World Anthropology* certainly then offer a substantial sample of world anthropology. It has been said that anthropology is at a turning point; if this is so, these volumes will be the historical direction-markers.

As might have been foreseen in the first post-colonial generation, the large majority of the Congress papers (82 percent) are the work of scholars identified with the industrialized world which fathered our traditional dicipline and the institution of the Congress itself: Eastern Europe (15 percent); Western Europe (16 percent); North America (47 percent); Japan, South Africa, Australia, and New Zealand (4 percent). Only 18 percent of the papers are from developing areas: Africa (4 percent); Asia-Oceania (9 percent); Latin American (5 percent). Aside from the substantial representation from the U.S.S.R. and the nations of Eastern Europe, a significant difference between this corpus of written material and that of other Congresses is the addition of the large proportion of contributions from Africa, Asia, and Latin America. "Only 18 percent" is two to four times as great a proportion as that of other Congresses; moreover, 18 percent of 2,000 papers is 360 papers, 10 times the number of "Third World" papers presented at previous Congresses. In fact, these 360 papers are more than the total of ALL papers published after the last International Congress of Anthropological and Ethnological Sciences which was held in the United States (Philadelphia, 1956). Even in the beautifully organized Tokyo Congress in 1968 less than a third as many members from developing nations, including those of Asia, participated.

The significance of the increase is not simply quantitative. The input of scholars from areas which have until recently been no more than subject matter for anthropology represents both feedback and also long-awaited theoretical contributions from the perspectives of very different cultural, social, and historical traditions. Many who attended the IXth Congress were convinced that anthropology would not be the same in the future. The fact that the next Congress (India, 1978) will be our first in the "Third World" may be symbolic of the change. Meanwhile, sober consideration of the present set of books will show how much, and just where and how, our discipline is being revolutionized.

The present book, and its companion volume, *Population, ecology, and social evolution,* edited by Steven Polgar, profited from a conference held in Oshkosh, Wisconsin, immediately before the Congress. Here scholars gathered from every continent to discuss the issues and to prepare their presentation to the Congress. Here also they took decisions which led to participation of anthropologists in the United Nations Population Conference in Bucharest a year later. Besides Dr. Polgar's companion volume there are in the whole *World Anthropology* series at least a dozen other books dealing with related questions of migration, reproduction, competition for resources, war, etc., as seen by anthropologists.

Chicago, Illinois   SOL TAX
July 11, 1975

Table of Contents

Introduction

MONI NAG

The articles published in this volume were prepared for the session on Population and Social Organization of the IXth International Congress of Anthropological and Ethnological Sciences held in Chicago during August and September of 1973. These articles were discussed in the Chicago session as well as in a pre-Congress seminar held at Oshkosh. The Center for the Study of Man (Smithsonian Institution) took the financial and administrative responsibility of bringing the participants together. Most of the authors were present both at Oshkosh and in Chicago.

The discussions at the Oshkosh seminar and the Chicago session were centered on the articles. They are not presented separately in this volume. Some of the authors have, however, made changes in their works as a result of the discussions.

Most of the articles were volunteered for the Congress prior to the decision to hold a session on Population and Social Organization. An interest in fertility and kinship was evident in the volunteered works. Although the subsequent invitees were informed of the broader title of Population and Social Organization, their contributions also reflect a similar interest. There is hardly any discussion of mortality, and there are only two articles on migration, one of which deals with the relationship between urbanization and fertility. The current interest of anthropologists in kinship and fertility is perhaps an indication of their readiness to deal with one of the most crucial problems of the contemporary world — the population problem. The articles, however, indicate that they are not preoccupied with family planning or fertility regulation.

The articles in this volume can be categorized under three broad headings: (1) Kinship, Marriage and Fertility, (2) Population Policy and Family Planning, and (3) Migration. I have elsewhere indicated the contributions already made and yet to be made by anthropologists in other aspects of the interrelationship between population and social organization (Nag 1973). It may be useful to give here very brief introductions to the individual articles included in this volume.

Marriage and Kinship in Relation to Human Fertility,
   by Moni Nag

The use of contraceptives, age at marriage, and practice of induced abortion are some of the very important variables which directly affect human fertility. These are, however, influenced considerably by sociocultural variables which include the institutions of marriage and kinship. Using primarily data regarding nonindustrial societies, my article examines the effects of the following aspects of marriage and kinship on fertility: forms of marriage (monogamy-polygamy), types of marriage (union), types of family, and types of descent groups.

Age Differential, Martial Instability, and Venereal Disease:
Factors Affecting Fertility among the Northwest Barma,
   by S. P. Reyna

Reyna draws attention to the "recruiting" function of marriage in addition to the "organizing" function which has been the focus of interest among a wide variety of anthropological theorists. The data he collected in 1970 among the western, southcentral Chad show that the two marriage-associated factors, namely age-differential between spouses and marital instability, are correlated with high female infertility and low fertility. The ethnographic evidence indicates that both these factors contribute towards the spread of venereal disease.

*Cultural Factors Inhibiting Population Growth among the Kafa of South-
western Ethiopia,*
    by Amnon Orent

Drawing upon field data collected in 1966–1967 Orent identifies a
few sociocultural factors which have affected the population size and
fertility level among the Kafa tribe of Ethiopia. The population size
is estimated to have declined from over 1,000,000 to 500,000 by
1897 and to about 230,000 in 1967. Orent thinks that the decline is
due to both high infant mortality and relatively low fertility. He
provides some quantitative data from his sample to support his contention. The ethnographic data collected by him indicate that the
following sociocultural factors may have contributed mainly to a
fertility level lower than its maximum biological potential: abstinence
due to various reasons, high rates of divorce, and polygyny.

*Some Aspects of Socioeconomic Change and Fertility Control among the
Emerging Elite of the Pathans,*
    by Karam Elahi

It is known that the highly educated professional class living in urban
areas of developing countries in Asia have fertility values similar to
those in developed countries. There are, perhaps, significant differences in this respect among developing countries in Asia, Africa, and
Latin America. In order to explain these differences it is necessary to
understand the social processes and factors which are related to the
change in fertility values and actual fertility levels as well as the
modernization process. Elahi analyzes these processes and factors for
the Pathan, an ethnic group of Pakistan to which he himself belongs.
He illuminates the demographic and historical data with anthropological insights regarding the effects of techno-environmental changes on family structure, marriage, and value systems.

The Economic Importance of Children in a Javanese Village,
    by Benjamin White

Anthropological literature is full of casual remarks about the contribution of children to the household economy of peasant societies.
A few ethnographies give some details about the nature of work done

by male and female children of different age groups. But quantitative estimates of the value of work done by children relative to their cost are almost absent from the literature, although economists have formulated elegant theories of fertility on the basis of questionable assumptions regarding the economic value and cost of children. In his article White questions the assumption that a reduction in fertility would constitute an economic benefit to parents in the overpopulated and impoverished peasant communities. His interviews and daily observations of children's productive activities in a Javanese village, although for a very brief period, enable him to support his viewpoint with quantitative data hitherto unavailable in any literature.

Factors Underlying Endogamous Group Size, by John W. Adams and Alice Bee Kasakoff

It has been a long time since the concepts of endogamy and exogamy have figured prominently in anthropological theories, but the article by Adams and Kasakoff shows the weaknesses of these concepts for quantitative use. It presents data from a preliminary sample of societies showing the effects of propinquity and population density on the sizes of groups of varying degrees of endogamy. The relevant conceptual problems are identified, facilitating the collection of useful empirical data.

Birth Planning: Between Neglect and Coercion, by Steven Polgar

Polgar tries to answer the question of why the population control and family planning programs got such astonishingly strong national and international support during the last decade. Citing historical evidence of the last two centuries from Britain and the United States, he argues that family planning by itself is neither a progressive nor a reactionary ideal. In order to evaluate it one has to look at the sociopolitical context in which it is pursued. It may be stimulated by the ideals of humanitarianism, liberalism, secularism, and utilitarianism. But it may also be a handmaiden of repressive and exploitative forces. The history of population control, according to Polgar, is more closely tied to repression than to liberation. He analyzes the circumstances under which the family planning movement brought together some strange bedfellows, such as the neo-Malthusian reactionaries and the feminist liberals, the neo-colonialists and the humanitarians.

Legislation Influencing Feritility in Czechoslovakia, by Olga Vidaláková

Almost all societies have laws which, although not intended to affect population characteristics and components, may nevertheless do so. Analysis of existing legislative provisions from this point of view is essential for the formulation of any population policy. Vidláková analyzes the Czechoslovakian laws regarding marriage, divorce, abortion, employment of women, and a few aspects of social welfare in terms of their possible effects on fertility.

The Marinal Family in Chile: Social Change and Woman's Contraceptive Behavior by Gerardo González-Cortés and Margarita María Errázuriz

Despite a large number of empirical studies in recent years, the relationship between the roles of women and their reproductive behavior is still not clearly understood. It has been demonstrated that the roles of women in a society may undergo considerable changes under the influence of changing political strategies. González and Errázuriz discuss on a theoretical level these complex relationships with reference to the strategies which three political parties applied to the marginal groups in Greater Santiago, Chile. Their analysis is based mainly on the results of a survey undertaken in 1966–1967 and on the official documents of the three political parties.

Kinship, Contraception, and Family Planning in the Iranian City of Isfahan, by John Gulick and Margaret E. Gulick

The limitations of the so-called KAP (Knowledge, Attitude, and Practice) studies in family planning are well-known. The need for more in-depth studies has been emphasized by many. The article by Gulick and Gulick illustrates very well what anthropologists can do in this respect. The statistical results and case histories provided by them from their intensive investigations among 175 working-class families in the city of Isfahan (Iran) illuminate the effect of some crucial variables related to fertility behavior and attitude (e.g. kinship, age at marriage, use of contraceptives, clinic treatment) more than the data that would be obtained through the usual questionnaire interviews.

Mass Acceptance of Vasectomy:
The Role of Social Interaction and Incentives in Social Change,
  by D. C. Dubey and A. Bardhan

The large-scale acceptance of modern fertility regulation methods is an aspect of social change which has not drawn adequate attention from the social scientists as yet. The sterilization program in India is a good example. In India more than 13,000,000 persons (mostly males) accepted sterilization during the period 1956–1973. Many of these were performed in "vasectomy camps" which were set up with widespread publicity. The success of these camps raised many questions of sociological importance. In order to answer these questions Dubey and Bardhan observed the behavior of acceptors, administrators, local leaders, and "motivators" in a few camps and interviewed a sample of them in depth. The findings presented in their article help us to understand the process of change in attitudes and values regarding fertility regulation.

Families to the City:
A Study of Changing Values, Fertility, and Socioeconomic Status among
Urban In-migrants,
  by Susan C. Scrimshaw

The process of urbanization has been of great interest to social scientists, particularly after World War II, but we still do not know much about the effects of urbanization on the fertility behavior of urban in-migrants. Scrimshaw asks the question: Do the urban in-migrants contribute more children to the next generation than their urban-born neighbors? She finds a negative answer from the data collected by her about the migrants from rural areas to Guayaquil in Ecuador. Besides presenting quantitative data, she examines the values involved in the relatively lower urban fertility and the process of acquiring these values. The combination of intensive anthropological investigation with a questionnaire survey obtained through interviews of a large sample contributes to a better understanding of fertility behavior than what could be gained by any one method.

Residential Patterns and Population Movement into the Farmlands of Yorubaland,
    by Philip O. Olusanya

The nature of migration from one rural area of a country to another is different from that of rural-urban migration and is perhaps a characteristic feature more of Africa than anywhere else. Olusanya describes such a migration in Nigeria with reference to the economic and social situation existing in the area of destination as well as the area of origin of the migrants. Although he uses the interview-survey data obtained from a sample of 853 households, his analysis rests heavily on information collected through anthropological techniques.

REFERENCES

NAG, MONI
    1973   "Population anthropology: problems and perspectives," in *Explorations in anthropology: readings in culture, man, nature.* Edited by Morton H. Fried, 254–273. New York: Thomas Y. Crowell.

PART ONE

Kinship, Marriage, and Fertility

Marriage and Kinship in Relation to Human Fertility

MONI NAG

PURPOSE AND SCOPE

Marriage and kinship constitute an area of human social organization to which cultural anthropologists have traditionally devoted their maximum attention. Another area of interest to them has been sexual behavior and attitudes (Ford and Beach 1951). But surprisingly little attempt has been made by cultural anthropologists to relate these areas to human reproductive behavior, particularly fertility. Perhaps this is due mainly to their general lack of sophistication in the techniques of population studies and a lack of interest in collecting and analyzing data in quantitative terms. Recently I have shown that it is possible for anthropologists to collect quantitative data on sex and reproduction which are necessary for a meaningful analysis of the relationship between sexual practices and fertility (Nag 1972).

Sexual behavior and attitudes are more directly related to fertility than are marriage and kinship. In their attempt to set forth an analytical framework for studying the relationship between social structure and fertility, Davis and Blake (1956) have identified eleven intermediate variables through which, and only through which, ANY cultural factor can affect fertility. Of these variables six affect exposure to sexual intercourse (e.g. age of entry into sexual union, voluntary abstinence, and coital frequency). The fertility level of a society is determined by the interactional effects of all the intermediate variables, which are influenced in varying degrees by social and cultural institutions. Our main concern here is to study cross-culturally the effects of a few aspects of marriage and kinship institutions on fertility through their influence on the intermediate variables. We shall focus primarily on nonindustrial societies in which modern contraceptives are not widely used.

One specific aspect of marriage that has been discussed by some anthropologists in relation to fertility is its form. The commonly distinguished forms of marriage are monogamy, polygyny, and polyandry. The societies in which polyandry is an ideal or approved form of marriage are rare in the contemporary world (Berreman 1962). In my cross-cultural study of nonindustrial societies, I found only two such societies, Toda and Jaunsari, for which some fertility data are available. Both are in India and had low fertility at the time of investigation. In both these societies fraternal polyandry combined with polygyny was practiced and the proportion of sterile women was quite high (Nag 1962: 92, 209). It was found, however, that there was no significant difference between the fertility levels of polyandrously married and nonpolyandrously married women of these two societies (Sen 1956: 66–7). Due to the paucity of relevant knowledge concerning polyandry, our discussion of the relationship between forms of marriage and fertility will be confined to polygyny and monogamy only.

There are differences of opinion among social scientists as to what a universally valid definition of marriage should be, a few even suggesting that it is not possible to find such a definition (Gough 1971: 365, 374–5; Leach 1971; 153–4; Marshall 1968: 10). In view of these differences, some have preferred the term "union" to denote relationships between a woman and a man which may or may not be legally/socially recognized as marriage, although the children born out of such relationships have full social recognition. The types of union generally distinguish the varying degrees of stability and recognition of the union. The most commonly used terms for them, particularly in the relevant literature for the Caribbean societies, are (1) visiting union, (2) common-law or consensual union, and (3) legal union (Roberts and Braithwaite 1960; Blake 1961: 249–50; Nag 1971: 113). We shall discuss the relationship between types of union and fertility.

Family is a kinship institution universally present in human societies, and reproduction occurs in the context of family. Societies vary in their dominant ideal regarding the type or composition of family. Also, for the same society at different times the dominant ideal may vary. The commonly distinguished types of family are: nuclear, stem, and extended. A number of variations can, however, be found within each type. One source of variation is the form of marriage. Each of the above three types may be present in societies with monogamy, polygyny, or polyandry as the ideal or approved form of marriage. In my discussion of the relationship between family type and fertility, I shall exclude the variations caused by polygyny and polyandry. My primary concern will be with nuclear and extended types of family, since very little relevant literature is available on the stem family. Besides reviewing the existing literature, I propose to analyse the relationship between family type and fertility, taking societies as units.

Another aspect of kinship institution that has been considered by some authors as having some effect on societal fertility level is the nature of the kin group larger than the family, particularly in relation to their linearity of descent and corporateness. Lorimer (1954) has provided a number of illustrations to show that the societies emphasizing corporate unilineal kinship groups tend to generate strong cultural motives for high fertility. The hypothesis has not been tested so far with cross-cultural data. I shall make an attempt to test a similar hypothesis stated in slightly different terms.

POLYGYNY AND MONOGAMY IN RELATION TO FERTILITY

The task of categorizing a society as polygynous is beset with several problems. Two of them are (1) a discrepancy between ideal and actual practice and (2) difficulty in setting up quantitative criteria regarding the incidence and intensity of polygyny. It is, therefore, extremely difficult to find out the distribution of the different forms of marriage in different regions or societies of the world, contemporary or past. Anthropological literature suggests, however, that most of the world's societies are characterized by a mixture of monogamy and polygyny, and that polygyny is more prevalent in Africa than in other regions of the world. Clignet (1971: 163) finds from an examination of the Human Relations Area Files that approximately three-fourths of the African societies included in the Files are characterized by general polygyny. My own calculations based on a random sample of 286 societies from Murdock's Enthnographic Atlas (Murdock 1967) show the following distribution of "Independent Polygynous" families in different regions of the world:
Africa: 38.5 percent
Circum-Mediterranean: 10 percent

East Eurasia: 0.0 percent
Insular Pacific: 7.7 percent
North America: 6.7 percent
South America: 10.9 percent

These figures are based on societies among which the extended family is NOT the "prevailing" type. Polygyny is practiced in some societies that have extended family as the "prevailing" type. The above estimates are useful to some extent for comparative purposes, but extreme care should be taken in interpreting them because of their serious limitations.

Sex-Ratio

There are examples in the anthropological literature of societies in which the prevalence of wide-scale polygyny is reported to be made possible through a great disparity between the relative numbers of men and women. The situation existing among the Baganda of East Africa during the early part of this century is often cited as an illustration. According to Roscoe (1965: 97), the Baganda women outnumbered the men by three to one as a result of the following customs and circumstances among others: (1) great numbers of men were killed in the annual wars the Baganda conducted with their neighbors; (2) men, never women, were required to be sacrificed in great numbers to the gods at appropriate ceremonies; and (3) large numbers of women were taken as booty in war expeditions. However, Roscoe's estimate of sex-ratio was based on what the Baganda people told him and was not quite reliable. Contemporary data on the population of African countries indicate a roughly equal sex-ratio (Clignet 1971: 171).

It has been found that the incidence of polygyny cannot be explained in terms of a higher proportion of females at birth or a higher proportion of females in the total population (Dorjahn 1954: 268; Lévi-Strauss 1968: 135). But a difference in the age-pattern of marriage between men and women may be a favorable condition for polygyny even when the sex-ratio is roughly equal. If men marry later than women on the average, which usually is the case in polygynous societies, there is a surplus of marriageable young women. It is estimated that if all men become eligible for marriage at twenty-two years but all women at sixteen years of age in a population with an exactly balanced sex-ratio at each age, and if one-fourth of all persons aged sixteen years and over are under twenty-two years of age, there would be four marriageable women for each three marriageable men (Lorimer 1954: 100). In some societies, however, the problem arising out of such a surplus is somewhat mitigated by a customary ban on remarriage of widows without a corresponding ban on remarriage of widowers.

Fertility

It is quite common to come across the view implying that polygyny tends to increase the fertility level or population size of a society. One of the reasons why the prophet Mohammed is reported to have approved polygyny is that he emphasized fertility and the expansion of Islamic societies (Lorimer 1954: 186–7). Recently the Government of Tunisia passed legislation abolishing polygyny, as one of the measures of controlling excessive population growth (United Nations 1968: 21). It is quite likely that the average number of children born to polygynously married men in a society is higher than that of children born to monogamously married men. It is also quite likely that in societies characterized by an excess of marriageable females over marriageable males (through differential mortality, emigration of males, military conquest, or a large sex differential in age at first marriage in a rapidly growing population) the potential loss of fertility is mitigated by polygyny (Munson and Bumpass 1973: 8; Lorimer 1954: 99). But the two important questions concerning the relationship between polygyny and fertility are (1) how to determine whether or not the population growth or fertility level of polygynous SOCIETIES is higher than that of monogamous SOCIETIES and (2) how to determine whether or not the polygynously married WOMEN in any society have higher fertility than monogamously married WOMEN in that society.

Almost all studies done so far represent an attempt to answer the second question and of these, all were done in African societies. One of the earliest studies, conducted in Ulanga of Tanganyika, found no relation between polygyny and fertility (Culwick and Culwick 1938, 1939). A similar conclusion was drawn from an investigation carried out among Gold Coast women in 1952 (Busia 1954: 347). A few official reports based on "sampling" investigations in the Belgian Congo showed, in contrast, that women in polygynous households had lower fertility than those in monogamous households (Congo

Belge 1951). Brebant (1954) also showed that in various regions of the Belgian Congo the "effective fertility rate" was lower among polygynous women than among the monogamous women by 25–42 percent. However, most of the statistics on the subject were not trustworthy (Lorimer 1954: 98).

After making a comprehensive and careful survey of the relevant literature on African societies, and on the basis of his own field investigation among the Temne, Dorjahn (1958) concluded that polygyny has the effect of reducing fertility. This conclusion was not based on any statistical test of significance (Gibson 1959: 892–3; Dorjahn 1959: 893–5). The methods of classifying the women of a society into polygynous and monogamous and the measures of fertility level used in the various studies surveyed by Dorjahn were not uniform. Perhaps these nonuniformities did not invalidate comparisons of the two sections of the same society as much as the lack of any control by age groups of women in most of the studies. Dorjahn's own study among the Temne controlled the age groups of women.

There are two other studies that controlled the age groups of women and supported Dorjahn's conclusion. In a survey conducted among the Beduin of the Negeb (Southern Israel) in 1946, Musham (1956: 9–12) found that the number of children aged zero to four years per 1,000 women of all ages was 735.8 in polygynous marriages (considering only the first and second wives) as against 1,076.6 in monogamous marriages. A similar difference was found when women of each five-year age-group were compared separately. There was a possibility of response error in this survey because of the cultural fact that the childlessness of a Beduin man is considered a serious disgrace. In order to correct the error Musham compared the fertility of polygynous and monogamous women who at the time of the survey had at least one of their children, of any age, living with them. The finding was similar to the above. In another comparative study of Central Nigerian Delta (a part of Mali), Congo, and Guinea, it has been found that, in all three cases, the age-specific fertility rates of women in polygynous marriage are generally lower at all ages than those of women in monogamous marriage (Van de Walle 1965: 304).

A few recent studies conducted in African countries showed, however, that either there were no significant differences between the fertility levels of polygynously and monogamously married women or that the findings were inconclusive. In a sample survey conducted in the municipal area of Lagos, Nigeria in 1964, Ohadike (1968: 388–9) found that the polygynously married women had a slightly higher average number of live births than the monogamously married women. There were more polygynously married women in the upper age groups, and the observed difference in fertility was much less when age groups were controlled. Henin (1969: 184–5) in a survey carried out among the Baggara and Kawahla of Sudan during 1961–62 found that the polygynously married women of the three age groups twenty to twenty-nine, thirty to thirty-nine, forty to forty-nine years had a generally lower average number of live births than the monogamously married women, but he did not consider the evidence as conclusive since the data were not controlled for other variables, e.g. age at marriage and proportion of childless women. In a survey conducted recently in the rural and urban areas of Ghana no significant difference was found in fertility level between the polygynously and monogamously married women (Pool 1968: 249). Another survey conducted in the rural and urban areas of Nigeria during 1966–67 also shows that when the effect of differences in marriage duration between the polygynously and monogamously married women is removed, the observed difference in fertility levels between the two groups virtually disappears (Olusanya 1971: 169–76).

All the studies described above, whether or not they took account of the variations in age or duration of marriage, had one common drawback: the cumulative fertility levels of women married polygynously or monogamously at the time of investigation were compared. Since a woman currently married to a polygynous or monogamous husband might have gone through other forms of marriage during her reproductive period, the differential effect of polygyny on fertility should not be inferred from this type of comparison. The analysis of survey data collected in 1969 from the rural and urban areas of Upper Volta took account of this particular problem besides controlling for other variables (Munson and Bumpass 1973: 8–10). In this case, the cumulative fertility level for the following two groups of women were compared: (1) those who had always been in monogamous marriage, and (2) those who had been in a polygynous marriage at any time. The average number of live births was less for the second group when the comparison was controlled for age, length of exposure to the risk of pregnancy ("span of fertility"), and sociostructural variables (e.g. education and religion).

So far, there has been only one study relating polygyny and fertility which takes societies as units instead of comparing two different sections of women in the same society (Nag 1962: 92–97). The main problem in taking society as a unit is in categorizing it as monogamous or polygynous or finding a scale of polygyny into which it can be fitted. Ethnographers have often stated whether or not polygyny is an ideal, preferred, approved, or permissible form of marriage in the societies investigated by them. For the purpose of relating polygyny to fertility it is preferable to use the data regarding actual practice, if available, rather than the emic data. There are few ethnographers who have gone beyond stating something to the effect that the practice is rare, moderate, or widespread. Even those who have done so are not uniform in presenting their statistics. For example, some have given the percentage of the total number of women in the married state who are polygynously married; some have given the average number of wives per adult man or husband. In the cross-cultural study mentioned above I used mainly the former as a criterion. If 20 percent or more of the total number of women in the married state in a society were polygynous at the time of investigation, it was designated as high on the scale of polygyny; otherwise it was designated as low. No ratings on the polygyny scale could be made for sixteen of the total sample of sixty-one nonindustrial societies for which the fertility level was known. The statistical test of significance done on the basis of these data did not support the hypothesis that polygyny is associated with reduced fertility (Nag 1962: 197–8).

The relationship between polygyny and fertility works through one or more of the "intermediate variables" of Davis and Blake (1956). Dorjahn (1959: 110–2), has identified five such variables: frequency of coitus, divorce or separation, postpartum abstinence, difference of age between spouses, and sterility. The logic underlying the assumptions of the association of each of these five variables with polygyny has been discussed previously by me in the light of relevant information from nonindustrial societies (Nag 1962: 94–7). The available data do not support the hypothesis of positive association between the incidence of polygyny and the following three variables: divorce or separation, childlessness, and postpartum abstinence. The association with the other two variables could not be tested statistically. A large variation in the frequency of coitus experienced by women may affect their fertility (Nag 1972: 231–3). But Olusanya (1971: 175) contends that the frequency of coitus experienced by polygynously married women is hardly ever so low as to affect their fertility in a significant way. No definite conclusion can, however, be drawn without some empirical evidence of quantitative type.

The above review shows that there are contradictory and inconclusive results obtained from various studies relating polygyny and fertility. The study done in Upper Volta (Munson and Bumpass 1973) is perhaps the most well-designed and statistically sophisticated. It concludes that polygyny reduces fertility. A majority of the studies done so far tend to support this conclusion. Very little is understood about the mechanism through which the reduction occurs. There is evidence from a number of societies that childlessness can be a cause of polygyny. Thus, the form of marriage may not only affect fertility, it also can be affected by fertility.

TYPES OF UNION AND FERTILITY

Types of Union

As mentioned earlier, in some societies three types of union between a man and a woman are distinguished: (1) legal, (2) common-law or consensual, and (3) visiting. The first type, as its name indicates, has full legal sanction and is the only one recognized as marriage. While it is the desired goal for most people it is realized most commonly by upper class individuals and by others at relatively late stages of their lives. The average ages at legal union of women in Jamaica, Barbados, and Grenada were respectively 28.6, 27.1 and 28.7 (Roberts 1955a: 205). This form is the most stable type of union.

In the common-law union a woman and a man have a steady conjugal relationship and share a common household but are not legally married. One main reason why common-law union persists without being converted into legal union or marriage is the inability of the man or the couple to save sufficient money for a proper celebration of the marriage, or for buying a house.

The visiting type usually implies that a woman is visited by a man regularly or occasionally at her parental or own home and has a sexual relationship with him. There is an expectation, particularly on the part of women, that the visiting union will ultimately become a legal union, but very often it does not. Visiting unions are quite unstable. One main reason for this instability is the purely casual motive of the man in the formation of the union. Alternately, in some cases women prefer to maintain their "single" status rather than live in common-law union because of their high esteem of legal union and their view of common-law union as an advertisement of non-material sexuality (Blake 1961: 150). Children born in any union do not suffer from any social stigma, although they are categorized as illegitimate in census and other official records.

The above description of the pattern of union is applicable mostly to the Caribbean countries although the consensual type of union is found in varying degrees in many other countries of the world. It is quite common in a number of Latin American countries (Mortara 1963) and perhaps in some countries of Africa and Asia, for example, Ghana (Pool 1968: 245–51) and Sri Lanka (Leach 1971: 160). But no figures regarding the union status of women and men are available for any others except a few Caribbean countries. Since 1943 the censuses of the latter countries have been recording the union status of each individual, although not exactly by the types described above. The categories used vary for different countries and for different censuses. They are not effective in the complete identification of the visiting type of union. Some comparative data are available for the other two types. For example, a comparison of the 1946 and 1960 censuses of Barbados shows that the percentage of fifteen to forty-four year-old women who were in legal union or married changed from 31.9 in 1946 to 27.3 in 1960, and the figure for common-law union changed from 12.4 in 1946 to 13.6 in 1960 (Nag 1971: 115).

The explanations attempted so far for the origin and persistence of the pattern of union in Caribbean countries may be grouped into two categories (Otterbein 1965: 68–79): (1) historical explanations which trace the pattern to its origin in West Africa (Herskovits 1943: 396), Western Europe (Greenfield 1966: 165–74), or eighteenth-century slave plantations (King 1945: 100–104), and (2) functional explanations that emphasize either the lack of economic opportunity for men (Greenfield 1966: 166) or the incidence of male absenteeism (Roberts 1955a: 219). It should be noted that the East Indians (persons of Indian descent) do not generally follow the pattern of union described above.

Fertility

In the early 1950's there was a widely held view in some Caribbean countries that their characteristic pattern of conjugal union was responsible for a high fertility level. Because all children born outside the legal union were recorded as illegitimate, there was a high rate of illegitimacy in these countries. This led some to believe that the general acceptance of marriage or legal union by the common people would have a restraining effect on reproduction. Demographers, however, started making an analysis of the census and survey data relating types of union to fertility and found that, in general, the reverse might be true (Roberts 1955a: 217; Ibberson 1956: 93).

Most of the fertility analysis for the Caribbean countries has been based on the census data regarding the number of children born to women of completed fertility. However, the census categories of the status of union are NOT legal, common-law, and visiting. The fertility data have been presented mostly in terms of the following categories: ever-married (which includes women currently in legal union or married, widowed, and divorced), common-law, and single. The "single" category includes women who are in the visiting union status as well as those who are genuinely single and therefore not at the risk of child-bearing. Hence a comparison of the average number of children per mother rather than the average number of children per woman is more meaningful for our purpose. Such comparative data for five Caribbean countries (excluding East Indians) computed from the 1946 census (1943 for Jamaica) are presented in Table 1.

Table 1. Average number of children born per mother of age 45 years and over in a few Caribbean countries

Union Status	Barbados (1946)	British Honduras (1946)	Jamaica (1943)	Leewards (1946)	Windwards (1946)
Single	4.14	4.73	4.74	4.41	4.58
Common-law	4.43	5.41	5.60	5.35	5.64
Ever-married	5.61	6.38	6.64	6.38	6.82

Source: Roberts 1955b: 255.

It may be observed from the above table that the fertility gradation by union status is similar for all the countries. The completed fertility per mother is highest for the ever-married type and lowest for the single type in each country. This indicates a pattern of differential fertility among the women living in legal, common-law, and visiting union at age forty-five years and over. A similar gradation is found when the following two other measures are used: (1) average number of children born per woman of age forty-five years and over, and (2) total fertility rate computed from the age-specific fertility ratio of mothers (Roberts 1955a: 215, 225).

Not much fertility analysis by union type for Caribbean countries has been done from the data collected in the subsequent censuses. Cumper (1966: 189–201) did a comparative study of the fertility of Jamaican women in 1943 and 1960 by using "age-specific birthrate" which is based on both census data and birth registration data. He found a similar gradation as above for both years, but the proportion of women of each age group in the common-law union as well as their fertility increased between 1943 and 1960.

In a sample survey conducted in 1956 among the lower-class Jamaican women of age fourteen to forty years in any union type, it was found that within each age group those who were currently in legal union had the largest number of pregnancies, those in visiting union had the least and those in common-law union had an intermediate number (Stycos and Back 1964: 148). In another survey conducted recently among the rural and urban women of Ghana it was found that within each age group the average number of live births for women living in "mutual consent" union was less than that for women living in "customary" and "religious" types of union (Pool 1968: 242).

One main deficiency in all the above census and survey studies, in terms of relating union type and fertility, is that while the union types of women compared were those in which they were living at the time of investigation, the fertility measure used was of a cumulative nature. It is well-known that a woman may very often start childbearing when she is "single," or in visiting union, and then may go through common-law and/or legal union. Hence the cumulative fertility of a woman currently in legal union may include the children born to her when she was living in another type or types of union. There is no way to overcome this difficulty completely. In their sample survey conducted in 1958 among the non-East Indians of Trinidad, Roberts and Braithwaite (1960: 965–78) tried to get over this difficulty at least partially by comparing the completed fertility of women grouped according to fifteen different patterns of union. They used the following approaches among others to get over this difficulty: (1) comparison of women on the basis of their union type at the initial stage of their childbearing period, (2) comparison of women on the basis of their union type at the termination of their childbearing period, (3) comparison of women who remained continuously in one of the three union types from the beginning to the end of their childbearing period, and (4) comparison of women who were in the same type of union at the beginning and end of their childbearing period, whatever might have been the type of union in the intervening years. The approaches (1) and (3) above showed common-law union to be associated with the highest fertility, while the approaches (2) and (4) showed the legal union to be associated with the highest fertility. But all these approaches showed the visiting union to be associated with the lowest fertility.

The existence of fertility differential by union type needs some explanation. Roberts (1955a: 217) states that the women living predominantly in visiting union belong to lower socioeconomic status, and that the lower fertility among them seems to run counter to the widespread patern of an inverse relationship between fertility and socioeconomic status. He thinks that a lower degree of exposure to childbearing among them, due to the absence of male partners, is the most important causal factor, although a higher incidence of venereal disease and induced abortion may also be contributory factors. Primarily, in other words, the higher the instability of the union is, the lower the fertility level.

The relevance of the pattern of union in relation to fertility arises from the fact that for a considerable period of time between successive unions the women are not at all exposed to the risk of pregnancy and for some additional periods the risk of pregnancy is less than that in a stable legal or common-law union. In two intensive investigations among small samples of lower class women, one in Jamaica and another in Barbados, attempts have been made to estimate the proportion of nonunion time to union time they experienced. From the data regarding reproductive and union history of eighty Jamaican women Blake (1955: 27–8) found that the total nonunion time spent by the women was 27 percent of the total time spent within unions, and that the corresponding figure was 40 percent when women in multiple unions only were considered. Nag (1971: 118–9) found from similar data regarding 124 women of Barbados that the total nonunion time spent was 13.3 percent of the total time spent within unions and that the corresponding figure was 20.8 percent when women in multiple unions only were considered. The observed difference between Jamaica and Barbados may be partly due to the methodological difference in the calculation of nonunion time in the two investigations and partly due to the fact that the prevalence of common-law union is lower in Barbados than in Jamaica. It is quite possible that the women separated from common-law union find it more difficult than the women in visiting union and take a longer time to get themselves attached to a new partner (Nag 1971: 199–20).

The evidence regarding the loss of reproductive period of women as a result of the characteristic pattern of union in Caribbean countries has given rise to the view that the increased acceptance of legal union or marriage by lower class women of these countries would raise the fertility level of these countries (Ibberson 1956: 99). Blake

(1961: 249–50) estimated from her study in Jamaica that

> other things being equal, were lower-class Jamaican sexual associations relatively stable, the island's fertility would be significantly, even spectacularly, higher than it now is — probably over 30 percent higher.

The above observations are made on the assumption of a balanced sex-ratio in Caribbean countries. But these countries have been mostly experiencing an unbalanced sex-ratio for a long time. For example, the number of males per thousand females in Barbados has varied from 675 to 849 from 1844 to 1960 and the male deficit has always been much greater in the potentially reproductive ages. The imbalance of sex-ratio in Barbados and other Caribbean countries has been primarily due to sex-selective emigration (Roberts 1955b; Marino 1970: 163–5; Nag 1971: 122–3). If the women in these countries were not allowed to have any union except monogamous and stable legal union or marriage, then under the situation of persisting male deficit, a considerable number of them would have been compelled to remain outside marriage for a portion or the whole of their reproductive lives. In other words, a shift toward conjugal stability would result in a decrease in the total number of unions. It would lead to a loss of reproductive potential of the women. Whether or not this loss would be higher or lower than the loss of reproductive potential caused by the characteristic pattern of union in the Caribbean countries is a subject worthy of further serious study, perhaps of the simulation type.

The investigations carried out in Jamaica (Blake 1961: 153) and Barbados (Nag 1971: 120) indicated that the termination of the visiting union of a number of women was synchronous with the event of their being pregnant. Some of them reported that their "boy friends" emigrated after making them pregnant. These reports may be interpreted to imply that pregnancy or begetting of children tends to weaken a union by stimulating the males toward desertion. In a more extensive investigation in Jamaica, Stycos and Back (1964: 161) have, however, found the following: (1) fertile unions tend to become more stabilized rather than less; (2) people believe that pregnancies have a tendency to lead to stabilization; and (3) pregnancy is not a significant explicit reason for dissolution of unions. They have, therefore, concluded that "perhaps not only does a stable union encourage fertility, but also fertility encourages a stable union."

FAMILY TYPE AND FERTILITY

Dependence of parents on their children in their old age is a character-istic feature of the extended family system. Freedman (1968: 222) has provided a striking illustration of the close relationship in Japan between the expectation of the parents in this respect and fertility. The crude birth rate in Japan fell from 28 to 17 per 1,000 between 1950 and 1961. Every two years within this period the following question was asked of a representative cross-section of the population: "Do you expect to depend on your children in your old age?" In 1950 more than 55 percent answered "definitely yes." In 1961 only 27 percent gave this answer, the proportion declining steadily in the intervening period.

Theoretical Propositions

Such statistical data relating family type and fertility, directly or in-directly, are rare, although some theoretical formulations appeared in the 1950's. Lorimer (1954: 201) stated that "the whole cultural con-text in which extended families tend to be idealized is likely to be con-ducive to high fertility." He was, however, not very consistent or convinced of the relationship. Although in one place Lorimer assert-ed (1954: 201) that "the extended or joint family, or any close-knit group of families, provides strong economic and social support for parenthood," in another place he stated (1954: 247) that the cohe-sive groups, such as extended families "do not necessarily stimulate high fertility, if disassociated from emphasis on competitive relations or sacred values that require high fertility." In most agrarian cultures under premodern conditions, according to him, extended families have generally tended to promote high fertility.

  Davis (1955: 34–6) has identified the following characteristics of extended families which are conducive to high fertility: (1) the cost and burden of childrearing do not fall on parents alone; (2) the mar-riage occurs early and universally because the husband is not required to be able to support his wife and children and because there are social, moral, and religious reasons for which the parents want their children to be married early; (3) the young wife is motivated to have many offspring and early since they raise her status and provide an outlet for her affection; and (4) the young husband is also motivated to have many offspring early because they raise his status, and in a patrilineal society the sons perpetuate his line and provide security in old age.

Goode (1963: 240, 250) thinks that the nuclear family is not necessarily associated with low fertility. Its fertility level can be high or low, depending on the circumstances that shape the interests of the couple.

Empirical Research

The above propositions have stimulated a number of empirical studies relating family type and fertility. Except for one in Guatemala, all such studies have been conducted in three countries of Asia: India, Taiwan, and Bangladesh. A few of them are reviewed here as illustrations.

A sample survey conducted in 1956 among 600 rural and 500 urban (Calcutta) households of West Bengal (India) showed that of the four types of families the one-generational extended family complex had the lowest fertility level (Poti and Datta 1960: 60–61). The data collected in 1960–61 by Uma Guha from 3,725 ever-married women living in seven villages of West Bengal and belonging to six groups of Hindu and Muslim castes revealed that for each group the average number of live births in extended families was less than that in nuclear families when women in all age groups were compared (Nag 1967: 162–3). However, computation of the age-standardized rates from the same data reduced the differential for five groups and reversed it for one (Pakrasi and Malaker 1967: 455). About 47.3 percent of the women in the sample lived in extended families. A sample survey conducted in 1956–57 among 1,018 married couples in Calcutta showed that, in general, the women living in extended families had a lower average of live births than those in nuclear families when the averages were standardized for marriage duration and social class. The differential was reversed for the lowest class in two of the four marriage duration categories (Pakrasi and Malaker 1967). The percentage of women living in extended families varied from 47.2 to 64.5 in the three classes. A few other studies conducted in India showed that the women living in nuclear families had slightly lower average fertility than those living in extended families (cf. Bebarta 1964; Driver 1960; Rele 1963).

One study, however, conducted recently in twenty-seven villages of Maharashtra (India) showed the reverse (Karkal 1972). It was found from a sample of 1,982 women belonging to nuclear families and 1,213 women belonging to extended families that when the data were standardized for both the age at marriage and the duration of married life, the average number of live births for women living in a nuclear family was 4.24, while the corresponding figure for those living in an extended family was 4.43.

It was found in a survey conducted in 1967 among 2,008 currently married women of fifteen villages of Bangladesh that the total marital fertility of women living in nuclear families was 7.31, whereas the corresponding measure for women living in extended families was 6.88 (Stoeckel and Choudhury 1969: 192–8). About 19.7 percent of the women in the sample were living in extended families. Another survey conducted in the same area in 1968 among 1,600 currently married women showed that the mean desired family size of the women living in nuclear families was 3.8 compared to 3.6 for those living in extended families (Mosena and Stoeckel 1972).

The results obtained from two Taiwan surveys are somewhat different from those stated above for India and Bangladesh and also from each other. It was found in a survey conducted in Taichung City during 1962–3 that the average number of live births was less for women thirty-five to thirty-nine years old living in nuclear families than for those living in stem or extended families (Freedman, Takeshita, Sun 1964: 24). The differences were larger in the average number of desired children and in the use of fertility control, including abortion and sterilization. A stratified sample of 49,000 women between fifteen and forty-nine years drawn from the 1966 population register of Taiwan showed that the age-standardized average number of children under five years within each type of community of residence (city, urban township, and rural township) was lowest for women living in nuclear families, intermediate in stem families and highest in extended families (Liu 1967a). The pattern of differences was less clear and consistent when a cumulative fertility measure, namely, the age-standardized average number of children ever born to the women was used. The percentages of women living in extended, stem, and nuclear families were respectively 9.2, 29.6, and 61.2. The category "stem family" in the above Taiwan study implied a family composition that represented a nuclear family plus one or more parents on either the husband's or wife's side (Liu 1967b). In Indian and Bangladesh studies this category was generally considered an extended family.

The only study relating family type and fertility conducted outside Asia was based on a 5 percent sample of 1964 census returns of

Guatemala City (Gendell and Burch 1970). In this study the two following types of extended family were distinguished: (1) a vertically extended type containing a head and either a parent or parent-in-law of the head, or a grandchild of the head, or both, and (2) a horizontally extended type containing a head with or without spouse or companion and "other relatives" (largely collateral). It was found from a sample of 9,469 women fifteen years and over that the average number of children born was higher for women living in vertically extended families than those living in nuclear and horizontally extended families. Age-specific cumulative fertility ratios showed that the difference was clearly greatest for the age group forty-five years and over.

Inadequacy of the Empirical Studies

The studies described above are far from adequate in testing the theoretical propositions stated earlier. The reasons for the inadequacy have been discussed by Burch and Gendell (1970) with special reference to the studies conducted in India and Taiwan. Four of them are briefly stated in the following:

1. SAMPLE SIZE AND CONTROL   Most of the studies were based on inadequate sample size. When samples were broken down into categories of age, duration of marriage, class or caste, the number of women in some categories was too small for a statistical test of significance. In most studies relevant data pertaining to the above categories, which should be used as controls for a valid comparison of fertility level among family types, were not collected.

2. DEFINITION OF FAMILY TYPE   All the studies described above took common dwelling or kitchen as a criterion of family rather than kin interaction. This was necessary because the data regarding kin interaction were more difficult to obtain and also would be harder to organize in terms of suitable units. But identification of family types in terms of kin interaction may be very important in relation to fertility. In India, for example, brothers living in separate dwellings after the death of their father may maintain a very close relationship among themselves with mutual obligations toward each other's children. The operational definitions used for nuclear and extended families in the above studies vary considerably.

3. CUMULATIVE MEASURES OF FERTILITY   All the studies described above related the cumulative fertility of women to the type of

family they were living in at the time of investigation. Many of them perhaps gave birth to children when they were living in some other type of family. This problem, arising out of the static concept of family type, was somewhat taken care of in Liu's (1967a: 368) Taiwan study by comparing the age-standardized average number of children under five years. For a better analysis of family type and fertility, it is necessary to have data regarding the residential history of women along with their reproductive history.

4. LEVEL OF ANALYSIS The theoretical formulations relating family type and fertility have been based generally on aggregate level using societies as units of analysis. But the empirical studies described above use individual women as units of analysis. An association between family type and fertility at one level of analysis does not necessarily imply an association at another level.

Analysis at Societal Level

Freedman (1961–62: 51) as well as Burch and Gendell (1970: 232) have emphasized the need for studies of family type and fertility at the aggregate level of analysis, for it is only at that level that certain issues arise. It has been argued, for example, that in a society where the extended family is dominant (numerically or ideologically), the higher fertility level of nuclear families may result from their interactions with the extended families and be quite different from the situation in which nuclear families are dominant.

No published literature is available so far relating family type and fertility at an aggregate or societal level. One of the main difficulties in doing so lies in identifying a society with a particular type of family. It is well known that even when the extended type of family is considered as ideal, the majority of families at any particular point of time may not be of that type because of the development cycle through which each family passes. Hence the numerical predominance of the nuclear family in a society is not a sufficient condition for the society to be identified as nuclear family oriented. The determination of the dominant ideal regarding family type in a society needs quantitative data plus some ethnographic investigation regarding behavior, attitudes, and values.

Contemporary industrial societies have the nuclear family as the dominant ideal, and their fertility level is generally low. But this does not imply a causal relationship between the nuclear family and fertility because these societies seem to have had a nuclear family ideal and a relatively high fertility level for a long time before industrialization began (Laslett 1972: 8; Goode 1968: 321). It seems that the association, if any, between family type and fertility can be detected better by a comparative study of nonindustrial societies which are somewhat controlled in terms of modernization processes.

In my cross-cultural study of factors affecting fertility in nonindustrial societies, it was found that the fertility levels of sixty-one societies varied considerably (Nag 1962: 169–78). The associations between fertility levels, categorized as high and low, and the various "intermediate variables" of Davis and Blake (1956) were tested statistically. The association between family type and fertility was not tested. In order to test this association here, the ethnographic literature pertaining to all sixty-one societies has been searched to find the ideal type of family prevailing at the period roughly corresponding to that for which the fertility data are available. The societies with polygynous or polyandrous families as the dominant ideal types have been categorized as such without making any attempt to identify them with nuclear or extended types. Stem family has been considered as a part of the extended family type. It has been possible to identify the family type of forty-one societies out of sixty-one. These are presented in Appendix A along with the information on fertility level data and the presence or absence of a corporate unilinear kin group (discussed in the next section). The association between family type and fertility level in the selected sample of nonindustrial societies can be studied from Table 2.

Table 2. Association between family type and fertility level in selected nonindustrial societies

	Family type	Extended	Nuclear	Number of societies
Fertility level *	High	8	17	25
	Low	4	12	16
		12	29	41

$i=d=8$, $x=b=4$, $y=13$, $a-d=4$, $z_1 > 17$
Not significant at 5 percent level
* Fertility level taken from Nag (1962: 176–177); both "very low" and "low" have been categorized as "low" here.

The association in the above and subsequent tables has been tested statistically by a method developed by Armsen (1955). It is claimed to be more sensitive than the chi-square test when the sample size is small. The data presented in the table, taking society as a unit, do not support the hypothesis that the extended family is associated with higher fertility when compared with the nuclear family. The hypothesis is also not supported by a statistical test of significance when the societies having a corporate unilineal kin group are separated from those without it. The results are similar to those found by Namboodiri (1967) except that he found a tendency toward higher fertility in societies with the extended family as the dominant ideal when only those having lineage organization were considered. Namboodiri used those societies from my sample of sixty-one for which kinship data were available in Murdock's (1962–66) Ethnographic Atlas. The kinship data used by Murdock do not correspond for all societies to the time period for which their fertility data are available.

The lack of a statistically significant association in the selected sample of nonindustrial societies should not be taken as convincing evidence for the rejection of the propositions of Lorimer and Davis regarding family type and fertility. The sample size is very small and the ethnographic data used are quite ambiguous, at least for some societies. Moreover, the effect of family type on fertility in any society may be offset by other factors. In order to test satisfactorily the isolated effect of family type on fertility, it is necessary to have adequate quantitative data on all other relevant factors for a reasonable number of societies with various types of family and fertility level. These are not available and are very difficult to obtain.

Intermediate Variables between Family Type and Fertility

In order to understand how family type may affect fertility, it seems worthwhile to discuss the relationship between family type and the following "intermediate variables": age at marriage, frequency of divorce or separation, proportion of widows not remarried, voluntary abstinence, involuntary abstinence, coital frequency, contraception, and other fertility control methods.

It has been stated above that Davis (1955: 34–6) identifies the early age at marriage as one important characteristic of the extended family system. Davis and Blake (1956: 215–8) have shown how a few characteristic features of the nuclear family system, such as the emphasis on marital rather than filial solidarity, which appear to have delayed marriage in Ireland and northwestern Europe, contrast sharply with the features that are related to early marriage in the extended family system. One relevant characteristic of societies emphasizing extended family is that the marriage of children is usually arranged by their parents. In these societies the parents may be eager to marry off their children quite early for several reasons (Davis 1955: 34–6; Nag 1962: 60). However, Davis-Blake (1967: 135–6) thinks that there is no empirical evidence to demonstrate that parental control over the marriage of children has been primarily associated with very early marriage.

In the cross-cultural study of nonindustrial societies (Nag 1962: 90) I did not find adequate evidence to support the hypothesis that the age at marriage of women is negatively associated with fertility. The association between family type and age at marriage in the same sample can be studied from Table 3.

Table 3. Association between family type and age at marriage of women in selected nonindustrial societies

		Age at marriage* High	Low	Number of societies
Family type	Nuclear	7	16	23
	Extended	3	8	11
		10	24	34

$i=d=7$, $x=b=3$, $y=13$, $a-d=1$, $z_1 > 18$
Not significant at 5 percent level
* Categorization of age at marriage as "high" and "low" taken from Nag (1962: 192–195).

The data presented in this table do not support the hypothesis that the nonindustrial societies with the extended family as a dominant ideal have a lower average age at marriage of women. The absence of statistically significant associations in both the tests may be due to the fact, among others, that the quantitative criterion of eighteen years and over for rating a society as high in the scale of age at marriage was not appropriate (Nag 1962: 89–90). A comparative study of average age at marriage around 1960 on a global scale shows that it tends to be lower in less industrialized countries (Dixon 1971: 216–18). These countries are known to have a higher level of fertility. It is also known that the extended family ideal has been more characteristic of these countries than of the industrial ones.

The relevance of nonmarriage or permanent celibacy to family type and fertility is similar to that of delayed marriage. Nonmarriage is expected to occur more in societies with the nuclear family as the dominant ideal for two reasons: (1) the rules of inheritance in these societies may make it very difficult for some individuals to make themselves economically eligible for marriage; and (2) marriage through courtship is more common than arranged marriage in these societies, and the possible competition for an attractive mate in the former may lead to nonmarriage for some. But nonmarriage or permanent celibacy in any society has never been as important a depressant of fertility as delayed marriage (Davis and Blake 1956: 222).

The frequency of divorce or separation is likely to be lower in a situation of arranged marriage compared to that of marriage through courtship for the following three reasons: (1) arranged marriage is very often associated with the payment of a dowry and "bride-price" which make divorce or separation difficult in various ways; (2) parents are more likely to make a better judgment when the marital partners are quite young; and (3) control by the kin group in the arrangement of marriage implies similar control over its dissolution. Because arranged marriage is more customary in societies characterized by the extended family the frequency of divorce or separation is likely to be less in these societies. Moreover, the nuclear family oriented societies may have a higher frequency of divorce or separation for another reason. Because marriage in these societies is often based on mutual attraction and dependence, the husband-wife relationship is expected to be very close and intensely emotional. Goode (1971: 374) thinks that this exclusive emotional dependence between husband and wife, without any recourse to dependency on a larger kin group, may lead to a high divorce or separation rate. However, he points out that in this situation generally the chances of remarriage are also high because there is no larger kin group to absorb the children or to prevent it. The association between family type and divorce or separation in my sample of nonindustrial societies can be tested from Table 4.

Table 4. Association between family type and frequency of divorce or separation in selected nonindustrial societies

		Frequency of divorce or separation*		Number of societies
		High	Low	
Family type	Nuclear	12	11	23
	Extended	2	8	10
		14	19	33

$i=d=8$ $x=b=2$, $y=9$, $a-d=4$, $Z_1=7$
Not significant at 5 percent level

* Categorization of the frequency of divorce or separation as "high" and "low" taken from Nag (1962: 200–202).

The data presented in this table do not support the hypothesis that the nonindustrial societies with extended family as the dominant ideal have a lower frequency of divorce or separation. The data from the same sample also do not support the hypothesis that divorce or separation is negatively associated with fertility, although they indicate a trend toward such an association (Nag 1962: 98).

Davis and Blake (1956: 226–7) argue that agrarian societies with the extended family as the dominant ideal exhibit a prejudice against widow remarriage for the following main reasons: (1) the custom of levirate, that is, the remarriage of a widow to her husband's brother or other close relative, would be structurally inappropriate, because the extended household is always subject to dissolution and the levirate marriage would increase the complications of such dissolution; (2) marriage in these societies is generally arranged by the kin of marital partners, and it is quite likely that neither the consanguineal nor the affinal kin of a widow would take interest in arranging her remarriage; and (3) remarriage of a widow outside the immediate kin of her husband would require her separation from them in a patrilineal society. There are, however, societies in which the extended family is a common feature, but the remarriage of widows is not only permitted but encouraged. For example, among the Tallensi of Africa levirate is usual, although the extended family seems to be the dominant ideal among them. Even old widows are sometimes married to their grandsons, as a matter of formality (Fortes 1949: 64, 239). The association between family type and the proportion of widows not remarried in my sample of nonindustrial societies can be tested from the data presented in Table 5.

The data in this table do not support the hypothesis that the non-

Table 5.   Association between family type and proportion of widows not remarried in selected nonindustrial societies

		Proportion of widows not remarried *		Number of societies
		High	Low	
Family type	Nuclear	3	22	25
	Extended	3	7	10
		6	29	35

$i=d=3$, $x=b=3$, $y=4$, $a-d=19$, $z_1 > 34$
Not significant at 5 percent level
* Categorization of the proportion of widows not remarried as "high" and "low" taken from Nag (1962: 204–206).

industrial societies with the extended family as a dominant ideal have
a higher proportion of nonremarried widows. Also, it was found that
there is no negative association between the proportion of nonremarried widows and fertility at a societal level (Nag 1962: 101). The lack
of a statistically significant association in cross-cultural tests should
not rule out the possibility of an effective relationship between family
type, widow remarriage, and fertility in any particular society. From
a study of the Indian census data 1901–41, Davis (1951: 80–2) concluded that the higher fertility level of the Muslims and Tribals in
India over the Hindus is due, in part, to their greater toleration of widow remarriage. However, a study conducted in 1960 among two Muslim groups and one Hindu group in rural West Bengal showed that
the average reproductive period lost per ever-married woman due to
widowhood was very small in all three groups and the variation
among the three groups was insignificant (Nag 1962: 54–55). But
the situation might have been different in earlier decades when the
mortality rate was much higher and women became widows at earlier
ages. The restrictions on the remarriage of widows have always been
observed more strictly in the higher castes of India among whom the
ideal of extended family is more prevalent. Social control is more effective among higher castes and in extended families. So the non-
remarriage of widows among Indian high castes may be an effective
mechanism through which the extended family system affects fertility negatively.

Davis and Blake (1956: 231–3) identify four types of voluntary
abstinence that may affect fertility: postpartum, occasional (including
ceremonial), gestational, and menstrual. Out of these, the postpartum
abstinence and occasional abstinence are likely to affect fertility negatively. In my cross-cultural study of nonindustrial societies, it has
been found that a long period of postpartum abstinence has a statistically significant negative association with fertility (Nag 1962: 79–
80). The association between family type and postpartum abstinence
in the same sample can be tested from the data presented in Table 6.
The data in this table do not support the hypothesis that the nonindustrial societies with the extended family as the dominant ideal
have longer periods of postpartum abstinence. This result comforms
with that of Saucier (1972: 246) obtained from Murdock's Ethnographic Atlas. It is, however, quite likely that the customary post-
partum or other types of abstinence, are observed more strictly in societies emphasizing the extended family than those emphasizing the
nuclear family. This may be true also at the family level within a so-

Table 6. Association between family type and period of post-partum abstinence in selected nonindustrial societies

		Period of post-partum abstinence*		Number of societies
		Long	Short	
Family type	Nuclear	6	16	22
	Extended	0	7	7
		6	23	29

$i=d=6$, $x=b=0$, $y=16$, a-d=1, $z_1=7$
Not significant at 5 percent level

* Ratings of the period of post-partum abstinence as "long" (more than one year) and "short" (one year or less) taken from Nag (1962: 78, 188–190).

ciety and explain partly the lower fertility level of women in extended families compared to those in nuclear families in the Indian studies described earlier.

One of the main causes of involuntary abstinence is the separation of couples due to migration which is not uncommon when plantation or mining is introduced, and the process of urbanization begins in a primitive or agrarian society. Under these circumstances, a man may stay away from his wife for long periods of time, thereby affecting her reproductive performance negatively. If he is a part of the extended family, his absence is less inconvenient to his wife and children than otherwise. In an agrarian society with increasing pressure of population on rural land resources, the patrilineal extended family encourages some of its male members to earn cash money in urban areas to supplement the family income. But very often it takes a long time, sometimes a few generations, for urban migrants to have sufficient income to enable them to bring their wives and children into urban areas. There are almost no quantitative data available regarding separation of couples due to migration and its relationship to fertility level or family type.

There are individual variations in the frequecy of coitus within a society and also perhaps societal variations (Nag 1962: 76). If these variations are large, fertility may be affected (Nag 1972: 231–3). There is no evidence to show that the frequency of coitus is associated with family type at the societal level. But it was found in the West Bengal rural study mentioned earlier that the average coital frequency for women living in nuclear families was consistently higher than that for those living in extended families. It was true not only when all groups and ages were considered together but also separately for almost every age category in each of the six Hindu and Muslim groups. The differences in average coital frequency were, however, not large enough to have any appreciable effect on fertility, but this cannot be ruled out as a possible factor responsible for lower fertility among the women living in extended families (Nag 1967: 161–3).

Very little is known about the relationship between family type and the use of contraceptives or other fertility control methods. It is generally assumed that in patrilineal societies, the mother-in-law and the old women of an extended family often have the power to decide whether a young couple may practice family limitation and that these elders often resist social change (United Nations 1971: 55). But the findings from a few studies conducted in India are not consistent. A fertility survey conducted in Bangalore city indicated that a slightly higher proportion of couples in nuclear families were practicing family limitation than those in extended families (United Nations 1961: 168). Bebarta (1967) found in a study of six villages near Delhi that the women of nuclear families exhibited a more favorable attitude toward family planning than those in extended families and that comparatively larger numbers of women in the former were aware of family planning. But with reference to a few villages in West Bengal, Mathen (1962: 43) states that the "force of the barrier against acceptance of family planning lessons due to the presence of mother or other relatives in the joint families was not so strong as supposed." It was found in a few other villages of West Bengal that the husband's indifference or opposition to family planning was a greater hindrance for a woman than her mother-in-law's.

It is generally considered shameful in agrarian societies, such as India and China, for the mother-in-law to bear children, particularly when she lives in the same household with her daughter-in-law. She is reported to practice abstinence or other fertility control methods.

In India the relative popularity of family limitation through sterilization in contrast to the spacing of children through contraceptive methods has been explained by Dubey (1967: 46–51) in terms of the prevalence of the extended family system. According to him, the couples living in extended families during the first stage of their family cycle do not have the motivation or decision-making authority for birth control. By the time they start living as a nuclear family they may find themselves burdened with too many children and would prefer a sure method such as sterilization.

The analysis of intermediate variables raises more questions about the relationship between family type and fertility than it answers. A few of these variables partly explain the findings in most Indian studies that the women living in extended families have slightly lower fertility than those living in nuclear families. But another possible explanation lies in the fact that fertility itself may affect the family type; that is, the dissolution and formation of families may depend on the number of children in them (Burch and Gendell 1970: 234). For example, Rele (1963: 197) suggests that in India the couples having a large number of children may live more frequently as nuclear families than those with fewer children.

CORPORATE DESCENT GROUP AND FERTILITY

In their study of kinship systems anthropologists have traditionally been more interested in the structure and function of descent groups rather than in those of family or household. There is sufficient evidence in the anthropological literature that the importance and corporateness of descent groups in nonindustrial societies may vary considerably. This variation may be in part a function of the ecological situation. Societies that need effective resistance against competition with others of the control of resources generally have a strong social organization emphasizing unilineal descent and corporate kin groups, such as clans and lineages. Lorimer (1954: 199–200) has hypothesized that such societies, whether patrilineal or matrilineal, tend to generate strong cultural motives for high fertility. According to him, the ego-group identification engendered by the corporate descent groups having common political and economic interests creates a strong sense of responsibility in individuals for childbearing and childrearing. He has provided a number of illustrative examples from anthropological literature in support of his hypothesis but has not attempted any statistical test to validate it.

Lorimer's hypothesis implies a comparison beween societies emphasizing corporate unilineal descent groups on the one hand with those emphasizing nonunilineal descent groups, and unilineal but noncorporate descent groups on the other. Since nonindustrial societies are more kinship oriented than industrial societies, a sample drawn exclusively from the former is appropriate for its valid testing. The main difficulty arises in getting adequate empirical data for such societies from which their motivation for children, actual fertility level, and nature of kin group can be assessed. I have categorized the societies used in my cross-cultural study of fertility (Nag 1962) as to the presence or absence of corporate unilineal groups. The categories are shown in Appendix A. The corporateness of the descent group has been assessed primarily on the basis of common economic and political interests of its members rather than on their cooperation in ritual affairs. Because the available literature is often incomplete or ambiguous, it has not been possible to avoid a certain amount of arbitrariness in deciding whether the corporate unilinear descent group was present or absent in a society at the time for which its fertility measure is available. The data regarding the nature of the descent group and fertility for fifty-nine nonindustrial societies are presented in Table 7 for a statistical test of association.

Table 7. Association between nature of descent group and fertility level in selected nonindustrial societies

		Corporate unilinear descent group		Number of societies
		Present	Absent	
Fertility level *	High	10	25	35
	Low	9	15	24
		19	40	59

$X^2 = 0.52$ Not significant at 5 percent level
Since $n > 50$ x^2 test is used (Fisher and Yates 1949, Table 4)
* Fertility level taken from Nag (1962: 176–177); both "very low" and "low" have been categorized as "low" here.

The data in this table do not support the hypothesis that the non-industrial societies with corporate unilinear descent groups have a higher fertility level than those without them. This finding, however, should not be interpreted as a direct repudiation of Lorimer's hypothesis which is stated in terms of motivation for fertility rather than actual fertility. It is not possible to assess the motivation for high or low fertility from the available literature. There may be societies with high motivation for children among their members which have quite low fertility levels. For example, among the Yakö, men desired a large number of children in order to strengthen their patrilineages which claimed collective rights to land (Forde 1941: 6), but the average number of children born to women of completed fertility was only 3.0 (Forde 1941: 96). The following factors may be responsible for the low fertility level of the Yakö: high frequency of divorce or separation (1941: 75); high incidence of polygyny (1941: 97); long period of postpartum abstinence (1941: 93).

The above illustration indicates that the high motivation for children in a society having a corporate unilineal descent group may not necessarily lead to an actual high fertility. Tables 8, 9, 10, and 11

Table 8.   Association between nature of descent group and age at marriage in selected nonindustrial societies

	Age at marriage*		Number of societies
	High	Low	
Corporate unilineal descent group — Present	0	17	17
Corporate unilineal descent group — Absent	11	18	29
	11	35	46

$i=d=1$, $x=b=0$, $y=18$, $a-d=6$, $z_1=0$, $z_3=2$
Significant at 1 percent level
*   Categorization of age at marriage as "high" and "low" taken from Nag (1962: 192–195).

Table 9.   Association between nature of descent group and frequency of divorce or separation in selected nonindustrial societies

	Frequency of divorce or separation*		Number of societies
	High	Low	
Corporate unilineal descent group — Present	10	4	14
Corporate unilineal descent group — Absent	11	18	29
	21	22	43

$i=d=10$, $x=b=4$, $y=7$, $a-d=8$, $z_1=8$
Significant at 5 percent level
*   Categorization of the frequency of divorce or separation as "high" and "low" taken from Nag (1962: 200–202).

Table 10.   Association between nature of descent group and proportion of widows not remarried in selected nonindustrial societies

	Proportion of widows not remarried *		Number of societies
	High	Low	
Corporate unilineal Descent group — Present	1	15	16
Corporate unilineal Descent group — Absent	6	27	33
	7	42	49

$i=d=6$, $x=b=1$, $y=26$, $a-d=9$, $z_1>18$
Not significant 5 percent level
*   Categorization of the proportion of widows not remarried as "high" and "low" taken from Nag (1962: 204–206).

Table 11.   Association between nature of descent group and period of post-partum abstinence in selected nonindustrial societies

		Period of post-partum abstinence*		Number of societies
		Long	Short	
Corporate unilineal descent group	Present	7	8	15
	Absent	5	21	26
		12	29	41

$i=d=7$, $x=b=5$, $y=3$, a-d$=14$, $z_1=17$
Not significant at 5 percent level
* Ratings of the period of post-partum abstinence as "long" (more than one year) and "short" (one year or less) taken from Nag (1962: 78, 188–190).

present data for testing the significance of the association between the nature of the descent group and the following four variables: age at marriage, frequency of divorce or separation, proportion of widows not remarried, and period of post-partum abstinence.

It can be observed from these tables that the presence of corporate unilineal descent groups is associated with low age at marriage and high frequency of divorce or separation. Both of these associations are statistically significant. The explanation attributed to the low age at marriage in societies emphasizing corporate unilineal descent groups is similar to that discussed earlier for societies emphasizing extended families. In fact, Lorimer (1954: 182) thinks that the principles of early and universal marriage in traditional agrarian societies of India and China

appear to be survivals, or culturally associated with survivals, from patrilineal lineage systems that had functional value in expanding tribal societies but do not have such functional value under the actual conditions of stable civilizations.

It is difficult to interpret the higher frequency of divorce or separation in societies emphasizing the corporate unilineal descent groups than that in societies not emphasizing them. There is, however, some evidence to support the hypothesis that the frequency of divorce is higher in societies with matrilineal descent compared to those with patrilineal descent (Lorimer 1954: 73–86). But it is not known whether or not the matrilineal descent groups tend to be more corporate in nature than the patrilineal descent groups. The statistically significant associations found in the data from the selected nonindustrial societies indicate the important mechanisms through which the nature of the descent group can affect the societal fertility level and should be considered as hypotheses for further empirical investigations rather than definitive conclusions.

Polgar (1973: 26) thinks that a high fertility may be a causal factor in the formation and persistence of corporate unilineal kin groups rather than the reverse, as hypothesized by Lorimer. According to him, the emergence of corporate lineage groups holding rights to productive resources is likely to have occurred during the period of rapid population growth (associated with transition to food production) when these groups had a high probability of surviving through time. It seems logical to speculate that there was a feedback relationship between the corporate unilineal kin group and high fertility.

CONCLUDING REMARKS

This article is an attempt to integrate the available anthropological, sociological, and demographic literature regarding the relationship between fertility and the following aspects of marriage and kinship, particularly in nonindustrial societies: polygyny and monogamy; types of union (legal, common-law, and visiting); family type (extended and nuclear); nature of descent group (corporate unilinear or not). There are two main difficulties in studying these relationships. First, there is a great deal of agreement on how to conceptualize and measure fertility but, in spite of anthropologists' long-standing interest in marriage and kinship, very little has been achieved so far in conceptualizing and measuring the important variables relevant to them. Second, the available fertility data for the nonindustrial societies which are of primary concern here are not satisfactory. However, a systematic review of the concepts, measures, and data related to marriage, kinship, and fertility is expected to be useful for various purposes.

The results obtained from various studies relating polygyny and fertility have been found to be contradictory and inconclusive. The relatively well-designed studies tend to indicate, however, that polygynously married women have lower fertility than monogamously married women. The mechanism through which polygyny can reduce fertility is very little understood.

There is a general agreement in the available literature regarding type of union and fertility. The visiting union is generally associated with the lowest fertility. In most cases, the fertility level associated with common-law union is lower than that associated with legal union or marriage. The differences can at least be partly explained by the variation in the proportion of nonunion time to union time experienced by women in different types of union. The relatively higher loss of reproductive period among the women in the visiting union would not necessarily mean than an increased acceptance of legal union by them would raise the societal fertility level. A shift towards conjugal stability, particularly in Caribbean societies, may result in a decrease in the total number of unions because of the large-scale emigration of males in these societies.

Contrary to some theoretical propositions, it was found in a number of studies in India and Bangladesh that the cumulative fertility of women living in extended families was somewhat lower than that of women living in nuclear families. In most cases there were inadequacies in conceptualization, sample size, and analysis. However, some explanations for the observed difference have been presented in terms of the effect of sexual behavior on fertility and the effect of fertility on family type. The results obtained from the studies in Taiwan **were less consistent. The** analysis of family type and fertility in all these studies was done at the individual level. This article presents some data on family type and fertility in a sample of nonindustrial societies, taking societies as units. The statistical tests based on these data do not support the hypothesis that the extended family is associated with higher fertility. The statistical tests also do not show any significant association between family type and the following "intermediate variables": age at marriage, frequency of divorce or separation, proportion of widows not remarried, and period of postpartum abstinence. The sample of nonindustrial societies was, however, very small and the data regarding them was not very satisfactory. It seems quite logical to assume that family type may affect fertility through its influence on some of the "intermediate variables," but the effects of these variables on fertility may not be in the same direction and sometimes offset one another.

There is a hypothesis that the societies emphasizing unilineal corporate descent groups tend to generate stronger cultural motives for high fertility than others. It is difficult to test this hypothesis because of the lack of empirical data and necessary methodology for measuring motivation for fertility. This article presents the data regarding actual fertility level and the nature of the descent group for fifty-nine nonindustrial societies. These data do not support the hypothesis that the societies emphasizing unilineal corporate descent groups have higher fertility than those without them. There are, however, some data to show that the emphasis on corporate unilineal descent groups is associated with low age at marriage and high frequency of divorce or separation. Since a low age at marriage is likely to have a positive effect on fertility, and high frequency of divorce or separation is likely to have a negative effect on fertility, the above associations indicate that the "intermediate variables" between the nature of descent groups and fertility may have opposing effects on the latter.

The conclusions made here are apparently based on data with serious limitations and should not be considered as anything more than suggested hypotheses. It is hoped that these will stimulate further refinement of concepts and collection of adequate data regarding marriage and kinship in relation to fertility.

APPENDIX: TABLE OF NONINDUSTRIAL SOCIETIES

Type of Family and Nature of Descent Group in the Nonindustrial Societies used by Nag (1962) for Cross-Cultural Study of Human Fertility
(Abbreviations used: H for high fertility; L for low fertility level; K for presence of corporate unilineal descent group; A for absence of corporate unilineal descent group; N for nuclear family; E for extended family; P for polygynous or polyandrous family)

Society	Fertility level	Nature of descent group	Family type	Reference
Alorese	H	K	N	Dubois 1944: 19, 20, 32
Apache	H	A	N	Opler 1941: 19, 24–25; Goodwin 1942: 168
Ashanti	H	K	P	Fortes 1954: 267–269, 287
Barbados	L	A	N	Nag 1971: 107
Bengali Hindu	H	A	E	Nag 1962: 48–61
Bengali Non-sheikh Muslim	L	A	E	Nag 1962: 48–61
Bengali Sheikh Muslim	H	A	E	Nag 1962: 48–61
Dinka	H	K	P	Roberts 1956: 323–330
Dusun	L	A	N	Glyn-Jones 1953: 1
Eskimo	H	A	N	Toshio Yatsushiro, personal communication
Fulani	H	K	N	Stenning 1959: 5, 38–41, 101
Ganda	L	A	N	Richards and Reining 1954: 381–384 Nag 1962: 69
Havasupai	H	A	N	Richards and Reining 1954: 369, 379
Haya	L	A	N	

Society	Fertility level	Nature of descent group	Family type	Reference
Hutterite	H	A	N	Eaton and Mayer 1954
Jamaica	L	A	N	Clarke 1957: 123, 182
Jaunsari	L	A	P	Majumdar 1955: 168
Juang	H	A	N	Elwin 1948: 25
Kanikkar	L	A	N	Nag 1954: 115
Kavirondo	H	A	P	Wagner 1939: 6–8, 40–44
Kapauku	L	K	N	Pospisil 1963: 36–40
Kgatla	L	A	E	Schapera 1941: 94, 109–110, 119, 219
Koreans	H	K	E	Osgood 1951: 37–40
Lesu	L	K	N	Powdermaker 1933: 33–34; 1931: 356
Lue	H	A	E	Moerman 1968: 122–123, 131
Masai	H	K	P	Merker 1904: 20–40; Leaky 1930: 201
Mende	L	K	P	Little 1951: 103, 140
Murut	L	No information	N	Rutter 1929: 63–64
Nasik	H	A	E	Sovani and Dandekar 1955
Navaho	H	K	N	Simmons 1950; Kluckhohn 1946: 54
Ngoni	H	A	P	Barnes 1951: 24, 50, 115
Nguni	H	A	E	Wilson et al. 1952: 47
Nkundo	L	A	P	Lorimer 1954: 120–121
North Chinese	L	K	E	Gamble 1954: 27, 54
Nupe	L	A	P	Nadel 1942: 33, 151
Ojibwa	H	A	N	Dunning 1959: 63–64, 77–79
Ovimbundu	L	A	P	Childs 1949: 30, 42
Pima	H	A	E	Grossman 1871: 415–416
Providencia	H	A	N	Peter Wilson, personal communication
Puerto Rico	H	A	N	Stycos 1955: 102
Purari	L	A	P	Maher 1961: 87, 99
Satudene	H	A	N	Cornelius Osgood, personal communication
Siane	L	K	N	Salisbury 1956: 3
Sinhalese	H	A	N	Ryan 1952: 364
Sioux	H	A	P	Macgregor 1946: 36–38; Hrdlicka 1931: 88, 213
Sukuma	H	A	P	Tanner 1956: 97–98; Cory 1953: 185–186
Tabar	L	No information	No information	
Taiwan	H	A	E	Barclay 1954: 174–184
Tallensi	H	K	P	Fortes 1949: 100–101
Tanoan Pueblo	H	A	N	Whitman 1947: 72–75

Society	Fertility level	Nature of descent group	Family type	Reference
Temne	L	A	P	Dorjahn 1958: 843–845
Tepoztlan	H	A	N	Lewis 1951: 58
Tikopia	H	A	N	Firth 1936: 117–118, 211–213
Toda	L	K	P	Rivers 1908: 515, 540
Tonga	H	K	P	Colson 1958: 41
Torres Straits	L	A	N	Rivers 1908: 9, 124
Ulithian	L	K	E	Lessa 1955: 61–62, 77–78
Walapai	H	A	N	Nag 1962: 69
Yakö	L	K	P	Forde 1941: 6, 97
Yao	H	K	P	Mitchell 1956: 131–136; Mitchell 1949: 297
Yapese	L	K	N	Hunt et al. 1949: 67, 109–110; Schneider 1955: 219

REFERENCES

ARMSEN, P.
   1955   Tables for significance tests of 2 × 2 contingency tables. *Biometrika* 42:494–511.
BARCLAY, GEORGE W.
   1954   *Colonial development and population in Taiwan*. Princeton: Princeton University Press.
BARNES, J. A.
   1951   *Marriage in a changing society: a study in structural change among the Fort Jameson Ngoni*. Cape Town: Oxford University Press.
BEBARTA, P. C.
   1964   "Family structure and fertility," in *Proceedings of the Fifty-first and Fifty-second Sessions of the Indian Science Congress*, part three. Calcutta: Indian Science Congress.
   1967   Attitude of women towards family planning: a study of differences by family types in six villages of Delhi. *Quarterly Journal of Indian Studies in Social Sciences* 1:78–93.
BERREMAN, GERALD D.
   1962   Pahari polyandry: a comparison. *American Anthropologist* 64: 60–75.
BLAKE, JUDITH
   1955   "Family instability and reproductive behavior in Jamaica," in *Current research in human fertility*, pages 24–41. Paper presented at the 1954 Annual Conference of the Milbank Memorial Fund. New York: Milbank Memorial Fund.
   1961   *Family structure in Jamaica*. Glencoe: The Free Press.

BREBANT, V.
1954 "Tendances de la fécondité au Congo Belge," in *Proceedings of the World Population Conference,* volume one, 775–793. New York: United Nations.

BURCH, THOMAS, MURRAY GENDELL
1970 Extended family structure and fertility: some conceptual and methodological issues. *J. of Marriage and the Family* 32:227–236.

BUSIA, K. A.
1954 "Some aspects of the relation of social conditions to human fertility," in *Culture and human fertility.* Edited by Frank Lorimer et al. 343–350. Paris: UNESCO.

CHILDS, GLADWYN MURRAY
1949 *Umbundu kinship and character.* New York: Oxford University Press.

CLARKE, EDITH
1957 *My mother who fathered me: a study of the family in three selected communities in Jamaica.* London: Ruskin House.

CLIGNET, R.
1971 "Determinants of African polygyny," in *Kinship.* Edited by Jack Goody, 163–179. Baltimore: Penguin.

CONGO BELGE
1951 "Démographie Congolaise 1950." Mimeographed manuscript. Leopoldsville: Services des AIMO du Gouvernment Général.

CORY, HANS
1953 *Sukuma law and custom.* New York: Oxford University Press (for International African Institute).

CULWICK, A. T., G. M. CULWICK
1938, A study of population in Ulanga, Tanganyika Territory. *Socio-*
1939 *logical Review* 30, 31.

CUMPER, GEORGE E.
1966 The fertility of common-law unions in Jamaica. *Social and Economic Studies* 15:189–202.

DAVIS, KINGSLEY
1951 *The population of India and Pakistan.* New York: Russell and Russell.
1955 Institutional patterns favoring high fertility in underdeveloped areas. *Eugenics Quarterly* 2:33–39.

DAVIS, KINGSLEY, JUDITH BLAKE
1956 Social structure and fertility: an analytic framework. *Economic Development and Cultural Change* 4:211–235.

DAVIS-BLAKE, JUDITH
1967 "Parental control, delayed marriage, and population policy," in *Proceedings of the World Population Conference,* volume two. Edited by United Nations Department of Economic and Social Affairs, 132–136. New York: United Nations.

DIXON, RUTH B.
1971 Explaining cross-cultural variations in age at marriage and proportions never marrying. *Population Studies* 25:215–233.

DORJAHN, VERNON R.
1954   *The demographic aspects of African polygyny.* Ann Arbor: University of Michigan Microfilms.
1958   Fertility, polygyny and their interrelations in Temne society. *American Anthropologist* 60:838–859.
1959   "The factor of polygyny in African demography," in *Continuity and change in African cultures.* Edited by Wiliam R. Bascom and Melville J. Herskovits, 87–112. Chicago: University of Chicago Press.
DRIVER, E. D.
1960   Fertility differentials among economic strata in central India. *Eugenics Quarterly* 7:77–85.
DUBEY, D. C.
1967   Family life cycle hypothesis and its importance in explaining fertility behaviour in India. *Journal of Family Welfare* 14(2):42–52.
DU BOIS, CORA
1944   *The people of Alor.* Minneapolis: University of Minnesota Press.
DUNNING, R. W.
1959   *Social and economic change among the northern Ojibwa.* Toronto: University of Toronto Press.
EATON, JOSEPH W., A. J. MAYER
1954   *Man's capacity to reproduce.* Glencoe: The Free Press.
ELWIN, VERRIER
1948   Notes on the Juang. *Man in India* 28:1–146.
FIRTH, RAYMOND
1936   *We, the Tikopia: a sociological study of kinship in primitive Polynesia.* London: Allen and Unwin.
FISHER, RONALD A., FRANK YATES
1949   *Statistical tables for biological, agricultural and medical research* (third edition). London: Oliver and Boyd.
FORD, C. S., F. A. BEACH
1951   *Patterns of sexual behavior.* New York: Harper and Row.
FORDE, DARYLL
1941   *Marriage and the family among the Yakö in south-eastern Nigeria.* Monograph on social anthropology 5. London: Percy Lund, Humphries.
FORTES, MEYER
1949   *The web of kinship among the Tallensi.* London: Oxford University Press.
1954   "A demographic field study in Ashanti," in *Culture and human fertility.* Edited by Frank Lorimer et al., 253–319. Paris: UNESCO.
FREEDMAN, RONALD
1961– The sociology of human fertility. *Current Sociology* 10–11:35–
1962   121.
1968   "Norms for family size in underdeveloped areas," in *Population and society.* Edited by Charles B. Nam, 215–230. Boston: Houghton Mifflin.
FREEDMAN, RONALD, JOHN TAKESHITA, T. H. SUN
1964   Fertility and family planning in Taiwan: a case study of the de-

mographic transition. *American Journal of Sociology* 70:16–27.
GAMBLE, SIDNEY D.
1954   *Ting Hsien.* New York: Institute of Pacific Relations.
GENDELL, MURRAY, THOMAS K. BURCH
1970   "Family type and fertility, Guatemala City, 1964." Paper presented at the Latin American Regional Population Conference, Mexico City, August 17–22. Organized by the International Union for the Scientific Study of Population.
GIBSON, GORDON D.
1959   On a common statistical fallacy. *American Anthropologist* 61: 892–893.
GLYN-JONES, MONICA
1953   *The Dusun of the Penampang plains in north Borneo.* Colonial Social Science Research Council.
GOODE, WILLIAM J.
1963   *World revolution and family patterns.* Glencoe: The Free Press.
1968   "The theory and measurement of family change," in *Indicators of social change.* Edited by E. H. Sheldon and W. E. Moore. New York: Russell Sage Foundation.
1971   "World changes in family patterns," in *Kinship.* Edited by Jack Goody, 365–383. Baltimore: Penguin. (Originally published 1963 in *World revolution and family patterns.* Edited by W. J. Goode. Glencoe: The Free Press.)
GOODWIN, GRENVILLE
1942   *The social organization of the western Apache.* Chicago: University of Chicago Press.
GOUGH, KATHLEEN
1971   "The Nayars and the definition of marriage," in *Readings in kinship and social structure.* Edited by Nelson Graburn, 365–377. New York: Harper and Row.
GREENFIELD, SIDNEY M.
1966   *English rustics in black skin.* New Haven: College and University Press.
GROSSMANN, F. E.
1871   The Pima Indians of Arizona. *Annual Reports of the Board of Regents of the Smithsonian Institution* 26:407–419.
HENIN, R. A.
1969   The patterns and causes of fertility differentials in the Sudan. *Population Studies* 23:171–198.
HERSKOVITS, MELVILLE J.
1943   The Negro in Bahia, Brazil: a problem in method. *American Sociological Review* 8:394–404.
HRDLIČKA, ALEŠ
1931   Fecundity in the Sioux women. *American Journal of Physical Anthropology* 16:81–90.
HUNT, EDWARD E., N. R. KIDDER, D. M. SCHNEIDER, W. D. STEVENS
1949   *The Micronesians of Yap and their depopulation.* Report to the Pacific Science Board, National Research Council, from the Peabody Museum, Harvard University, Cambridge, Massachusetts.

IBBERSON, DORA
1956   Illegitimacy and the birth rate. *Social and Economic Studies* 5: 93–99.
KARKAL, NALINI
1972   "Family type and fertility." Paper presented at the Indian Census Centenary Seminar held at New Delhi in October 23–29, 1972. New Delhi: Office of the Registrar General, Government of India.
KING, CHARLES E.
1945   The Negro maternal family: a product of an economic and a cultural system. *Social Forces* 24:100–104.
KLUCKHOHN, CLYDE, DOROTHEA LEIGHTON
1946   *The Navaho.* Cambridge: Harvard University Press.
LASLETT, PETER
1972   "Introduction: the history of the family," in *Household and family in past time.* Edited by Peter Laslett and Richard Wall, 1–86. Cambridge: Cambridge University Press.
LEACH, E. R.
1971   "Polyandry, inheritance and the definition of marriage," in *Kinship.* Edited by Jack Goody, 151–162. Baltimore: Penguin.
LEAKY, L. S. B.
1930   Some notes on the Masai of Kenya colony. *Journal of the Anthropological Institute* 60:185–210.
LESSA, WILLIAM A.
1955   Depopulation of Ulithi. *Human Biology* 27:161–183.
LÉVI-STRAUSS, CLAUDE
1968   "The family," in *Studies in social and cultural anthropology.* Edited by John Middleton, 128–155. New York: Thomas Y. Crowell.
LEWIS, OSCAR
1951   *Life in a Mexican vilage: Tepoztlán restudied.* Urbana: University of Illinois Press.
LITTLE, K. L.
1951   *The Mende of Sierra Leone.* London: Routledge and Kegan Paul.
LIU, PAUL K. C.
1967a "Differential fertility in Taiwan," in *Contributed Papers to the Sydney Conference of the International Union for the Scientific Study of Population, August 1967.* Edited by International Union for the Scientific Study of Population, 363–370.
1967b *The use of household registration records in measuring the fertility level in Taiwan.* Taipei: Institute of Economics, Academia Sinica.
LORIMER, FRANK
1954   "General theory," in *Culture and human fertility.* Edited by Frank Lorimer et al., 156–159. Paris: UNESCO.
MACGREGOR, GORDON
1946   *Warriors without weapons: a study of the society and personality development of the Pine Ridge Sioux.* Chicago: University of Chicago Press.
MAHER, ROBERT F.
1961   *New men of Papua.* Madison: University of Wisconsin Press.

MAJUMDAR, D. N.
1955 Demographic structure in a polyandrous village. *Eastern Anthropologist* 8:161–172.
MARINO, ANTHONY
1970 Family, fertility and sex ratios in the British Caribbean. *Population Studies* 24:159–172.
MARSHALL, GLORIA A.
1968 Comparative analysis. *International Encyclopedia of Social Sciences* 10:9–16.
MATHEN, K. K.
1962 "Preliminary lessons learned from the rural population control study of Singur," in *Research in family planning*. Edited by Clyde V. Kiser, 33–50. Princeton: Princeton University Press.
MERKER, F.
1904 *Die Masai.* Berlin: D. Reimer.
MITCHELL, J. CLYDE
1949 An estimate of fertility in some Yao hamlets in Liwonde district of southern Nyasaland. *Africa* 19:293–308.
1956 *The Yao village.* Manchester: University of Manchester.
MOERMAN, MICHAEL
1968 *Agricultural change and peasant choice in a Thai village.* Berkeley: University of California Press.
MORTARA, G.
1963 "Les unions consensuelles dans l'Amerique Latine," in *International Conference, New York, 1961*, volume two, 264–273. London: International Union for the Scientific Study of Population.
MOSENA, PATRICIA W., JOHN STOECKEL
1972 Correlates of a desired family size in a rural area of Bangladesh. *Journal of Comparative Studies* 3:207–216.
MUNSON, MARTHA LITTLE, LARRY L. BUMPASS
1973 "Determinants of cumulative fertility in Upper Volta, West Africa. Working paper 73–76, mimeographed manuscript. Madison, Wisconsin: University of Wisconsin.
MURDOCK, GEORGE PETER
1962– Ethnographic atlas. *Ethnography* 1–5.
1966
1967 Ethnographic atlas: a summary. *Ethnology* 6:109–236.
MUSHAM, H. V.
1956 The fertility of polygamous marriages. *Population Studies* 10:3–16.
NADEL, SIEGFRIED F.
1942 *A black Byzantium: the kingdom of Nupe in Nigeria.* London: Oxford University Press.
1954 *Nupe religion.* London: Routledge and Kegan Paul.
NAG, MONI
1962 *Factors affecting human fertility in nonindustrial societies: a cross-cultural study.* Yale University Publications in Anthropology 66. New Haven: Yale University. (Reprinted in 1968, New Haven: Human Relations Area Files.)

1967 "Family type and fertility," in *Proceedings of the World Poplation Conference, 1965,* volume two. New York: United Nations.

1971 "The influence of conjugal behavior, migration, and contraception on natality," in *Culture and population: a collection of current studies.* Edited by Steven Polgar, 105–23. Cambridge, Massachusetts: Schenkman.

1972 Sex, culture, and human fertility: India and the United States. *Current Anthropology* 13:231–267.

NAMBOODIRI, N. KRISHNAN
1967 "Fertility differentials in nonindustrial societies." Unpublished manuscript.

OHADIKE, P. O.
1968 "Marriage, family and family growth in Lagos," in *The population of tropical Africa.* Edited by John C. Caldwell and Chukuka Okonjo, 379–92. London: Longmans, Green.

OLUSANYA, P. O.
1971 The problem of multiple causation in population analysis, with particular reference to the polygamy-fertility hypothesis. *Sociological Review* 19:165–178.

OPLER, MORRIS E.
1941 *An Apache life-way.* Chicago: University of Chicago Press.

OSGOOD, CORNELIUS
1951 *The Koreans and their culture.* New York: Ronald Press.

OTTERBEIN, KEITH F.
1965 Caribbean family organization: a comparative analysis. *American Anthropologist* 67:67–79.

PAKRASI, KANTI, CHITTARANJAN MALAKER
1967 The relationship between family type and fertility. *Milbank Memorial Fund Quarterly* 45:451–460.

POLGAR STEVEN
1973 "Cultural development, population and the family." Paper presented at the Symposium on Population and the Family, Honolulu, August 6-15, 1973. United Nations Economic and Social Council Number E/Conference 60/Symposium II/3 dated 15 June 1973.

POOL, D. I.
1968 Conjugal patterns in Ghana. *Canadian Review of Sociology and Anthropology* 5:241–253.

POSPISIL, LEOPOLD
1963 *Kapauku Papuan economy.* Publications in Anthropology 67. New Haven: Yale University.

POTI, S. J., S. DATTA
1960 "Pilot study on social mobility and differential fertility," in *Studies in family planning.* New Delhi: Government of India, Director General of Health Services.

POWDERMAKER, HORTENSE
1931 Vital statistics in New Ireland (Bismarck Archipelago) as revealed in genealogies. *Human Biology* 3:350–375.

1933 *Life in Lesu.* New York: W. W. Norton.

RELE, J. R.
  1963 Fertility differentials in India: evidence from a rural background. *Milbank Memorial Fund Quarterly* 41:183–199.

RICHARDS, AUDREY I., PRISCILLA REINING
  1954 "Report on fertility surveys in Buganda and Buhaya, 1952," in *Culture and human fertility*. Edited by Frank Lorimer et al., 351–403. Paris: UNESCO.

RIVERS, WILLIAM H. R.
  1908 "Regulation of marriage," in *Society, magic and religion of the eastern islanders*. Edited by A. C. Haddon. Reports of the Cambridge expedition to Torres Straits, volume six. Cambridge: Cambridge University Press.

ROBERTS, D. F.
  1956 A demographic study of a Dinka village. *Human Biology* 28:323–349.

ROBERTS, GEORGE W.
  1955a Some aspects of mating and fertility in the West Indies. *Population Studies* 8:199–227.
  1955b Emigration from the island of Barbados. *Social and Economic Studies* 4:245–288.

ROBERTS, GEORGE W., LLOYD BRAITHWAITE
  1960 Fertility differentials by family type in Trinidad. *Annals of the New York Academy of Sciences* 84:963–980.

ROSCOE, JOHN
  1965 *The Baganda: an account of their native customs and beliefs* (second edition). London: Frank Cass.

RUTTER, OWEN
  1929 *The pagans of north Borneo*. London: Hutchinson.

RYAN, BRYCE
  1952 Institutional factors in Sinhalese fertility. *Milbank Memorial Fund Quarterly* 30:359–381.

SALISBURY, RICHARD F.
  1956 Unilineal descent group in the New Guinea highlands. *Man* 2:2–7.

SAUCIER, JEAN-FRANÇOIS
  1972 Correlates of the long post-partum taboo: a cross-cultural study. *Current Anthropology* 13:238–248.

SCHAPERA, I.
  1941 *Married life in an African tribe*. New York: Sheridan House.

SCHNEIDER, DAVID M.
  1955 "Abortion and depopulation on a Pacific island," in *Health, culture and community*. Edited by Benjamin D. Paul, 211–238. New York: Russell Sage Foundation.

SEN, D. K.
  1956 Some notes on the fertility of Jaunsari women. *The Eastern Anthropologist* 10.

SIMMONS, DONALD C.
  1950 "The Alamo Navaho kinship and sib systems." M.A. thesis. Yale University, New Haven, Connecticut.

SOVANI, N.V., KUMUDINI DANDEKAR
1955 *Fertility survey of Nasik, Kolaba and Satara (north) districts.* Gokhale Institute of Politics and Economics Publication 31. Poona.
STENNING, DERRICK J.
1959 *Savannah nomads.* London: Oxford University Press.
STOECKEL, JOHN, MOQBUL A. CHOUDHURY
1969 Differential fertility in a rural area of East Pakistan. *Milbank Memorial Fund Quarterly* 47:189–198.
STYCOS, J. MAYONE
1955 *Family and fertility in Puerto Rico.* New York: Columbia University Press.
STYCOS, J. MAYONE, KURT W. BACK
1964 *The control of human fertility in Jamaica.* Ithaca: Cornell University Press.
TANNER, R. E. S.
1956 A preliminary enquiry into Sukuma diet in the Lake Province, Tanganyika Territory. *East African Medical Journal* 33:305–324.
UNITED NATIONS ECONOMIC AND SOCIAL COUNCIL
1968 *Family planning and the status of women.* Interim report of the Secretary General. Number E/Conference 6/497. New York.
UNITED NATIONS, DEPARTMENT OF ECONOMIC AND SOCIAL AFFAIRS
1961 *The Mysore population study.* Population studies 34. New York.
1971 *Human fertility and national development: a challenge to science and technology.* New York.
VAN DE WALLE, ÉTIENNE
1965 The relation of marriage to fertility in African demographic enquiries. *Demography* 2:302–316.
WAGNER, GUNTER
1939 "The changing family among the Bantu Kavirondo." Supplement to *Africa,* volume twelve.
WHITMAN, WILLIAM
1947 *The Pueblo Indians of San Ildefonso.* New York: Columbia University Press.
WILSON, MONICA, *et al.*
1952 *Social structure.* Keiskammahoek Rural Survey, volume three. Pietermaritzburg.

Age Differential, Marital Instability, and Venereal Disease: Factors Affecting Fertility among the Northwest Barma

S. P. REYNA

If divergence in biological evolution consists of dissimilar responses of related organisms to varying environmental situations, then, by analogy, the thought of Lowie, White, Murdock, Steward, Radcliffe-Brown, and Lévi-Strauss would be an example of divergent intellectual evolution. There is, however, an interesting parallelism in their work. All regard marriage as fulfilling an "organizing" function. Marriage for the Americans organizes nuclear families or relations between affines (Lowie 1948: 65–66; Murdock 1949: 1; Steward 1963: 119; White 1959: 94, 110). The Radcliffe-Brownians see the exchange of bride-wealth and jural rights as organizing stable relations between pairs of affines who normally represent different descent groups (Radcliffe-Brown and Forde 1950: 40). Alliance theorists devise ideal state models that utilize marriage exchange as the major logical modality of formal systems possessing the property of reciprocity.

There is nothing wrong in considering marriage in terms of its organizing activities. It is, nevertheless, a remarkable case of "the emperor wears no clothes," i.e. of ignoring the obvious. If human groups are to survive transgenerationally, they must have methods for recruiting new members. Variables associated with marriage control whether a person is married, when he is married, and how long he is married. Others have noted that marriage is a major way for people to jurally "have" children (Malinowski 1930: 35; Radcliffe-Brown and Forde 1950: 5). The three former factors can regulate the variety and incidence of coitus, and the latter factor legally allocates children to social groups. Marriage, then, fulfills not only an organizing function but a further "recruiting" function. Clearly, the latter function of marriage is equally as important as the former. Presumably, it is to a population's benefit to possess some shreds of organization, but obviously, and equally urgently, it is in its better interests to possess some members. The ethnologist's *idée fixe* with marriage's "organizing" function is paralleled by his almost complete ignorance of marriage's "recruiting" function.

This article discusses marriage's recruitment activities among the northwest Barma of the Republic of Chad. Specifically, it hypothesizes that marriage-associated variables operate in conjunction with venereal diseases to reduce Barma fertility. Marriage-associated variables means those which can be measured only if a Barma marriage has occurred. The two marriage-associated variables treated are age differential between spouses and marital instability. It will be shown that high age differential between husband and wife and a high number of divorces in women are correlated with high female infertility and low fertility. These associations will be interpreted as resulting from marriage-associated variables acting in two ways to lower fertility. These ways are (1) that the large differential in age between husbands and wives and the high incidence of divorce act to spread venereal disease, increasing the number of infertile women, and (2) that divorce leads to decreased coital frequency.

RESEARCH TECHNIQUES AND BARMA BACKGROUND

The data were collected between July, 1969 and November, 1970, using survey techniques and participant observation. The latter occurred in the villages of Bougoumen and Guera. Survey procedures were utilized to collect demographic and marital information. A total of 208 presently married Barma women between the ages of fourteen and forty-nine were interviewed in four villages and the capital of Chad. The 208 women interviewed represent the most northwestern area of Barma habitation. Map 1 shows the location of the towns studied.

The Barma (numbering about 34,500 in 1970) reside in western, south-central Chad. Their language is included in Greenberg's Central Sudanic (1966: 109ff.). The majority of the Barma are distributed along the Chari and Bahr Erguig Rivers between Bousso and Fort Lamy in the Préfecture of Chari-Baguirmi in a sahelo-sudanic climatic zone. The area receives annually between 500 and 900 millimeters of rain coming during a four- to five-month period from May or June until September. The vegetation is predominantly wooded savannah.

A most important cultural influence in the region has been Islam. Perhaps 300 years ago the Barma adopted the Koran, and with it a sudanic,

Muslim state, becoming rulers of the polity Baguirmi. The autonomy of
Baguirmi was completely vitiated in 1912 when she was incorporated into
what was to become French Equatorial Africa. Barma economy resembles
that of her Muslim neighbors — the Kanuri, Hausa, and Wadaians —
with whom there has long been contact. Most Barma are extensive subsistence farmers of millets. They keep no cattle, though they include dairy
products in their diet by regularly exchanging their grains for the milk
products of neighboring pastoralists. Many Barma fish, and trading is
well developed. Barma lack unilineal descent groups. They reside in
households whose ideal composition is some form of the patrilineal
extended family. Groups of frequently agnatically related households
form villages. If a village is a large one, it may be subdivided into wards.
Villages range in size from about fifty people to about a thousand. A
large number of Barma have migrated to Fort Lamy, the capital of Chad.
Barma fertility has been described as rather low and her infertility as high
for a nonindustrial population (Nodinot 1956; INSEE 1966). Of the
women surveyed, 25 percent were classified as infertile (Reyna 1972: 89).
Barma are painfully aware of their low fertility and observe that "a
woman without children is like a tree without leaves."

AGE DIFFERENTIAL

Age Differential and Fertility

There is a considerable differential in age between husbands and their
wives among the Barma. Husbands were on the average 10.8 years older
than their wives (Reyna 1972: 214). Table 1 shows the mean number of
live births for northwest Barma women in their present marriage with
varying age differentials. Figure 1 depicts the same information graphic-
ally. Both Table 1 and Figure 1 each exhibit two peaks of high fertility,
one in the women 6–8 years younger, and the other in the women 18 or
more years younger than their husbands. Our first concern is to account
for these two peaks of fertility.

The high fertility for the total population in these two age differentials
does not appear to be due to differences in the ages of the women. The
average age for the total population of women 0–8 years younger than
their husbands is 29 years, and the average age of women 9–18 years or
more younger than their husbands is 30 years. The average age for women
in the 6–8 year age differential is 1 year younger than the average for the
smaller age differentials (0–8) as a whole, while the average age for women

in the 18 and over age differential is the same as the average for the higher age differentials (9–18 and over). Thus, the ages of women in the two age differentials with the highest fertility deviate little from the average age in the other age differentials.

Table 1. Mean number of live births occurring in present marriages in northwestern Barma with varying age differentials

Age differential from husband	Total population			First marriage		
	Total number of women	Number of children born	Mean number of children	Total number of women	Number of children born	Mean number of children
0–2	12	24	2.0	4	10	2.5
3–5	44	94	2.1	25	64	2.6
6–8	27	70	2.6	18	61	3.4
9–11	18	42	2.3	14	39	2.8
12–14	18	22	1.2	10	18	1.8
15–17	9	4	0.4	5	3	0.6
18 &+	35	72	2.1	25	69	2.8
0-8			2.3			3.0
9-18&+			1.8			2.4

The lowest age differentials for the total population are associated with higher divorce than the higher age differentials, for fully 48.2 percent of the women 0–5 years younger than their husbands have been divorced (see Table 2). The high percentage of divorced women in the lowest age differentials may mean that divorced women tend to marry men closer to them in age.

Table 2. Divorce and age differentials for the total population

Age differentials									
Divorced	0–2	3–5	6–8	9–11	12–14	15–17	18 and over	0–8	9–18 and over
Number divorced	8	19	9	4	8	4	10	36	27
Total number	12	44	27	18	18	9	35	83	80
Percent divorced	66.7	43.2	33.3	22.2	44.4	44.4	28.6	43.4	33.7

It should be noted that the lower age differentials are associated with lower sterility than the higher age differentials (see Table 5), but that the 6–8 year age differential has the lowest percentage of sterile women of all the age differentials. It may be suggested that the women 6–8 years younger than their husbands have the highest fertility because so few of them are barren (only 2 out of 27).

The 35 women who are at least 18 years younger than their husbands include a fair number who are sterile (37 percent in Table 5), but a large

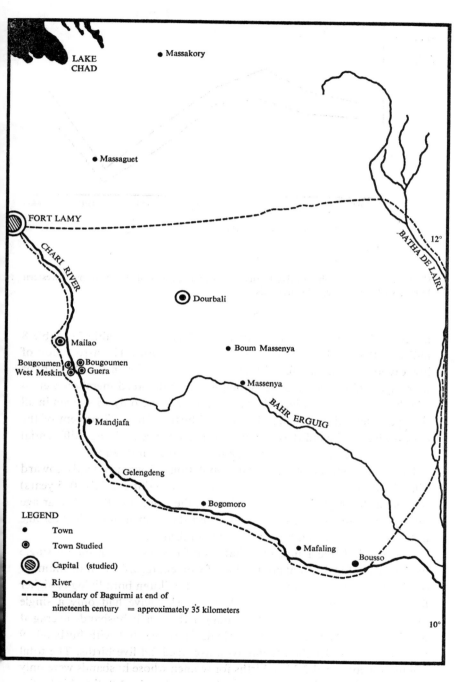

LAKE CHAD

● Massakory

● Massaguet

FORT LAMY

CHARI RIVER

BATHA DE LAIRI

12°

◉ Dourbali

◉ Mailao

● Boum Massenya

Bougoumen West Meskin ◉ ◉Bougoumen Guera

● Massenya

BAHR ERGUIG

● Mandjafa

● Gelengdeng

● Bogomoro

LEGEND

● Town

◉ Town Studied

◎ Capital (studied)

〜 River

---- Boundary of Baguirmi at end of nineteenth century = approximately 35 kilometers

● Mafaling

Bousso

10°

Map 1. Location of towns studied in Barma

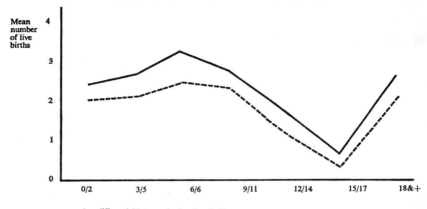

Figure 1.   Mean number of live births occurring in present marriage in northwestern Barma with varying age differentials

number who have never been divorced (71 percent in Table 2). Table 8 indicates that as divorce increases fertility decreases. The association of low divorce and higher fertility may be accounted for in the 18 years or more age differential because among its never divorced members were 4 who had had over 7 children born alive. There were only 15 women in all the age differentials who had had over 7 births. Thus, 27 percent of the extraordinarily fecund Barma women surveyed were in the age differential with women 18 years or more younger than their husbands.

Hence, the graph of the total population of women tends toward bimodality because the women in the lowest age differentials (0–5 years) possess such a high frequency of divorce; the women in the 6–8 year age differential possess such low sterility; and the women of the highest age differential have such a high percentage of fertilly.

In general, Table 1 indicates that both for women with only a single marriage and for the total population of women, regardless of the number of divorces contracted, the mean number of children born living is higher for the smaller age differentials. Women who have had only a single marriage who are 8 years or less younger than their husbands averaged 3.0 live births. Women of only a single marriage, but with husbands 9 years or more older than themselves, averaged 2.4 live births. The total population averaged 2.3 live births for women whose husbands were only 8 years or fewer older than themselves; and only 1.8 live births for women in the total population whose husbands were 9 years or more older than themselves.

The higher average number of live births for the women with age differentials of eight years or fewer is more impressive when one realizes that higher differentials are associated with marriages of longer duration. Table 3 presents the average duration of marriages (in years) for women in first marriages and the total population by the age differentials between husband and wife. Marriage duration of the present marriage was 9.2 years for the total population of women with age differentials of 8 years or less, and 11.7 years for single marriage women with age differentials of 8 years or less. Women with age differentials of 9 years or more averaged durations of 11.6 years for the total population and 13.1 years for single marriages (see Table 3). In general, women with higher age differentials

Table 3. Average marriage duration for women in present marriage in different age differentials among the northwest Barma

Age differential	Total population			First marriage		
	Number of women	Total number of years married	Average number of years in present marriage	Number of women	Total number of years married	Average number of years in present marriage
0–2	12	118	9.8	4	62	15.5
3–5	44	390	8.9	25	251	10.0
6–8	27	256	9.4	18	235	13.1
9–11	18	241	13.4	14	195	13.9
12–14	18	194	10.7	10	120	12.0
15–17	9	71	7.9	5	56	11.2
18 and +	35	422	12.4	25	336	13.4
8 or under			9.2			11.7
9 or +			11.6			13.1

had been married for longer periods of time than those with lower age differentials. The fertility of the women studied increased with the length of time they had been married, as is reported in Table 4.

The women with age differentials of 8 years or fewer have been married for shorter periods than women with age differentials of 9 years or more, and the longer women are married the more children they have, but the women with the lower age differentials still manage to produce more children than the females with the higher age differentials. Clearly then, higher fertility is associated with lower age differentials. The likelihood of a northwestern Barma woman having more children is greater the less her age differential.

Table 4.   Average number of children born alive by marriage duration among the northwest Barma

Marriage duration	Single marriage average number of children	One or more divorces average number of children
0–4	0.77	0.21
5–8	2.40	0.61
9–12	3.13	1.83
13–16	2.15	1.20
17–20	4.61	–
21–24	6.67	2.50
25–28	6.42	7.00*
29–32	3.50	–
33–35 and over	5.50	–

*   Figure based on only one representative

Age differential and Sterility

Table 5 reports on the incidence of sterility for women in the total population and for women married only once in terms of the age differentials of the population studied. Table 5 indicates, both for the total population and for those married only once, that as age differentials increase, in general, sterility increases. Women with age differentials of 8 years or less have only 8.5 percent of their members sterile if it is their first marriage, and 16.9 percent sterile in the total population as opposed to 27.8 percent of the numbers sterile for women with age differentials of 9 years or more if it is a first marriage, and 38.8 percent sterile for the total population. Fully 79 percent of the sterile women with only one marriage had age differentials of 9 years or more; while 68.9 percent of the sterile women in the total population had age differentials of 9 years or over.

The X^2 test was utilized to determine whether age differential and sterility were related by chance. The X^2 was applied both to women with a single marriage (see Table 6) and to women in the total population (see Table 7). The X^2 resulting from both tests is high enough, with the proper degrees of freedom, to indicate that the null hypothesis may be rejected, and that the relationship between sterility and age differential is not one of chance.

Adolescent Subfecundity, Age Differential, and Sterility

It is possible that sterility is positively associated with age differential because marriages with high age differentials are ones where the wife is

Table 5. Incidence of sterility in marriages of northwest Barma with varying age differentials

Age differential	Total population			First marriage		
	Total number of women	Number of women sterile	Percent sterile	Total number of women	Number of women sterile	Percent sterile
0–2	12	2	16.7	4	0	–
3–5	44	10	22.7	25	3	12.0
6–8	27	2	7.4	18	1	5.6
9–11	18	7	38.9	14	4	28.6
12–14	18	7	38.9	10	2	20.0
15–17	9	4	44.4	5	2	40.0
18 and over	35	13	37.1	25	7	28.0
Total making response	163			101		
Number do not know	45			28		
Percent of total do not know	21.6			21.7		
Number do not know sterile	6			1		
Percent do not know sterile	13.3			3.6		
Percent 8 years or less sterile	16.9			8.5		
Percent 9 years or more sterile	38.8			27.8		
Percent of sterile women with 9 and over age differential	68.9			79.0		

Table 6. Age differential and sterility among the northwest Barma surveyed with only a single marriage

Age differential	Sterility		
	Sterile	Not sterile	Total
9 years and over	15	39	54
8 years and under	5	43	48
			(N = 102)

$X^2 = 4.211$; $P < .05$.

Table 7.   Age differential and sterility among the total northwest Barma population surveyed

	Sterility		
Age differential	Sterile	Not sterile	Total
9 years and over	31	49	80
8 years and under	14	69	83
			(N = 163)

$X^2 = 9.950$; P < .005.

very young, so young that one would expect adolescent subfecundity. The mean age of the women with husbands 9 years or more older than themselves in the population surveyed was 29.7 years. There were only six women with these age differentials aged 17 or younger. Similarly, it is possible that the women surveyed and judged to be sterile are so because they are very young. The mean age of the women defined as sterile in the population studied was 32. There were no sterile women aged 17 or less.

Adolescent subfecundity would not appear to be a factor in the sterility of the population surveyed, or in the association of sterility with high age differential.

Relationship between Age Differential, Sterility, and Fertility

The relation of fertility to age differential and sterility is discussed after the relations of the latter two variables have been considered. Among the northwestern Barma studied, a higher incidence of sterility occurs in the higher age differentials. Evidence will be cited to suggest that marriages with high age differentials result in increases in sterility.

Elsewhere I have reported that age differentials between husband and wife, for one part of the population studied, could be shown to be largely contingent on the inability of young males to muster the resources necessary to successfully make bridewealth payments (Reyna 1972: 214). Young men do not perform the economic tasks that would provide them with the commodities necessary to make bridewealth payments. Lacking the goods to pay brideprices, men must postpone their marriages. There is nothing hindering the marriage of a woman once she has reached puberty. Accordingly, women marry for the first time at the mean age of 14 to husbands reporting a mean age of 26 (Reyna 1972: 212).

A high incidence of venereal disease has been documented for the entire Barma region where one person in every thirty-three reported venereal illness in 1970 (Reyna 1972: 131). Gonorrhea occurs roughly two and a half times more frequently than syphilis in the Barma region. Untreated gonorrhea often scars the fallopian tubes, resulting in female sterility. As no other major determinant of female sterility has been identified in the Barma area, it is suggested that the high incidence of infertile women reported for the northwestern Barma is due to venereal disease.

It has also been suggested that northwest Barma sexual morality is procoital. Both never married and previously married males would be expected to have sexual intercourse. Their sexual intercourse would not be expected to be restricted to single partners. Most likely candidates for partners would be previously married Barma females and prostitutes (Reyna 1972: 161ff). Matings of unmarried males with previously married females would result in increased exposure to and contraction of venereal illnesses. The greater the age differential, the older the husband, the longer the duration of such matings, the more probable the contraction and repeated contraction of venereal diseases. Marriage with an older man for a Barma woman increases the risk of exposure to venereal infection. Thus, a major consequence of a high age differential between husband and wife is an increase in the likelihood of venereal disease, with its attendant hazards of female sterility.

The association of high sterility and high age differential may be interpreted to follow from increased incidence of female infertility resulting from venereal illness contracted as a result of marriage to men considerably older than their wives. The argument is depicted diagrammatically in Figure 2. Bridewealth costs are shown to lead to a situation where hus-

Figure 2.   Hypothesized relationship between age differential and female sterility

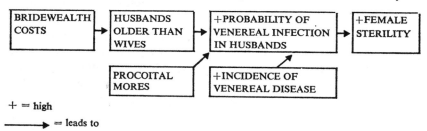

bands are considerably older than their wives, while the high incidence of venereal disease and the procoital mores are shown to operate with the greater age of the husbands to increase the probability of male contraction of venereal disease, which is shown to be transmitted to the wife. The situation diagrammed is more likely to obtain in cases of high age differential when the marriage is to a never previously married wife. For both a previously married woman and a never married woman, marriage with an older man is similarly interpreted. In both cases the high age differential means time — time for the husband to contract a venereal disease before he marries.

Attention is turned to the relationship between fertility and age differential among the northwest Barma. The lower mean number of live births with the higher age differentials may be interpreted as attendant on the increased sterility resultant from high age differentials.

DIVORCE

Divorce and Fertility

The incidence of divorce among the Barma is high, as has been documented elsewhere (Reyna 1972: 223ff). Among the women surveyed 35 percent had been divorced at least once. In the villages of Bougoumen and Guera, 80 percent of the men and women over age forty-five had been divorced at least once. Table 8 reports the mean number of live births for the

Table 8.   Mean number of children born living by divorce among the northwest Barma women of all age groups

	No divorces	One divorce	Two divorces	Three divorces
Number of women	132	56	14	6
Number of children born	356	134	28	5
Mean	2.7	2.4	2.0	0.8

women studied under varying conditions of marital stability. Stability is defined in terms of the following categories: women with no divorces; those with one divorce; those with two; and those with three or more. The table indicates that the mean number of live children women bear decreases as the number of divorces incurred increases. Women with no divorces average 2.7 live births; those with one divorce 2.4 live births; those with two divorces 2.0 live births; and those with three or more divorces 0.8 live births.

Divorce and Sterility

Table 9 notes the incidence of sterility among the northwest Barma women according to the number of divorces they have undergone. The table indicates sterility to be associated more frequently with divorce — 54.9 percent of the sterile women were those who had been divorced at least once. The percentage of those sterile who had never been divorced was 17.4 percent; 32.1 percent for those divorced once; 35.7 percent for those with two divorces; and 83.3 percent for those with three or more divorces.

Table 9.   Incidence of sterility among the northwest Barma by marital stability

	No divorces	One divorce	Two divorces	Three or more divorces	Ever divorced	Total
Number in category	132	56	14	6	76	208
Number sterile	23	18	5	5	28	51
Percent sterile	17.4	32.1	35.7	83.3	36.8	

The X^2 test was used to ascertain whether the relationship between divorce and sterility was one of chance. Table 10 presents the result of the test applied to marital stability and sterility where stability is defined as ever divorced and never divorced women. The X^2 for the test indicates that the null hypothesis may be rejected. Note that 48 of the 76 ever divorced women, or 63 percent, were not sterile, and that 23 of the 51 sterile women, or 45.1 percent were never divorced. These figures indicate that a sizable number of nonsterile women divorce, and that a fair number of sterile women do not divorce. Consider further that 109 of the 132 never divorced women, or 83 percent, were not sterile and that 48 of the 157 nonsterile women, or 31 percent, were ever divorced. These figures indicate that while sterility is associated with marital instability, fecundity is more strikingly associated with marital stability.

Table 10.   Marital stability and sterility among the northwest Barma

	Sterility		
Marital stability	Sterile	Non sterile	Total
Ever divorced	28	48	76
Never divorced	23	109	132

$X^2 = 9.528$; $P < .005$.

Table 11 gives the results of the X^2 test applied to marital stability and child production per marriage. The latter variable is defined as a marriage in which either children were produced or children were not produced. In Table 11 the X^2 test is applied to determine whether marriages terminated by divorce and childlessness are more than chance occurrences. The X^2 resultant from the test indicates that the null hypothesis may be rejected. Note that 37 of the 102 ever divorced women, or 36 percent, had not been childless in their marriages terminated by divorce. These figures indicate that a relatively small percentage of marriages with children are terminated by divorce, but that one-half of the childless marriages do not terminate in divorce. Observe further that 141 of the 206 marriages with no divorce, or 68 percent, are marriages with children, and that 37 of the 178 marriages with children, or 21 percent, have been terminated by divorce. These figures indicate that, while marital instability manifests itself in one out of every two cases of childless marriage, marital stability is very strong in marriages in which children have been produced.

Table 11.   Child production in marriage by marital stability among the northwest Barma

Marital stability	Child production Marriage with no children	Marriage with children	Total
Ever divorced	65	37	102
Never divorced	65	141	206
			(N = 308)

$X^2 = 29.1$; $P < .005$.

Relationship between Divorce and Sterility

The data presented in Tables 8, 9, 10, and 11 will be interpreted to indicate that one effect of female sterility is divorce, and that a consequence of divorce is increased sterility. The former hypothesis is considered first. We have already argued that at least some of the female sterility results from high age differentials. The Barma, as is true of many nonindustrial populations, regard childnessness as a ground for divorce (Reyna 1972: 112). Getting divorced is a simple matter among the Barma requiring little time, expense, or formality (Reyna 1972: 215–217). Accordingly, in situations of barren marriage, divorce being easy and childlessness being a ground for divorce, we would expect that divorce would frequently occur (see Table 11).

Table 11 indicates that there were sixty-five barren marriages not resulting in divorce. It is likely that some percentage of these marriages are of such recent duration that sufficient time has not elapsed for divorce to occur. But it must be observed that marriages take a considerable outlay of resources. Any man who divorces, unless he is polygamously married, must expect to have to gather the resources necessary for making a remarriage. It should further be remembered that divorce in the situation of a barren marriage was considered to be difficult (Reyna 1972: 113). So it is quite possible that some barren marriages are not terminated because the spouses have affection for each other and regard divorce as cruel. It is equally possible that some barren marriages are not terminated because the husband does not wish to bear the additional economic burden of paying bridewealth for a new wife. Additional economic responsibilities and the realization of the difficulty of divorce should be considered to be two factors operating to maintain some childless marriages.

The forty-eight nonsterile divorced women in Table 10 will now be discussed. It should be appreciated that the Barma have no way of knowing whether a person is sterile or not sterile. Barma only know if people have or do not have children. Some of the forty-eight women who now have children may well have been childless in the marriage(s) terminated by divorce. Further, it may reasonably be asserted that the Barma divorce for more reasons than simply childlessness, which would account for the other nonsterile women divorced.

Our arguments may be summarized by two hypotheses accounting for (1) women with stable marriages under conditions of childlessness and (2) divorced women under conditions of both childlessness and non-barrenness. The factor of sterility will not be sufficient to result in divorce under conditions of disinclination to assume the economic responsibility of divorce by the husband or dislike of the cruelty of divorce in a barren marriage. In the absence of these conditions, the factors of easy divorce and the belief that barren marriages should be terminated in divorce will be, in some cases, sufficient to result in divorce. In other cases of divorce, marriage termination will result from other factors not identified and called 'X' factors.

The Divorce-Sterility Cycle

Now we turn to examine the mating possibilities of divorced women to argue that a consequence of divorcing is increased sterility. In so doing, we shall describe possible relationships between age differential, divorce, sterility, and fertility; and the possibility of a cycle maintaining divorce and sterility within the northwestern Barma.

The average time between marriages terminated by divorce for the entire population was one year, seven months (Reyna 1972: 231). Women between marriages are frequently called *kedabogos* and are not expected to remain celibate. Possible mates for *kedabogos* are described below. Married Barma males might be less frequent sexual partners with divorced women because of some (admittedly mild) negative sanctions against such mating. Furthermore, matings with non-Barma males might be less frequent owing to lack of spatial propinquity with such males. Thus, the most likely partners for *kedabogos* are previously married and never married Barma men. Matings with these partners would carry no negative sanctions and would be facilitated by propinquity.

Two categories of *kedabogos*, varying in their reasons for divorce, are

(1) those divorced because of a barren marriage, and (2) those divorced because of the 'X' factor. The two categories of *kedabogo* and the two categories of their most probable mates each have different probabilities of having contracted a venereal infection. The category of divorced, sterile women have a high probability of having contracted a venereal infection. Indeed, the reason they are sterile is probably because they have had a venereal infection. The 'X' factor women have not run this risk. The never married males are less likely to have contracted a venereal infection than the previously married men. These males are younger and have had less coital experience than their elders; they have accordingly had less time and fewer partners from whom to contract venereal infections.

The two categories of *kedabogos* have four mating possibilities:

1. A divorced, sterile woman with a previously married male
2. A divorced, sterile woman with a never married male
3. A divorced, 'X' factor woman with a previously married male
4. A divorced, 'X' factor woman with a never married male

In the first mating possibility, both partners are likely to have previously contracted venereal illness. In the second mating possibility, the never married male may contract a venereal illness from the divorced, sterile woman. In the third mating possibility, the divorced, 'X' factor woman may contract a veneral disease from the previously married male. In the final mating possibility, the likelihood is the greatest that neither party would contract a venereal disease.

Divorce creates two categories of Barma individuals freed from conjugal bonds: previously married males and females. Both males and females, when divorced, are not expected to remain celibate, and both would be expected to find a wider variety of mates than when married. Some divorced, sterile women would mate with never previously married men, while some previously married men would mate with divorced, 'X' factor women. Such mating patterns would favor the spreading of venereal illness.

Next, let us concentrate our attention on the women with whom these never married males who have had experience with *kedabogos* are likely to mate. These never married men are the same young men we described in the section on age differential, sterility, and fertility. They are men waiting to gather sufficient resources to marry. When they marry some will marry women who were never previously married. Some of these never previously married men will have contracted venereal illnesses. The marriage of a never married male with veneral illness to a never married woman is likely to cause the latter spouse to contract the illness, and its attendant risks of sterility. Should this occur, the same sequence of events would begin anew. This newly sterile wife runs a risk of being divorced. As a divorced, sterile woman, she is likely to mate with a never married male.

Those matings that do occur as described above, result in a cyclical situation where divorce at time T_1 creates previously married, sterile women who mate with never married males, who, consequently, run a high risk of contracting venereal disease. Some of those never married males who have contracted venereal disease marry never married women, who, then in turn, run a high risk of contracting a venereal infection. Some of these women married to never previously married men become sterile, and at the time T_2, divorce occurs. The cycle begins anew, theoretically at least, repeating itself until an unknown T_n. This mating cycle is diagrammatically presented in Figure 3.

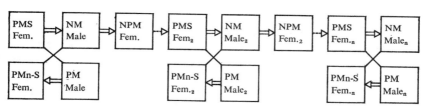

PMS Fem.   = Previously married, sterile female
NM Male   = Never married male
NPM Fem.   = Never previously married female
PMn-S Fem.   = Previously married, non sterile female
PM Male   = Previously married male
⇒   = Mating likely to result in venereal infection (direction of arrow indicates who is infecting whom)
——   = Mating

Divorce and Coital Frequency

Divorce has effects other than the reduction of fertility through increasing sterility. There were forty-eight divorced women who were not sterile in the population studied. Previously, it was mentioned that on the average, the population surveyed spent 1.7 years between divorce and remarriage. This means that ever divorced women would spend less time in marriage than their never divorced counterparts. Table 12 presents the average amount of time spent in marriage by different age groups of women according to the number of divorces they have incurred. The table confirms that, in general, divorced women have less total married time. Although the divorced woman is under no compunction to remain celibate while divorced, it is probable that mating is less frequent than when she was married. Thus, divorced women, while they probably mate with

Table 12.   Mean total marriage duration according to age group and marital stability among the northwest Barma

| Age group | Marital stability (mean duration) | | | | |
	No divorces	One divorce	Two divorces	Three or more divorces	Ever divorced
45–49	33	27	–	–	27
40–44	25	20	16	–	18.5
35–39	21	21	19	26*	21
30–34	15	14.5	18	18.5	16
25–29	12	11	10	15*	11
20–24	7	7	–	–	7
15–19	3	–	–	–	–

* Category is represented by only one individual.

a greater variety of partners, mate with a lesser frequency than married women.

This reduction in coital frequency comes at a crucial time. The average age of women at their first divorce is 19; 24 at the time of their second divorce; and 25 at the time of their third or more divorce (Reyna 1972: 230). Fertility is the highest in younger female age groups, with the highest percentage of births to take place in the 15–24 age group (Reyna 1972: 85). These are precisely the ages when women are divorcing. Thus, northwest Barma women who were studied were reducing mating frequency at precisely the ages when they had the greatest chance of having a live birth.

It may reasonably be inferred that divorce results in a situation of reduced coital frequency at precisely the time most likely to result in children, which accounts for the diminished fertility of the divorced, nonsterile women.

CONCLUSION

An association has been reported for the northwest Barma of both high age differential between husband and wife and high marital instability with high infertility and low fertility. These associations have been interpreted as resulting from (1) the spreading of venereal infection due to young men seeking mates, who are likely to have such infections, after their marriages have been postponed to collect the goods necessary for bridewealth payments, (2) the spreading of veneral infection after divorce due to the matings by previously married males and females with new partners (either never previously married men or women) and (3) the reduction in coital incidence presumed to occur when men and women are divorced.

Marriage-associated variables at least partially regulate the number of partners with whom coitus occurs and the frequency with which coitus occurs among the northwest Barma. Postponement of male marriage while collecting commodities for bridewealth payments and the high incidence of divorce ensure that matings occur among a relatively large number of partners. The high incidence of divorce means that there will be many people who mate less frequently because they are not married. Marriage-associated variables are hypothesized to reduce the recruitment of Barma to social groups by increasing the variety of mates and decreasing the incidence of coitus.

Thus, for the Barma, both increasing mate variety (by increasing risks of venereal infection) and decreasing frequency of intercourse both act to lower the likelihood of successful conception, lowering fertility, and reducing recruitment to social groups.

REFERENCES

GREENBERG, J. H.
  1966 *Languages of Africa* (second revised edition). The Hague: Mouton.
INSEE
  1966 *Enquête démographique au Tchad, 1964. Résults définitifs.* République Française. Paris: Secretariat d'Etat aux Affairs Etrangeres.
LOWIE, R. H.
  1948 *Social organization.* New York: Rinehart.
MALINOWSKI, B.
  1930 "Parenthood: the basis of social structure," in *The new generation.* Edited by V. F. Galveston and Samuel Schmalhausen, 113–168. New York: Macauley.
MURDOCK, G. P.
  1949 *Social structure.* New York: Macmillan.
NODINOT
  1956 *Une vieille société dirigeante baguirmienne au contact d'une poussée démographique de non-Baguirmiens,* M.S. Paris: Memoirs ENFOM.
RADCLIFFE-BROWN, A. R., D. FORDE
  1950 *African systems of kinship and marriage.* London: Oxford University Press.
REYNA, S. P.
  1972 "The cost of marriage: a study of some factors affecting northwest Barma fertility." Unpublished manuscript. Ann Arbor University Microfilms.
STEWARD, J.
  1963 *Theory of culture change.* Urbana: University of Illinois Press.
WHITE, L. A.
  1959 *The evolution of culture.* New York: McGraw-Hill.

Cultural Factors Inhibiting Population Growth among the Kafa of Southwestern Ethiopia

AMNON ORENT

INTRODUCTION

In a recent analysis of health practices in Ethiopia it has been shown that the birth rate is very low: twenty–five to thirty per 1,000 population as compared to forty per 1,000 for other agrarian societies. Furthermore, studies show that the infant mortality rate is 152 deaths per 1,000 live born and that 59 percent of this loss takes place within the first two months of life. A series of medical reasons have been offered to explain this low rate of population maintenance (Torrey 1967).

Our purpose here is to show how certain cultural factors inhibit the normal population growth of the Kafa people of Ethiopia. Customs and habits with regard to sexual intercourse, postpartum care of infants, and ritual taboos concerning menstruation are factors which inhibit the chances for pregnancy and the survival of the newborn in the first six months of its life. The marriage and divorce customs, i.e. rotation amongst the wives (the Kafa are polygynous) and the high divorce rate are also factors which decrease chances for a rise in the birthrate in the near future.

The eighteen months of fieldwork (1966–67) which allowed me to collect the data for this paper were sponsored by the Foreign Area Fellowship Program, Ford Foundation. The Central University Research Fund of the University of New Hampshire supported the writeup period of an earlier draft of this paper in 1970. To both of these institutions I offer my gratitude; however, I alone am responsible for anything in this article that does not match up to the standards of reason and clear thinking.

KAFA: THE PEOPLE AND THEIR SURROUNDINGS

The peoeple of Kafa live due north of the Omo River bend in southwestern Ethiopia. They are an agricultural people who also raise cattle. Their main crops include maize, *teff*, (an African cereal grass), millet, and *ensete* (Abyssinian banana). The Kafa social organization is based on the activities of the patrilineal, patrilocal, and territorial lineage. They also have dispersed clans which are socially stratified into a hierarchy of high clans and low clans. Kafa society has in addition a series of outcaste groups (hunters of monkeys, crocodile, and hippopotamus and potters and leather tanners), but these people play a very small part in the normal activities of village organization.

Politically speaking, the Kafa are no longer the independent kingdom that they were before 1897, when they were conquered by the Ethiopian armies. They are administered by the central government today, and two members of their tribe sit in Ethiopia's parliament. Very few of the daily habits and familial patterns have changed in Kafa since the conquest. Although the Ethiopians brought Christianity with them and converted most of the Kafa people, spirit worshiping still plays a dominant role after seventy years. Their pantheon of spirits ranges from *ek'k'o* spirits, which are summoned by spirit mediums, to *baro* spirits, which are worshiped on particular feast days throughout the year.

Hamlets in Kafa consist of dispersed homesteads and because the men are polygynous, they have houses in different parts of the hamlet. Each houseowner lives on part of a *gasha* of land (an Ethiopian measurement of eighty hectares), and if he is well-to-do he will have relatives or friends living on the land with him. The countryside is forested heavily with tropical trees and exotic vegetation. One of the things that strikes the eyes of the traveler is that much of the forest is secondary growth, many of the trees being no older than thirty years or so.

The people in Kafa claim that they were once much more numerous but that the wars and bandits of the last few decades killed many of their people, and the conquerors took a large proportion of their people into slavery. The climax of these events occurred in 1897 when the Kafa lost their independence and their monarchy to the expansionist empire of Menelik II, then emperor of Ethiopia. Further devastation of the region followed in a long period of lawlessness, when many people died and the land was left barren to grow the secondary forests of today. References in the literature for these times claim that prior to the war of 1897 the Kafa numbered over a million people and that in the eight months of the war they were reduced to half that number. My own current estimates indicate that the Kafa people may number only approximately 230,000 people.[1] It appears then, that since 1897, if we are to take the population estimates of the European travelers of the time, the Kafa people have been reduced by 77 percent. At the moment we have no accurate way of checking the authenticity of this assumption. Nevertheless, my firsthand evidence indicates that the Kafa were once a much larger tribe than they are today. Moreover, their present customs further inhibit the possibility of any rapid population expansion which would allow them to reach the numbers of the kingdom of the past.

SEXUAL INTERCOURSE

Kafa men say that sexual intercourse is a man's prerogative although women can be quite demanding in their own right. Men generally have coitus three times per week; at least I was so informed by different people. About 21 percent of Kafa unions are polygynous and the custom continues that a man must spend one week with each wife. When a woman begins to menstruate she moves to a small hut for four days. She is not allowed to prepare any food that others may eat; she cannot come into direct contact with any other person; nor is she allowed to enter any house. Usually, another wife takes over the chores. However, often it may be a clan sister or a neighbor. In any case, the Kafa man is obliged to keep up his sexual prowess in a polygynous marriage, whereas in a monogamous marriage he has some respite.

Although sex is a subject which causes a great deal of mirth in Kafa, male attitudes do in fact reflect some ambivalence, and the men make

[1] Friedrich Bieber, who was in Kafa in 1905, writes that the Kafa tribe was decimated from one million to half that number in 1897. (Bieber 1920: 33.) Other travelers who went through Kafa in the first quarter of this century attest to the slaving and general reduction in the population. (Bieber 1920: 20; Montandon 1913: 113–116; Hodson 1927: 146; Grühl 1932: 184).
My own estimate of the size of the population is based on the following data. From the eleven communities which I studied I determined the average size of a Kafa community. I divided the total sample of 3214 people by eleven communities, which came to 290 people per hamlet. (See Table 1 in the Appendix.) From an intensive survey of tax records I found that the subprovince of Kafa Awraja contains 800 hamlets. Multiplying these two quantities I arrived at the total estimated population of 232,000.
The 1965 estimates of the total population of Kafa Province, which includes many other tribes than the Kafa, was 657,000 people (Torrey 1967: 3). This means that the Kafa tribe, which is limited to its own subprovince, numbers approximately 35.2 percent of the provincial population. Seen against the total population of Ethiopia in 1965 (22,590,500) they are approximately 1.03 percent of the population.

equivocal comments when one approaches the subject. It is felt that coitus interferes with good farming practices because it drains a man's energies. This is especially true for the plowing season for *teff* (the unique grain of Ethiopia) and when preparing the fields for the maize planting. Men fear that if a man has intercourse frequently he will become a "weak man" — not only in the physical sense but mentally as well. Frequency of intercourse is connected also with the amount of sperm that a man can generate. Men believe that the greater the amount of sperm in an ejaculation the more likely that the woman will conceive a son. Therefore, because men want sons, a more moderate frequency of intercourse is considered to have definite advantages.

The preferred position for intercourse is a sideway position, the prone position being both uncomfortable for the woman and too demanding on the man. (The beds are made of bamboo poles with false–banana leaves as mattresses.) A man must lie on his left side between the legs of his woman and stimulate her vulva with his penis before actual intercourse. It is not unusual, although I have never witnessed such a case, for a woman to complain to the elders of her community that her husband was not satisfying her desires. The elders generally try to solve the problem quietly. If they feel that he is overworking — and this is the cause of his "weakness" — they will see to it that he does not get drafted for corvee labor gangs which are summoned often by regional chiefs. The real fear for every man is that his wife will make a "public accusation" (she will disguise it in some mundane manner) and everyone will guess at his sexual laxness.

FREQUENCY OF COITUS

According to normative statements from Kafa men, having sexual relations three times per week is average. Actually, if the Kafa people live up to their code of ritual purity in worshiping communally as Christians or in attending the feast days of the various spirits which abound in every hamlet, they probably engage in sexual relations less than twelve times each month. Taking into consideration that women menstruate for at least four days every month, Kafa couples probably engage in coitus even less frequently than that. Furthermore, during the months of June, July, August, and September the number of times men have intercourse may be even fewer because of the intense agricultural activities.

Just as a comparative comment, we might note that the Bena and Hehe tribes of East Africa "claim" that they have coitus twelve to twenty-one times per week (Swartz 1969). If we cut that claim in half it is still twice that of the Kafa. More believable perhaps is that the Bena and Hehe also say that during the agriculturally active periods of the yearly cycle they decrease their sexual activity. I believe that the statements of the Kafa men who informed me of the number of times they had coitus each week are relatively accurate and fall somewhere between those of the American and Bengali groups mentioned by Nag (1972).

MENSTRUATION

The Kafa consider menstrual blood very dangerous. A woman is said to bleed only four days per month. If she flows more than four days then she is being punished by her *ek'k'o* spirit or her family lineage spirit for some misdeed. This misdeed may be related to her behavior during a prior menstrual period when she was not careful enough to avoid the pathway to the spirit house. This indiscretion may have been the cause of her excessive bleeding, or it may have given her other ill-nesses such as fits of hysteria, headaches, or a vaginal discharge.

Men keep away from their wives at the time of menstruation for at least seven days because they fear contamination from any stray blood which might still be in the woman's vagina. Men can be just as easily punished by the spirits for having touched a contaminated woman prior to entering a spirit-worshiping house. The sanctions from the *ek'-k'o* spirits are very real and men try to pay close attention to the dura-tion of their wives' periods.

Since the latter part of the nineteenth century Christianity has made many inroads into Kafa customs. There are both Catholic and Ethio-pian Orthodox churches in Kafa (five Catholic churches and seventy-two Orthodox). The churches are actually an extension of the spirit-worshiping houses in Kafa. In form and function they simply fit into the pantheon of spirits; e.g. Mary, Michael, Gabriel, and Jesus reward and punish just as do the *ek'k'o* and *baro* spirits. Only the names differ. For our purposes it is important to understand that a man or woman who has had sexual intercourse in the twenty-four hours prior to a church feast day (Sundays and commemorative days for the many saints) or prior to a spirit feast day, may not partake of that feast day. The same applies to a woman who has just completed her period. Because these feast days play such an important part in the lives of most Kafa people, by and large they adhere to these rules. Perhaps more pertinent are the sanctions which these supernatural powers can send down to mortal men, e.g. blindness, barrenness, death, etc.

KAFA PREFERENCES FOR SEX OF OFFSPRING

Potential fathers express ambivalence when stating their preference for the sex of the child. Male children are desired in Kafa because as youngsters and young men they are very helpful to their fathers. But in the long run they must compete against their fathers and brothers for the main natural resource of the region, i.e. land. Most men are aware of and can articulate this fear and for this reason many men say that they prefer daughters. Daughters cook and clean when the woman of the house is indisposed, and daughters never compete with their fathers or paternal males for land rights. More important, daughters eventually bring their fathers wealth in the form of the brideprice, which usually consists of cattle. A man's status is increased immeasurably if he then uses the cattle to obtain another wife for himself.

The other side of the picture is that a man needs sons in order to have them make sacrifices to the *baro* spirits. One does not say "a *baro* spirit" in Kafa. The only correct form of reference to a spirit is "my father's *baro*." The *baro* spirits protect the living and honor the dead and every man wants to know that his sons will continue to honor him after he dies.

According to some recent research by Shettles and Kleegman, there are certain cultural practices which are conducive to conceiving either male or female children (Rorvik and Shettles 1970).

Shettles has noted that Orthodox Jews in New York produced a statistically significant higher proportion of boys than did the rest of the population. He determined that this is in part due to the Jewish injunction against sexual intercourse from the onset of menstruation to a full week after termination of the period. This brings the possibility of conception very close to ovulation time and therefore, because of the abstinence of the male and the consequent increase in sperm count, it increases the chances for conceiving a male child. He also says that the deeper the penetration during coitus the more likely the woman will conceive a male.[2]

---

[2] It "... helps insure deposition of the sperm at the entrance of the womb ... this is desirable because the secretions within the cervix and womb will be highly alkaline (and therefore) ... most favorable to androsperms," which are most conducive for conceiving males (Rorvik and Shettles 1970: 39). Clinical tests of Shettles' ideas show 80 percent success.

Summary Statements on Sexual Intercourse, Frequency of Coitus, and Menstruation

It can be stated from the preceding data that:

1. Kafa men engage in coitus infrequently. This infrequency is due in part to their attitudes toward the demands of physical labor during their agricultural activities and to their belief system in the realm of the supernatural.

2. According to rough calculations based on cultural practices, the Kafa have intercourse very close to ovulation time, which increases the chances for conception.

3. The sexual practices of the Kafa are also interesting when examined in the light of recent research on the cultural and biological reasons for conceiving male or female children.

These three summary statements must now be examined in light of statistical data which follow.

BIRTH AND DEATH RATES IN KAFA

For a detailed analysis of birth and death rates in Kafa I have chosen two communities in the Decha Warada district, these being the hamlets of Shapa and Malio. The total population of these two communities is 949 people (see Table 2). I was able to get relatively reliable data on the ages of the people; however, data on death of children and death in general were rather difficult to come by. This is due in part to the accepted belief in Kafa that premature death is due to some punishment from an *ek'k'o* or *baro* type of spirit.

The mean crude birth rate of these two hamlets for a three–year

Table 1. Comparative data for birth and death rates in a few agrarian societies[a]

Country	Year or period	Birth rate	Infant death rate
Brazil	1960–65	41 — 43	170
Ghana	1960	47 — 52	156
India	1951–61	42	139
Indonesia	1962	43	125
Pakistan	1965	49	142
Turkey	1966	43	161
Ethiopia	1965[b]		
Kafa	1964–66	32	386

a All data except for Ethiopia and Kafa are from the Statistical Office of the United Nations, New York (see United States Bureau of the Census 1969: 59).
b Torrey (1967: 4).

period was thirty–two per 1,000 population which in comparison with other agrarian societies in the developing countries is rather low (see Table 1).

Table 2 shows the birth and death rates for Shapa and Malio in Kafa. The steady increase in the crude birth rate after 1962 might be due to an upswing in the use of local clinics (two in Shapa, three in Bonga). The increased use of the clinics might in turn be related to the increase in the dissemination of information about these services. In any case

Table 2. Birth and death rates for Shapa and Malio communities, Decha Warada, Kafa Awraja, Ethiopia

Year of birth	Male	Female	Total	Crude birth rate N = 949	Infant mortality M	F	T	Infant mortality per 1,000 births
1944	9	10	19					
1945	1	4	5					
1946	1	–	1					
1947	6	10	16					
1948	2	5	7					
1949	8	5	13					
1950	6	7	13		3			
1951	6	2	8		4			
1952	9	4	13		7			
1953	8	2	10		6			
1954	6	7	13		5			
1955	4	5	9		4			
1956	8	6	14		6			
1957	17	9	26		8			
1958	8	11	19		5			
1959	8	10	18		6			
1960	9	16	25		3	4c		
1961	3	10	13	13.7	3	2c		
1962	11	11	22	23.7	4	2c		
1963	13	12	25	26.4	8	3c		
1964	12	14	26	27.4	4	5	9	346
1965	10	16	26	27.4	6b	5	11	423
1966	21	14	35	37.0a	6	3	9	389
Unknown	55	30	85	–	–	–	–	–
Totals	241	220	461					
Percentages	52	48	100					

– Blank spaces indicate information unknown or highly questionable.
a A mean figure for the last three years is thirty-two. The figures for the last three years are by and large the most reliable.
b The deaths for the 1964–66 period occurred within the first year of life, and most were within the first six months.
c Female deaths were determined only for Shapa.

these figures are for live births. Of particular interest in Table 2 is the higher birth rate for boys over that for girls and the high infant death rate for male children.

The really shocking comparative data are in the infant mortality rate. Out of thirty–five births in Shapa and Malio in 1966, nine children (38,9 percent) died in the first year of life. Computing deaths per thousand live births, using a mean for three years, we come up with the astronomical rate of 386. Table I indicates that this figure is more than twice that of any other agrarian society in the developing countries including that of Ethiopia.

POSTPARTUM CARE OF INFANTS

Apart from the general problems of hygiene, malnutrition, and diseases,[3] the very high infant mortality rate in Kafa may be due in part to a series of cultural practices. These have to do with the customs of clitoridectomy, circumcision, infant tooth removal, and uvula removal.

Circumcision in Kafa is relatively new. The northern Ethiopians, Amhara and Western Galla, who conquered Kafa in 1897 brought with them many new customs. Once the Kafa people were convinced that the Ethiopian government was going to stay in their territory, they started to convert to the dominant religion of the conquerors, i.e. Orthodox Chistianity. One important custom of these northerners is the traditional biblical injunction of circumcision. The Kafa are very anxious to conform to Ethiopian standards of the "good person," i.e. being Christian, and therefore most male babies are in fact circumcised. However, I have been told that the Kafa have not as yet learned the art of successful circumcision, and consequently, many male infants die after the procedure. I do not know in fact how many infants die from this operation nor do I know how accurate this view of circumcision among the Kafa is. Admittedly this information was given to me by prejudiced informants, i.e. European doctors and by Amhara administrators in government and health services in Kafa. Nevertheless, the fact does stand out that twice as many infant boys die in Kafa in the first year of life than do girls. Clitoridectomy is also practiced in Kafa, but it is not as common as circumcision. In any case my informants felt that this custom, too, was new in Kafa and that "the old lady who does it" doesn't know what she is doing. I knew some of the elder-

---

[3] For a discussion of the rates of death as a result of the conditions and the customs related to health practices in Ethiopia see Torrey 1967.

ly women in the community where I was living, and one in particular had scabies on her body. This is perhaps a small example of the very unhygienic conditions during such operation.

Another common custom in Kafa is the removal of tooth buds from infants. Because the Kafa believe that when infants are born with white gums the teeth are already showing their impetus to come forth, these infants have their gums cut open and the milk teeth removed. In my eighteen–month stay in Kafa I saw two such infants and in both cases the whole area of the mouth was terribly infected indicating advanced stages of blood poisoning. This custom of tooth extraction is also biased in favor of boys. Kafa men believe that if a male child shows its teeth too early it will steal its patrimony prior to what is considered to be the proper time. If the teeth are removed in time, the fathers believe, the threat is thwarted. A percentage of the infant population is certainly affected by this custom. Much to my regret I have no statistics to elaborate this particular point.

Kafa elders are divided on the issue of whether or not the custom of removal of the uvula was introduced by the Amhara. Linguistic analysis indicates that it may be indigenous to the Kafa because their word for the uvula is *kilo,* whereas the Amhara use the word *intll.* In any case the Kafa believe that if an infant is not taking its food properly it is probably due to the interference of the uvula which in their view blocks the passage of food. The *kilo* operation, which is done with a bamboo sliver or with a metal spoon which has been sharpened at one end, causes a great deal of blood letting and I hesitate to guess at its effect on the infant population of Kafa.

SUMMARY STATEMENTS ON BIRTH AND DEATH RATES IN KAFA

1. It becomes apparent that the Kafa birth rate is very low and the infant death rate is very high when compared to other similar agrarian societies.

2. The male-female birth ratio is in fact not very different from other areas in the world. For example, in Kafa, from 1944 to 1966, the ratio was 52 percent male and 48 percent female. In the United States, in 1967, it was 51.2 percent male and 48.8 percent female (United States Bureau of the Census 1969: 58). The data raise some very serious questions for either Shettles' work or my own ethnography.

THE CYCLE OF MATES

There are several ways in which one can examine the divorce rate of a given population. A limiting factor, of course, is the type and quality of data. Because I did not go to the field primarily to study divorce my data are somewhat limited. For instance, Table 3 shows the cycle of mates for a sample of 643 men and completely leaves out comparable data for women. I also did not get information on duration of union and reason for divorce. I much admire Cohen's (1971) exemplary study of divorce amongst the Kanuri of Nigeria, but in comparison my data are sadly lacking. However, I have enough information to shed some light on certain aspects of Kafa divorce frequencies.

Table 3. Frequency of marriages and divorces in a sample of 643 men in Kafa

Frequency per person	Total married	Percent	Total divorced	Percent	
0	0	–	434	67.60	
1	355	55.20	149	23.10	
2	174	27.10	41	6.37	32.4 percent
3	81	12.60	11	1.71	were
4	23	3.57	6	.91	divorced
5	6	.91	2	.31	at least
6	2	.31	0	–	once
7+	2	.32	0	–	
Totals	643	100.00	643	100.00	

Table 4. Divorce rates from a sample of African tribes[a]

	Divorce rates in percent
Urban Kafa (men)	52
Rural Kafa (men)	32
Urban Kanuri (men)	75
Rural Kanuri (men)	56
Bakweri (women)	54
Yao (women)	41
Ngoni (both sexes)	37

[a] The number of divorces as a proportion of all marriages except those ending in death (adapted from Cohen 1971: 125).

Table 5 shows the different combinations of unions which Kafa men engage in through their married years. It seems that the thirty-one to sixty age group has the greatest number of polygynous marriages. In the sample, however, it is also the largest group of people who have been divorced at least once. The figures for the same table may be broken down in another way. Thus we can say that 643 men were

Table 5.   The cycle of mates for men in Kafa: by age[a]
(including eleven communities and thirty neighborhoods)

The cycle of mates[b]	Ages: -20	21–30	31–40	41–50	51–60	61–70	71–	Totals	Percent
1. c	15	139	95	41	33	6	4	333	52.
2. cc	1	7	21	20	10	5		64	10.
3. ccc			2		1	1		4	< 1.
4. cd		27	28	14	10	3	3	85	13.2
5. cdd		2	8	11	8			29	4.5
6. cddd			1	4	3	1		9	1.4
7. cdddd			2		1	1		4	< 1.
8. ccd		4	5	12	8			29	4.5
9. ccdd			2		2		1	5	< 1.
10. ccddd				1				1	< 1.
11. ccdddd		1						1	< 1.
12. c... d...				1	1			2	< 1.
13. cdD			2	3	1	4		10	1.5
14. cddD				1	2	1	1	5	< 1.
15. cdddD					1			1	< 1.
16. cddddD					1			1	< 1.
17. ccdD				1	1	1		3	< 1.
18. ccD			2	2	1	2		7	1.
19. cD		4	2	2	7	3	3	21	3.3
20. cDD							1	1	< 1.
21. cDDd							1	1	< 1.
22. d	1	9	3	1	3		1	18	2.8
23. dd		1						1	< 1.
24. dD				3				3	< 1.
25. ddD			1					2	< 1.
26. D		1		1	1	1		4	< 1.
Total	17	195	174	118	95	29	15	643	

[a]   The total number of households was 721. Out of these 721 households thirty-eight were with women lacking mates and forty were with men who have never had more than a transitional union. Therefore, this table includes only the 643 men who are heads of households and who have had some kind of stable mate at one point.
[b]   c = current wife, d = divorced, D = deceased. The cycle of mates as itemized above did not necessarily occur in these sequences.

engaged in 1,094 unions with women. If we subtract all those unions that were terminated by the death of the wife (sixty in number) we remain with 1,034 unions. Adding up all the divorces we get a figure of 298. Thus we can say that 28.8 percent of all unions ended in divorce.

Cohen (1971: 125) has suggested that we may break down divorce data in another way, i.e. by individual frequency of divorce. Table 3 shows that 32.4 percent of my sample were divorced at least once in their lives and 9.3 percent at least twice.

Two other authors who have worked in Kafa have some divorce data on townsmen (less than one percent of the total population) which confirm the theory that in urban settings divorce is markedly increased. For example, they write that in Bonga, the regional capital of the Kafa Warada district, 52 percent in a sample of 311 men have been married more than once (Giel and van Luijk 1968a: Table 8). Seen in the perspective of Cohen's analysis the Kafa fall somewhat short of other African tribes (see Table 4).

According to my survey 48 percent of Kafa men are married at least twice in their lives and many of their marriages overlap (see Table 6: 21 percent of my sample were polygynous). However, my data as seen in Table 5 are somewhat misleading. Approximately 78 percent of my sample is under fifty years of age (504/643 x 100). My experience in Kafa indicates that most of those men will divorce and remarry at least once if not twice in the years ahead. My sample is of a limited nature in time and space and I believe that I was simply not informed of many marriages which had been dissolved by the older group of men. The attitudes of Kafa men toward the misfortunes of their previous spouses (those who were divorced because of having various diseases) are laden with fear about the causes of these misfortunes. It is believed that a woman is cursed by a malevolent spirit because of her own misdeeds. These

Table 6. Summary of basic demographic data on eleven communities comprising thirty neighborhoods) from Decha and Gimbo Warada (districts), Bonga, Awraja, Kafa, Ethiopia

	Communities I–XI including those six neighborhoods which are on church lands	Communities I–XI excluding those six neighborhoods which are on church lands
Head of household (male)	683	534
Spouses	745	604
Head of household (female)	38	23
Percentage of female heads of household	(5.2 percent)	(4.3 percent)
Children living at home	1496	1209
Percentage of children living at home	(46.7 percent)	(48.0 percent)
Nonmembers of family of procreation	252	150
Percentage of nonmembers of family of procreation	(7.8 percent)	(5.9 percent)
Total population	3214	2520
Number of polygynous households	114	111
Percentage of polygynous households	(16.7 percent)	(20.8 percent)

deeds can reflect the familial situation in her husband's house, and men are somewhat reluctant to speak of divorces which had to do with interference from the spirit world. Therefore, I feel that my data are quantitatively low in their estimate of divorce in Kafa. Women retain their clan identification and in fact are referred to by their clan name in terms of address and reference. Their bond with their husband's clans are weak, and as Table 2 above shows, 2.9 percent of married men have their sisters living with them. By and large these are divorced sisters who are looking for a new mate, and the only place they can turn to once their parents are deceased is to a brother's house.

Divorce, in terms of the rate of fertility of a given population, may be a means by which the population eventually screens out sterile women. The divorce rate in Kafa is about 32 percent (my own data) and the number of sterile women is about 27 percent (in a sample of 106 women, Giel and van Luijk 1968b: Table 40). A high divorce rate in effect allows for circulation of women and thus for a greater chance for sexual compatibility (from the fertility point of view). The highest divorce rate in Kafa occurs in the twenty–one to forty age group for men. This is generally the most fecund age group and these men are most desirous of having children. If a woman does not get pregnant in the first two years of marriage the union usually ends in divorce. But, the woman soon remarries and thus enters the potential gene pool again.

In writing about the high rate of divorce in modern western society some scholars have referred to the phenomenon of "serial polygyny." The Kafa data on divorce rates suggests that what they have in fact is "serial polygyny." The question of the relationship between polygyny and fertility has been raised by many authorities. Dorjahn (1959: 109) writes: "Most writers, both official and unofficial, who take note of the relationship between polygyny and fertility agree that this practice results in fewer children born." Although Dorjahn writes that we must be wary of other variables when it comes to generalizing about polygyny and fertility rates, he states that of twenty–three studies analyzed only five show the polygynously married women to have been as fertile or more fertile than the monogamously married women (1954: 368, Table 229). Furthermore he says "...that the fertility differentials... may be the result of differences in divorce frequency, sterility, age differentials between spouses, or abstinence rather than the coitus rate differential (per wife per year)" (1959: 110). And finally, with regard to divorce and fertility, Dorjahn makes a good guess that fertility decreases as family instability increases (1959: 110).

SUMMARY STATEMENT ON DIVORCE IN KAFA

1. Compared to other African tribes the divorce rate appears somewhat low.

2. The turnover of women in marriage unions in rural areas (32 percent) allows for some reflection on its contribution toward increasing or decreasing the rate of population growth. According to other authors the frequent changing of wives either through polygyny or divorce adversely affects the birth rate.

Table 7. Incidences of relatives of head of household living with his family of procreation[a]

Relationship to head of household	Total	Percentage out of 252 relatives	Percentage out of 721 households
Mother	82	32.5	11.4
Mother's child	5	1.9	< 1.
Mother's sister	1	< 1.	< 1.
Mother's sister's child	2	< 1.	< 1.
Mother's husband	1	< 1.	< 1.
Mother's mother	5	1.9	< 1.
Father	2	< 1.	< 1.
Father's son	1	< 1.	< 1.
Father's mother	1	< 1.	< 1.
Father's sister's child	2	< 1.	< 1.
Wife's child	26	10.3	3.6
Wife's daughter's child	1	< 1.	< 1.
Wife's mother	4	1.5	< 1.
Wife's sister	1	< 1.	< 1.
Wife's sister's child	4	1.5	< 1.
Wife's brother	2	< 1.	< 1.
Brother	16	6.4	2.2
Brother's son	2	< 1.	< 1.
Sister	21	8.3	2.9
Sister's child	12	4.7	1.7
Son's wife	2	< 1.	< 1.
Daughter's child	13	5.1	1.8
Relatives	10	3.9	1.4
Christian — God relations	2	< 1.	< 1.
Servants	34	13.5	4.7
Total	252		

[a] Out of a population sample of 3,213 people (721 households) 252 people were not members of the family of procreation.

CONCLUSIONS

Nag (1972) recently has shown, by comparing selected communities in India and the United States, that the frequency of coitus is not necessarily the reason for a high birthrate. My own data for the Kafa tribe in Ethiopia indicate that the rate of sexual intercourse per month must have some effect on the birthrate. The Kafa people have sexual customs which are optimum for a high birthrate. The time of the month, as defined by the woman's menstrual cycle, in which a man may have intercourse with his wife, and the position of intercourse, are in theory, very good for conception. However, because of additional days of abstinence each month the chances for conception are greatly reduced.

Nag's work among Bengali groups shows the many cultural reasons for their abstinence from coitus. However, none of the reasons given has anything to do with the menstrual cycle. It is in fact the menstrual cycle which controls the ability to conceive. The Kafa people fulfill all the rules for a high rate of fertility and yet they are far below the average for nonindustrialized societies. It would appear, then, that the cultural factor requiring abstinence during many days each month (for conserving strength, for being able to offer sacrifices to spirits, and for attending Christian services) is the deciding factor. Nag's references indicating that the rate of coitus is directly linked to the frequency of conception provide the most pertinent evidence for confirming my own findings. Authors have noted that polygyny and divorce (family instability) also contribute to maintaining low fertility rates.

My initial purpose here was to explain the reasons behind the low population growth of the Kafa. Now that I have summarized and explained the data on the low birthrate, a crucial factor in maintaining populations, a few words must be said about the very high infant mortality rate.

From my sample data it appears that the infant (under five years) mortality rate is very high in Kafa, 38.6 percent. Nevertheless the fact remains that about four out of every ten live infants die by the time they reach five years of age in Kafa. Aside from reasons of malnutrition (Torrey 1967), which are universal for Ethiopia, it would appear that a series of cultural practices add their share to the infant mortality rate. All these data add up to the fact that the Kafa people have had a difficult time in reproducing their population in the last few decades.

REFERENCES

BIEBER, FRIEDRICH J.
1920 *Kaffa: ein Altkuschitisches Volkstum in Inner-Afrika.* Anthropos-
1923 Bibliothek 1 (1920, Munster). Anthropos-Bibliothek 2 (1923, Vienna).

COHEN, RONALD
1971 *Dominance and defiance: a study of marital instability in an Islamic African society.* American Anthropological Association, Anthropological Studies 6. Washington, D.C.

DORJAHN, VERNON R.
1954 "The demographic aspects of African polygyny." Ann Arbor: University of Michigan Microfilms.
1959 "The factor of polygyny in African demography," in *Continuity and change in African cultures.* Edited by William R. Bascom and Melville J. Herskovits. Chicago: University of Chicago Press.

GIEL, R., J. N. VAN LUIJK
1968a "Patterns of marriage in a roadside town in southwestern Ethiopia." Mimeograph.
1968b "Psychiatric morbidity in a small Ethiopian town." Mimeograph.

GRÜHL, MAX
1932 *The citadel of Ethiopia.* Translated by Ian F. D. Morrow and L. M. Sieveking. London: J. Cape.

HODSON, A. W.
1927 *Seven years in southern Abyssinia.* Edited by C. L. Leese. London: T. F. Unwin.

MONTANDON, G.
1913 *Au pays Ghimira: recit de mon voyage à travers le Massif éthiopien,* 1909–1911. Paris: Neuchatel.

NAG, MONI
1972 Sex, culture, and human fertility: India and the United States, *Current Anthropology* 13 (2):231–237.

RORVIK, DAVID M., LANDRUM B. SHETTLES
1970 *Your baby's sex: now you can choose.* New York: Bantam.

SWARTZ, MARC J.
1969 Some cultural influences on family size in three East African societies. *Anthropological Quarterly* 42:73–88.

TORREY, E. FULLER, *editor*
1967 *An introduction to health and health education in Ethiopia.* Addis Ababa: Artistic Printer.

UNITED STATES BUREAU OF THE CENSUS
1969 *Pocket data book – U.S.A. 1969.* Washington, D.C.: Government Printing Office.

Some Aspects of Socioeconomic Change and Fertility Control among the Emerging Elite of the Pathans[1]

KARAM ELAHI

INTRODUCTION

The relationship between economic change and fertility has been subjected to careful examination and debate. There have been two major schools of thought regarding their interaction. The first considers that economic development has an inhibiting effect on fertility, which is evidenced by the demographic transition that occurred in Western countries. The second school has a Malthusian framework; its view is that economic development promotes fertility. I will attempt to examine the relationship between fertility and economic development from both these perspectives (Heer 1965).

This case study of the Pathans seeks to identify the role of economic development by locating the direction of its impact. Approaching this problem through the study of socioeconomic changes is deemed appropriate because of the apparent role of economic development in initiating changes in the traditional social structure. Economic development appears to start a process of structural differentiation and the creation of specialized role structures distinct from and based upon entirely different criteria from the traditional multifunctional structures.

I am grateful to Miss Tasneem Quraishi, Senior Lecturer in Child Development, College of Home Economics, University of Peshawar, for carrying out the interviews with the women of the Gharibabad village.
[1] The concept of elite used in this analysis is in a more general sense. By emerging elite is meant Western-educated technocrats who are distinct from traditional chiefs or *khans*. It was considered essential to use the word "emerging" to convey appropriate meaning because they are in the process of becoming the future elite in diverse fields of activity.

The separation and specialization of roles is a consequence of expanding social and economic activity that creates a new opportunity structure. The opportunity structure in turn is functionally related to and provides a basis for reorientation of individual units of the primary family. These combined sets of conditions encourage more "goal-oriented" behavior patterns and strengthen a sense of efficacy in contrast to the traditional fatalistic outlook on life.

Methodologically the schemes for empirical verification of the effects of socioeconomic development are usually based on the demonstrable fall in birthrates, which is causally linked to such indices of development as a rise in per capita income, increases in percentage of literacy, changes in type and level of employment and finally the overall level of culture reflected by these indices.[2] But the Pathan society with which I deal here is still in the initial process of economic change. There is no apparent fall in the birthrate. The absence of the indicators of demographic transformation make it difficult to adopt any straightforward approach to demonstrate the causal link between socioeconomic change and demographic transformation. What is essential in this case is to find

[2]   This can be further refined by using the statistical test of coefficient correlation. It is easy to demonstrate, for example, that crude birthrates and illiteracy are positively correlated. It may yet be further put to multiple coefficient of correlation R 1 2 3 4 (1 = general fertility level, 2 = percentage of those without education, 3 = per capita national income, 4 = percentage of urban population). But Pathan society is still in the initial process of economic change. The literacy rate is extremely low. Literacy among women is 2.2 percent and overall 7 percent. This shows 93 percent as illiterate. Thus the birthrates which are obviously related to this high percentage of population have no use of such refined tools as mathematics. Another reason which is still more important is that there is no indication of the fall in birthrates. The very basis of assumption — that a fall in the birthrate is related to socioeconomic change — is not there.

It would be possible to compare crude birthrates and fertility rates of the provinces or regions. The Northwest Frontier Province is comparatively less industrialized. It has less urban population, lower rate of literacy, lower per capita income. But the crude birthrates are comparatively low. For example West Pakistan's estimated crude birthrate is 53 per thousand. (Yusuf Farhat 1967; also Pakistan Family Planning Council 1967 gives the crude birthrate as 42; adjusted 53.) To cite Khalid (1967): "utilizing the average fertility rates obtained for the towns of Sialkot, Lyallpur, and Multan, the 1951 birthrate for Pakistan comes to 51 per thousand." He further gives birthrates for West Pakistan 1960–65 as 43.5 and 1965–70 as 43.5. This means that Punjab, the Northwest Frontier Province, and West Pakistan do not show significant differentials, though there is great economic disparity. In the absence of indicators of variation, it seems that the elements of this system of population are constantly reflecting stable high growth trends. The demographer can safely predict the future population. To the social demographer the persistent configuration of the elements constituting the social system is logically coherent in their interconnection with the demographic pattern. The demographic phenomena in this case would show a remarkable consistency with patterns of regularity in social and individual units of human behavior.

a tendency that reflects oncoming changes which cannot yet be demon-- strated by the mathematical quantifications.

I shall examine those characteristics of the traditional system to which the majority of the population is still bound, and their relevance to the existing demographic situation, thus helping to explain the "why" of persisting high fertility. Then the model is exposed to induced dynamic changes. The impact of these changes is traced by describing how these changes affect traditional stability. The ultimate determinants in this process, according to Reed (1955) "are sought in the organized sub-group of goal-directed people who comprise the institutional isolate in every human society. . . ." It will then be necessary to see how this group emerges.

Anthropological studies of various population groups have concentrated on stable models based on the concepts of equilibrium, in which population fluctuations are accommodated in a variety of ways that tend to restore the balance (Reed 1955).[3] The balance of the indigenous population gets disrupted only through the introduction of foreign elements. For instance, these societies are commonly subject to a high deathrate, a result of diseases, epidemics, and child mortality. The introduction of preventive cures in preindustrial societies has led to "superabundant fertility" and falling mortality. The Pathan society, in this respect, is no exception. It is therefore essential to see how Pathan society has responded to this superabundant fertility. A lack of response in such societies is explained by sociologists in terms of time lag between the surge in population growth and the subsequent change in cultural and normative elements. Although the realities of danger are long over, the continuing belief that group existence is threatened by mortality finds its expression in fatalistic beliefs and the value system of the culture. This suggests two explanations: (1) the interpretation of demographic behavior as a response to absolute needs; and (2) the

---

[3] Professor Nag (1973) has challenged the modern theory of demographic transition which explains the population dynamics of western countries in the post industrial period. The theory postulates that "from high levels of both mortality and fertility in the pre-industrial period, the population of these countries settled down to low levels of mortality and fertility through a transitory stage of low mortality and high fertility levels. One of the underlying assumptions of this theory is that both mortality and fertility levels of all pre-industrial societies were generally high." Nag questions this assumption and has demonstrated that there is "great variation in the fertility levels of contemporary non-industrial societies."

I am not concerned here with this debate, however. The population dynamics and social dynamics are deemed as mutually interdependent processes. This article explores these processes in the case study of Pathans where economic change has just started.

idiosyncrasy of a particular culture and its customs and value systems (Davis 1963).

Both these explanations have implicit danger of oversimplification. In Davis' words (1963),

... such as the assumption that population is simply a matter of two capacities – a "reproductive urge" on the one side and "means of subsistence" on the other – or at the opposite extreme, that demographic behavior is a function of a "traditional culture" or "value system."

The explanation of demographic change, accordingly, he emphasizes:

is not to be found in some inflexible biological or economic law or in some particularistic cultural idiosyncrasies, but rather in the main features of the operating social organization on the one hand, and, on the other, in the changing conditions which arise from past performance and the altering international politico-economic environment (1963: 345).

PATHANS' TRADITIONAL SOCIETY

Social Structure and Higher Fertility

The Pathans' demographic behavior can be analyzed within the context of the traditional institutional framework and its remarkable continuity, on the one hand, and induced changes that interact producing counter effects on the other. It needs relatively more emphasis on the understanding of the entire complex of interacting forces presently governing the societal replacement. The continuity of traditional mechanisms of the institutional complex, carrying a high fertility value, indicates an essential common feature of preindustrial societies — a high birthrate.

About such societies Davis (1955) and Davis and Blake (1956) have postulated that corporate kinship system, clan, and lineage organization tend to motivate universal early marriage and consequently higher marital fertility. Davis (1955) asserts that the structural features of such societies are conducive to early marriages because the nuclear family is subordinate to and dependent on a wider kinship structure. This structure is manifested through authority patterns and economic solidarity and provides economic security making early marriage possible. The corporate kin groups are further motivated by their desire to establish links with other family lines. The desirability of more children in this case is apparent, because they strengthen the family line and establish status. The applicability of these propositions to the Pathans will be examined.

Pathan traditional social organization and economic system and its relevance to higher fertility can be understood in terms of its features, similar in character to that constructed, as an analytical framework, by social demographers. The key social structure variables which provide a guideline, are extended family, corporate lineage, and economic solidarity and authority structure and are congruent to a maximum degree with the Pathan system. The Pathans live in the Northwest Frontier Province of Pakistan which is divided administratively into two zones, tribal areas, and the adjoining settled district. The homogeneity of the population is evidenced by the fact that they speak a common language, Pashto, and follow the same code of life. The Pathans are divided into lineages. The lineages are occasionally localized groups but are often dispersed. The lineage is composed of joint families, the most visible grouping. It is the joint family which is most significant in the overall social structure of the Pathan tribe. The joint family is prevalent because the land and immovable property keep the family, a closely knit economic unit, integrated. It may be a coresidential (members living under the same roof or sharing the same dwelling) or coproperty (members sharing the same landed property) unit, or both.

The joint family consists of spouses (husband and wife), unmarried daughters, married sons, and their offspring. Socialization is also carried out within this unit. The children are socialized by the mother until puberty, at which time the boys associate themselves with the male members and girls with the female members of the family. In the division of labor between sexes it is apparent that the boys go to work with the father, and girls perform household duties. The members of a joint family also perform *rites de passage* on occasions of birth, circumcision, marriage, and death, elaborately carried out to establish the member's new status. For instance, a bachelor does not enjoy a recognized social status because he has not passed through the ceremonies. He is called *landar,* meaning that he is not as responsible a member as a married person.

The father, who is the senior man by age or generation in the joint family, is the headman of the unit. Jural and economic authority are vested in him. He is dominant in the Pathan social system because inheritance and descent are traced from him to his offspring.

The institution of marriage is of the highest value because it entitles a husband to a set of rights in his wife's sexual and procreative capabilities and assures perpetuation of the lineage.[4] A woman's fertility is

---

[4] My own observation based on field study of Pathans of the Northwest Frontier Province.

so important that if she does not bear a child within a short span of time, the son may be pressured to marry another woman. In the majority of cases of polygyny observed, the reason given by the husband was that his first wife had not given him a child.[5]

After marriage he has the option either to stay and work with his father or to separate from his parents. Upon the death of the father, each son becomes head of his own family. The father is the main unifying link in the family. On his death the unifying link is gone and the joint family disintegrates. His death usually comes, however, at a time when the joint family has already attained a huge group structure through the addition of children and grandchildren, so that from the fragmentation units emerge that are not nuclear but of the joint family type. They construct their dwellings near the ancestral house and divide the landed property. Thus the household keeps on dividing until finally a village settlement emerges. This process meets all those criteria set in terms of economic solidarity of the joint family and authority vested in the head of the joint family.

The economic system has characteristics which further reinforce the stability of the joint family. The system is agrarian and in addition to agricultural laborers it requires smiths, muleteers, tanners, etc. Job specialization is attained through socialization in the family. The son of a smith learns his techniques from his father and the same is true for all the others. Thus the *kasab* [occupation] is perpetuated through the family. There are no institutions other than the family to teach any specialist techniques. The high degree of differentiation of roles, and the prescription of rights and duties for the person in a particular role are essential to the maintenance of the productive system, because at the peak of the production cycle no person can afford to perform two roles simultaneously, without jeopardizing his commitment to his original duties and obligations.

This system is a closed one. It does not have the capacity to go on absorbing the continual addition of more and more members. Davis has suggested that it is the continuing high fertility along with a decline in the deathrate which explains the rapid growth of population in India and Pakistan. Understanding the demographic situation thus requires an understanding of fertility: the actual trend in birthrate and those factors responsible for it.

---

[5] This fact is also apparent in the Family Laws Ordinance which provides for a second marriage subject to these conditions: (a) the couple has no children; (b) the wife's consent is essential for a second marriage. The second condition was simply a built-in mechanism for restriction.

At the operational level, the traditional social organization makes for a higher fertility level. And because of the inheritance law, the units of production get smaller and smaller with the passage of time.[6] This phenomenon forces the Pathans to make readjustments. Thus, in a majority of villages a small landowning class has emerged, but due to a deterioration in their economic position, they have to work the land themselves — not a desirable situation.[7]

Table 1.   Decennial birthrate per thousand in Northwest Frontier Province

1901	1911	1921	1931	1941	1951	1961
29.5	38.1	27.3	28.0	42.0	43.5	45.5

The birthrates given in Table 1 are taken from census records of India.[8] The table shows that up to 1931 the birthrates are greatly underestimated. The discrepancies in registration of births have been a dilemma for the census authorities from the start of the century and still continue to be. The birthrates for 1941, 1951, and 1961 were computed from census records using a reverse survival method to bring the table up to date. It shows the upward trend in birthrates.

Traditional Response, "Hiving Off," Migration and its Ineffectiveness

It has been recorded that various societies have responded to their ex-

[6]   Most of the farm area is fragmented into small parcels and the size of the farm as an operating unit is small as a consequence of growing pressure of population and the Islamic law of inheritance.
[7]   My data for this observation come from two main sources: (1) *Jumabandi* is a record book maintained in every village by the local revenue officer known as *Patwari*. In this book the entries about the ownership of land and its sale and transfer are recorded. (2) *Khasra Gardawari* is another document, prepared by *Gardawar*, the immediate superior of the *Patwari*. This contains the record of on-the-spot verifications by revenue officers about the crops: who cultivates and who owns particular land plots. This is done normally once or twice a year. *Khasra Gardawari* provides evidence as to whether a plot of land is cultivated by a tenant farmer or the owner himself. When a plot of land has been regularly cultivated by the same tenant for a number of years (I do not know the exact period), the tenant's occupancy right is established. He then cannot be ejected by the owner.
[8]   The information in this table is from the *Census Report of India*, 1911, 1921, 1931. Due to nonavailability of birth and death records, the birth records were computed from census records using the reverse survival method for 1941, 1951, and 1961. The enumerated population below ten years of age are the survivors of birth in the census period. The terminology adopted is that Nx persons enumerated at age X are the survivors of

$$\frac{Lo}{Lx} \times Nx.$$

The factors Lo and Lx are taken from life tables of the 1961 census. The number of persons enumerated in 1961 as aged 0–1 are the survivors of birth in 1960, under operation of mortality prevalent in the group. The estimated birthrates by means of population are divided by mean population of 1951–1961.

cessive population growth in a variety of ways, from the drastic one of trading off a number of people to the actual infanticide or neglect of female infants, according to the level of the culture. The Japanese in modern times have shown a "multiphasic" response, using all possible measures, including migration, celibacy, and abortion to control the birthrate. It appears that the motivation is in the nature of a threat perceived by the society facing the situation.

The Pathan situation is alarming compared to worldwide standards. We will now examine the extent to which this threat has been realized and what methods have been adopted to cope with it. The nature of these methods, or the response, would reflect how far the indigenous people show competence to handle it effectively.

There are certain cultural symbols which illustrate the degree of consciousness prevalent among the people. The harshness of the environment, which demands hard work and creates poverty, is apparent in day-to-day expressions. When a Pathan meets another Pathan he greets him by saying *satari mushê* [I hope you won't get tired]. The reply is *khawar mushê* [I hope you don't become impoverished]. This is meaningful when we keep in mind the harsh environment and perennial dearth of resources. There is a further expression revealing the ever-present fear of child mortality. When a boy addresses someone who is working, he also says *satari mushê,* but the reply is *loi shê* [I hope you may become an adult]. When the expressions are analyzed the conclusion is that the awareness of poverty forces the Pathans to work hard. Child mortality is another factor that tends to deprive the society of its working population.

When we say this, however, it doesn't mean that the Pathans have a perpetual fear of the precariousness of group existence. The threat of overpopulation is also understood and is portrayed in the proverbs and folk songs such as *Nin da ka saba da rana pata da watan da da lasa da janan.* The young Pathan sings to his peers, saying shortly he will have to leave his country for the sake of his beloved. Beloved here is the symbol of life aim. This aim cannot be attained because things have become difficult. Its implication on the economic side is that the person has lost all that was prized in life due to economic impoverishment and consequent loss of status. The other interpretation of this phrase is in terms of feudalistic chivalry, when the knight or khan leaves his country to undertake a romantic adventure in far distant lands for some ideal lady of his love. Thus, it can be stretched to encompass a variety of references, but the empirical referent is certainly economic impoverishment.

As another response to excessive population growth, Pathans have migrated to cities of the Indo-Pakistan subcontinent. This migration continues to increase from 1921 onward. This is clearly indicated by *Census Reports of India* from 1911, 1921, and 1931. The outflow in 1901 was 54,858; in 1911, 65, 476; in 1921, 67,642; in 1931, it ran to 90,681. The outflow in 1941 was much larger but as it was during World War II, many people of the Northwest Frontier Province joined the Indian Army. It was due to the historic incidence of war and, therefore, is not very relevant to our present discussion. However, in the following decade, Pakistan's first census showed that 250,000 Pathans were living outside the Province in the cities of other provinces. The in-migration to the Province from 1901 to 1931 is also excluded here because the majority of inmigrants were the soldiers of the Indian army. The breakdown of these figures suggests that Nepalese, Punjabis, Scots, and others who were counted as inmigrants were actually soldiers of the British Indian army stationed at various strategic places and in encampments (*Census Reports of India* 1911:60, 1921:59, 1937:64).[9]

There is a falling in the mortality level after 1931, according to the mortality graphs (*Census Reports of India* 1931, volume one). The outflow after independence increased to the level of 3 percent of the base population per year. There is a continuous increase of 7 percent in outflow and it is projected to continue increasing. This post-independence exodus is rather remarkable and is consistent with the pull-factor. Previously the Pathans left the Northwest Frontier Province for scat-

---

[9] Discussion of outmigration in the *Census Report* of 1911 is reproduced for reference. Emigrants only amounted to 29 per thousand of actual population of border districts. At the same time, while in-migration was contracting, emigration was becoming more common. This is understandable enough. The same cause, namely the extension of cultivation and growth of population within the province which have operated to check the streams of migration towards it, have been effective to induce the native population to tend to look for outlets elsewhere. There is not yet, of course, any such pressure of population as to drive any large number to look beyond the province for livelihood. At the same time, whatever the cause (and it is presumably not unconnected with the growing density at home and increasing opportunities of getting away), those who turn their eyes to the areas outside are increasing. Migrants from the province to other areas in India have increased by 10,618, 19 percent since 1901.

Also see *Census Report of India* (1921: I, 61) with regard to in-migration: "The total number of immigrants from other provinces of India is 118,395 ... The Punjab, which always supplies the largest number of immigrants, tops the list not only because it is contiguous to this province, but also because most of the immigrants consist of the troops concentrated in the province and the majority of the Indian army is recruited from the Punjab ... The imigrants from the Punjab advanced from 67,132 to 97,624 during the decade, a gain of 45 percent, which is accounted for by the presence of an unusually large number of military forces in the Province."

tered cities of the Indo-Pakistan subcontinent. In a majority of cases, this practically amounted to abandoning the local community, the distance being long and communications cumbersome.

In the post-independence period, the improvement of communication between villages and cities of Pakistan made rural-urban movement easier. But it became much more difficult to move out of the country to the cities of the subcontinent or beyond because after independence the countries which had formed the British Empire were now independent nation states. Thus the movement became restricted to much smaller areas and within the border of Pakistan. Now outmigration from the Province to cities of Pakistan is more like a rural-urban movement within the country. It is this exodus which is of interest here. I therefore take up post-independence census records.

In 1951 according to the census report, the population of the areas comprising Peshawar Division, i.e. Hazara, Peshawar, Morden, Kohat, and adjoining tribal regions, was 4,970,000, growing at the rate of 2.6 percent; the population ran 6,372,000 in 1961. Of those 6,372,000, the settled areas accounted for 3,413,000 or 52.6 percent and 2,959,000 or 46.6 percent was tribal population. In 1970 this population was estimated at 7,957,000 and it is estimated that by 1985 the total population will be 11.5 million. The age and sex composition is expected to conform to 1961 (Khan 1970). (See Table 2.)

Table 2. In/out migration

	1951	1961	Variation Number	Percentage
1. Born in Peshawar Division (counted outside)	167,260	250,220	82,960	+ 49
2. Born outside Peshawar (counted inside)	61,028	67,009	15,901	+ 9.
Excess of one over two net outmigration	106,232	183,211	76,979	+ 72.

From 1951 to 1961, the outmigration as given in the tables (Khan 1970) was 82,960 persons; thus some 3 percent of the 1951 population left this area. The net outmigration of 76,979 is equal to 2.8 percent of the population. The outflow rate is assumed to remain the same for the population exodus during 1961–1970, which was estimated at 91.8 thousand, the net exodus being 85.5 thousand. The exodus, as suggested by the same source, was expected to decrease after 1970, due to expansion in manufacturing, commercial, and other nonagricultural sectors in general. Agricultural improvement is also being planned. It is forecast that the exodus will start diminishing at the same rate as it increased, and by 1983 the outmigration will stop altogether. Table 3, giving the projection of exodus, is adopted from Khan (1970).

The outflow of population is caused by overpopulation on the one hand, and the availability of alternative sources of employment in the cities of Pakistan on the other. It is a process of redeployment of surplus population of the working-age group. When these aggregates of outflow are closely examined, the composition of the group migrating is found to be comparatively younger. (This is based on my own observations in Karachi.) They travel as bachelors even if married. The reason for this is that not until they find employment are they economically in a position to have their families with them. This is evidenced by

Table 3. Projection of gross/ net exodus from Peshawar division 1970–1989

		(Number in thousands)				
		Gross exodus		Net exodus		
Year	Popu-lation	Rate: percent per annum	Num-ber	Rate: percent per annum	Num-ber	Total out-living population
1	2	3	4	5	6	7
1961–69	3,413a	0.300	91.8b	0.280	85.5b	342.0c
1970	4,157	0.285	11.8	0.260	10.8	353.8
1971	4,248	0.270	11.4	0.240	10.2	365.2
1972	4,341	0.255	11.1	0.220	9.5	376.3
1973	4,436	0.240	10.6	0.200	8.9	386.9
1974	4,533	0.225	10.2	0.180	8.1	397.1
1975	4,633	0.210	9.7	0.160	7.4	406.8
1976	4,735	0.195	9.2	0.140	6.6	416.0
1977	4,839	0.180	8.7	0.120	5.8	424.7
1978	4,945	0.165	8.0	0.100	4.9	432.7
1979	5,053	0.150	7.6	0.080	4.0	440.3
1980	5,164	0.135	7.0	0.060	3.1	447.3
1981	5,277	0.120	6.3	0.040	2.1	453.6
1982	5,393	0.105	5.7	0.020	1.1	459.3
1983	5,511	0.090	5.0	0.000		464.3
1984	5,632	0.075	4.2			468.5
1985	5,755	0.060	3.4			471.9
1986	5,881	0.045	2.6			474.5
1987	6,010	0.030	1.8			476.3
1988	6,142	0.015	1.0			477.3
1989	6,277	0.000	0.0			

a   1961 Census population
b   Exodus during 1961–1969 (nine years total)
c   Estimated at the end of 1969

the circumstances of the families of migrants. The heavy demands made on the traditional system by conspicuous consumption often contributes to impoverishing the families.[10]

The occasion for spending may be for such initiation ceremonies as circumcision, marriage, or death, or for feasts. The common peasantry normally do not have enough savings. If there are no savings available, property may be mortgaged or, to pay off the debt, the younger male members travel to industrial centers in hopes of finding employment. When they do find jobs they save and send money back to the parents. But it takes time before a family is in a position to arrange a marriage for the younger members if they have traveled as bachelors or if they were married before migrating, to enable them to be reunited with their families. It can also create a situation of voluntary abstinence from sexual union. The family economic solidarity remains but this solidarity has a reverse effect in terms of the obligation to support the parents.

There is even a chance that a bachelor living in a city and working there may be asked to take care of a younger sibling while the latter is going to school. This further increases the period of bachelor life. The fact that marriages take place at a later age must produce a significant

---

[10]   Such conspicuous consumption on certain occasions is carried out by all peasant societies; yet there are other misfortunes such as crop failure during a bad season. In the Indo-Pakistan subcontinent, agriculture is mostly dependent on natural seasonal variation. The possibility of impoverishment of peasant families due to these natural calamities is not ruled out. But even the normal season cannot provide much surplus over and above the subsistence level. For conspicuous consumption either debt is incurred or land is mortgaged to a moneylender. In British times it led to a very severe crisis. The government then legally banned the purchase of land by moneylenders or merchants. The people who were not professional agriculturalists could not buy land. (See revenue records of the Northwest Frontier Province, Office of the Director of Government Archives, Peshawar.)

Recently the government of Pakistan felt that this overspending on conspicuous consumption was basically part of continued traditionality, which poses a serious problem. The government-sponsored seminar on eradication of social evils has particularly emphasized strong measures to stop this. Hashmi (1961: 54) points out that "the series of ceremonies that precede and follow the actual wedding such as gift exchanges, dowries, feasts, large parties and rituals involve a lot of spending beyond family means." He says he is not "against rituals and ceremonies but the extravagance which reduces parents to bankruptcy is most objectionable."

I participated in the marriage rites of many peasant families in Hazara District, Tanawal, Lora, and Dhund areas on behalf of parents, and was shocked in many of these areas at the huge number of guests and the number of feasts that were held. The gold ornaments, jewelry, and dresses offered to the girl's family were of very high quality. Even the embroidery work on the bride's dress might have cost thousand of rupees. In three of the above cases, the bridegroom's parents had mortgaged their entire land. When the guests were leaving for their homes, the bridegroom had already planned to leave his new wife with his parents and go to Karachi to get a job.

effect on demographic performance. But to affect the aggregates, the percentage of population that migrates is still too insignificant. Also, the age may be raised from the traditional marriage age by four or five years, but this does not make any significant difference because marriage is still within the age limits characterized by normal fertility.

Thus the effects of migration and consequent rise in age at marriage, or of abstinence, is not likely to reduce sharply the birthrate even within this group. This, however, needs further research to determine the impact of migration, but so far no study of Pathan migrants has been carried out. There is every likelihood that if younger men migrate from an area the age structure of the population changes, the consequences being reduction in fertility and increase in area mortality. But this happens when the number of younger migrants is considerably larger: the continuing high growth rate of the population of the Northwest Frontier Province defies this assumption. The society needs more measures to check high fertility, such as the use of contraceptives and family planning. But the use of contraceptives and such measures as abortions or celibacy are against the cultural ethos of the society.[11] The situation is both alarming and unbalancing, and the Pathan traditional response of moving out is not enough to cope with it.

ECONOMIC DEVELOPMENT AND DEMOGRAPHIC CHANGE

Historical Background

So far we have dealt with the static situation, the factors that tend to generate change in a traditional system and the result of changes induced by the economic development program. This program has its multidimensional impact. On the one hand, as expected, it diversifies the resource potential and increases employment opportunities, and on the other, it tends to disintegrate the traditional economy of the community which hitherto was stable but now is incapable of yielding the desired living standard.

When we talk of changes and developmental activities, the normal

---

[11] I had the privilege of attending a seminar on birth control and family planning held under the auspices of VAID Department, Campbelpur, in 1961. This area was then a part of Peshawar Division. The VAID workers almost all were of the opinion that local people disapproved of birth control. They suggested that the people had traditional methods of controlling birth and even do abortions in the case of illegitimate conception.

impression gathered, and rightly so, by the various scholars who have worked in the developing world of Asia and Africa, is that these changes are the result of cultural contact with the Western world. The frontal attack by Western institutions on indigenous institutions has resulted in the uprooting of certain local institutions and the substitution of Western ones. The developing world now looks like a matrix of culturally mixed institutions. The theoretical implications of these statements are that interactions among institutions are an initial step towards disruption of the local cultural framework (Kessing 1955).

In the Pathan case this theory can be applied only with caution for various reasons. First, because Pathan contact with the British was characterized by hostility and resistance, there was a conscious attempt to fight back the erosion of local institutions.[12] This is manifest in Pathan opposition to British education, for instance. Second, the introduction of political, legal, administrative, and educational institutions did not create an impact so profound as to penetrate to the mass level. The selected few who participated in these institutions and worked with the British were a class of people who opted for Western education primarily in order to get jobs. The khans, or chiefs (and very few of those), sent their children for education only to reinforce their positions. They rose through the civil service in the British administration. On attaining certain positions or ranks they were given titles like Khan, Khan Bahadur or Nawab (knighthood), with fiefs given as a reward for meritorious service rendered to the British Crown. This title gave the civil servants a position of prestige in an entirely indigenous hierarchy of gradation within the feudal framework of Pathans. This did not amount to a change in the system of roles, but instead introduced an additional mechanism to attain a position within the existing system of stratification. This class in turn was locally viewed as an agent of or collaborator with imperialism. So Western education was considered a way of creating British loyalists.

The Northwest Frontier Province remained economically the same agrarian society. The only change was that settled areas directly administered by the British found British magistrates, revenue collectors,

---

[12]   The reference here is to the Pathans' continued struggle against the British. It should not be assumed that the Pathans fought battles as the tribal people did, against the colonizing imperial forces. The local leaders, chiefs, and mullahs like Hade Mullah, Haji of Tarrangzai, not only fought battles but also preached against British education. Sir Salahzada A. Qayam, who worked for the establishment of the University of Peshawar, was a civil servant and had to name the institution *dar ul aloom Islamia* [Islamia College] to attract Pathans. The evidence is scattered in various books and articles.

and policemen among them. If the disputes among various factions could not be settled locally, then the government courts were approached. This created the tendency among the disputant factional groups to approach the formal legal institutions — not to get justice done but to use the institutions for prestige reasons. The litigation continued among disputants, not because they did not know who was legally right or wrong but because nobody would accept defeat. Therefore, even though they brought in a complex new legal framework and process, the British did not significantly erode the traditional forms and values.[13]

The change from colonial rule to national government in 1947 brought three new elements: (1) the economic development program with emphasis on mass education; (2) the restriction placed by the change of government on migration to cities in countries formerly included in the British Empire; and (3) the mass evacuation of Hindus, a trading and commercial class which had acted as middlemen between the producer Pathans and the market. They controlled through their agents at the village level the movement of goods between cities and the villages of the frontier. Their evacuation created new opportunities for some people to take their place. At this time people from India were also coming to Pakistan, but these refugees did not concentrate in the frontier. Rather, they settled primarily in the Punjab and the city of Karachi. These factors are highly relevant to the Pathan situation discussed below.

Economic development was started in the Northwest Frontier Province by the national government, which initiated many developmental projects simultaneously. The first thing worth noting was the installation of sugar factories in Mardan and Charsadda; tobacco processing factories at Mardan, Akora Khutak and Naushura; the Adamji Chemical, Ferozson's Pharmaceutical Laboratories, and textile mills and cardboard mills at Naushura. This created an incentive for farmers to shift to cash crops instead of food grains. The areas under sugar cane and tobacco increased enormously. This in turn created a shift from paying rewards for service to working the land for cash payments instead of for a fraction of the produce. Some petty landlords rented land from others for a fixed sum of money to be paid annually, known as *aja ra*. This

[13] These are my own observations. We must not, however, assume that the national government of Pakistan had opted for a different model of development. The point here is that when the British left, the rulers in Pakistan planned developmental programs according to Western models and were assisted by the developed countries of the West. The participation of Pathans in national activities then increased.

meant a profitable investment. The land was cultivated, and after paying off the work team, net profit from the cash crop was very high.

At the same time a big dam construction project was undertaken as a joint venture with the government of Canada under the Colombo plan. In the heart of the tribal area are the narrow mountain gorges through which the Kahal River emerges into the Peshawar Valley. The project involved highly technical work, with the manual labor supplied by Pathans who came by the thousands. These workers learned on the job to handle various kinds of equipment. Some became electricians, others learned to drive heavy trucks, while still others worked with earth-moving machinery. The labor had to be transported for every shift from Peshawar and the adjoining villages. The tribal Pathans bought trucks and converted them into buses which plied between the city and the damsite. This was their first exposure to an industrial and technically modern work situation, and the tribal Pathans acquired new skills.

After completion of this dam, another earth-filled dam was started in the Punjab, a much bigger project, financed by the World Bank. The same workers were recruited to work on it. Simultaneously, an air base and other construction work were going on in the frontier, financed by the United States. All of this was an introduction of a new and external element in the traditional setup. Many of the Pathans who earned money reinvested it in buses and transportation companies. Others, whose land was taken over by these projects, were paid by the government; they also went into commerce and business. Locally, a class of businessmen — construction and building contractors — was emerging. But the majority of those who were comparatively younger and had found work on these projects, after the projects' completion either were absorbed by business firms or started finding jobs in various other centers.

This created further momentum for labor migration. At present, it is usual for boys to go to an industrial center. They have their co-villagers in the center, with whom they can stay. If the destination is Karachi, the ethnic ties may be used first for help in finding a manual job in a textile mill, and then later, gradually to pick various trades. The factories provide on-the-job training. The situation becomes exactly like the normal industrial process of labor differentiation. Those who are now entering may start from the lowest position and move upward with the passage of time and acquisition of skills.

The Consequences of Economic Change: Structural Breakdown

The newly skilled workers *(kasabgars)* find the change very favorable. They leave the traditional setup for the urban center. A carpenter may easily find a job as a joiner in city furniture factories. A blacksmith may find it easier to learn lathe turning; all that he has to do is learn to handle the new tools. Former muleteers have opened small shops and entered into the trade. The sons of tenants may learn to drive buses or trucks by being apprenticed to the bus owner. In the new setting the availability of these roles has upset the traditional pattern of relationships. Its impact on the rural agricultural society is significant, for many in rural and village occupations are no longer dependent upon the landlord. By earning money one can improve his status, and new economic changes provide chances for mobility and change which hitherto were impossible. This process has social implications of high consequence. It has set in motion the forces that interact with indigenous social organization and the first impact is on the family, and through it on the whole set of relationships. The economic and social training functions previously performed by the family are now increasingly performed by separate nonfamilial institutions. The kinship groups have no control over the assignment of roles or occupational status. This gives impetus to a further breakdown of traditional ascriptive criteria, to be replaced by more flexible ones that are suitable to accommodate the increasing upsurge in social mobility.

The Role of Education and Creation of a New Class

Education plays a predominant role in filtering out a group of people who constitute a Western-educated class. It was pointed out that economic development necessitates manpower training to meet the growing need for technically skilled labor. This is done through educational institutions. The post-independence period is characterized by increasing participation of Pathan rural youth in educational activity. Mass literary schemes were launched by multiplying the educational institutions to provide facilities for education at the village level. There were also additions of colleges and high schools, and finally the opening of a university. The real advancement in education is indicated by the percentage of the total school- and college-age population attending the educational institutions.

In 1961 only 18.3 percent of the total population aged five to nineteen was attending school or college but in 1968 the figure rose to 29.9 percent. These figures indicate the growing interest in education. This large number of high school students and graduates in various branches of knowledge cannot find jobs in the rural areas. They have to leave their homes for urban centers where they can find work. The opportunities for highly qualified graduates is not as good as for the average literate person, but what is important is that expectations are rising and there is increasing demand for creating more job opportunities for the growing technically-trained, educated manpower. Those of the educated group who do find jobs usually find permanent jobs, and therefore have left the rural areas permanently.

The increasing number of school- and college-age children who are attending school add to the expenses of the family. The children in the traditional system start helping their parents with the work and thus also learn their respective occupations. But when education and training are imparted by specialized institutions the parental family is not only deprived of the help of younger members but it adds to the burden when they have to support the children's education. It makes the family realize the burden of having children. (At the national level this realization is always there because of the relatively high percentage of school-age population.) After the completion of education the young tend to seek employment in towns and cities away from rural areas,[14] and become economically independent.

The joint family depended on the income of the property owned by the head of the family. After marriage, the son had an option to leave the home of his parents, but he was bound for economic reasons to the joint family. In present circumstances when dependence on parental income is no longer essential, nuclear families tend to separate. It has been observed that parents' investment in children's education and training is motivated to some extent by expectations of future support from the children. These expectations create tensions in the joint family relationship. When the newly married couple was dependent on parental property jointly held by the family, the mother-in-law exercised an unquestionable authority over her daughter-in-law who was expected to perform household tasks assigned to her by the mother-in-law. Major decisions were in the hands of the parents. The division of roles by sex was prescribed. The strict segregation of conjugal roles, a normative imperative, could not be violated. The daughters-in-law, whether they

---

[14] The West Pakistan government had to make rules for certain educated groups like doctors to serve in the rural areas for some years. But for others there was no possibility of such rules because the rural areas have no employment opportunities.

liked that position or not, had to accept it out of dire economic and social necessity.

Now, when the son becomes employed, the situation is reversed; the parents expect the new family to help them. This changes the position of the daughter-in-law because she is not on the receiving end. But now she seems to be the one who is responsible for segmentation of the family. She is also looked upon by her mother-in-law as the one who monopolizes her son. The tension is aggravated and becomes apparent when these rival elements demand the fulfillment of the young man's obligation toward both. The individual stands in a situation of dual commitments: loyalty to his parental family and to his own wife and children. This leads to various conflicts. The girls now prefer to marry a man who has some job and can support his family: first, because they do not want to be subordinate to another woman; second, because an employed husband will take his wife away and establish his own house, which would be exclusively managed by the wife without any interference; third, the mother-in-law will not be in a position to exert her influence over a son who may be residing at a distance not in easy reach of his parents. The new family tries to leave the village to live in the industrial towns, or in places where the husband has to stay because of his job commitments.

It is not only the job commitment that divides the nuclear family, but the increased interest in the individual marriage. This is evident from the fact that the frequency of visits to the parental family decline considerably and become only occasional. It is further interesting to note that these families have visitors from among friends or co-professional colleagues rather than from members of the kin group. The economic independence of the nuclear family weakens the hold of parental authority and with it the influence of kinship. The offspring of these families have a different environment and consequently the orientation and education are aimed at goals other than the traditional.

The social consequence of technological development is disintegration of community structure and the emergence of new structures which differentiate themselves. A chain of causation can be noticed at both the macro- and micro-level: through social structure to parental authority to childhood environment. The disintegration of the traditional social structure induced by economic change upsets those sets of conditions which constitute the "societal variable" outside the boundary of the primary family unit. The family is a dynamic action system within the broader social structure. The changes necessitate reorientation of individual participants in this system in accordance with new societal imperatives. The individuals bring into their interaction orientations which reflect these imperatives (Sussman 1967). The decision to have a child depends on the goals and imperatives of the individuals. The filtered group is assumed to be goal-directed. Their attitudes toward family size are determined by their orientations and manifest themselves in fertility differentials prevalent in the same society among various groups. The downward trend in the overall fertility level is not yet visible because the numerical strength of this educated group is still very small. But this does not minimize its importance.

The Modern Subgroup

Pushing the scheme further to include the dynamic effects of socio-economic development, it seems appropriate to concentrate on this subgroup which has been filtered out of the traditional mass through the process of education and resource mobilization. This group within tradition-bound society has demographic behavior characteristics more resembling those in developed societies. It is involved in the process of social reintegration through substitution of new bonds of affiliation. This middle class, Western-educated group is ethnically heterogenous yet integrated by the functional forces of modern industrialization. Their attitude toward family circumstances has direct bearing on the decisions that are made with regard to the procreation of children. It is therefore essential to examine in detail those circumstances to understand how this group's goal is set in terms of its response to demographic transformation. It is through them that one can hope that a change may come.

The Impact of Family Circumstance: Rise in Age at Marriage

The families of this new group send their children to schools, colleges, universities, or other institutions catering to technical specialization. The parents plan for their children desirable careers. The responsibility which starts with procreation of offspring goes on extending to the various stages of life that the offspring have to pass through to settle finally in their careers. Before they are so settled the question of marriage does not arise: it is career first and then marriage. The process of education is time-consuming. After high school it requires a minimum of seven years to obtain from a university a first degree in medicine or engineering, or master's degree in education, arts, or sciences. Normally a boy or girl of seventeen years gets through high school. An additional seven years for completion of education makes their age twenty-four years when they start looking for jobs. The job, when they obtain it, may take another year of two, as it may need further specialization. The doctors or teachers go abroad or elsewhere in the country for higher degrees or specialization. Science and arts graduates who are selected for the Civil Service of Pakistan (CSP) may be sent for training in the academies before finally filling vacancies. The army and air force en-roll officers after completion of pre-engineering or pre-medical training, or students of the arts prior to obtaining degrees, but they have to start military training in various training establishments. On leaving their training establishment, they obtain degrees and a commission in the forces. But the army regulation is hard on marriage. It says that no one who is under the age of twenty-five and married can be accepted.

In spite of these factors, marriage can take place at an early age, but the most important factor is the selection of a mate. This matter is still the purview of the elders; the parental family makes the contacts and arranges the marriage. In traditional rural cases, the available mates are well known, because marriage is endogamous, preferentially among cousins. Whenever the elders are in a position to arrange marriage they do it immediately. In the above-mentioned group, the real problem is finding a suitable match. The family or parents may have somebody in view but the boy may not want to marry that girl or vice versa.

On the one hand, family or elders try to find a match based primarily on compatible values. On the other hand, the husband and wife must accept this choice because without their acceptance the marriage cannot be successful. Both individual and family considerations, which are not always the same, have to be kept in view. There is still no institutional mechanism or approved norm of allowing younger adults to establish premarital liaisons to select mates mutually acceptable to each other.[15] The families go on trying and it takes time, and in the majority of cases, a great deal of time. This extends the marriage age still further.

The joint family had a built-in mechanism of stability. The endoga-mous marriage among cousins not only reinforced its solidarity, but also provided a way to increase the number of its members by early

[15] There is a general trend among the younger generation to have the right of choosing their own lifelong partners, and they refer to Islamic principles that guarantee them this right; yet due to strict segregation of males and females, a centuries-old tradition and practice, it is difficult to find in what way people could exercise this right. There is only one possibility, that of having some contacts with coeds, but coeds, too, do not freely mix with each other.

marriage. The female members were potential mothers; their procreative capability was an asset to the group. It was preferable that this asset be retained in the group rather than allowed to be passed on to another lineage. The Pathan feels the wife-giving position is dishonorable or lower than that of wife-receiving, which is just opposite to that of the Mayo-Dama of Kachin. Thus intermarriage among cousins was a safeguard against lowering oneself to others. More hands were needed by the lineage to perpetuate as well as to have political equality, if not a dominating position, vis-à-vis others. In the case of marriage outside the lineage, the *Mehr* [dower] amount was high and other terms of exchange more severe.

The exact statistics about the number of persons married to their cousins is not known. There has been no survey carried out to determine this. But it is generally observed that the first choice is a cousin, and in certain cases it is obligatory to marry a cousin.

Marriage was a social concern rather than an individual one. The right to select and arrange marriage was the exclusive concern of the parents and elders of the group. The legitimate sexual union could only be brought into effect by the elders' agreement among themselves with or without the knowledge of adults who have to marry each other. There are empirically noticeable deviations. The important cause for deviation is the hostility between mother-in-law and daughter-in-law. The unmarried siblings who are on the side of their mother are also hostile to their sister-in-law. One of the causes of hostility is the mother-in-law's authoritative role in the joint family and the subordinate role of the daughter-in-law. For future decisions about intermarriage among cousins, the nature of this relationship becomes important. The higher the degree of hostility between these relatives, the less the chances of continuing intermarriage.

The stability of the joint family is on the decline for various reasons. First, the authority structure of the joint family is becoming more conflict-generating; second, its economic solidarity is on the decline; and third, the reorientation of individual members in the modern educational system has created another important element. They challenge the right of parents and elders with respect to the selection of mates. Thus for the younger generation, marriage is for individual consideration and the right of choice belongs to them. The altercation over these matters in families is very frequent. This creates a sort of polarization of views within a primary cohesive group.

When a marriage is finally arranged, the new couple is again faced with multifarious problems. The wives normally want husbands to be more interested in the nuclear family, and wish them to look for support to the wife's family. But the husband also feels an obligation to his parents. The men who have been brought up in families where the authority structure was such that the mother had a subordinate position, after a while start to reassert their position in an identical way to their fathers. This leads to tensions and quarrels in the families. But the educated and highly-placed persons would like to always avoid these conflicts. It is this consideration primarily which promotes the formation of nuclear families. Also, since husband and wife in the nuclear family have to live together as lifelong partners, parents are led by this consideration to arrange marriages acceptable to them. Thus they try to avoid imposition of their own choice. The number of such people is relatively small but their influence has created an effect and now even in the villages, the rural Pathans do give consideration to individual choice.

Factors that Lead to Planned Parenthood

The new family has to establish itself, if acquiring a separate new house. They have contacts with other families or friends who pay visits frequently. For prestige reasons, the house is desired to be an ideal one because otherwise people will certainly circulate gossip in the social circle against the wife of the man. If pregnancy occurs, all prenatal problems are to be undergone independently without any assistance from the parental family. If something is beyond the understanding of the couple, they seek professional advice from prenatal clinics. The child's birth disrupts the family considerably; the family has to provide nursing care for the mother and infant. In rare cases, such as at military or missionary hospitals, nursing care is provided by the hospital. Government hospitals do have nurses, but their time is preempted by serious patients. Hence, nursing care normally devolves on the family. This forces the nuclear family to depend on the parental family, particularly the mothers-in-law, to care for the mother and child. Once home, the new parents are beset with congratulatory callers, all of whom have to be entertained. The mother no longer has other family members to help with the care of the infant, and the responsibility for its care descends on the mother before she, herself, is fully recovered from the delivery. Having another child immediately would multiply the pressures already described, and so subsequent births are delayed until the family can cope with them.

The urban housewife is caught, on the one hand, with a lack of servants, who formerly were cheaply available, and on the other with few labor-saving appliances, which also are too costly. She is left to manage as best she can by herself. Entertaining, formerly the responsibility of the husband's mother, now must be handled by the young wife. Because the government schools are overcrowded, the family will attempt to keep the children in private schools which will require the mother to spend much time taking the children to and from schools. Also not to be overlooked is the cost of this kind of education. These stresses also tend to limit family size.

The reproductive cycle if unchecked would certainly endanger the resources of the family including its leisure and other social activities. The family would have to care for more children and its standard of living might be lowered relatively. The more children the greater the division of parental attention, and as a result the offspring might not be able to do well in their career. This could in turn mean that they might have a comparatively low standard of living (Husain 1968).[16] These are the possible exigencies which the parents have in their view. A member of one of the families remarked: "It is not a simple matter to have a child. He does not grow when left to himself. He needs upbringing and remains on the mind until he becomes an adult and starts his own career." Another woman said: "All that we want is that our children should be prosperous and happily settled in their careers." These families have no pressures from any group, as in the case of the joint family members of the Pathans. The number of children in this case is the result of family decisions. And the decision, for the reasons quoted above, tends to control the number of births. It becomes, therefore, essential to see how their actual performance is influenced by their attitude toward fertility.

ATTITUDES TOWARD CHILDREN AMONG MODERNS — AN EMPIRICAL REPORT

The foregoing discussion of socioeconomic changes and their impact on Pathan society identified a group of people which is being filtered out as an "institiutional isolate." The observation of their family circum-

---

[16] As Dr. Husain (1968: 51) observes: "The higher stage of development is characterized by the achievement oriented society and emergence of a substantial middle class. The upward movement on a social scale becomes a function of achievements and aspiration. This movement becomes easier for those who travel light, hence inverse relationship between fertility and socio-economic status develops ... Fertility among socio-economic groups is largely related to the degree of motivation for limiting the size of the family."

stances leads to certain assumptions that fertility level depends on family decisions. These decisions are taken in the light of the families' perceptions of their situation. This group is a Western-educated class. Their attitude toward family size and fertility is the consequence of both social and economic forces. To test these assumptions empirically a sample of 200 families of upper-class specialists of various kinds working in Peshawar (the capital of the Northwest Frontier Province) was studied.

The Sample

The 200 specialists all have educated wives. Their composition by educational standard is given in the table below:

Table 4. Education of wives and profession of husbands in 200 upper class families

Education of wives	
No education	0
Primary education	5
Secondary education	50
B.A., B.Sc. and higher	145
Total	200
Profession of husbands	
Doctors	30
Engineers	50
Professors	50
Civil servants	20
Business executives, other	50
Total of all professions	200

The Growing Realization that Bringing Up Children is More Expensive

Changes in society have created a pressure for education, particularly among elites. In addition to the cost of maintaining a child in school there is the loss of the child as an economic asset. This inevitably causes the child to be seen as a financial liability. To confirm this assumption the question was asked: DO YOU THINK THAT IT'S MORE COSTLY TO BRING UP CHILDREN NOW THAN BEFORE? As opposed to the traditional way of bringing up children, the modern way is the substitution of infant formula, cereal, and other diets instead of simple breast-feeding. The prices of infant formula more than doubled in 1968 to 1972, not to mention the other diets for which the mothers have to buy fresh vegetables and meats and process them for the children. This is time-consuming and tedious. And infant formula has to be continued for a longer time due to the scarcity of pasteurized milk. Their attitude toward children is evidenced from the fact that 99 percent of the sample considered children to be a burden.

After looking into the results it became apparent that the sample (Table 4) was too small, although it originally was intended to examine the attitude of this group alone. So it was thought essential to extend the sample after stratifying the group on income and age criteria. But within the group, the income level and age level of the respondents varied considerably. It was therefore planned to administer the same questionnaire to surrounding villages of Peshawar. A Gharibabad sample of 1,000 families was taken but again due to the shortage of time only 500 families could be contacted. The two samples were analyzed separately. Table 5 presents the consolidated results from both groups.

Table 5 indicates that among the high specialists children were considered to be a burden to 99 percent of the sample, while in the village sample, 73.4 percent of the respondents considered children a burden. In this group, 90 percent of the literate women without formal education considered children a burden while 95 percent of those with primary education and 100 percent of those with a secondary education thought so. The attitude of village white-collar professionals (98 percent) was along similar lines to the high specialist group. This realization of the burden by a majority of the people is the result of ongoing changes in Pathan society.

The impact of these changes is being felt at least by those who are nearer to the urban centers. These villages are nearer to Peshawar and hence have daily communication with it. For example, the white-collar people were almost all working in Peshawar. The businessmen and traders were in constant touch with the city. Actually, they carried on daily transactions with the Peshawar market. The farmers were also influenced by the fact that all their families somehow are within range of direct contact with the city.

The Attitude Toward Family Size

The question asked was: DO YOU THINK IT IS GOOD TO HAVE A LARGE FAMILY, I.E., ONE WITH MANY CHILDREN? Responses to the question regarding family size show an apparent fall in the percentages of the village sample from 73.4 percent to 49.2 percent. In this case, although the white collar workers still favor a small family, women educated at the

Table 5. Change in women's attitudes toward children as they become more expensive to raise

Random sample of women of Gharibabad village

Educational level of wives	Number	Percentage seeing children as a burden
No education	240	68
Literate without formal schooling	108	90
Primary	19	95
Secondary, or higher	10	100
Total	367*	73.4
Husbands' occupation		
White collar	49	98
Village occupation	48	60
Shopkeeper, business	48	80
Farmer, laborer	222	71.5
Total	367*	73.4
Sample of urban middle class		
No education	—	—
Primary	4	80
Secondary	49	98
B.A., B.Sc. or higher	145	100
Total	198*	99
Husbands' occupation		
Doctors	30	100
Engineers	49	98
Professors	50	100
Civil servants	20	100
Business executives, others	49	98
Total	198*	99

* Not everyone in the sample responded to all questions.

primary level were 60 percent and at the secondary level 70 percent, but this fall may be seen with two distinct sets of conditions. The women living in joint families might have perceived the question as if the intention were to know whether they wanted to segment the larger family or not. The interviewee, in the presence of family members, could not possibly say that she did not want a larger family, because a majority of women live with their in-laws, and to say that they do not want larger families would provoke the mother-in-law. The relationship between mother-in-law and daughter-in-law is characterized by hostility.

The daughters-in-law generally prefer to live by themselves. The women also do not have a fixed opinion on numbers of children because a majority of the women have a fatalistic attitude despite the fact that they consider childbearing troublesome.

The urbanized middle-class group shows practically no change as almost none want a large family. This further confirms that this group understood well what was meant by a large family (see Table 6).

Table 6.   Women who did not want a large family

Random sample of women of Gharibabad village

Education level of wives	Number	Percentage not wanting a large family
No education	161	46
Literate without formal education	66	55
Primary	12	60
Secondary	7	70
Total	246	49.2
Husbands' occupation		
White collar	46	92
Village occupation	42	52.5
Business	31	51.7
Farmer	127	40.9
Total	246	49.2
Sample of urban middle class		
Primary	4	80
Secondary	50	100
B.A., B.Sc. or higher	145	100
Total	199	99.5
Husbands' occupation		
Doctors	30	100
Engineers	50	100
Professors	50	100
Civil servants	20	100
Business, other	49	98
Total	199	99.5

The next question asked was: HOW MANY CHILDREN WOULD YOU LIKE TO HAVE? (PLEASE GIVE EXACT NUMBER OF CHILDREN DESIRED ASSUMING THAT THEY WOULD ALL GROW UP TO BE ADULTS.) This was a direct question to know the ideal family size.

Table 7. Number of children wanted: Gharibabad village

Number wanted	Illiterate	Percentage
1	—	—
2	—	—
3	20	5.7
4	40	11.5
5	80	22.9
6	90	25.7
7	25	7.1
God*	95	27.1
Total	350	
Average 5.7		

Number wanted	Literate without formal education	Percentage
1	—	—
2	2	1.6
3	10	8.3
4	15	12.5
5	25	20.9
6	20	16.9
7	18	15.0
God*	30	25.0
Total	120	
Average 5.6		

Number wanted	Primary	Percentage
1	—	—
2	1	5
3	3	15
4	5	25
5	6	30
6	1	5
7	—	—
God*	4	20
Total	20	
Average 4.7		

Number wanted	Secondary	Percentage
1	—	—
2	2	20
3	3	30
4	2	20
5	1	10
6	1	10
7	—	—
God*	1	10
Total	10	
Average 3.9		

Number wanted	White collar	Percentage
1	—	—
2	5	10
3	12	24
4	10	20
5	10	20
6	4	8
7	4	8
God*	5	10
Total	50	
Average 4.4		

Number wanted	Village jobs	Percentage
1	—	—
2	—	—
3	10	12.5
4	40	50.0
5	10	12.5
6	7	8.7
7	—	—
God*	13	16.3
Total	80	
Average 4.6		

Number wanted	Traders	Percentage
1	—	—
2	—	—
3	8	13.3
4	6	10.0
5	30	50.0
6	4	6.7
7	2	3.3
God*	10	16.7
Total	60	
Average 5.1		

Number wanted	Farmers	Percentage
1	—	—
2	—	—
3	6	1.9
4	6	1.9
5	62	20.0
6	97	31.3
7	37	11.9
God*	102	32.9
Total	310	
Average 6.1		

* "As many as God wills."

Table 8. Number of children wanted by urban wives

Number wanted	Primary	Secondary	Graduate	Doctors	Professors	Engineers	Civil servants	Businessmen
1	—	—	—	—	—	—	—	—
2	1 (20%)	25 (50%)	96 (66.2%)	25 (83.3%)	41 (82%)	40 (80%)	10 (50%)	6 (12%)
3	3 (60%)	15 (30%)	40 (27.6%)	4 (13.4%)	5 (10%)	5 (10%)	8 (40%)	36 (72%)
4	1 (20%)	10 (20%)	9 (6.2%)	1 (3.3%)	4 (8%)	5 (10%)	2 (10%)	8 (16%)
5								
6								
7								
God's will	—	—	—	—	—	—	—	—
Total	5	50	145	30	50	50	20	50
Average number of children	3.0	2.6	2.4	2.2	2.2	2.3	2.6	3.0

The women who were illiterate tend to indicate a preference for a larger number of children. No one in the sample said they wanted only one child; only five families wanted two children. This number is deemed risky. In contrast, 132 women of the higher-placed professional group wanted two children and considered three to be the ideal number. The illiterate women constituted the highest among those who considered the number of children up to God's will. This proportion goes on declining with an increase in education. Among the wives of white-collar workers only five indicated the belief that it was up to God alone to determine the number of children. Among craftsmen this was thirteen; traders and shopkeepers, ten; and farmers 102. It is obvious that traditionality is proportionately higher in the illiterate group. With literacy and advance in education the traditional beliefs are modified.

The average number of children wanted by the group shows an inverse differential to education. The illiterate wives' average was 5.7, literate without formal education 5.6, primary 4.7, secondary 3.9. From an occupational standpoint, the farmer was highest with 6.1, traders 5.1, holders of village jobs 4.6, white-collar workers 4.4. Among high-class specialists' wives: with primary education 3.0, secondary 2.6, and graduates 2.4. Among the professionals, doctors, professors, and engineers had 2.2 as an average number, civil servants 2.6, businessmen 3.0. In this group it was difficult to decide exactly what was the ideal number. It was the civil servants who were just a bit higher but the proportion of civil servants being very low, this could not be of much significance. The business executives and others had a proportionally higher number. Knowing the limitations of the survey it can only reflect a tendency.

CONCLUSION

In general, the attitude towards fertility and family size of the Pathan community as a whole does not seem to have changed considerably. However, the small but growing group of modernizing Pathans does show attitudes towards fertility and family planning very different from those of the traditional community. The traditional economy of the community type gets jolted with the introduction of economic development and technological change. The education and technical orientation of a number of individuals who opt for new employment opportunities provided by changes have to reconstruct their links of social relationships. The kinship ties and lineage group ties are replaced by a new kind of tie apparently more in the functional framework. The weakening of traditional bonds on the one hand tends to disintegrate the traditional structures and on the other becomes conducive to growing new structures.

Those who are involved in this process find their attitudes conditioned by techno-environmental realities. The normative imperatives which concerned traditionality and reinforce the traditional social structures consequently become invalid. The group that opts out of the traditional system primarily has status based on achievement and not only birth criteria. The standard of living is reached and maintained by hard efforts. The upbringing of children and family size are viewed by this group in the light of its own circumstances. It therefore has an unfavorable attitude toward excessive child-bearing and is highly rational in its perception of socioeconomic realities. Their decision to have a manageable number of children obviously has pragmatic overtones. The personality traits of this group would reveal the impact of the aggregate environmental complex created by transition from traditional state to economic growth.

REFERENCES

BARTH, F.
1960   "System of social stratification in Swat," in *Aspects of caste in South India, Ceylon and North West Pakistan*. Edited by R. E. Leach. Cambridge Papers in Social Anthropology 2. Cambridge: Cambridge University Press.
BEAN, LEE L., MASHIHURREHMAN
1967   "Interrelationships of some fertility measures in Pakistan," in *Seminar on population problems*. Karachi: Pakistan Institute of Development Economics.
DAVIS, KINGSLEY
1955   Institutional patterns favoring high fertility in underdeveloped areas. *Eugenics Quarterly* 2:33–39.
1963   The theory of change and response in modern demography. *Population Index* 29(4).
DAVIS, KINGSLEY, JUDITH BLAKE
1956   Social structure and fertility: a theoretical framework. *Economic Development and Cultural Change* 4:211–235.
FARHAT, YUSUF, *editor*
1967   *Seminar on population problems*. Karachi: Pakistan Institute of Development Economics.
FAMILY PLANNING COUNCIL OF PAKISTAN
1967   "Efforts in reduction of fertility through family planning," in *Seminar on population problems*. Karachi: Pakistan Institute of Development Economics.

HASHMI, DALAM
1961   Report of "Seminar on the Eradication of Social Evils," held under the auspices of the Bureau of National Reconstruction, West Pakistan, Lahore. Karachi: Government Printing Press.
HEER, DAVID M.
1965   *Economic development and fertility.* World Population Conference, volume two. United Nations.
1968   *Society and population.* Englewood Cliffs, New Jersey: Prentice-Hall.
HUSAIN, I. Z.
1968   "An urban fertility field." Demographic Research Center, Lucknow University.
KHALID, HAYAT
1967   "Growth rate in two models for population of Pakistan, with high specific birthrates and declining age specific death rate," in *Seminar on population problems.* Karachi: Pakistan Institute of Development Economics.
KHAN, AHMAD
1970   *Human resources.* Peshwar: Peshwar University Press.
KESSING, FELIX M.
1955   "Population patterns in stable societies," in *Proceedings of the World Population Conference, Rome, 1954.* New York: United Nations.
LIU, WILLIAM T., *editor*
1966   Family and fertility. *Proceedings of the Fifth Notre Dame Conference on Population.* University of Notre Dame, South Bend, Indiana.
NAG, MONI
1973   "Population anthropology: problems and perspective," in *Exploration in anthropology.* Edited by Morton Fried. New York: Thomas Y. Crowell.
POLGAR, STEVEN, *editor*
1971   *Culture and population.* Cambridge, Massachusetts: Schenkman.
REED, STEPHEN W.
1955   *Proceedings of the World Population Conference, Rome, 1954,* volume four: *Cultural dynamics and demographic change in preliterate societies.* New York: United Nations.
SUSSMAN, MARVIN B.
1967   "Family interaction and fertility," in *Family and fertility.* Edited by William T. Liu, 101–111. Proceedings of the Fifth Notre Dame Conference on Population, December 1–3, 1966. Notre Dame: The University of Notre Dame Press.
SZABADY, EGON, *editor*
1968   *World views of population problems.* Budapest: Akadémiai Kiadó.
WORLD POPULATION CONFERENCE
1967   *Proceedings of the World Population Conference, Belgrade, 1965,* volume two. New York: United Nations.

The Economic Importance of Children in a Javanese Village

BENJAMIN WHITE

While there has been comparatively little research in Java on fertility attitudes and practices, there are several quantitative and qualitative studies which indicate the prevalence among both rural and urban couples of the desire for large numbers of children, matched in practice by a high level of marital fertility (see, for example, Gille and Pardoko 1965; IPPA 1969a, 1969b; Geertz 1961; Koentjaraningrat n.d.). These studies on the whole confirm Jay's impression that "The value that Javanese society places upon a family full of children can scarcely be exaggerated. ... Across the entire social spectrum ... children are desired in abundance" (Jay 1969: 97).

In view of the acuteness of the population problem in Java, one's first impulse perhaps is to regard the desire for children "in abundance" as totally out of step with the reality of Javanese economic life, as a prime example of the "irrationality" that social scientists so frequently describe in peasant life. In the aggregate or statistical sense — that is, from the point of view of the Javanese economy as a whole — there is ample justification for the view that high fertility will in the foreseeable

Field research (beginning in August 1972 and still in progress at the time of writing) was carried out in a village in Kabupaten Kulon Progo, special district of Jogjakarta, as part of a project on "The economic cost and value of children in four agricultural societies" under the general direction of Dr. Moni Nag, Columbia University. The project was funded by the National Institutes of Health — National Institute of Child Health and Development, under Contract Number NIH — NICHD–71–2209. I am very grateful to Moni Nag and Anne Stoler for advice and encouragement at all stages of the research; also to Drs. Masri Singarimbun, Hanna Papanek and Mely G. Tan for the opportunity to present earlier versions of this paper in seminars at Gadjah Mada University, Jogjakarta and University of Indonesia, Jakarta.

future mean only more mouths to feed in that crowded island and more children to educate, who when they reach potentially productive age, will add themselves to an already overcrowded and underproductive labor-force. Population growth certainly implies for the large majority of the children born each year, increasingly bleak economic prospects. However, because the basic unit of demographic behavior (and likewise, in Java, of economic behavior) is the family, if we wish to examine the economic rationality or otherwise of demographic behavior, we must transfer our attention from large-scale statistics to individual couples in their individual economic environments. In doing so, we should not assume that the Javanese family economy merely replicates in miniature the Javanese economy as a whole. In this paper, I hope to question the view that rural overpopulation implies that prospective Javanese parents have no economic justification for producing large families of potential child laborers.

Such a view, I think, is based on dubious assumptions concerning the implications of overpopulation in terms of labor opportunities and the value of children's labor within the family. Overpopulation and the existence of a labor surplus in the Javanese rural context does not mean that large numbers of people are reduced to complete idleness for long periods of time ("idleness" in the sense of having no opportunity to work at all, is perhaps a peculiar characteristic of the unemployed in industrial economies, as depicted in the cry of America's depression years, "How can I work when there's no work to do?"). On the contrary, people are forced by population pressure into increasingly marginal and UNDERproductive activities, (that is, activities with increasingly low returns to labor) and must therefore work increasingly LONGER hours to achieve the required minimal returns. Labor is abundant, and cheap in the market, but since it is the only resource available to so many Javanese families, it is still for them a valuable resource. Under these conditions, rather than assuming *a priori* that the economic costs of children to their parents outweigh the economic benefits, we should consider carefully the extent to which Javanese parents may derive benefit (although their children, and the economy as a whole, do not) from the production of large numbers of children as a potential source of labor. In what follows, with the aid of preliminary results from field research in a Javanese village, I shall attempt to outline some of the economic benefits arising from high fertility, considered from the parents' point of view.

No systematic research on this topic has yet been done in Java, or in other agricultural societies so far as I know; but there are some studies which, though not specifically concerned with the cost and value of children, give us some general information about the ages at which Javanese children begin participating in production, and the kinds of tasks they engage in. Slamet, for instance, estimates (1965: 173) that by the age of eight children in Java have begun to join in all the subsistence activities and daily work of their parents. Koentjaraningrat (n.d.: 146ff.) notes that in Tjelapar (South Central Java) regular school attendance is rare; instead, girls are engaged in household tasks, cooking, pounding paddy, or caring for younger sibs, while boys are sent by their parents to collect branches and leaves from the woods (for use as wrappers or for weaving), to help in garden cultivation, etc. A majority of boys and girls also earn wages herding water-buffalo, cows, goats, or ducks. The conflict between children's education and the need for their labor is mentioned also by Budi Prasadja (1972: 46), who notes that in Gegesik (West Java) economic pressures often force small farmers and landless laborers to neglect their children's education, because they need their labor, especially in the case of male children. Gille and Pardoko note that "As soon as he reaches school age [six or seven years] every child born into a farmer's family is put to work on the land during the peak periods of planting and harvesting, when all available labour is used" (Gille and Pardoko 1965: 503–504). In rural Modjokuto (East Java) Jay wrote that he

... observed children to be industrious, even at an early age, in picking up small piecework jobs such as hulling peanuts or sorting and bundling onions. ... As the children move into adolescence, their labour of course becomes more valuable. A daughter in particular is able to carry much of the load of housework and also to work with the mother in the fields for cash wages when there are opportunities. Sons are helpful not so much for the work they may do with the father, which in my observation was minimal, but for the exchange labour they can perform as a young male of the household (1969: 69).

In small-town Modjokuto, "little girls [i.e. pre-adolescent] . . . soon learn to do the whole family shopping alone, and — if the mother sells in the market — may take over the mother's stand for short periods." During adolescence, boys may start to earn money

by occasional farm-work, as a labourer in a shop making cigarettes, as a ticket-collector on one of the many jitneys [or] as apprentice to a tailor or carpenter. Girls rarely work except in the mother's business . . . they usually remain at home, occupied with a continual round of domestic duties (Geertz 1961: 116, 118ff.).

While these observations are of interest, much more quantitative research is necessary if we wish, for instance, to compare the Javanese case with Clark's estimate that children in Asian peasant societies may become "net producers" (i.e. produce more than they consume) at ages as low as seven years (Clark 1970: 226). Indeed, the question turns out to be a very complex one on closer examination.[1] In order to compare the "economic cost" with the "economic value" of children, we require a substantial amount of data from families of various sizes and economic levels on at least the following points. With regard to the COSTS of children, we would need to know as a minimum: (1) the economic costs of pregnancy and childbirth; (2) the cost of feeding, clothing, educating, and otherwise caring for a child at various ages; (3) the cost of all the social and ritual obligations incurred from the time of the mother's pregnancy until the child reaches adulthood (in Java these costs are considerable); and (4) the opportunity costs involved in the production and rearing of an extra child, e.g. the time lost by the mother in pregnancy, childbirth, and nursing when she might otherwise be productively employed. In addition, we should determine from current mortality levels (5) the probability that a child will survive to a given age, and thus the costs "lost" on children who fail to reach productive age. Turning to the economic VALUE of children, two kinds of values should be considered: (6) the value of children as sources of security for parents in old age (a factor whose resistance to quantification does not negate its importance in the shaping of reproductive decisions); and (7) the value of children as a source of productive or useful labor in the household economy. Since it is clearly impossible to deal with all of these questions here, I shall confine myself almost entirely to the last one. This question itself requires data on the following points: (1) At what ages do children of either sex become CAPABLE of performing various productive or useful activities? (2) How does their output at various ages compare with that of an adult? (3) Granted a given level of POTENTIAL of children in productive or useful activities, what is the ACTUAL extent of their involvement in the household economy? — in other words, to what extent does the over-populated, "labor-surplus" economy still allow room for the participation of children.

It is important to remember that while the POTENTIAL of children for various kinds of economic activity depends largely on physiological factors (levels of health and nutrition, etc.), the extent of their actual

[1]   Various approaches to the study of the economic value of children in agricultural societies, and some relevant ethnographic data, are discussed in Nag (1972).

participation in the economy depends upon a number of additional factors specific to the particular economy and society in question. Thus, before providing any data on children's economic activities, I shall attempt to put the material in an economic framework with a brief description of the economy of the village sample studied, and the available opportunities for productive activity.

Economic Characteristics of the Population Studied
The population studied consists of several hamlets in a village complex approximately twenty-five kilometers northwest of the city of Jogja-karta. Basic demographic and economic data were obtained from about 500 households, but I shall deal here with only forty households which were selected for detailed research on the participation of children in the household economy. This small sample (which at a later stage of research was increased to 100 households) consisted of small farmers and landless laborers and the households selected con-tained at least one child of potentially working age (over six years) so that the average household size (6.3) was considerably larger than the average for the village as a whole (4.5). Average land-holdings per household and per capita are shown in Table 1.

Table 1.   Average land-holdings in the forty household sample (in hectares)

	Per capita	Per household
Sawah (irrigated rice-fields)	0.0170 hectares	0.1066 hectares
Pekarangan and *tegalan* (house-compounds and dry fields)	0.0289 hectares	0.1811 hectares
Total:	0.0459 hectares	0.2877 hectares

In the region in question, the varying quality of *sawah* (mostly rather low) and an uncertain water supply make for equally uncertain yields, so that it is not easy to estimate how much *sawah* is necessary to supply the average household's rice needs. However, taking 125 kilograms of hulled rice as the average per capita requirement per year (see Penny and Singarimbun, 1972: 83) and thus almost eight quintals as the annual requirement of a household of average size in our sample, we can be certain that at the very least, all households with less than one-tenth hectare (that is, almost three-quarters of the forty-household sample) fall in the category of those unable to meet their rice require-ment from their own land in normal years. Garden crops are also sold for cash or in exchange for rice, but there are no households in our sample whose primary source of income or subsistence is garden cultivation. The large majority of our sample, then, are compelled to rely on activities outside the "family farm" for a major part of their basic subsistence. I shall briefly describe the most important of these other subsistence activities.

Sharecropping   With this system, the land-owner usually provides none of the inputs (cost of seeds, fertilizer, cultivation, etc.) although he usually pays the land tax, and receives as rent one-half of the total yield. It can thus be said that from the sharecropper's point of view, the returns to his inputs of cash and labor are approximately one-half what they would be were he cultivating his own land. There are nine sharecroppers in our forty-household sample.

Agricultural wage-labor   Irrigated rice, besides requiring almost continual attention, demands large amounts of labor over short periods of time at three stages in the cycle (hoeing, planting, and harvesting); even small holders can rarely provide this labor from their own families, and must therefore seek outside labor. Some small farmers enter reciprocal (*gotong-royong*) labor exchange arrangements for this purpose, but the large majority engage hired labor. At the time of my research, wages for these tasks were as follows:
Male labor (ground preparation): thirty to forty rupiah for three to four hours
Female labor (planting): fifteen to twenty-five rupiah for three to four hours; (harvesting): one-sixth to one-tenth of the total rice she harvests.
A day's harvesting yields more in rice than other kinds of wage labor (Anne Stoler's research in the same village showed the average share or *bawon* received by harvesters to be 3.5 kilograms of unhulled rice), and this partly explains why planting wages are so low; those who have participated in the planting expect later to be invited, or at least allowed, to join in the harvest. Some do not even ask for planting wages, in the hopes that their *bawon* at harvesting will be increased. Wages are quoted for half-day periods of three to four hours because labor is normally engaged by the half-day, and only at peak periods can laborers obtain an occasional full day's paid labor.

Handicrafts for cash sale   The main handicrafts for cash sale are *tikar* [pandanus sleeping-mats], woven by women, and *kepang* [split-bamboo mats], used often for drying rice, and usually woven by men. Almost all the households studied engage in mat weaving as a part-time occupation. Some also gather, cut, boil, and soften pandanus-leaves for sale to *tikar*-weavers. Most of the *tikar*-weavers produce on an average one *tikar* each five days, weaving for about four hours each day; the cost of materials is thirty-five rupiah, while the finished product sells for sixty to 120 rupiah depending on size, quality and on the season. Thus the weaver makes only one to four rupiah per hour; returns to labor for a *kepang*-weaver are only slightly higher.

Small trading   In the forty households, a large number of women and a few men are engaged in small-scale trade as a permanent or seasonal source of income; carrying loads of goods or produce, usually on foot and occasionally by bicycle, from home to market, from market to town, or from market to market over a range of up to thirty kilometers, for very small profits. Given the distances covered, this is a very time-consuming occupation (a minimum of four hours daily, and a maximum of twenty-four hours in the case of the distant markets). Most of these small traders or *bakuls*, with a working capital of 500-1000 rupiah, earn perhaps fifty to a hundred rupiah on their selling days.

Animal husbandry   The forty households own and care for a large number of animals: altogether 298 chickens, 61 ducks, 46 goats or sheep, 32 cows, and 4 water-buffalos. Chickens generally find their own food, apart from being fed kitchen scraps, but all other animals require a considerable amount of labor to care for and feed. Ducks must be fed and taken to water for extended periods each day; goats, sheep, cows, and water-buffalos all require fodder which is generally cut and brought to them from gardens, roadsides, river banks, irrigation channels and the edges of rice fields. In addition, cows and water-buffalos must be taken to water. For those households with enough labor to care for them, these animals provide an important means of storing wealth, besides a regular source of income in the case of laying chickens and ducks, and a seasonal source of income in the case of working cows and water-buffalos. An idea of the value of the larger beasts is given by two common practices. First, a household with enough labor to care for a beast but not enough capital to purchase one will often undertake to care for animals belonging to a richer household. The animals remain the property of the original owner, but half of their offspring become the property of the "sharecropping" household. Second, a cow or water-buffalo requires at least one large basket of green fodder each day, mixed with another of paddy-stalks; an owner who cannot provide the labor from his own household will pay from thirty to fifty rupiah per day (compare this with the wages quoted above) for that amount of fodder. It should be noted that here, as elsewhere in rural Java, animal husbandry does not provide a significant source of meat or eggs for home consumption; 95 percent of the eggs, and virtually all the animals, are sold. The major source of protein is the much cheaper *tempe* [fermented soy-bean cakes].

Production of food for sale   Twelve of the forty households are engaged in the production of various food items for cash sale, mostly in the collection of coconut-palm sap and the process of boiling it down to produce *gula Djawa* [palm sugar]. A man will climb the trees twice daily (about two hours in all) to collect the sap (*nderes*), while his wife will boil the sugar (*nites*) for about four hours. Also, up to two hours daily will be necessary to provide sufficient firewood. These labor-inputs (figures are for a household tapping four trees) produce a daily yield of sixty to eighty rupiah. Other items produced for sale are *tempe* (the fermented soy-bean cakes mentioned above) and *dawet* [boiled drink made from rice or arrowroot flour, coconut milk, and *gula Djawa*]. Both of these require comparable amounts of labor in preparation, as well as firewood. To these labor-inputs should be added the hours spent in selling the finished product — a whole morning at the market, unless the product is bought in the house, at a lower price, by neighbors or small traders.

The above summary indicates some important characteristics of household economy in rural Java. If we compare wages or returns to labor from the activities described above with an individual's rice needs (about 1/3 kilogram daily) and with the local price of rice (which rose gradually throughout the research period, from forty to seventy-five rupiah per kilogram), it is clear that though the returns from those activities may meet or even sometimes surpass the rice-requirement of one adult, they definitely fail even to nearly meet the requirements of a whole household of four to six people; even more so if we include a household's other daily expenditures on kerosene for lamps, tobacco, tea, etc. In such conditions, ALL family members in addition to the household head must take whatever labor opportunities there are in order to meet the household's needs. For those households with insufficient land resources and without enough capital to engage in large-scale trade, the most profitable activity in terms of returns per hour is agricultural wage-labor, particularly harvesting with the *bawon*-system. This is confirmed by the common practice of stopping or reducing all other activities during the busy agricultural seasons in order to avail oneself of the more profitable opportunity. But because of the strictly limited nature of such opportunities, all family members must usually spend a large majority of their time in the less productive sectors mentioned above, however low the returns may be, or in other words, WHATEVER THEIR COST IN LABOR TIME to produce the necessary minimal return. The question we now turn to is to what extent under such conditions a married couple may expect to derive economic benefit from the accumulation of large numbers of children as sources of labor.

The Value of Children in the Household Economy

Age of beginning various economic activities   First we need some idea of the ages at which children are capable of performing various economic activities, and the ages at which they begin regularly performing them. A total of 146 household heads were asked at what age their children had begun performing ten types of activity; fetching water, care of chickens or ducks, care of goats or cattle, cutting green fodder, hoeing irrigated rice fields, hoeing dry fields, transplanting rice, harvesting rice, care of younger siblings, and wage-labor of any kind. I have included such activities as fetching water and child care under the heading of "economic activity" (and later shall include others, such as cooking and other housework) because, while not strictly productive, these tasks are necessary for the maintenance of the household, and may frequently be indirectly productive when performed by young children through the freeing of an older household member for more productive labor. The results are summarized in Table 2. From the table it can be seen that while there are isolated cases of children beginning various tasks at five or six years of age, most children begin them at a somewhat later age. This is confirmed by more detailed observations described below. Thus for the sake of simplification I have omitted children below the age of seven years from further consideration in this paper, because the majority of them cannot be considered significantly productive or useful to their parents before that age. But from ages seven to nine, it appears, children of both ages will have begun regular performance of such tasks as water-carrying, animal care, fodder-collection and (in the case of the girls) rice-planting and harvesting; while the heavier tasks of hoeing a wet or dry field (boys) and all kinds of wage labor (both sexes) are not generally begun until thirteen years. An exception to this last is harvesting for a *bawon*-wage, which as we shall see is often performed by very young girls.

Table 2.   Numbers of children engaged regularly in various productive or useful tasks, age of beginning (youngest case) and average age of beginning (from a sample of 146 households)

Activity	Number of children Boys	Number of children Girls	Age of beginning (youngest case)	Average age of beginning
Fetch water	29	66	5 years	8.8 years
Care of chickens/ducks	38	18	5	7.9
Care of goats/cattle	58	9	6	9.3
Cut fodder	80	4	6	9.5
Hoe *sawah*	41	—	8	13.0
Hoe dry field	39	—	10	13.1
Transplant rice	—	50	5	9.9
Harvest rice	8	61	7	9.7
Care of younger sibs	36	35	5	8.0
Wage labor	12	8	8	12.9

Productivity of children's labor   With this information as a beginning, we next need to know how the productivity per hour of children at various ages compares with that of adults in various tasks. Relative productivity, in all kinds of manual occupations, depends on a combination of skill and strength (in the forty households there was only one man, a teacher, engaged in non-manual work). So far as skill is concerned, very few of the tasks commonly performed by members of our sample can be classed as skills which take great lengths of time to acquire (the exceptions are tasks performed almost exclusively by adults, such as ploughing and perhaps certain kinds of trading). In agriculture, for example, a boy can do all the tasks involved in preparing a rice field (apart from ploughing) with as much skill as an adult after about one season's experience. This does not mean, of course, that farming is not a highly skilled occupation, demanding years of experience of differing weather conditions, crop varieties, pests, market conditions, and many other variables. The point is that these skills lie largely in deciding what is to be done and when to do it, rather than in the actual performance of the tasks once the crucial decisions have been made.

From detailed observation of daily activities in the forty-household sample (the methods used are described below), some interesting facts emerged with regard to the productivity of children's labor, if the level of wages received can be taken as an indication of productivity. In the case of wage-labor by boys aged thirteen to fifteen years (hoeing *sawah* or *pekarangan*, and weeding), the wage was in every case the same as that received by adults; for girls of thirteen to fifteen, from a much larger number of observed cases, the wages for planting were in all cases the same as the adult wage. There were also two cases where a girl of eight years received the same wage as her mother, for the same hours of work, in the same field. In the case of harvesting with *bawon-*payment, Anne Stoler's research shows that the *bawon* received by girls below ten years and in the eleven to fifteen age group averaged 3.0 kilograms of unhulled rice, while that of the over-fifteen age group was 3.5 kilograms. These data indicate that the productivity per hour of children's agricultural labor of the most common kinds, at least from the early teens, is not much lower than that of adults. The same appears to be true of non-agricultural wage labor, from the few cases that we observed. Boys of fourteen years regularly received an adult wage for a full day's labor in construction projects, and girls of fifteen weaving on handlooms in a small local factory, though paid at piece-work rates, took home the same wages as their adult counterparts.

For other tasks, particularly those in which younger children are engaged, it is much more difficult and in some cases impossible to estimate absolute or relative productivity per hour. In the case of cutting fodder (the most common of all male children's tasks), it frequently occurred that an adult male would one day cut grass for two hours to feed the household's animals, while a few days later a boy in the ten to twelve or thirteen to fifteen age group would spend the same amount of time to feed the same number of animals. For those below the age of ten, productivity in this task may be somewhat lower, because the basket in which they carry the cut grass is usually smaller than that which adults and older children use. Girls of thirteen and above seem to be able to weave *tikar* with the same speed as their mothers, although the quality may be somewhat lower if they have only recently begun weaving, and may thus fetch a lower price. But what of the productivity of young children in such tasks as taking cattle to bathe, herding goats or ducks, scaring birds from a field of ripe paddy awaiting harvest, or staying at home cooking, caring for younger children and keeping chickens from a *kepang* full of rice drying in the sun, while the mother is working in the fields or trading at the market? The most that can be said is that these tasks are very frequently performed by extremely young children; that they involve long periods of time but little physical effort; that although these tasks in themselves may not be productive, they are all NECESSARY in the sense that they must be done if the household in question wishes to keep animals, to save its rice from depredation, or to free an older household member for more productive labor. Furthermore, there is nothing in my observations to suggest that an adult could perform these tasks any better or faster than a small child, although on the other hand, there are many OTHER tasks in which an adult can be more productive than a small child, if he or she is freed from these "necessary but unproductive" tasks. The same would be true of many other tasks such as fishing in streams and irrigation channels to supplement the family's diet, collecting firewood, fetching water (an extremely time-consuming task in the dry season, when water must be scooped in coconut shells from a seep-hole by the water's edge, the river water not being clean enough for household use without this filtering). It is thus interesting, though not surprising, to see that small children spend large amounts of time every day in these "adult-freeing" tasks (Table 3).

Many other cases concerning other tasks could be mentioned if space allowed, each of them suggesting the same conclusions. First, there are a large number of economically useful, sometimes necessary, but not very productive tasks — both in household maintenance and in the productive effort itself — in which small boys and girls from ages as low as six in some cases, and generally by the age of nine, can be virtually as productive or efficient as their adult counterparts could be. However, they remain largely children's tasks because adults and older children can be more productively occupied in other ways. Second, most of the more productive tasks (such as mat weaving, cutting fodder, planting, harvesting, hoeing) can be performed by children thirteen to fifteen years old with a productivity virtually equal to that of adults.

Extent of children's participation in household economy   Given this POTENTIAL for the participation of children in household economy and production, we turn to the question of their ACTUAL contribution to the total production of the household. In other words, having estimated their relative productivity per hour in various kinds of work, we must discover how many hours per day they actually spend in these tasks compared with adults, because a given potential of children, however great, is of no practical significance unless the household economy, and the larger framework of the "labor-surplus" village economy surrounding it still leaves room for the actual exercise of that potential. In order to ascertain the average number of hours spent daily by children and adults of various ages in various kinds of activity, a regular series of visits was made to each of the forty selected households in order to ask each family member how he or she had spent the twenty-four hour period immediately preceding the interview, and the time of beginning and ending each activity. The households were each visited every six days over a period of several months (although I am using here only the data from the first two months, because the remainder were not yet processed at the time of writing). The six-day interval was chosen so that visits should not coincide either with the Javanese five-day market week or with the seven-day week which might have affected the pattern of daily activities, for instance, in trading and school attendance respectively.

Because the writer could not attend each interview, a majority of the interviews was delegated to a team of local secondary-school children or secondary-school graduates, who came from the same hamlets as the small group of households they interviewed and thus were already well acquainted with their subjects.

A number of questions may be raised concerning the accuracy of data collected in this way, particularly in regard to the extent to which the household members, possessing no clocks or watches, will have known with any accuracy the duration of each of their activities. So far as it has been possible to check independently the accuracy of the information recorded, it seems that while there have undoubtedly been omissions and inaccuracies, the general level of accuracy is much higher than I had expected. Omissions that could be easily checked (involving activities that must be done every day, such as cooking, cutting fodder, etc.) were very rare, while irregular or unusual activities (such as *gotong-royong* labor) are of course much more easily recalled. With regard to the accuracy of the times recorded, I found to my surprise that the majority of people whom I asked could correctly estimate the time of day to within a quarter of an hour. It is interesting to note that several features of everyday Javanese village life combine to give both old and young a considerable awareness of the time of day. One might mention the relatively invariable time of sunrise and sunset in a region close to the equator; the practice of gong-beating by hamlet heads at various relatively fixed times of day and night to announce that all is well; the close attention to how many hours are spent in agricultural labor, since the pay varies in accordance with the time spent; the presence in the middle of crowded hamlets of primary schools whose classes begin and end at specific times; and finally the five obligatory daily Moslem prayers, which although performed by only a few of our sample, at least were performed by some of their neighbors. What inaccuracies there are will probably have occurred throughout the whole sample, so that the material, whatever its absolute errors, can be used with some confidence for internal comparisons.

It should be noted that the two months of data used here (from mid-October to mid-December 1972), covering the end of the dry-season harvest and the beginning of the rainy season, are from a relatively peak period of labor-inputs in agriculture. Subsequent data will determine how much the levels of productive activity are decreased, or channeled into different types of activity, at other times of year.

In order to present the results simply, all economic activities have been grouped into eight broad categories as follows:

A1 *Care of small children*

A2 *Household* (includes fetching water, house cleaning, washing clothes and kitchen implements, drying paddy and other crops, all kinds of food preparation)

A3 *Collect firewood*

B *Production outside agriculture* (weaving and all other handicrafts, food preparation for sale, trading, fishing)

C *Animal care and feeding* (cutting fodder, collecting other food for chickens, ducks, cattle etc., herding and bathing of animals)

D *Non-agricultural wage-labor* (weaving in a small factory, carpentry, construction, carrying goods for a wealthy trader, etc.)

E *Exchange or communal labor* (unpaid labor building or repairing a neighbor's house etc.; does NOT include reciprocal agricultural labor — see category F — and does NOT include non-productive labor such as serving guests at a neighbor's ceremonial)

F *Agriculture* (all agricultural labor, on one's own or another's land, whether unpaid, paid in cash or with *bawon*, etc.)

Taking the data from a series of eight days and ordering them in the above eight categories, I have divided the totals by eight to give a picture of the average number of hours spent *daily* by individuals according to age group, sex, and type of activity. The results are presented in Table 3. From this table it can be seen that the average time spent by adults in "work" each day is nine hours (men) and twelve hours (women), or if we exclude care of small children, nine hours (men) and eleven hours (women).[2] Girls of age thirteen to fifteen and sixteen to eighteen almost equal the adult contribution, while children in the other groups contribute about one-half as much, with the exception of boys of seven to nine who contribute only one-fourth of the adult working hours. Looking more closely, we see that children exceed the adult contribution in some important tasks both in the "useful" (A1 -

---

[2]   These figures confirm the view of Koentjaraningrat (n.d.: 355) that Javanese villagers "need no enticement or encouragement to work hard." Rather, they need help that can increase the productivity of their work.

Table 3. Average hours per day per person devoted to various tasks, according to age, sex and type of activity (N = forty households, eight days of observation per household)*

Age group, sex, and number in the sample: Activity:	7–9 M (N=18)	7–9 F (10)	10–12 M (14)	10–12 F (10)	13–15 M (18)	13–15 F (11)	16–18 M (9)	16–18 F (12)	19–29 M (6)	19–29 F (12)	30+ M (39)	30+ F (42)
A1 Care of small children	0.2	1.2	0.5	1.7	0.5	1.5	0.3	0.1	—	0.6	0.4	1.2
A2 Household	0.1	1.2	0.3	1.1	0.2	2.3	0.2	2.8	0.1	3.1	0.3	4.3
A3 Collect firewood	0.7	0.2	0.6	0.3	0.7	0.5	0.2	0.1	0.1	0.1	0.3	0.1
B Production outside agriculture	0.2	1.3	0.4	0.2	0.8	1.9	0.2	4.9	3.2	4.8	1.8	4.9
C Animal care and feeding	1.2	1.0	2.7	0.5	2.2	0.1	1.6	0.1	0.8	—	0.8	0.1
D Non-agricultural wage labor	—	0.1	—	—	0.1	0.4	1.7	0.3	2.1	1.3	1.1	—
E Exchange or communal labor	—	—	0.2	—	0.2	0.1	0.7	0.2	0.4	0.3	0.6	0.1
F Agriculture	0.1	0.8	0.7	0.7	1.1	2.1	3.2	2.3	2.6	2.3	3.7	1.6
Total hours of "work" per day	2.5	5.8	5.4	4.5	5.8	8.9	8.1	10.6	9.3	12.5	9.0	12.3

* Because these per-person, per-day averages are derived from a sample of at least nine individuals in each group, and from a total of eight days of observations, they do NOT give a realistic picture of one day in the life of one individual. In reality, each member of the sample spends a greater amount of time in a smaller number of activities each day.

A3) and "productive" (B - F) categories. Children of ALL age-groups spend more time on the average than adults in child care, with the result that only a little of the adults' time is spent in this way; an example of the function of children in freeing adults for more productive labor. The collection of firewood and animal care are clearly in large part the responsibility of children rather than adults. In all kinds of "productive" activity (categories B, C, D, and F) boys and girls of sixteen to eighteen years almost equal, and in some cases exceed, the contribution of adults, so that if all these activities are counted together, we find that the totals of productive activity almost equal those of adults in the case of girls, and exceed them in the case of boys. Recalling the observation of Jay (1969) that male children frequently replace the adult in fulfilling *gotong-royong* (communal or reciprocal labor) obligations, it appears that boys in the ten to twelve and thirteen to fifteen age groups regularly engage in *gotong-royong* labor, but that their contribution is small compared to that of the sixteen to eighteen age group, who slightly surpass the adult contribution in this activity. The table also shows that during the two months covered, girls of thirteen and over spend as much time as adult women in agriculture, but that girls of seven to nine and ten to twelve spend only one-third of that time; there is, however, a possibility that when the period is extended to cover the whole of a harvest season, the contribution of small girls will be much greater. Anne Stoler's research during the 1973 wet season harvest, with the same forty households, found that the number of days spent harvesting according to age group was as follows: up to ten years of age, 12.6 days on the average per person (N = 12); eleven to fifteen years, 21.1 days (N = 11); sixteen years and over, 14.5 days (N = 56).

Having compared the contributions of the various age groups and sexes, it is interesting to see if there are any significant differences to be found WITHIN those groups; for example, it is important to know whether children from large families do more or less work, and what kinds of work, compared with children from small families. This question is very closely related to that of the "cost and value" of high versus low fertility. In the economic environment of "labor-surplus," it might easily be supposed that the larger the family size, the smaller the productive contribution of each child in the family must be, because the household can only provide strictly limited labor opportunities for them. Or possibly we might find that although children in large families work for long periods, the greater the family size, the greater the likelihood that children's work will be less productive. In this case even the elder children would be engaged in the less productive activities in large families, simply because the household cannot provide them with the chance to be more productive, although they are potentially capable of being so. If this were the case (i.e. if the number of children in the family varied inversely with their productivity), we would have to conclude that increasing the number of one's children results in economic "loss" to the parents, because of the effect hypothesized above. In order to examine the validity of such an argument, the sample was divided into two further groups of children: (1) children with only one, or no sibs in the potentially productive age group seven to eighteen years, i.e. "children from small families" and (2) children with two or more sibs in that age group (i.e. "children from large families"). Dividing these new categories into only two age groups (so as to retain a sufficiently large sample in each group), and calculating per-person averages in the same manner as previously, some interesting results emerge which are presented in Table 4.

Table 4. Average hours per day devoted to various tasks by children according to age, type of activity, and number of siblings (N = 102 children in forty households, eight days of observation per household)*

Age, number of sibs in that age group, and number in the sample: Activity:	7–12 years		13–18 years	
	0–1 sibs N = 15	2 or more sibs N = 37	0–1 sibs N = 15	2 or more sibs N = 35
A1 Care of small children	0.5	0.9	0.8	0.5
A2 Household	0.4	0.6	1.3	1.2
A3 Collect firewood	0.5	0.5	0.3	0.5
B Production outside agriculture	1.9	1.1	1.9	2.4
C Animal care and feeding	0.7	1.2	1.4	1.0
D Non-agricultural wage-labor	—	0.1	0.5	0.5
E Exchange or communal labor	—	0.1	--	0.4
F Agriculture	0.3	0.6	1.3	2.2
Total hours of "work' per day	4.3	5.1	7.5	8.7

*   Those in the left-hand column of each age-group have one or no sibs in the potentially productive seven to eighteen age-group, and are referred to in the text as "children from small families"; those in the right-hand columns, with two or more sibs in that age-group, are referred to as "children from large families."

Taking the children of seven to twelve years first, it can be seen that children from the larger families (those with many sibs) do MORE work in ALL types of activity (excepting "non-agricultural production") than do their counterparts from the smaller families. In the case of the older children of thirteen to eighteen years, the children from large families also do more work (comparing the total work-hours daily), and that difference is due to the fact that children from large families work more in the directly productive categories of B - F, while those from small families work more in the useful but nonproductive categories of A1 - A3 (with the exception of animal care and feeding). If these differences can be taken to indicate a significant trend (which can be subsequently tested by the calculation of similar totals from a total of a hundred households over a period of several months), then they clearly tend to refute the argument examined above, leading us instead to the conclusion that CHILDREN FROM LARGE FAMILIES TEND TO BE NOT LESS, BUT MORE PRODUCTIVE THAN THOSE IN SMALL FAMILIES. Perhaps the reasons for this might be as follows: first, that children with many sibs are encouraged by the presence of elder sibs to participate in all kinds of work, and using their elder sibs as examples, begin performing each task at an earlier age than usual; and second, that children with many sibs, precisely because of their younger sibs' earlier participation in the useful but unproductive chores, are themselves liberated from those chores and free to engage in more productive activity.

In any case, there seems to be a strong possibility that in the village studied, high fertility does not reduce the productivity of children in the family economy, but rather tends to raise it. For the majority of households whose land and capital resources are severely limited — for whom the large part of their income must be sought in the application of their labor in whatever opportunities are available outside the household's own resources — the productivity of labor is determined by the population-resources ratio of the larger economic environment, over which they themselves have no significant control. In other words, productivity depends on the general demographic and economic conditions obtaining OUTSIDE the individual family, not on the size of that particular family. Certainly, the situation might improve if EVERY family were to limit the number of its children, but in the absence of this it is possible that individual parents may derive relative economic benefit from producing large numbers of children, in direct conflict with the needs of the economy as a whole, whose difficulties stem in large part precisely from a century and a half of steady and continuing population growth.[3]

A great deal more research is necessary before the question of costs and benefits of high versus low fertility to Javanese parents can be resolved, particularly in the area of costs of children, which I have not attempted to cover here. However, I hope at least to have suggested the value of further research along these lines, both in rural and urban communities. For example, one imagines that urban children in Java are considerably less productive than their rural counterparts, but there are certainly no data to prove this. The streets of Jakarta and other cities teem with small boys, collecting bags full of cigarette ends for "recycling," selling old magazines, shining shoes, or simply begging; how does their "productivity" compare with the cost of their keep, and with that of their rural cousins, cutting grass and bird-watching in the *sawah*? Finally, we should consider whether there are any practical conclusions to be drawn from the data and preliminary conclusions presented above, from the point of view of the effort to reduce fertility in Java through the Indonesian National Family Planning Program. Suppose it were confirmed in further research that high fertility does tend to result in net economic gain from the parents' point of view. Such a conclusion does not necessarily imply bleak prospects of success for the family planning program; for, although I have been narrowly considering the economic consequences of high fertility from the parents' point of view in this article, it is not at all the case that these are the only factors entering into reproductive decisions. Even casual research shows that Javanese parents are extremely anxious for their children's future economic welfare as well as for their own, and that they are acutely aware that whatever the consequences of high fertility for themselves, the consequences for the welfare of their children are disastrous. In this case, perhaps the argument for family planning most likely to succeed is not so much "limiting the number of your children will benefit YOU" (an argument which may not be valid), but rather "limiting the number of your children will benefit your children" — an argument which is known to be true, and therefore might be easily received by the generation of prospective Javanese parents who must make the crucial reproductive decisions.

---

[3] For those readers interested in population history, I have suggested a basically similar hypothesis to account for Java's demographic growth under colonial rule in White (1973).

REFERENCES

BUDI PRASADJA, A.
1972 "Pembangunan desa dan masalah kepemimpinannja." Unpublished thesis, University of Indonesia.

CLARK, COLIN
1970 "Economic and social implications of population control," in *Population control*. Edited by A. Allison, 222–237. London: Penguin.

GEERTZ, HILDRED
1961 *The Javanese family*. Glencoe: Free Press.

GILLE, H., R. H. PARDOKO
1965 "A family life study in East Java: preliminary findings," in *Family planning and population programs*. Edited by Bernard Berelson et al., 503–523. Chicago: University of Chicago Press.

IPPA
1969a "KAP survey, knowledge, attitude and practice of family planning, Djakarta, Indonesia, 1968." Draft Report of the Preliminary Findings. Indonesian Planned Parenthood Association, Jakarta.
1969b "Hasi 12 Penelitian Pengetahuan-Sikap-Praktek Keluarga Berentjana, Kabupaten Bekasi 1967." Indonesian Planned Parenthood Association, Jakarta.

JAY, ROBERT
1969 *Javanese villagers*. Cambridge: MIT Press.

KOENTJARANINGRAT
n.d. "Tjelapar: sebuah desa di Djawa Tengah Bagian Selatan," in *Masjarakat Desa di Indonesia Masa Ini*. Edited by Koentjaraningrat, chapter eight. Jakarta, Yayasan Penerbit Fakultas Ekonomi, University of Indonesia.

NAG, MONI
1972 "Economic value of children in agricultural societies: evaluation of existing knowledge and an anthropological approach," in *The satisfactions and costs of children: theories, concepts, methods*. Edited by James T. Fawcett. Honolulu: East-West Center.

PENNY, D. H., MASRI SINGARIMBUN
1972 *A case study in rural poverty*. Bulletin of Indonesian Economic Studies 8(2):79–88.

SLAMET, INA A.,
1965 *Pokok² Pembangunan Masjarakat Desa*. Jakarta: Bhratara.

WHITE, BENJAMIN
1973 Demand for labour and population growth in colonial Java. *Human Ecology* 1(3):217–236.

Factors Underlying Endogamous Group Size

JOHN W. ADAMS and ALICE BEE KASAKOFF

Endogamy is the tendency of people to mate within their own group. Endogamous groups are important as a social universe in which all sorts of basic interaction go on; the study of endogamy is therefore the study of social communication in the broadest sense. This article describes the range of sizes of endogamous groups and some of the reasons for variations that exist within this range. It discusses to what extent and by what forces the social horizon of man is confined; for confined it is, and our evidence indicates that even modern society, with its sophisticated means of transport and communication, fits quite nicely into the set of conclusions we have reached for primitive groups.

What we are able to present here are no more than first approximations; the statistical information about marriage upon which we have had to depend is not available for most societies of the world and what is available is limited. But more important are the many methodological and conceptual problems that exist and are partly responsible for these deficiencies in the data. The purpose here is as much to explore these with a hope of guiding further work as it is to present a broad outline of the nature and sizes of the groups within which endogamy occurs.

We came to this topic from an attempt to describe the marriage patterns of the Gitksan, a group on the Northwest Coast among whom

We would like to thank Michael Karpinko for drawing the tables that accompany this paper.

we had done fieldwork. We were interested in whether any of the models Lévi-Strauss had discussed applied; that is, if there were marriage to particular kinds of relatives. But we soon found that to determine this statistically we had to delineate a marriage universe for our sample. There were strong preferences to marry within the same village and within a set of villages which formed a dialect group. Yet there were also flows of people both between villages in the same dialect group and between the two different (minor) dialect groups we had studied.

We discovered, however, that the marriage universe of most individuals was very small. Because of this, many of the statistical techniques that had been developed for demonstrating marriage patterns were difficult to apply (see Kasakoff 1974). The size of the marriage universe, the endogamous group, limited the number and type of marriage patterns that could be found within it, and thus our attention turned to the problems of delineating marriage universes themselves.

PROCEDURES

It was important to know how the Gitksan compared with other societies but we soon found that little work had been done on this topic. Limited as we were by the way other ethnographers had tabulated their data, we began with the simplest and most obvious ways of describing marriage universes. We plotted the sizes of endogamous groups reported by ethnographers against the percentages of endogamy they reported for these groups. Next, we plotted the percentages of endogamy against the distances traveled for spouses. We made no attempt to draw a systematic sample — this would have been difficult in any case because only half the ethnographies we consulted had any information on endogamy at all, and only about half of those had information that could actually be used — but we used twenty-one societies of a variety of economic types from all over the world.

We were interested in answering the question, "Of the people who belonged to a group before marriage, how many subsequently married someone who also belonged to that group before marriage?" The relevant information was reported quite differently by different ethnographers and it was not always easy to get an accurate answer from the data provided. Usually ethnographies contain statistics compiled from a census made when the fieldwork was done, giving the origin of the spouses living in a local group at that time. The most obvious way to compute an endogamy rate from such data would be to take the percentage of the total that were endogamous.

But there are problems with this method. Because the local group described was rarely a closed marriage universe, individuals who were in it before marriage have left it to marry elsewhere; their marriages were not included in the figures. If one uses a percentage of extant marriages as the endogamy rate, one is, in effect, substituting the choices of people who moved to the group upon marriage for those of people who left it. This rate does not give a true picture of the choices of people from the local group.

It would be acceptable if one could assume that all the similar local groups in the region had the same endogamy rates and that the people coming in were in fact balanced by those going out, but this is surely never the case. For example, the different barrios of Tepoztlán (Lewis 1951) have different endogamy rates. They range from 14–42 percent (computed by the method to be described below) for the outlying barrios. This might be supposed to be the result of the small size of these barrios (the average is 186 persons), but the central barrios which average 793 persons also have varying rates (from 34–50 percent).

Rather than combine information on members of different local groups, we decided to use information only on individuals who had been part of the group before marriage. Each marriage was conceived of as *two* marriage choices and we counted only the choices of individuals from the local groups for which complete information was provided. For example, Leach's information on Pul Eliya (1961: 82) states that in 1951 there were thirty-nine "extant marriages of living residents of Pul Eliya (including latest marriages of widows, widowers, and divorced males)." The totals appear in Table 1.

Table 1.   Extant marriages of living residents of Pul Eliya*

Diga marriages, wife from another village	21
Diga marriages, wife from Pul Eliya	5
Binna marriages, husband from another village	8
Binna marriages, husband from Pul Eliya	5
	39

* *Diga* marriages are virilocal; *binna* marriages uxorilocal.

There is information about the marriage choices of 18 (5 + 8 + 5) women and 31 (21 + 5 + 5) men originally from Pul Eliya. The denominator is the sum, 49. The numerator is 20, since there are 10 endogamous marriages, each of which involves two choices. The percentage of endogamous marriage choices for Pul Eliya is 20 out of 49, or 41 percent. We used this method to arrive at all figures quoted in the article and entered on the charts.

If we had taken the endogamy rate to be a percentage of extant marriages it would have been 10 out of 39, or 26 percent, for Pul Eliya. However, this is no more accurate than our method because Pul Eliya has not engaged in a balanced exchange of spouses with other villages. This can be demonstrated by a second set of figures where Leach has tabulated the marriages "extant at various dates between 1850 and 1954 of which at least one partner was born in Pul Eliya" (1961: 83). Here he has followed people who left Pul Eliya at marriage and we have the information we need to answer the question we posed; the endogamy rate from these figures is 34 percent. Our method, therefore, slightly OVERESTIMATES endogamy. This is because the people who left the village at marriage are left out of our count. Endogamous marriages are counted twice, as it were, while exogamous marriages are counted only for the partner who remains in the village.

This type of distortion was minimal for societies where data for a relatively closed marriage universe were provided because very few people left the sphere of reporting and almost everyone could be "followed" from his original local group to the group into which he had married. This sort of information was available for Tikopia (Firth 1959), Tiwi (Goodale 1971; Hart and Pilling 1962), San Bernardino Contla (Nutini 1968), and Tepoztlán (Lewis 1951); for all of these societies full information was provided on the marriages of a group with over 90 percent endogamy. Distortion was a little greater for two societies for which information on groups with 67 and 69 percent endogamy was given: Telefolmin (Craig 1969) and the Negev (Marx 1967). In all these societies we averaged the rates for groups of the same type: for example, we averaged the rates for the barrios of Tepoztlán and used the average on our charts.

The information for the rest of the societies came from tabulations of the marriages in communities that had lower rates of endogamy. If figures which followed people who left those communities were provided, as was the case if marriage information came from genealogies rather than censuses, we used such figures for our estimates and the rates are an accurate answer to our question, with no distortion, for the community that was the focus of the study. (But such a rate is probably not representative of similar communities in the region.) The societies for which such "following" figures were available were Turkey (Stirling 1965), Pul Eliya, Round Lake Ojibwa (Rodgers 1968),

Enga (Meggitt 1965), Daribi (Wagner 1969), and Maring (Rappaport 1969).

But for the remaining nine communities in our sample, we did not have information on the people who had left at marriage, and our method of counting overestimated endogamy. The difference of 7 percentage points between the two estimates for Pul Eliya is probably characteristic of the magnitude of the overestimate for groups of about 30 percent endogamy in these societies. For the larger groups in those societies, the more inclusive groups with higher endogamy rates, the overestimate is probably smaller.

It might have been possible to compensate for the different types of ethnographic reports and use different ways of counting for each one, but rather than expend this effort on information that was so obviously faulty in other ways, we decided to go ahead with the method we have described — a method that kept information from different local groups separate unless it was possible to have virtually complete information on the choices of several comparable groups in a region. Our goal was simply to get some rough estimates of basic parameters rather than to arrive at final conclusions.

SEMICLOSED GROUPS

The concept of a 100-percent endogamous group did not prove to be very fruitful in our research. Such groups are extremely rare and when they do occur they break down into smaller semiclosed groups. We came to refer to these as "80-percent groups" because usually the rate of endogamy for such groups is about 80 percent though it can range from 70 to 90 percent. When ethnographers report higher rates of endogamy these rates usually refer to very large groups, such as an entire ethnic group or a nation. The 80-percent group we are speaking of here can be recognized by the fact that after the rate of endogamy that defines this group is reached, group sizes increase almost astronomically for very small increases in rates of endogamy. The 80-percent groups typically range from several hundred to 10,000 individuals.

We found such groups in all the societies we had information about. Even isolated island societies like the Tiwi and Tikopia have *two* 80-percent groups, clearly separated geographically. This is all the more remarkable because travel to all points in their social space is not difficult and the overall population of these societies is quite small.

It is almost as though a society has to have another one, very similar to it, nearby.

In effect, 80-percent groups are semiautonomous social microcosms within which a large proportion of daily interaction occurs. They are always local groups of some kind: the Tiwi occupy two islands, each of which is an 80-percent group, and the Tikopia have two districts on different sides of the island. For pastoralists, the 80-percent group is typically the "tribe" the ethnographer studied. In the New Guinea highlands it is a valley, while in peasant societies it is either a set of small villages near each other or a neighborhood within a large settlement. For the Gitksan it was a set of three (or four) villages which were also a subdialect group.

Marriages outside of this group are made either by high-status individuals who "represent" their locality in some larger system or by persons who live close to other 80-percent groups. But villages on the border between two 80-percent groups confine most of their marriages to one of them, even though the rate may be slightly lower than it is for localities which are near the centers. The 80-percent groups, therefore, appear to be discrete, although the degree of discreteness may depend on geographical barriers.

ENDOGAMOUS GROUP SIZE

When we plot percentages of endogamy on a vertical axis, against size of group on the horizontal we find that (1) the majority of societies are bunched together, but (2) a few bunch closer to the vertical, i.e. high endogamy in small groups, and (3) a few closer to the horizontal, i.e. low endogamy in large groups.

Those nearer the vertical in our sample are the Ojibwa, Tiwi, Basseri (Barth 1961), and peasants of the Negev; those nearer the horizontal are villages in China (Diamond 1969; Baker 1968) and Japan (Nakane 1967) and densely populated societies in the highlands of New Guinea (see Figures 1, 1a).

The societies near the vertical furnish some information on the limits of endogamy in human beings. Due to the difficulty of finding spouses of suitable age in small groups, there is a lower limit on the sizes of groups that can have certain percentages of endogamy. The most endogamous society we have record of is the Round Lake Ojibwa in which 50 percent of the marriage choices were reportedly made within a group of fifty individuals and 80 percent within a group of 150.

While this sounds extreme (and, quite frankly, we question whether it is indeed possible to keep this rate up for a long period of time), the existence of societies which come close to these figures in other parts of the world does seem to lend them some credence. For example, among the Basseri 68 percent of the marriage choices are made within a group a little smaller than 150, and among both peasants in the Negev and the Telefolmin, approximately 60 percent of the marriage choices fall within a similar-sized group. The figures on Tiwi and Tikopia are not very different: 52 percent in a group of 180 (Tikopia) and 55 percent in a group of 200 (Tiwi).

The Round Lake Ojibwa do seem to be exceptional in the small size of their 80-percent group, however, since there is no other society that comes even close to making this percentage of their marriage choices in such a small group (150 people). The next largest group we have for this percentage is among the Tiwi who make 80 percent of their marriage choices within a group of 500. This latter figure compares quite well with the physical anthropologists' notion of size of the isolate in hunting societies, which Birdsell (1968) has suggested was 500 for aboriginal Australia. But in the majority of societies the 80-percent group is much larger than this and ranges from 850 to 55,000.

In fact, the estimate of a physical anthropologist (Bunak, quoted in Spuhler 1967: 251) that "many contemporary rural populations of Europe, North America, and Negro Africa are composed of demes numbering 1,500 to 4,000 individuals, with about 80-percent endogamy" is borne out by our work. And, if we amend this statement to say the demes range from 850 to 10,000 individuals, we shall include every society in our sample except the Ojibwa, the Tiwi, Tikopia of 1929, some sparsely populated societies in New Guinea, but also rural Japan, which is unique in having an 80-percent group of approximately 55,000 people (but see below).

Thus, there appears to be an upper as well as a lower limit on endogamous group size. Even in societies where it is possible to come in contact with a very large number of people, as is the case in the more densely populated areas in our sample, and even where such contact is actually maintained through markets and the like, the marriage universe is probably limited to groups of 10,000 at the most.

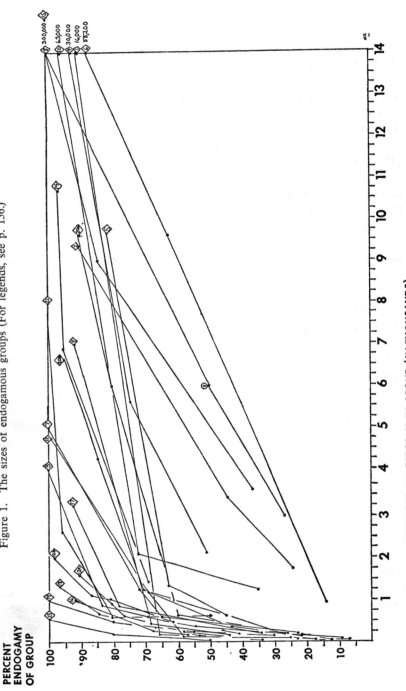

Figure 1. The sizes of endogamous groups (For legends, see p. 156.)

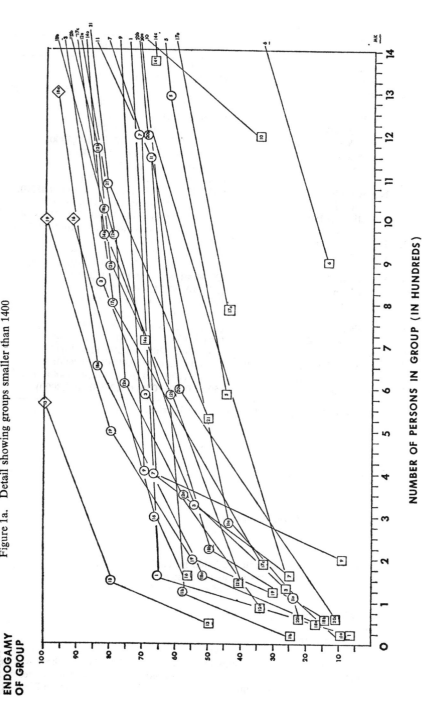

Figure 1a. Detail showing groups smaller than 1400

Table 2.   Entries in Figures 1 and 1a

Societies	(Percent endogamy, group size)
1. Basseri	(7,25) (66,143) (91,16000)
2. Chimbu	(24,1700) (44,3400) (90,9350)
3. Daribi	(26,130) (54,325) (69,585) (83,845) (100,4000)
4. Enga	(51,2100) (75,5600) (92,30000)
5. Hal-Farrug	(45,580) (63,1290) (82,9800)
6. Japan (rural)	(14,900) (63,9600) (88,55200)
7. Konda Valley Dani	(25,160) (67,400) (72,1200) (100,5000)
8. K'un Shen	(25,3000) (50,6000) (100,300000)
9. Maring	(44,204) (68,408) (92,7000)
10. Melpa	(35,1200) (73,1960) (96,63000)
11. Negev (a) Bedouins	(9,23) (24,109) (43,285) (69,1150) (99,4830)
(b) Peasants	(25,23) (58,121) continue with (69,1150)
12. Pul Eliya (a) 1931	(34,87) (58,348) (76,609) (80,957) (91,1566)
(b) 1954	(41,146) (62,584) (81,884) (85,1168) (98,1898)
13. Round Lake Ojibwa	(50,50) (80,150) (100,550)
14. Contla*	C: (68,1373) (95,6863) (97,10699)
	O: (70,714) (82,959) (94,3836) (97,10,699)
15. Sheung Shui	(37,3600) (86,9000) (100,14,080)
16. Telefolmin	(57,160) (67,312) (92,1000)
17. Tepoztlán*	O: (33,186) (80,800) (93,3200)
	C: (44,790) (80,2300) (93,3200)
18. Tikopia (a) 1929	(17,49) (52,165) (84,645) (97,1300)
(b) 1952	(16,65) (50,227) (83,1026) (98,1750)
19. Tiwi	(30,100) (55,200) (80,500) (100,1000)
20. Turkish Villages (a) Sakaltutan	(11,60) (60,600) (80,6000) (90,9600)
(b) Elbasi	(23,60) (70,1200) (84,4200) (94,6600)
21. Zinacantán	(50,523) (80,1086) (96,2583) (100,8000)

* C refers to central barrios; O to outlying barrios.

Legends for Figures 1, 1ᵃ, 2, and 2ᵃ:

Numbers refer to societies which are listed in Tables 2 and 3.
The symbols used in the figures are as follows:

☐   entry with the lowest percentage of endogamy for each society

◇   entry with the highest percentage of endogamy for each society

◯   intermediate entries.

The lines connect endogamous groups from the same society. Where there was no direct information given on the distance travelled for spouses, the entries for Figure 2 were calculated from population density and the sizes of groups in Figure 1.

THE EFFECT OF POPULATION DENSITY

The size of endogamous groups is related to population density which in turn is related to the type of subsistence economy. Societies with the smallest 80-percent groups are those with the lowest population densities: hunters and gatherers, pastoralists, and sparsely populated horticultural societies in the New Guinea highlands. The largest 80-percent groups are found in peasant societies and in the most densely populated societies in the New Guinea highlands, all societies whose livelihood is based on farming. There are exceptions to this relationship: Tikopia, for example, has a very high population density but quite small 80-percent groups, doubtless due to its island situation. Also, the Mexican cultures, Tepoztlán, San Bernardino Contla, and Zinacantán (Vogt 1970), have smaller 80-percent groups than other societies with similar population densities. But in general the relationship holds and suggests that the size of the 80-percent group is the outcome of the opportunity to travel. And, indeed, we find that when we plot the percentages of endogamy against the radii of circles within which each percentage of marriage choices is made, the differences between most of the cultures disappear: in societies with large and small endogamous groups people seem to go the same distance for their spouses; 80–100 percent of spouses are found within a day's journey, that is, seven miles, and usually the distance is under four miles (see Figure 2 and Table 3).

The only exceptions are the Ojibwa, the Basseri, the Bedouins of the Negev, and the Tiwi, who are very sparsely settled. These people have to travel much farther for their spouses (twenty-five to thirty miles) than those in the majority of societies. But, even though nomadic pastoralists do travel farther, this is compensated for by their means of transport, horse or camel rather than on foot, and so for them the spouses are also within a day's travel. It is only the hunting and gathering populations that are very sparsely settled, e.g. the Tiwi and the Ojibwa, for whom it often takes longer than a day to go and return from relatives by marriage.

Incidentally, the societies we have studied are not very different from urban populations of today. The results of eight propinquity studies made in a variety of American cities at different dates show that over half the people found their marriage partners within twenty-one city blocks, that is, roughly two and a half miles (Katz and Hill 1963: 43). This is true of all of the societies we studied as well, except for the nomadic pastoralists and hunters and gatherers. Thus, in societies quite different in scale and population density, and even in those like our own, with sophisticated means of transport, most marriages are made within a small geographical area of about the same size.

There are, then, three important "constants" that appear to determine the sizes of endogamous groups, each important for societies with different population densities. In those with very low densities the important factor is the minimum size for a viable human population. In these societies people will have to travel far to make contact with another community. In most such societies people don't have to go all the way to their spouse's abode; instead, the mating process is facilitated by periodic meetings at a convenient place either for reasons of subsistence or for ceremonials.

But for societies with higher densities, in which the minimum number of people live close by, the important constant would seem to be the distance traveled easily in a day. There the minimum population is always exceeded and the size of the 80-percent group depends almost entirely on population density. It is as though a grid determined by the daily walking distance were laid down and the sizes of 80-percent groups resulted from the number of persons in each space on the grid.

The tribes discussed in *Pigs, pearlshells and women* (Glasse and Meggitt 1969) illustrate this dramatically. They have quite different endogamous group sizes. But this is due almost entirely to their different population densities. When that is held constant, which occurs when the percentages of endogamy within particular groups are plotted against the land area those groups occupy, the societies fall neatly into a straight line. What is more, the number of clans in groups at each percentage of endogamy is nearly the same in all the societies.

And for societies with very high population densities, the important constant is the upper limit on the sizes of 80-percent groups. Theoretically, this suggests that at very high densities people travel even less than they could in a day to find their spouses. Actually, however, in societies of high density travel patterns no longer seem to limit the sizes of endogamous groups. Instead, social class restrictions take over. This may explain why Mexican villages do not have as large endogamous groups as one would expect from their population densities (although this may also be due to their being located in valleys).

Table 3.   Entries in Figures 2 and 2a

Societies	(Percent endogamy, distance)
1. Basseri	(7,0) (66,0) (91,25)
2. Chimbu	(24,1.18) (44,1.84) (90,3.08)
3. Daribi	(26,0) (54,2.32) (69,3) (83,3.75)
4. Enga	(51,2.35) (75,3.85) (92,8.95)
5. Hal-Farrug	(45,0) (63,0) (82,2)
6. Japan (rural)	(14,0) (63,3.1) (88,7.4)
7. Konda Valley Dani	(25,1.30) (67,2.32) (72,3.52) (100,7.3)
8. K'un shen	(25,0) (50,1) (100,10)
9. Maring	(44,1) (68,1.41) (92,5.84)
10. Melpa	(35,2.64) (73,3.08) (96,17.83)
11. Negev (a) Bedouins	(9,0) (24,0) (43,4.36) (69,8.95) (99,17)
(b) Peasants	(25,0) (58,0) continue with (43,4.36)
12. Pul Eliya (a) 1931	(34,0) (58,1.5) (76,3) (80,6) (91,10)
(b) 1954	(41,0) (62,1.5) (81,3) (85,6) (98,10)
13. Round Lake Ojibwa	(50,17.9) (80,30.9) (100,59,2)
14. Contla*	C: (68, .375) (95,1.5) (97,3.56)
	O: (70,0) (82, .75) (94,2.25) (97,3.56)
15. Sheung Shui	(37,6) (86,6) (100,6)
16. Telefolmin	(57,0) (67, .75) (92,10)
17. Tepoztlán*	O: (33,0) (93,1) C: (44,0) (93,1)
18. Tikopia (a) 1929	(17,0) (52, .125) (84, .875) (97,1)
(b) 1952	(16,0) (50, .125) (83, .875) (98,1)
19. Tiwi	(30,8) (55,12) (80,17) (100,31)
20. Turkish villages (a) Sakaltutan	(11,0) (60,0) (80,3.5) (90,7.7)
(b) Eibasi	(23,0) (70,0) (84,5) (94,8)
21. Zinacantán	(50,0) (80, .5) (96,1) (100,3.6)

*   C refers to central barrios; O to outlying barrios.

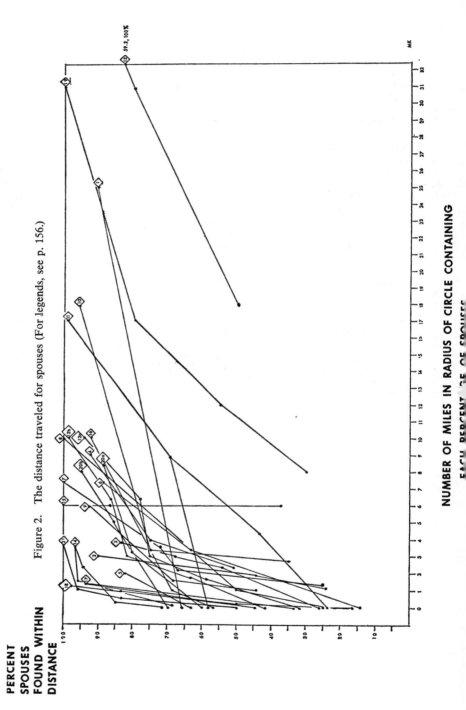

Figure 2.   The distance traveled for spouses (For legends, see p. 156.)

PERCENT
SPOUSES
FOUND WITHIN
DISTANCE

NUMBER OF MILES IN RADIUS OF CIRCLE CONTAINING

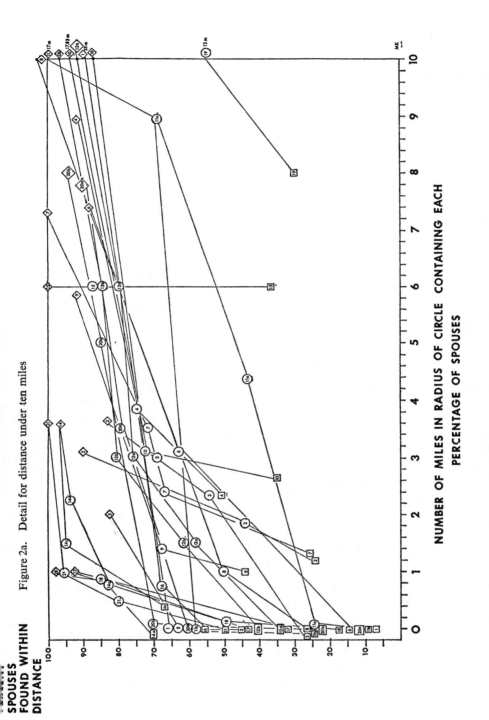

Figure 2a. Detail for distance under ten miles

162   JOHN W. ADAMS, ALICE BEE KASAKOFF

REGIONAL PATTERNS

From this it might seem as though propinquity were a prime determinant of endogamous group sizes, but this is in part due to the lack
of other data. Most anthropologists start with a single community as
the focus of study and move outward from there. The result is a set
of concentric circles centered on the community: higher and higher
percentages of endogamy occurring within circles with larger and
larger radii. For the first few societies we looked at, the rates of
endogamy were 30 percent for the local group, 50 percent for the
immediate neighborhood of the local group, and 80 percent for the
geographical region. (These were Tiwi, who had 30–50–80; Gitksan
and Zinacantán both of whom had 50- and 80-percent groups; and
Tikopia who had 27–50–80. These figures are not arcane, however.
They simply represent the likely rates if there really were endogamy;
for 30 percent is more than half of 50 percent, which is more than
half of 80 percent. Moreover, not all societies report these particular
rates.

The concentric circle approach seems to be the most readily available way of ordering marriage data when the ethnographer has nothing
"interesting" to report by way of kinship preferences. Indeed it is
almost an anthropological folk model of endogamy. The result is
almost certainly a very partial view of endogamy. Often ethnographies mention social groups which, on reading between the lines,
appear to structure marriage, but the endogamy rates are not reported
in those terms. For example, in Mexican societies bride and groom
must often contribute equally to marriage payments (Lewis 1951;
Nutini 1968). This should foster marriages of economic equals, yet
figures on social class are lacking; we have endogamy rates for the
barrios instead. In other societies, data on disputes indicate the existence of factions which have as cores what appear to be endogamous
kindreds. Yet because these groups are relatively amorphous, and,
indeed, may perhaps be defined better by marriage than by any other
criterion, they are usually not explicitly described, let alone used as
the basis for the tabulation of marriage choices. The fact is that ethnographers do not set out to describe marriage choice and groups
based on it; therefore, they mention it only when it coincides with
groups formed on other bases.

And, rarely do ethnographers report rates of endogamy for the
entire set of subgroups that constitute a semiclosed region. But in the
studies that do give more details, we can see that the marriage patterns

cannot be characterized by concentric circles. Factors other than propinquity come into play. The "circles" are different for different subgroups.

We will illustrate the sorts of regional patterns that one finds by describing three societies in detail: the Ojibwa, a hunting and gathering group of low population density (data are from Dunning 1959); Bedouins of the Negev (Marx 1967), a pastoralist society also with low population density; and Hal Farrug (Boissevain 1969a, 1969b), a village in Malta where the population density is very high.

The Ojibwa

Among the Ojibwa marriage choices are motivated largely by manpower requirements. Traplines must be worked by at least two adult males (and the upper limit seems to be about eleven). Normally a father and son or two brothers provide the men needed but due to demographic accidents, etc., some men may have no sons to pass their line to. If they have daughters the men who work the line will usually be sons-in-law. Thus, within the band, choices are not made at random but from economic considerations. Families with large numbers of brothers send some of them to live uxorilocally while families with few brothers or with all young children may have to rely on men from other families for their trapping manpower. Marriages between sibling groups with complementary characteristics seem to be preferred, and in each generation sexually skewed sibling groups seem to have a tendency to form endogamous enclaves.

Some marriages between bands are caused by pressure on resources. Men who marry into other bands for this reason reside uxorilocally. The result is that sibling groups consisting largely of women are more exogamous than those that are more evenly balanced. Other marriages between bands are caused simply by the shortage of women of appropriate ages.

In sum, even in a small society like the Ojibwa, marriages at certain distances are not simply the result of casual social encounter. How far away one marries depends, in part, at least, on the minimum number of people needed to make this particular system work. Here there are so few encounters outside the band, and the band is so small, that one suspects that one creates many encounters in order to be able to make marriages. Unlike the situation on our frontier, there were no mail-order brides. One used one's relatives in other bands instead of the advertisements, and these people also could vouch for a bride's suitability: if one comes from outside there is always the danger of getting a leftover from the local marriage market, someone left over for good reason. Thus, marriage choices did not result solely from proximity, and proximity, together with the social encounters that went on with neighboring bands, was kept up at least partly to provide marriage partners.

Moreover, even in this situation economic needs divide the people in one local settlement into endogamous enclaves which, though dependent on demographic accidents and thus constantly shifting from generation to generation, are nevertheless real. And, these needs also result in some types of people — those in sexually skewed sibling groups — marrying farther out than others.

Bedouins of the Negev

Bedouins marry either very close by or very far away, skipping over their middle-distance neighbors in a checkerboard pattern. The marriages close by are largely political, to link the smallest units of the society together into larger groups, often incorporating peoples who originated from quite far away, several generations back. The result is a subtribe knitted together by marriage ties which are carefully allotted to keep all of the segments united, usually through marriages to the group of the chief, which is the largest in size. Furthermore, the subtribe belongs to a tribe whose territory extends in a band across two major ecological zones, hilly country and plains. In dry years one might have to move one's flocks into the hilly country because the wells in the plains dry up. Therefore, subtribes that own land predominantly in the plains marry into subtribes in the hilly area, often into the zone of a different tribe. These are the only marriages that occur outside of the subtribe, except for a few far-flung marriages of polygynous chiefs. Thus, one will have relatives in the other subtribes of one's own zone only at two generations removed or through the polygynous chief of one's subtribe. Here is a case, then, where proximity is avoided in order to take out a certain type of ecological insurance and complex marriage rules thus force people out of their local groups, often quite far away, to find wives.

A different form of uncertainty prevails in Greece. The Sarakatsani (Campbell 1964) were the only society examined that could not be put on our charts because the only statistic reported on them was that virtually all marriages took place with other Sarakatsani. There were no "circles of endogamy." A closer look revealed that there were no local groups because shepherds had to make new leases for pasture every year. Pasture land was scarce and the best strategy seemed to be for a family to marry spouses from as many areas as possible so as to be able to get the best pasture arrangement. This would also help in marketing produce, getting favors from the settled people, etc. Here the uncertainty is not in the natural environment, but in the human one: the situation of being a landless group in a complex, economically differentiated, modern society.

All of these societies would fall outside of the proximity range talked about above: they go more than a day's journey for their spouses. Among the Ojibwa this seems to be due simply to very low population density and the need to find a minimum group, but in the other societies there is also a conscious desire to marry people from far away and people close to home are "turned down." Even in the Ojibwa case there are people living in one's own band whom one could marry if there were not extensive, quasi-moiety rules of exogamy to follow. That two of these societies should be mobile pastoralists and the other mobile hunters and gatherers suggests that the need to avoid proximity may be limited to certain types of economies. On the other hand, the case of the Sarakastani shows that ethnic enclaves of quite different economies might have to follow this strategy in order to cope with the dominant society.

Hal Farrug

A third example, Malta, is a society in which the local group is divided into classes that are more or less endogamous. Here, then, physical proximity gives way to social proximity in making marriage choices. Not only is this society densely populated in the extreme but communication by bus with other parts of the island is frequent. In fact, many work outside their village, commuting every day to another community. Nevertheless, marriage ties are separate from work ties and it seems to be the girl of one's own locality whom one marries. Casual encounters occur all the time with a huge number of people, but spouses are chosen from the local community only. Thus, marriages do not come automatically from a certain *amount* of social mixing. There are different *kinds* of social mixing and marriages result from only one kind.

There are four occupational classes: farmers, manual laborers, skilled laborers, and a bourgeoisie of architects, doctors, teachers. These four groups are more or less endogamous. Furthermore, there are also factions which are even more endogamous than the classes. One faction is made up of more people from higher classes than others, but there are people from all four classes in every faction. Paradoxically, breaking down the population to such an extent results in the same problem we saw among the Ojibwa: in the smallest class, the bourgeoisie, people have trouble finding spouses close to home and must move far away to find them. These people have the money and power to get the ban on first-cousin marriages lifted by the church, so their strategy is either to marry more closely than the other classes, or to go farther afield to find suitable partners. Not only is their marriage universe smaller than those of the other classes, but due to their low population density they must also go farther afield.

The middle groups are larger than the higher (and lower) classes. But even though they seem to be able to find spouses in their village and faction, the group is larger than the minimums we have from the Ojibwa and many other societies, and they seem to want to marry into the six closest neighboring villages even though they could probably find spouses in their natal villages. The reason for this is far from clear.

On the other hand the lowest group, the farmers, is again small, though not so small as the highest class. They, too, appear to marry into the neighboring six villages but in their case it might well be a question of simply finding enough available people of the proper social category and faction. (Note: the factions are found only within the community, and there is no data on whether they structure marriage outside of it, but it seems that one might avoid marrying into a family into which a member of the opposing faction of one's own community had married).

In Malta, therefore, not only is the local group broken down into endogamous enclaves, both classes and factions, but this results in different pressures on different classes to marry out. The highest and lowest classes are too small to be endogamous within a single village, even though the highest group has changed the kinship rules to permit them to have a smaller endogamous group. The middle groups appear to marry into a larger endogamous group than they have to. They marry out presumably for quite different reasons than the other classes, though the ethnographer does not tell us why.

BEYOND PROPINQUITY

These case studies indicate that there is probably no society in which proximity alone determines marriage choice. For within local groups different segments make different choices and thus belong to different endogamous enclaves; moreover, in some societies there is a conscious attempt to avoid making choices on the basis of proximity in order to spread marriage ties more evenly throughout a larger area (see Yengoyan 1968).

The *actual* group from which a person selects his mate is probably quite a bit smaller than those we have discussed in the first part of this article. Those figures probably represent simply the outer limits on marriage choice, the largest number of people from whom a spouse is chosen. The percentages express the chance that a person picked at random from a local group finds his spouse within that group. Actually, however, to take the extreme case, no one in Japan actually chooses from 55,000 people. Since the groups are inclusive, that segment of the 55,000 who are in an individual's 30-percent group are the ones most likely to be chosen. Of the rest, many are slated to marry into their own 30-percent and 50-percent groups. More important, people are not picked at random to marry. Many factors narrow down choice, a selection of which we have tried to provide in the preceding case descriptions.

We doubt if we will actually find that the small group of possible mates is always the same size, but the few studies which have made estimates of this (Dyke 1971; Goldberg 1967; and our own unpublished materials on the Gitksan) have come up with strikingly similar results. This is all the more suggestive since each society had different criteria for choosing mates, most of which were used by the researchers in making up their lists of potential spouses. It is difficult to make the figures exactly comparable, but fifteen to thirty would probably encompass all three estimates. (This is the number of *unmarried* individuals who meet various age and relationship criteria.) And if allowance were made for enclaves that might exist within the local groups which were the bases for these studies, the number might be even lower. Lest it be thought that the similarity is the result of these all being "small-scale" societies, the following quotation from a study of marriage in present-day Seattle is well taken:

American students, taking a course in marriage and the family sometimes react ethnocentrically when they learn of such exotic mate selection practices as go-betweens, family-arranged marriages, etc. On the other hand, the sociologist may sometimes overemphasize the cultural relativity of marriage norms by exaggerating the extent of cultural variability. Taking arranged marriage as one extreme and the American image of unrestricted individualism and romantic love as the other extreme, the range of variation in degrees of freedom in mate selection appears to be from one to infinity. The propinquity studies suggest that the actual range from one cultural extreme to the other may be only from one to about half a dozen or so. (Catton and Smircich 1964:529)

CONCLUSIONS

To review what we have said briefly:

1.   Endogamous groups are semi-closed, not completely closed.

2.   This means that there are always at least two marriage patterns in every society: marriage within the group and marriage outside of it. To understand endogamy, then, we have to take account of the variety of rules that characterize a society rather than assigning only one marriage pattern to each.

3.   Endogamous groups form systems of interlocking subgroups which extend over regions.

4.   Their sizes are closely tied to population density; but there are also upper and lower limits which set sizes at high and low densities, respectively.

Most anthropologists see marriage in terms of *rules* that guide behavior. They have implicitly followed Lowie (1961: 17) in seeing the tendency to marry people nearby as universal; thus, they consign it to the realm of "natural" tendencies that are not properly the study of anthropologists. Only if the rule is as extreme as the caste system found in India or other places is it worthy of study.

Another common view is to speak of endogamy in terms of marriage to relatives. Here again anthropology stresses rules that vary between cultures and that in some sense go against nature. The work of Lévi-Strauss (1953), of course, comes to mind here. From our point of view, his distinctions seem quite arbitrary. The different elementary structures produce marriage universes of the same size. And, father's brother's daughter marriage, which he excludes from his typology, can result in marriage universes that are similar in size to those of societies where marriage is an exchange between different unilineal groups. Furthermore, his distinction between elementary and complex structures is not the result of a difference in scale as he suggested. In both types of societies actual marriage choices are made within a relatively small group of people. We find that the groups that are most highly endogamous — which are also those with the lowest population densities — are the ones most likely to have preferences for kin (see Cavalli-Sforza 1958: 401). It is a moot point, therefore, whether they are small because of the preference, or have preferences for kin because they are so small. In any case, there is no correlation found so far between type of preference and degree of endogamy.

Romney (1971) has discussed the requirements of a mathematically satisfying proof of marriage preferences. But, as he himself has pointed out, anthropologists have rarely collected the data necessary to carry out such proofs. Because of their focus on a single community, they do not have the information on intermarriage between a set of communities that would be needed to demonstrate mathematically that their community is endogamous. We are trying to develop a new set of hypotheses about what natural marriage systems look like. After we do so, if the data are available, we would like to test mathematically whether, for example, the villages in a region are endogamous and arrive at a notion of the actual percentage that characterizes them — probably using Romney's method.

It would be important to find out what effect the existence of semi-closed groups would have on the algorithm. But at this point the application of his method would be premature: we must instead take the hints available in ethnographies and synthesize from them a new set of models of marriage systems based on endogamy rather than exogamy. If marriage systems are communication systems, as Lévi-Strauss has pointed out (1953: 536), we ought to know more about their boundaries.

Geographers and physical anthropologists have already devoted a great deal of effort to the mapping of marriage over distance. And, curves we obtained resemble curves of phenomena involving interaction over distance these other disciplines have examined. They are all highly leptokurtic, that is, very peaked: studies of migration distances, distances separating spouses before marriage, distances separating the birthplace of the parents and that of the child, number of phone calls between two places — all have shown this form. (For a sampling of such findings see Cavalli-Sforza and Bodmer 1971; Morrill and Pitts 1967; Stewart 1947; Sutter 1963; Zipf 1949).

The same sorts of distributions characterize gene dispersal in species other than man (Bateman 1963) and, interestingly, it has been shown mathematically that the leptokurtosis results from different rates of dispersal for different individuals, the same phenomenon as the different marriage patterns within the same society that we have stressed. Geographers interested in diffusion of inventions have used measures such as these to create a "mean information field," a set of probabilities that a person will learn about a certain invention from people at varying distances from himself (Hägerstrand 1965).

We would like to underscore the finding of these researchers that, despite the simplicity of the fact that interaction is very intense nearby and falls off rapidly the farther one gets from an individual, the underlying mechanisms that produce such curves are quite complex (Cavalli-Sforza and Bodmer 1971). Certainly the attitude among anthropologists such as Lowie that these things are the same the world over and can be factored out of cultural descriptions is not correct.

Different researchers have found that their data fit different theoretical distributions (see Sutter 1963). Some have had to combine two distributions to account for their findings (Morrill and Pitts 1967; Thanh and Sutter 1963). We have shown that the scale of distances for these curves varies from society to society depending on travel opportunity and population density. Moreover, there are always subgroups in society whose boundaries are not set by proximity. And in the same society existing under identical technological restrictions different subgroups marry different distances from home. The data we have had to work with are too crude to tell whether the *forms* of the curves differ from society to society (and from subgroup to subgroup) but this does seem to be the case. The size of a village and its distance from others does affect the shape of the curves.

The explanations that have been given for these different curves are circular. Sometimes they are little more than descriptions of a behavioral regularity (Harvey 1969: 110–111, 159). They result from an insularity of approach in the different fields, so that one field explains the curve with concepts central to a second field, while that field, in turn, is found to have explained it with concepts central to the first. Thus, geneticists explain their curves of marriage distances as having to do with the probability of interaction at various distances, but the sociologists and geographers base their formulations of the "laws" of interaction on the very same data that the geneticists use.

In reality, then, all that any of the disciplines have are a variety of sets of data showing that interaction, a frequent example of which is marriage, decreases sharply with distance. Most often the theory advanced is an economic one, that the time and resources invested are less if interaction is nearby rather than far away: to stay put is cheaper.

A more sophisticated idea, Stouffer's theory of intervening opportunity (1940), which states that besides the sizes of places and the distance one must take into account the number of opportunities between two places that would deflect interaction away from the more distant points, has recently been shown to be inadequate to account for the data on marriage distances (Catton and Smircich 1964), though it is useful in other applications.

In order to break out of this circularity we ought to abandon the egocentric point of view of the geographers and physical anthropologists and the community-centered point of view of the social anthropologist and adopt a regional approach. Our remarks here are intended to give some idea of the kind of regional organization one finds in marriage systems. We need a theory complementary to Central Place Theory for marriage choice. Only then will we be able to see how different subgroups intermarry to create a regional marriage pool; in effect we will be able to see how semiclosed groups arise and what factors lead them to be only semiclosed: why some people go farther than others. Only with such an approach, we feel, can we arrive at a more precise idea of the sizes of endogamous groups than we have been able to outline here.

REFERENCES

BAKER, HUGH
 1968 *A Chinese lineage village.* Stanford: Stanford University.
BARTH, F.
 1961 *Nomads of South Persia.* Boston: Little, Brown.
BATEMAN, A. J.
 1963 "Data from plants and animals," in *Les déplacements humains.* Edited by Jean Sutter, 85–91. Paris: Hachette.
BIRDSELL, JOSEPH B.
 1968 "Some predictions for the Pleistocene based on equilibrium systems among recent hunter-gatherers," in *Man the hunter.* Edited by Richard B. Lee and Irven DeVore, 229–240. Chicago: Aldine.
BOISSEVAIN, J.
 1969a *Saints and fireworks.* London School of Economics Monographs on Social Anthropology 30. London: Althone.
 1969b *Hal-Farrug, a village in Malta.* New York: Holt, Rinehart and Winston.
BROWN, PAULA
 1969 "Marriage in Chimbu," in *Pigs, pearlshells, and women; marriage in the New Guinea highlands.* Edited by R. M. Glasse and M. J. Meggitt, 77–95. Englewood Cliffs, N.J.: Prentice-Hall.
CAMPBELL, J. K.
 1964 *Honour, family, and patronage.* Oxford: Clarendon.

CATTON, WILLIAM R., R. J. SMIRCICH
1964   A comparison of mathematical models for the effect of residential propinquity on mate selection. *American Sociological Review* 29:522–529.

CAVALLI-SFORZA, L. L.
1958   "Some data on the genetic structure of human populations," in *Proceedings of the Tenth International Congress of Genetics*, 390–407.

CAVALLI-SFORZA, L. L., W. F. BODMER
1971   *The genetics of human populations*. San Francisco: W. H. Freeman.

CRAIG, RUTH
1969   "Marriage among the Telefolmin," in *Pigs, pearlshells, and women; marriage in the New Guinea highlands*. Edited by R. M. Glasse and M. J. Meggitt, 176–197. Englewood Cliffs, N.J.: Prentice-Hall.

DIAMOND, NORMA
1969   *K'un Shen, a Taiwan village*. New York: Holt, Rinehart and Winston.

DUNNING, R. W.
1959   *Social and economic change among the northern Ojibwa*. Toronto: University of Toronto.

DYKE, BENNETT
1971   Potential mates in a small human population. *Social Biology* 18: 28–39.

FIRTH, RAYMOND
1959   *Social change in Tikopia*. London: Allen and Unwin.

GLASSE, R. M., M. J. MEGGITT, editors
1969   *Pigs, pearlshells, and women: marriage in the New Guinea highlands*. Englewood Cliffs N.J.: Prentice-Hall.

GOLDBERG, HARVEY
1967   FBD marriage and demography among Tripolitanian Jews in Israel. *Southwestern Journal of Anthropology* 23:176–191.

GOODALE, JANE
1971   *Tiwi wives*. American Ethnological Society Monograph 51. Seattle: University of Washington.

HÄGERSTRAND, TORSTEN
1965   *Aspects of the spatial structure of social communication and the diffusion of information*. Regional Science Association, Papers and Proceedings 16.

HART, C. W. M., ARNOLD R. PILLING
1962   *The Tiwi of North Australia*. New York: Holt, Rinehart and Winston.

HARVEY, DAVID
1969   *Explanation in geography*. New York: St. Martin's.

KASAKOFF, ALICE
1974   "Lévi-Strauss' idea of the social unconscious: the Gitskan case," in *The unconscious in culture: the structuralism of Levi-Strauss in perspective*. Edited by Ino Rossi. New York: Dutton.

KATZ, A. M., R. HILL

1963   "Residential propinquity and marital selection: a review of theory, method and fact," in *Les déplacements humains.* Edited by Jean Sutter, 41–61. Paris: Hachette.

LEACH, E. R.

1961   *Pul Eliya, a village in Ceylon.* Cambridge: Cambridge University.

LÉVI-STRAUSS, CLAUDE

1953   "Social structure," in *Anthropology today.* Edited by A. L. Kroeber, 524–553. Chicago: University of Chicago Press.

LEWIS, OSCAR

1951   *Life in a Mexican village.* Urbana: University of Illinois Press.

LOWIE, ROBERT H.

1961   *Primitive society.* New York: Harper Torchbooks.

MARX, EMANUEL

1967   *Bedouin of the Negev.* New York: Praeger.

MEGGITT, M.

1965   *The lineage system of the Mae-Engae of New Guinea.* Edinburgh: Oliver and Boyd.

MORRILL, RICHARD L., FORREST R. PITTS

1967   Marriage migration and the mean information field: a study in uniqueness and generality. *Annals of the Association of American Geographers* 57:401–422.

NAKANE, CHIE

1967   *Kinship and economic organization in rural Japan.* London School of Economics Monographs on Social Anthropology 32. London: Althone.

NUTINI, HUGO

1968   *San Bernardino Contla; marriage and family structure in a Tlaxcalan municipio.* Pittsburgh: University of Pittsburgh Press.

O'BRIEN, DENISE

1969   "Marriage among the Konda Valley Dani," in *Pigs, pearlshells, and women; marriage in the New Guinea highlands.* Edited by R. M. Glasse and M. J. Meggitt, 159–175. Englewood Cliffs, N.J.: Prentice-Hall.

RAPPAPORT, ROY

1969   "Marriage among the Maring," in *Pigs, pearlshells and women; marriage in the New Guinea highlands.* Edited by R. M. Glasse and M. J. Meggitt, 117–137. Englewood Cliffs, N.J.: Prentice-Hall.

RODGERS, EDWARD S.

1968   "Band organization among the Indians of the eastern subarctic Canada," in *Contributions to anthropology: band societies.* Edited by David Damas, 21–50. National Museums of Canada Bulletin 228. Ottawa: Queen's Printer.

ROMNEY, A. K.

1971   "Measuring endogamy," in *Explorations in mathematical anthropology.* Edited by Paul Kay, 191–213. Cambridge, Massachusetts: M.I.T. Press.

SPUHLER, J. N.
1967   "Behavior and mating patterns in human populations," in *Genetic diversity and human behavior.* Edited by J. N. Spuhler, 241–268. Chicago: Aldine.

STEWART, JOHN Q.
1947   Empirical mathematical rules concerning the distribution and equilibrium of population. *Geographical Review* 37:461–485.

STIRLING, PAUL
1965   *Turkish village.* New York: Wiley.

STOUFFER SAMUEL A.
1940   Intervening opportunities: a theory relating mobility and distance. *American Sociological Review* 5:845–867.

STRATHERN, ANDREW, MARILYN STRATHERN
1969   "Marriage in Melpa," in *Pigs, pearlshells, and women; marriage in the New Guinea highlands.* Edited by R. M. Glasse and M. J. Meggitt, 137–158. Englewood Cliffs: Prentice-Hall.

SUTTER, JEAN, *editor*
1963   *Les déplacements humains.* Paris: Hachette.

THANH, LUU-MAU, JEAN SUTTER
1963   "Contribution à l'étude de la répartition des distances séparant les domiciles des épous dans un département français. Influence de la consanguinité," in *Les déplacements humains.* Edited by Jean Sutter, 123–139. Paris: Hachette.

VOGT, EVON Z.
1970   *The Zinacantecos of Mexico.* New York: Holt, Rinehart and Winston.

WAGNER, R.
1969   "Marriage among the Daribi," in *Pigs, pearlshells, and women; marriage in the New Guinea highlands.* Edited by R. M. Glasse and M. J. Meggitt, 56–76. Englewood Cliffs, N.J.: Prentice-Hall.

YENGOYAN, ARAM
1968   "Demographic and ecological influences on aboriginal Australian marriage sections," in *Man the hunter.* Edited by Richard B. Lee and Irven DeVore, 185–199. Chicago: Aldine.

ZIPF, G. K.
1949   *Human behavior and the principle of least effort.* Reading, Massachusetts: Addison-Wesley.

PART TWO

Population Policy and Family Planning

Birth Planning:
Between Neglect and Coercion

STEVEN POLGAR

Between 1962 and 1972, large-scale programs for natality regulation have changed from something that few people would support (or even talk about) to a major policy instrument of the United States government for poor people both inside the country and abroad. Several European countries, particularly Britain, Sweden, Holland, and Denmark, as well as the United Nations and its associated agencies, have also become involved in population and family planning programs. This rapid metamorphosis is indeed astonishing. International funds available for bilateral and multilateral efforts in this field are fast approaching the magnitude of expenditures for all other health programs, and, within the United States Agency for International Development, have already surpassed them. Why has this change occurred?

Some would look to "factual" and humanitarian causes: that population was growing in a number of countries almost as fast as average income; that the export of "death control" from the metropolitan countries was a double-edged sword if "birth control" was not exported as well; that new techniques of contraception made mass programs feasible; that surveys showed families in many "developing" countries wanted fewer births than was the average they would have by the end of the childbearing period; that infant mortality could be reduced if births took place further apart; and so on.

Others see less praiseworthy reasons: the preservation of the privileged status of the industrialized countries; a distraction from efforts to liberate and develop the economies of ex-colonial nations; the brainchild of a small interlocking directorate of reactionaries and their helpmates; the prelude to a new wave of colonization from the rich countries occupying sparsely populated areas in the Third World; an attack on the virility and femininity of politically emergent people; a cheap substitute for more positive types of international assistance; and so forth.

To answer my own question about the causes for this sudden change I first will take a quick and rather ethnocentric[1] excursion into the history of birth planning,[2] and then analyze some of the forces operating on the current scene. It is appropriate, I think, before proceeding, to sketch in my own background in this field. In 1956 while I was studying public health, one of my professors argued, convincingly to me, that the population problem was the most important problem in public health. When I joined the faculty of a school of public health in 1959 I wanted to do a study on family planning. My boss demurred because both the head of the university and the governor of the state were Catholics; if we wanted to be accepted as behavioral scientists in this school, family planning would be a poor topic for research. So the study came to focus on prenatal care, but I did ask some questions about prior contraceptive use. In 1963 I joined the Planned Parenthood Federation of America as its Director of Research. And since 1967 I have been affiliated with the Carolina Population Center, working for the last two years mainly with universities in Africa. Thus I think it is fair to say that I am an "insider" in population family planning circles. But as birth planning has attracted an increasingly large and vocal following, I have come to feel more and more a member of a shrinking minority of "non-Malthusians" within this circle.

BIRTH PLANNING BEFORE 1800

The cultural regulation of reproduction, as I have stressed elsewhere (Polgar 1972), has been a very long-standing feature of human groups. In the gathering-hunting stage of evolution, apart from the increases when new ecological zones were entered, cultural and biological forces kept natality close to the replacement level. With the change to food production, local birth rates increased perhaps as much as a hundredfold over a period of a few thousand years. The development of state societies,

---

[1]   I will concentrate on Britain and the United States because I am most familiar with the literature in English, because Malthusianism is most prominent in these two countries, and because of the Anglo-American influence in the Third World today on population matters.

[2]   "Birth planning" is a term coined by Edward Pohlman (1969); it combines birth control and population planning. The two latter concepts should be clearly distinguished in many contexts; sometimes, however, it is efficient to combine them.

empires, colonialism, and mercantilism spurred further increases, but due to the less radical alteration of the subsistence base and to the ravages of great epidemics, populations increased "only" about tenfold. Industrialization and economic colonialism in recent times have led to further growth — at a rate which is now causing much alarm.

The proselytizing religions which developed in state societies all include exhortations such as "be fruitful and multiply and replenish the earth" to promote natality. Notice the term "replenish" which is presumably a reference to catastrophic population losses. But more fundamental, I think, is the pressure exerted by the central authority in a redistribution system to expand the numbers of those paying tribute, taxes, and tithes. Economic decisions are largely centralized, but reproduction, necessarily, still takes place in individual conjugal units.

The Judeo-Christian tradition has an additional feature that is relevant here because it is the tradition of Malthus and of most population/family planning advocates today. This has to do with sexuality. Although pronatalist statements occur in all the major religions, the Judeo-Christian tradition has been unique in linking contraception to "immorality." The Biblical passage on Onan, for example, can be interpreted as showing divine displeasure with a man who refuses to follow the rules of the levirate, but most commentators have regarded the "sin" at issue as contraception (coitus interruptus, in particular, although many use "onanism" to refer to masturbation). A major impetus against contraception in Christianity came with the influence of Thomas Aquinas, who strongly argued that intercourse not aimed at the generation of offspring was a vice against nature. The opposition from Christian denominations was unbroken until 1925 when the Quakers declared themselves in favor of birth control under certain conditions. Then in 1929 the Federal Council of Churches of Christ in America advocated fewer children for each mother and in 1930 the highly significant Lambeth Conference of Anglican Bishops held the sex act to be as important for marital love as for procreation (a theological position adopted also by the Second Vatican Conference three decades later).

Egyptian developments from before 1000 B.C. are customarily accorded a place by Western writers in the history of their own civilization. Thus Himes's monumental review of contraception (1963) starts the chapter on "Contraceptive technique in antiquity (Western World)" with descriptions of Egyptian papyri that contain information on vaginal plugs and other contraceptives. The "ancient" Greeks discussed the question of ideal population size, as well as contraception and abortion, in quite a few writings (Hutchinson 1967: 9–13). The prohibition on prescribing an abortifacient, preserved in the modern-day Hippocratic oath, referred to post-"animation" abortions only and was apparently one of several conflicting opinions on the subject. Of the many Greek and Roman writers of "antiquity," Himes is most impressed with Soranus of Ephesus who described many methods of birth control, distinguished between contraception and abortion, and discussed indications and contra-indications for each (1963: 88–92).

In the Middle Ages the scientific tradition with which Westerners identify was maintained by Islamic scholars who also wrote quite a bit on birth control. Ibn Sina (Avicenna) was clearly among those who "considered the prevention of conception a legitimate part of medical practice" (Himes 1963: 142). In European writings from the Middle Ages and through the eighteenth century, Himes was able to find little more than magical means for preventing conception, and he turned instead to the folk traditions of peasants in the late nineteenth and twentieth centuries and to the history of the condom, which was used to prevent infection rather than pregnancy (1963: 170–206). In their extensive search of the French literature Bergues et al. (1960: 75–119) found medical writings on the mechanisms of conception, the causes of sterility and abnormal offspring, and the determination of gender and accidental abortions, but nothing on birth control. Evidence that induced abortion, contraception, and infant abandonment were practiced at this time, mostly in illicit unions before the seventeenth century and increasingly among married couples thereafter, can be found in other types of historical sources (Bergues, et al. 1960: 121–189; Fryer 1966: 24–32).

MALTHUS, POVERTY, AND INDUSTRIAL CAPITALISM

I noted that population dynamics had been discussed by some "ancient" Greeks; it was also a topic for Islamic scholars such as Ibn Khaldun in the Middle Ages, Machiavelli, and many others. The symbolic significance of Malthus, however, for our current population policies in the Western world surpasses that of all previous writers as well as of most subsequent ones (see Hutchinson 1967 for a review of population theories in the Western tradition prior to 1900). Malthus's writings on population theory were by no means original, but his ideas found large receptive audiences from 1800 on for reasons I will try to indicate.

Malthus's primary concern was not the regulation of population in general, but the regulation of the poor (Beales 1959; Meek 1971). In contrast to some utopians of his day (against whose arguments he explicitly aimed the first edition of his *Essay on the principle of population* published in 1798) Malthus wrote that poverty stems from the laws of nature. The discrepancy, he argued, between the powers of reproduction and the possible expansion of food production will inevitably frustrate all attempts at obtaining equality among men. To give relief to the poor would only encourage them to have more children; rather they should be exhorted to delay marriage. Malthus saw population control as important to forestall revolutions such as the one of 1789 in France.

Demographers and economic historians have argued endlessly about whether the growth of population in England after 1740 was due to a rising birth rate or a falling death rate and whether it was stimulated by industrialization or allowed industrialization to happen (see Glass and Eversley 1965). One of the most convincing analyses of population growth during this period is that of Langer (1963) who assigns a major role to the spread of potato cultivation. Langer shows that despite numerous epidemics and the widespread abandonment of infants, population grew from 1750 to 1850, very fast relative to earlier periods, not just in England but also in many European countries which did not industrialize until quite a bit later.

Malthus's writings should be seen in the context of this spurt in population and of the rise of industrial capitalism. Polanyi (1944) has argued that by 1800 both land and money, but not yet human labor, had been transformed into market commodities. As the feudal system became weaker, the cultivators started to move away from the manor, both socially and physically. In the towns the guilds had little ability to absorb new entrants beyond their own descendants. The Elizabethan poor laws were stretched to cover more people, including many who were able-bodied, and at the same time vagrancy laws were made more severe and workers' associations were prohibited (Beales 1959; Chambliss 1964). As more and more of the commons came under enclosure and as agricultural prices, colonialist successes, and long-distance trade fluctuated, the problem of unemployment became worse. On the manor the peasants may have starved, but they were not categorized as "poor." Poverty was not only a low level of consumption, but also the social condition of being unattached. Punitive laws, aid-in-wages, and make-work schemes were only stop-gap measures.

When Malthus wrote his *Essay* industrial capitalism even in England had not yet fully developed. Colonialism and mercantilism, together with the enclosure movement and the rise in population, were crucial in the transformation of human labor into a commodity:

The explanation [of increasing poverty] lies primarily in the excessive fluctuations of trade in early times which tended to cover up the absolute increase in
trade. While the latter accounted for the rise in employment, the fluctuations
accounted for the much bigger rise in unemployment. But while the increase in
the general level of employment was slow, the increase in unemployment and
underemployment would tend to be fast. Thus the building up of what Friedrich
Engels called the industrial reserve army outweighed by much the creation of
the industrial army proper (Polanyi 1944:91).

The final and necessary step in creating a working class and a market
economy was the poor law reform of 1834:

The new law provided that in the future **no** outdoor relief should be given....
Aid-in-wages was, of course, discontinued. The workhouse test was reintro-
duced, but in a new sense. It was now left to the applicant to decide whether he
was so utterly destitute of all means that he would voluntarily repair to a shelter
which was deliberately made into a place of horror.... (Polanyi 1944:101–102).

Malthus's influence, both through the general arguments of his *Essay* and
through his specific opposition to Samuel Whitehead's reform bill (Malthus 1959), was "the spirit behind the Poor Law Amendment Act"
(Beales 1959).

Engels and Marx, in numerous places in their writings between 1841
and 1882, condemned Malthus as a plagiarist, an advocate for the interests of the landed aristocracy and, for the most part, a shoddy economist.
For them a "superfluous" population (the "reserve army of the unemployed") was both a product of capitalism (through mechanization, boom-
and-bust cycles, urban migration, etc.) and essential to its system of
exploiting workers (Meek 1971).

MALTHUSIANS AND NEO-MALTHUSIANS IN BRITAIN
AND THE UNITED STATES: 1797–1939

Malthus, of course, was adamantly opposed to contraception. But not so
some of his contemporaries. Jeremy Bentham in 1797, a year before the
first edition of Malthus's *Essay* was published, advocated the use of birth
control (with the sponge method) to reduce the birth rates of the poor
(Himes 1963: 211). Francis Place, who published "Illustrations and proofs
of the principle of population" in 1822 and a number of handbills addres-
sed to working people, was, according to Himes, the founder of the birth
control movement (1963: 212). Although Place, who started as a journey-
man breeches-maker and later became a prosperous tradesman, repeated
some of Malthus's arguments, he not only recommended several methods

of contraception, but also asserted that birth limitation would help raise the workers' wages, reduce hours of work, and allow earlier marriage without fear of having too many children (Fryer 1966: 45–57). Some of Place's immediate followers were working-class reformers of a radical bent, such as Carlile, Hassell, and Campion, who were sent to jail on free-thought charges, but not for advocating birth control (Himes 1963: 220–222).

Several people in the United States were influenced by Place and Carlile. Most prominent among them were Robert Dale Owen (son of Robert Owen) who published *Moral physiogie* in 1830 and Charles Knowlton (a philosophical materialist and physician who was prosecuted several times). Knowlton's *Fruits of philosophy* was probably the most important publication on contraception in the nineteenth century. R. D. Owen saw contraception as a step in the progress of mankind toward rational liberty; Knowlton advocated it on medical, eugenic, social, and economic grounds (Himes 1963: 224–230; Fryer 1966: 99–106).

Judging by the literature in English he had researched, Himes felt that "with the passage of the Reform Bill in 1832 and the Poor Law in 1834, the public agitation for birth control died down" (1963: 231). Population growth, colonial expansion, and the development of industrial capitalism all accelerated in the next half century. With the demand for cheap labor growing both in the industrializing countries and in the colonies, it is not surprising that attention to death control was much greater than to birth control. And working-class people, while buying some of the pamphlets on contraception, saw unionization (chartism) as a more relevant solution to their most pressing problems (Fryer 1966: 107).

Upwardly mobile middle-class families in England in the latter half of the nineteenth century intensified their efforts to reduce childbearing (Banks 1954) as did some groups of small landowners in several areas on the continent (Carlsson 1966; Demeny 1968). In France, of course, the birth rate had been declining steadily since the 1770's, with large segments of the population joining the new trend toward smaller families after the 1789 revolution. In neither France nor Britain, however, was there much heard from the medical profession, the one exception being George Drysdale who advocated Malthusianism on economic grounds but was a radical on the subject of marriage (Himes 1963: 233).

In 1873 the federal Comstock Law was passed in the United States (followed by many similar state laws) which included literature on contraception and abortion among obscene materials whose dissemination was prohibited. Edward Bliss Foote, a doctor who had started out as a printer, was prosecuted and fined in 1876 for advocating contraception in various publications (Himes 1963: 277). In England in 1877 and 1878, Edward Truelove (an elderly free-thought publisher), Charles Bradlaugh (a publisher and member of Parliament), and Annie Besant (a writer) were brought to trial on charges connected with disseminating Knowlton's *Fruits of philosophy* The publicity related to these trials apparently helped to increase greatly the sale of this and other writings on birth planning.

The Malthusian League was founded shortly after the trial in 1878, with Dr. Charles Drysdale (brother of George) and Mrs. Besant its first officers. The League sponsored lectures and distributed pamphlets. Although no medical services were given, a Medical Branch was formed and an International Medical Congress held in London in 1881 (Himes 1963: 256–257). Drysdale, Foote, Bradlaugh, Besant, and their associates were clearly "Neo-Malthusian" in orientation, combining a concern for overpopulation, particularly among the poor, with strong advocacy of contraception. They also had some ties with the feminist movement, e.g. the active part taken in the Malthusian League by Dr. Alice Drysdale-Vickery, who was married to Dr. Charles Drysdale (however, see Banks and Banks [1964] on the divergent programs of the two groups in Victorian England).

Despite the interest of a few physicians, including at least one highly placed figure in Holland (Himes 1963: 258), official medical circles ranged from neutral to hostile on the issue of contraception, not only in the nineteenth century (Himes 1963: 282–284; Fryer 1966: 119–131) but well into the twentieth (Fryer 1966: 198–199; Kennedy 1970: 172–217).

The story of Margaret Sanger is well known. Daughter of an upstate New York stonemason, trained nurse, briefly an eclectic socialist, she became a tireless crusader for birth control (an expression she and a group of friends originated). By her own account, the turning point that launched her on this crusade was the death, from an attempted abortion, of Sadie Sachs, a resident of a tenement on New York's Lower East Side (Kennedy 1970: 16–17). Margaret Sanger was influenced by the radical ideas of Emma Goldman, Rosa Luxemburg, and Anatole France, tutored in the history of Malthusianism and contraception by Havelock Ellis, and swayed by Dr. Johannes Rutgers of The Hague to favor the Mensinga diaphragm fitted in birth control clinics (Kennedy 1970: 20–32). From a "woman rebel," advocating sexual liberation and scorning the bourgeois capitalist order of society, Margaret Sanger moved rapidly to the right in the 1920's and 1930's, using Malthusian arguments on overbreeding among the poor and eugenicist appeals about the "menace of the feeble-minded"; she even spoke for the substitution of the "efficient technique of stock-breeding" for welfare legislation (Kennedy 1970: 112–117). Yet she remained steadfast to the idea that birth control was an essential and powerful factor in the sexual emancipation of women (Kennedy 1970: 127–135).

In England the Malthusian League concentrated on antinatal propaganda until just before World War I, when it finally started to disseminate information on contraceptive methods (Fryer 1966: 235–240). Marie Stopes, botanist, poet, and playwright, was above all interested in freeing women to use their bodies as they saw fit; she opened the first birth control clinic in Britain in 1921, where the stress was on healthy children, and a somewhat anti-Malthusian position was taken (Fryer 1966: 223–234).

Holland was probably the country where systematic clinical work in contraception started (Himes 1963: 309). A great deal was published in nineteenth century Germany, both on Malthusianism and birth control (Himes 1963: 322–323). In Austria it is noteworthy that some anarchists (as in France, Britain, and the United States) were strongly favorable to birth control during the 1910's and 1920's (Himes 1963: 325).

PHYSICIANS, CLINICS, AND TAX-SUPPORTED SERVICES

Despite the handful of physicians in the ranks of the Malthusian movement, the existence of clandestine medical abortionists, and the important role of a few pioneers in developing new methods of contraception, it is clear that the medical contribution to the spread of natality regulation prior to 1960 was small. Himes wrote that "the failure of the medical profession to accept leadership in contraceptive instruction has undoubtedly played a part in the tremendous increase in recent years in the commercial and sometimes anti-social dissemination of such advice" (1963: 326). Even as late as 1957, among women in metropolitan areas of the United States, only 16 percent of those using a method of contraception said they chose it because of a physician's recommendation (Westoff, et al. 1961: 364).

A study of private physicians in six localities in the northern part of the country by Cornish, Ruderman, and Spivack (1963) produced congruent results: only 27 percent of the medical men themselves thought most women got their information on contraception from doctors (1963: 19); only 29 percent of non-Catholic physicians (and 4 percent of the Catholics) thought providing contraceptive advice and information should be a standard procedure in the practice of medicine (1963: 31); and only 40 percent of non-Catholics (and 10 percent of Catholics) said they often or very frequently introduced the subject of contraception in the course of the premarital medical examination (1963: 48). In sum, this study showed that physicians were reluctant to provide help with family planning unless the patients specifically asked them and the patients in turn were reluctant to ask (1963: 66–67).

A survey of British physicians ten years later (Cartwright 1968) showed that only 23 percent would introduce the subject of birth control themselves with a woman just getting married, although 90 percent would do so with one who was married, had mitral stenosis, and two children. More recent studies in the United States, however, show considerable change in favor of a more active role among some groups of physicians (Wright, et al. 1968).

Kennedy (1970: 172–217) attributes the resistance to family planning among physicians in the United States in the 1920's and 1930's to a combination of factors: their attempt to build themselves up as scientific practitioners (trying to live down the widespread nineteenth-century criticism of quackery while birth control was associated with "troublemakers" like Margaret Sanger); their middle-class attitudes toward sexuality; their fear of being prosecuted under the Comstock laws; and the lack of contraceptives of proven safety and effectiveness. The sole methods they favored were abstinence ("Let Jake sleep on the roof" the doctor had said to Sadie Sachs, according to Margaret Sanger) and sterilization.

With accumulating knowledge about such methods as rhythm and the diaphragm and in response to the enormous growth in commercial sales of birth control materials, physician opposition relented somewhat in the 1930's, particularly in the prescription of birth control where "medical indications" were present. Such indications, of course, had been found with great facility when it came to performing hysterectomies on poor and black women. Sterilization as a "eugenic" measure has long enjoyed the favor of Social Darwinists in the United States (Hofstadter 1955; Paul 1967). Constructive (to use Marie Stopes' phrase) family planning services in tax-supported health facilities, in contrast, are still not accessible to many poor people. Clandestine abortion, meanwhile, has been widespread and those who could afford it could obtain it from qualified physicians.

In the United States, the number of birth control clinics affiliated with the Clinical Research Bureau and the American Birth Control League increased slowly from 1923 to 1939, when the two organizations merged. Then, with the war years, there was a sharp decline. In 1959 the Planned Parenthood Federation of America had ninety-four local affiliates while at the time of the merger the two organizations between them had 417 local units (Rein 1962: 17).

The various attempts to run family planning clinics in the United States, Britain, continental Europe, and elsewhere fell far short of expectations. In most cases the clientele consisted of women with a higher average level of income and education than the clinics' sponsors would have liked. Some clients were working class or poor but their numbers remained small until quite recently. (I have tried to show that this was largely due to factors in the methods offered and other aspects of the services, rather than to "lack of motivation" to plan births [Polgar 1966]; see also the critiques of clinics by Lafitte [1962]; Stycos [1963]; and Chandrasekaran and Kuder [1965].)

With federal funds appropriated for maternal and child health (and some support from Dr. Clarence Gamble's Pathfinder Fund) in 1937 and 1938, seven Southern states and Puerto Rico started to offer family planning services through local health departments. The number of people attracted to these tax-supported services remained very small. New clients admitted to the combined Charlotte and Mecklenburg County Health Departments in North Carolina, for example, fluctuated between 139 and 339 annually in the 1945–1961 period, but then rose quickly to over 1,500 in 1965 following the introduction of orals and IUD's (Corkey 1966).

A significant political battle was fought in New York City in the late 1950's concerning the unwritten ban on providing contraceptive services (and even discussing family planning) in municipal facilities. Sterilizations, of course, were done in most hospitals. Starting with quiet efforts by Dr. Louis M. Hellman to provide services in Kings County Hospital, Brooklyn, and a series of articles by Joseph Kahn in the *New York Post*, the controversy developed into an open confrontation between a broad alliance of medical, religious, and other community leaders orchestrated by Planned Parenthood versus the Catholic Archdiocese and ended with the lifting of the ban (Best 1959). But by the time the ban was lifted, the diabetic woman with two Caesarian sections who was the "test case" in the dispute had been sterilized. Spurred on by this victory and under an increasingly professionalized leadership, the Planned Parenthood Federation of America launched a nationwide campaign to stimulate more health departments to offer family planning services. Some prominent members of the American Public Health Association and other medical, religious, and welfare organizations were also instrumental in this effort. Responses to a questionnaire sent to state health departments show a gradual expansion of such services in the middle 1960's, particularly in the South and in California (Eliot, et al. 1966). Yet, the first really comprehensive review of the extent to which needed services were being met by organized programs shows that by 1967–1968 in two-thirds of the 3,072 counties in the nation, public health departments still provided no services (Center for Family Planning Program Development 1968: 8). Even in those counties where some services were reportedly offered, the number of clients usually remained very small.

Realizing that obstetric clinics might be a superior channel for reaching a large number of clients, both Planned Parenthood (Jaffe 1964, 1967) and the Population Council (Taylor and Berelson 1968) started to focus on large hospitals. In 1967–1968, however, of the nation's 4,305 nonprofit general care hospitals only 435 reported offering regular family planning services (Center for Family Planning Program Development 1969: 8). In the five years since this time substantial progress has been made, particularly in the large metropolitan areas. Thus, combining the reports for public and private clinics, hospitals, and private physicians, it was estimated that about one-half of all low-income women in need of subsidized services for family planning in the United States were receiving some medical help in 1971–1972 (Guttmacher 1973).

The fascinating combination of advocacy, indifference, and opposition to the expansion of family planning services is illustrated in a 1969 study of ten North Carolina counties. The author, a Canadian physician, identified eleven leaders who were instrumental in promoting the programs: six welfare officials, four health professionals and one president of a women's club (Measham 1972: 43). County commissioners approved of public family planning care because they thought it would reduce the cost of public assistance ('welfare'); in this context discriminatory attitudes were directed more toward the poor in general than specifically toward blacks (1972: 49–52). Opposition to the programs came from private physician groups who were concerned about the possible decrease of their income, and disliked "government medicine," although they favored family limitation for the indigent (1972: 52–54).

In Britain, the advocates of birth control services show a similar mixture of intentions. Secularism and anarchism provided the underlying philosophy for Richard Carlile and Guy Aldred, women's emancipation for Marie Stopes, liberalism for H. G. Wells, utilitarianism for Jeremy Bentham, and reactionary Malthusianism for Charles Drysdale and many others. There was a slow growth of private clinics in the 1920's (Fryer 1966: 250–256), but a campaign was also started to include family planning at government maternity and child welfare centers.

In 1924 two London boroughs controlled by the Labour Party set up birth control clinics in their maternity centers, but were stopped by the

Ministry of Health (Dowse and Peel 1965: 184–185). A bill in the House of Commons, introduced by a Labour member of Parliament in 1926, obtained 40 percent of Conservative, 47 percent of Labour and 33 percent of Liberal votes in favor of disseminating birth control through maternity and child welfare centers (Dowse and Peel 1965: 187). In 1930 these centers were permitted to give contraceptive advice to married women on medical indications, and the newly merged birth control organizations set about to persuade local councils to translate policy into action.

While the number of clinics increased and indications for service were liberalized in subsequent years, Dowse and Peel conclude that once it came close to achieving the goals set decades earlier, the family planning movement was reluctant to relinquish its control over services. And, as in the United States, surveys show that until recently clinics and physicians probably had a very limited impact on the contraceptive behavior of most British couples (Lewis-Fanning 1949: 50–55).

COERCION, POPULATION CONTROL AND THE NEW COLONIALISM

(Le) paternalisme colonial crée les mêmes réflexes malthusiens que le paternalisme familial ou national: *du moment que les sujets deviennes des charges, l'accroissement de leur nombre devient un sujet de préoccupation;* une limitation parait souhaitable, sinon du nombre lui-meme, du moins du rythme de son développement. (Sauvy 1963:145. Original emphasis.)

The idea of using various kinds of constraints to prevent people from having children is, of course, not new. Although castration was not done for Malthusian purposes and chastity belts had nothing to do with the "iron law" of wages, C. A. Weinhold, a German Malthusian of early nineteenth-century vintage, urged that boys be required to wear a kind of ring over the penis from the age of fourteen until they had sufficient income to marry and have children (Himes 1963: 320).

In Britain and the United States the boundaries between eugenic and Malthusian proposals were not always distinct. There is indeed a close similarity between arguments put forward in the 1920's, like the one of the Committee to Study and Report on the Best Means of Cutting Off the Defective Germ-Plasm of the American Population that "Society must look upon germ-plasm as belonging to society and not merely to the individual who carries it" (see Paul 1967: 295), and those of current spokesmen such as Garrett Hardin:

How can we reduce reproduction?... But in the long run a purely voluntary system selects for its own failure: noncooperators outbreed cooperators. So what restraints shall we employ? A policeman under every bed?... We need not titillate our minds with such horrors, for we already have at hand an acceptable technology: sterilization.... If parenthood is only a privilege, and if parents see themselves as trustees of the germ plasm and guardians of the rights of future generations, then there is hope for mankind (Hardin 1970; see also Hardin 1968).

It is easy to guess, even if one did not know what Hardin was saying in private, that he is hinting that the white middle- and upper-class majority should impose sterilization on the poor, the blacks, and other minorities. Reviewing the history of sterilization in the United States in the twentieth century, Julius Paul (1967, 1968) shows how its intended victims are being shifted from the presumably feebleminded or mentally ill to parents receiving Aid for Dependent Children, particularly if the children are "illegitimate." While none of the punitive sterilization laws introduced in many state legislatures have so far been enacted and most judicial decisrions on giving mothers a choice between being sterilized or going to jail were overturned, the agitation against AFDC and for "Zero Population Growth" has so intensified in the last five years that such proposals might well succeed in the near future.

There can be no doubt that racism has played an important part in the movement to expand birth control in the United States. Several large private donors to Planned Parenthood (including some members of the Mellon and Du Pont families) earmarked their gifts for "inner city" programs or for the hiring of Spanish-speaking staff. The first appropriation in Congress in 1962 for an explicitly designated family planning program was for Washington, D.C. (Piotrow 1973: 119); it was pushed through by the congressional committee on the District of Columbia on which bigoted Southerners are heavily represented. One should never forget, however, that liberals like Senator Gruening and Congressman Scheuer also played big roles in federal legislation in support of family planning (Piotrow 1973: 103–111). Time and again, political battles on natality regulation have brought together some strange bedfellows!

For a long time, most academics concerned with demographic phenomena have remained largely aloof from those trying to provide organized services for family planning. At the 1927 World Population Conference in Geneva, from which the International Union for the Scientific Study of Population emerged (Fryer 1966: 219), Margaret Sanger was given no official recognition even though she was the primary organizer, and the topic of contraception was barred from the agenda (Kennedy 1970: 103). During the first ten years of its existence the Population Council, brought

into being by John D. Rockefeller III in 1952 (Piotrow 1973: 13), acted
for the most part as if family planning services existed only on the planet
Venus. And Robert Cook of the Population Reference Bureau character-
istically printed a report on the important 1960 Growth of American
Families study totally ignoring the half of the volume which dealt with
contraception (Solomon and Cook 1966).

Apart from the distaste of most academic demographers (like that of
most physicians) for the open political battles of Margaret Sanger and her
group, many are also convinced that the means by which natality regulation is accomplished are of no consequence — only the motivation to
limit births matters (see Polgar 1968). This conclusion is ostensibly based
on their studies of nineteenth-century Europe and of natality trends during the 1930's in the United States. The bitter attacks by Davis (1967) and
Blake (1969) on family planning services are very much in this tradition.
Davis decries the emphasis on voluntary action at the family level in programs abroad and misrepresents the program planners as promoting a
purely technological approach. Blake insists, despite voluminous evidence
to the contrary (see Harkavy, et al. 1969), that the goal of family planning
services in the United States is population control, obfuscates the difference between opinions and actions, and favors an attack on the family
because it enforces pronatalist norms. Davis and Blake also advocate the
creation of extrafamilial roles for women, but manage to transform even
this progressive policy into a punitive one by extolling its virtue in creating
role conflict for the mother. (I hold no special brief for the modern
Western form of the family myself, but I do deplore policies that deliberately advocate widespread suffering.)

The Davis-Blake brand of repression is relatively mild, but it adds to
the political strength of the social Darwinists like Hardin and the latest
group of strident Malthusians, the bug-killer types. The climate of public
opinion has apparently been so well prepared that one can now openly
publish articles on the "earthpest" explosion (Corbet 1970) and on " man
the pest" (Eyre 1971).

The concept of the population "bomb" has been publicized for quite a
few years by Hugh Moore, founder of the Dixie Cup Company (Piotrow
1973: 18). The picture of our planet as a bomb, which decorated his
pamphlets and advertisements, was symbolic of Moore's shock tactics.
Also prominent in the campaign he started right after World War II was
the linking of the population "explosion" with the threat of communism.
I never saw this man at a Planned Parenthood meeting, but he was a
strong supporter of the Population Reference Bureau and the major force
behind the disgusting newspaper publicity of the Campaign to Check the

Population Explosion (analyzed by Barclay, et al. 1970). He was also instrumental in convincing the formidable General Draper and many other businessmen to join the population control movement (Piotrow 1973: 18, 37–38).

What Hugh Moore has done in the world of big business, the lepidopterist Paul Ehrlich did, perhaps even more successfully, in academic circles. His *Population Bomb* (Ehrlich 1968), with the help of advertisements paid for by Moore, quickly became a basic text of the young "ecofreaks" and "ZPG-ers" (ecology freaks and Zero Population Growthers). Although Ehrlich clearly thinks of himself as a political liberal (he opposed the Vietnam war, for example) he extolled William and Paul Paddock's *Famine 1975!* ("the Paddocks deserve immense credit for their courage and foresight in publishing *Famine 1975!*, which may be remembered as one of the most important books of our age" (Ehrlich 1968: 161), and adopted their proposal of using the military triage concept for allocating U.S. assistance in food. *Famine 1975!* ought to be quoted from the original:

Before the end of the 1970's the interplay of power politics will be based on who is starving and who is not, who has extra food to send to others and who has not. Food will be the basis for power. Here the sophistication will lie in the need for the "food nations" to select which countries, out of the many hungry ones, will receive its limited food stock, which countries will be left in the miseries of their starvation...

During the coming Age of Food that nation which has the most food will be, if it uses that food as a source of power, the strongest nation. This will be, then, clearly an era which the United States can dominate — if the United States picks up the challenge (Paddock and Paddock 1967:232).

This sophisticated vision of grainboat diplomacy had its trial run when Nixon held up food shipments to India two years ago.

Typically, Paul Ehrlich has done almost nothing to encourage the provision of voluntary family planning services; on the contrary, he is clearly enthusiastic about the negative and coercive writings of Blake, Davis, Hauser, and Ketchel, and disdainful towards Harkavy, Jaffe, and "Wishnick" (Ehrlich and Ehrlich 1970: 233-258, especially 257–258).

Government actions regarding international aspects of population can best be understood in the light of commercial, military, and labor force considerations. These concerns, after all, antedate Malthus, Ibn Khaldun, and Plato and are still very much with us today. Early empires depended on tribute and slaves coming in and soldiers and administrators going out. Slavery was eventually supplanted by indentured and contract labor, colonial wars were fought over trading areas, and migratory workers nowadays provide a large part of the manpower for the mines of South

Africa, the factories of West Germany, and the produce fields of southern California.

In the wake of the disastrous population declines set off by early European expansion, a primary concern of colonial administrators became the supply and productivity of labor on plantations and in the mines. Theologians, meanwhile, debated the status of the laborers' souls. Once Western Europe, the United States, and Japan became industrialized, a new consideration emerged: the market for manufactured products. Despite the rapid demise of administrative colonialism after 1945, the metropolitan powers remained anxious to find new customers for their exports as well as safeguard their sources of cheap raw materials and maintain opportunities for highly profitable foreign investments.

The post-World War II foreign aid program of the United States (particularly the Marshall plan) however, was not mainly designed to serve these ends; altruism and the expiation of guilt were probably more important. But if famine relief and health programs in the past had been a response to both humanitarian motives and the need to maintain labor pools for the production of cheap raw materials, the latter purpose had become largely irrelevant under postwar conditions. Many synthetic substitutes had been developed for the raw materials whose imports were uncertain during the war, and the trend towards automation had accelerated even in the foreign-owned production facilities in the Third World. And some Westerners like Hugh Moore had come to believe that population growth in Asia, Africa, and Latin America was contributing to political discontent, which might help the interests of the Soviet Union (see the discussion by Barclay, Enright, and Reynolds [1970] which is among the better recent leftist critiques of Malthusian programs, despite the naiveté of its analysis of the population lobby). And, last but not least, the poverty of the masses in the Third World precluded any great expansion there in the sales of manufactured products. The subjects have become burdens!

Piotrow's highly detailed account (1973: 55–65) of how population policy was handled in the State Department and the Agency for International Development during the early 1960's makes but the briefest mention of one development I consider highly significant. Economists at this time were beginning to attack the foreign aid expenditures for health programs because, by increasing the rate of population growth, mortality reduction was hindering the possibility of raising the average level of income (and purchasing power). Piotrow may be superficially correct in linking the sharp reduction in AID assistance for health programs to the bureaucratic reorganization ordered by the Kennedy administration (1973: 63).

But she hints at a more important factor, I believe, when she notes that the reorganization "put priority on government-directed income and job-producing investments" (1973: 63). In other words, the Keynesian economists were put in charge! The Truman Point Four program of reconstruction and humanitarian assistance was largely over, the bad conscience of the United States over its destructive acts appeased, and the "foreign aid" program could settle down to the major business of helping the interests of American capital.

I have already noted that the first direct appropriation by Congress for birth control in 1962 was for the District of Columbia, where over half of the population is black. Students of internal colonialism will be interested in another "first" three years later:

American Indians, Eskimos and natives of the islands the United States holds in trust in the Pacific have been made the beneficiaries of the first Federal program offering direct help in family planning and birth control. The announcement by Secretary of the Interior Udall that contraceptive advice and services will be made available, where desired, on reservations and in trust territories encourages hope that the taboo against birth control programs will also crumble in such domestic undertakings as the war on poverty (*New York Times*, June 21, 1965).[3]

The irony of Secretary Udall's policy was not lost on the Navajo:
"We had Washington's stock reduction program forced on us, now it would seem that they are trying to sell us a people reduction program" *(Indian Voices* 1965). And in the same year, Langston Hughes wrote in his column on how his protagonist "Simple" was reading the papers

"... in which I see a lot these days about the population explosion and how we ought to be doing something about it"
"What we?" I asked.
"We white folks," said Simple...
"Suppose ... they sent a Sterilization Wagon to Harlem ... They better send that Sterilization Wagon to Viet Nam ..."
"But suppose the Viet Cong captured a lot of our Sterilization Wagons and then used them against American troops?" I said.
"Negotiations for peace would begin at once," said Simple.
"White folks are not thinking about being sterilized, neither in war nor peace. It is India, China, Africa and Harlem they is considering ..." (Hughes 1965).

By attending family planning service units in large numbers, once the orals and IUD's became available, Amerindians and blacks have demonstrated that they do want to regulate their own natality, but, as sociologist

---

[3]   That "taboo" did indeed soon crumble, but recently Nixon, on the one hand, killed the Office of Economic Opportunity (OEO) altogether and, on the other, prohibited the medical corps of the U.S. armed services from performing abortions for servicewomen and dependents.

Charles Willie has stressed in his testimony to the Commission on Population Growth and the American Future, if a national population policy is to

gain the cooperation of black people, such a policy must gather up the goals which blacks themselves have identified as important. A national population policy must demonstrate that it is more concerned about the HEALTH and WEALTH of black people than it is about the number of children they have. (Willie 1972:2. Original emphasis.)

Many United States officials (like their British counterparts) regard Third World people as "*des charges*" — to refer back again to the quotation from Sauvy at the beginning of this section — and the current political situation has selected out or silenced those who might favor a partnership aimed at making substantial improvements in the "health and wealth" of the Third World masses.

From 1965 to 1972 the budget for population activities at the disposal of the United States Agency for International Development rose from two million to one hundred million dollars. As the political base of support increased and included more and more people outside of the family planning lobby, Congress and AID defined the work to be done in increasingly Malthusian terms.

As money is poured into the birth control programs of those countries and agencies that are willing to accept a definition of the population problem in terms of the Malthusian analysis, the leadership of the more humanitarian, health-oriented people is being challenged by those who favor mass campaigns of "motivation," incentive schemes, and even compulsory sterilization. But fortunately the field has not yet been completely preempted by the Malthusians. Some organizations involved in international assistance, including the Swedish International Development Agency, the Canadian International Development Agency, the (Quaker) Friends Service Committee, and the World Health Organization have concentrated on positive programs involving family planning services and medical education. Furthermore, opposition to externally stimulated population control has come not only in the form of nationalist exhortations (from both the political right and the left) but is also based on non-Malthusian philosophical and economic analyses of a scholarly nature (e.g. Amin 1971; Bahri, et al. 1971; Pradervand 1970; Raulet 1970).[4]

---

[4] I will not attempt here to even indicate the various policies pursued by socialist countries or the directions of the writings from these countries on population and family planning. I am simply not well enough informed to do so at this time.

CONCLUSION

Birth planning as such, I would submit, is neither a progressive nor a reactionary idea; to evaluate it one has to look at the context in which it is pursued. The deliberate modification of natality by an individual, a couple or a kinship unit, i.e. family planning, has a very long history in human evolution. Physicians have often been concerned with family planning and in recent years have made great contributions to the improvement of its technology. That European (and American) medical men were unconcerned with, and even hostile to, contraception and abortion from the thirteenth to well into the twentieth century can be attributed to the influence of the Judeo-Christian tradition and to the changing status of their profession in society. The almost complete failure to provide voluntary family planning services through public medical care channels has been quite injurious to poor people who wanted to regulate their own childbearing, but did not even have recourse to the relatively safe (but expensive) abortions performed by clandestinely practicing physicians. By the same token, poor people were quite frequently sterilized without their prior knowledge or consent.

Voluntary parenthood by safe and effective means has a very important role in family health and welfare and particularly for the liberation of women. Many of the pioneers in the birth planning movement recognized this and so do most socialists today. By contrast, birth control offered in the context of Malthusian schemes of regulating the poor, with only a superficial veneer of charity, and provided on a voluntary basis only because more compulsory programs are not considered politically feasible at the time, is a cruel hoax.

Population control, like natality regulation, is not a new idea. Unlike family planning, however, its history is more closely tied to repression than to liberation. Malthus's ideas originally became popular among the European elite just after the French revolution and as the process of transforming human labor into a marketable commodity was culminating. Today, as Third World people are fighting for and beginning to win their freedom from political and economic exploitation by the big industrial powers, another wave of Malthusian reaction is pouring forth. "Overpopulation" is once again blamed as the cause of poverty, crime, hunger, and war. And there is a new ingredient: the concern for the environment. The sincere worry of many people about the damage of pollution and resource depletion is being manipulated by Malthusians and industrialists who hope to deflect attention from the fact that it is the rapacious and thriftless processes of extraction, manufacturing, and selling by the metropolitan powers which are the major causes of environmental degradation. Population policies can be regarded as progressive if aimed, for example, at slowing the rate of influx to large cities where employment is scarce and public services are not yet adequate or if concerned with slowing growth rates while educational facilities are still insufficient. In the future, if the distribution of resources becomes more equitable, stabilizing population in order to maintain environmental quality for all the people and to preserve the complex biosphere of the earth will also be a positive measure. None of these population policies, however, can be seen as progressive if isolated from, or put ahead of, more comprehensive measures to promote human equality and the development of people's creative potential.

So why did the policies concerning population and family planning programs change so drastically in the last decade? As in late eighteenth-century Britain, population has been growing rapidly. The expanding numbers of Third World people, who are no longer dutiful subjects toiling in their mines and fields and are not consumers either for an ever-expanding flow of manufactured products, have become a burden for the industrial powers. They are not only a burden, but also a threat, for, as in the time of Malthus, a great revolution is taking place.

But there is another side also. New freedoms have been declared: from all-too-frequent illness and death, from the oppression of women by men, from the high risks of clumsy abortions and the cruel pain of burying an infant. Among the pioneers of family planning there were idealists and anarchists, not just elite privilege seekers. By 1962 the rich already had a number of relatively safe and effective ways to plan their families — and humanitarians wanted to offer this opportunity also to the poor.

The uneasy alliance of rightist and democratic forces has succeeded in greatly increasing attention to birth planning. Today, as the voices of the population "hawks" rise louder and louder demanding that coercion be instituted and that all is lost if birth rates do not immediately tumble, the alliance is no longer tenable. Were the humanitarians used as a tool by the reactionaries? When I visit a well-run family planning service, I don't think so. When I read of an "earthpest explosion" I despair. In another ten years, perhaps, we may have a clearer answer as to what really happened in the 1960's.

REFERENCES

AMIN, SAMIR
1971 "Population policies and development strategies: underpopulated Africa." Paper given at the meeting on Population Dynamics and Educational Development in Africa, Dakar, November 29 to December 4, 1971. UNESCO Regional Office for Education in Africa, Dakar, Senegal.

BAHRI, AHMED, et al.
1971 "A new approach to population research in Africa: ideologies, facts and policies." Position paper given at the African Population Conference, UNESCO, Accra, Ghana, December 9 to 18, 1971.

BANKS, J. A.
1954 Prosperity and parenthood: a study of family planning among the Victorian middle classes. London: Routledge.

BANKS, J. A., OLIVE BANKS
1964 Feminism and family planning. Liverpool: Liverpool University Press.

BARCLAY, W., J. ENRIGHT, R. T. REYNOLDS
1970 Population control in the Third World. North American Congress on Latin America Newsletter 4:1–18.

BEALES, H. L.
1959 "The historical context of the Essay on population," in Introduction to Malthus. Edited by D. V. Glass, 1–24. London: Frank Cass.

BERGUES, H. et al.
1960 La prévention des naissances dans la famille. Institut National d'Etudes Demographiques, Travaux et Documents. Cahier 35. Paris.

BEST, W., editor
1959 The anatomy of a victory. New York: Planned Parenthood Federation of America.

BLAKE, J.
1969 Population policy for Americans: is the government being misled? Science 164:522–529.

CARLSSON, G.
1966 The decline of fertility: innovation or adjustment process. Population Studies 20:149–174.

CARTWRIGHT, A.
1968 General practitioners and family planning. The Medical Officer 120: 43–46.

CENTER FOR FAMILY PLANNING PROGRAM DEVELOPMENT
1969 Need for subsidized family planning services: United States, each state and county, 1968. New York: Planned Parenthood Federation of America.

CHAMBLISS, W. J.
1964 A sociological analysis of the law of vagrancy. Social Problems 12: 67–77.

CHANDRASEKARAN, C., K. KUDER
1965 Family planning through clinics. Bombay: Allied Publishers.

CORBET, P. S.
1970 "Pest management: objectives and prospects on a global scale," in

Concepts of pest management. Edited by R. L. Rabb and F. E. Guthrie, 191–208. Raleigh: North Carolina State University.

CORKEY, E. C.
1966 "The birth control program in the Mecklenburg County Health Department," in *Public health programs in family planning.* Edited by S. Polgar and W. B. Cowles. *American Journal of Public Health* 56 (2): 40–47.

CORNISH, M. J., F. A. RUDERMAN, S. S. SPIVACK
1963 *Doctors and family planning.* National Committee on Maternal Health Publication 19, New York.

DAVIS, K.
1967 Population policy: will current programs succeed? *Science* 158:730–739.

DEMENY, P.
1968 Early fertility decline in Hungary: a lesson in demographic transition. *Daedalus* (Spring): 502–522.

DOWSE, R. E., J. PEEL
1965 The politics of birth control. *Political Studies* 13:179–197.

EHRLICH, P. R.
1968 *The population bomb.* New York: Ballantine.

EHRLICH, P. R., A. H. EHRLICH
1970 *Population resources environment: issues in human ecology.* San Francisco: W. H. Freeman.

ELIOT, J. W., C. HOUSER, R. WHITE
1966 "The development of family planning services by state and local health departments in the United States," in *Public health programs in family planning.* Edited by S. Polgar and W. B. Cowles. *American Journal of Public Health* 56 (2):4–16.

EYRE, S. R.
1971 "Man the pest: the dim chance of survival." *New York Review of Books* (November 18, 1971): 18–27.

FRYER, P.
1966 *The birth controllers.* New York: Stein and Day.

GLASS, D. V., D. E. C. EVERSLEY, *editors*
1965 *Population in history.* Chicago: Aldine.

GUTTMACHER, A. F.
1973 *President's Newsletter* 65:3. New York: Planned Parenthood Federation of America.

HARDIN, G.
1968 The tragedy of the commons. *Science* 162:1243–1248.
1970 Parenthood: right or privilege? *Science* 169:427.

HARKAVY, O., F. S. JAFFE, S. M. WISHIK
1969 Family planning and public policy: who is misleading whom? *Science* 165:367–373.

HIMES, N. E.
1963 *Medical history of contraception.* New York: Gamut Press. (Originally published 1936.)

HOFSTADTER, R.
1955   *Social Darwinism in American thought* (revised edition). Boston: Beacon Press.
HUGHES, L.
1965   "Population explosion." *New York Post*, December 10.
HUTCHINSON, E. P.
1967   *The population debate*. Boston: Houghton Mifflin.
INDIAN VOICES
1965   Rosebud Herald speaks out on birth control. *Indian Voices* (August): 4–5.
JAFFE, F. S.
1964   Family planning and poverty. *Journal of Marriage and the Family* 26: 467–470.
1967   Family planning, public policy and intervention strategy. *Journal of Social Issues* 23:145–163.
KENNEDY, D. M.
1970   *Birth control in America: the career of Margaret Sanger*. New Haven: Yale University Press.
LAFITTE, F.
1962   *Family planning and family planning clinics today*. Birmingham: Birmingham University.
LANGER, W. L.
1963   Europe's initial population explosion. *American Historical Review* 69: 1–17.
LEWIS-FANNING, E.
1949   *Report on an enquiry into family limitation and its influence on human fertility during the past fifty years*. Papers of the Royal Commission on Population 1. London: His Majesty's Stationery Office.
MALTHUS, T. R.
1959   "A letter to Samuel Whitehead Esq., M.P., on the proposed bill for the amendment of the poor laws," in *Introduction to Malthus*. Edited by D. V. Glass, 183–205. London: Frank Cass. (Originally published 1807. London: J. Johnson.)
MEASHAM, A. R.
1972   *Family planning in North Carolina: the politics of a lukewarm issue*. Carolina Population Center Monograph 17. Chapel Hill: University of North Carolina.
MEEK, R. L.
1971   *Marx and Engels on the population bomb* (second edition). Berkeley: Ramparts Press.
NEW YORK TIMES
1965   "More headway on birth control." *New York Times*, June 21.
PADDOCK, W., P. PADDOCK
1967   *Famine 1975!* Boston: Little, Brown.
PAUL, J.
1967   Population "quality" and "fitness for parenthood" in the light of state eugenic sterilization experience, 1907–1966. *Population Studies* 21: 295–299.

1968   The return of punitive sterilization proposals: current attacks on illegitimacy and the AFDC program. *Law and Society Review* 3:77–106.
PIOTROW, P. T.
1973   *World population crisis: the United States response.* New York: Praeger.
POHLMAN, E.
1969   *The psychology of birth planning.* Cambridge, Massachusetts: Schenkman.
POLANYI, K.
1944   *The great transformation: the political and economic origins of our time.* Boston: Beacon Press.
POLGAR, S.
1966   Sociocultural research in family planning in the United States: review and prospects. *Human Organization* 25:321–329.
1968   "Malthus, magic and motivation." Chapel Hill: University of North Carolina, Carolina Population Center (processed).
1972   Population history and population policies from an anthropological perspective. *Current Anthropology* 13:203–211.
PRADERVAND, P.
1970   Les pays nantis et la limitation des naissances dans le tiers monde. *Développement et Civilisations* 39–40:4–40.
RAULET, H. M.
1970   "Population policy, economic development, and social structure in South Asia: a critique of the neo-Malthusian perspective." Paper given at the Annual Meeting, American Anthropological Association, San Diego, November 1970.
REIN, M.
1962   "An organizational analysis of a national agency's local affiliates in their community contexts: a study of the Planned Parenthood Federation of America" (excerpts from doctoral dissertation). New York: Planned Parenthood Federation of America (processed).
SAUVY, A.
1963   *Théorie generale de la population*, volume one. Paris: Presses Universitaires de France.
SOLOMON, G., R. C. COOK
1966   "Boom babies" come of age: the American family at the crossroads. *Population Bulletin* 22:61–79.
STYCOS, J. M.
1963   Obstacles to programs of population control — facts and fancies. *Journal of Marriage and the Family* 25:5–13.
TAYLOR, H. C., B. BERELSON
1968   Maternity care and family planning as a world program. *American Journal of Obstetrics and Gynecology* 100:885–893.
WESTOFF, C. F., *et al.*
1961   *Family growth in metropolitan America.* Princeton: Princeton University Press.
WILLIE, C. V.
1972   A position paper, presented to the President's Commission on Popu-

lation Growth and the American Future. Population Reference Bureau Selection 37.

WRIGHT, N. H., G. JOHNSON, D. MEES

1968 "Report on a survey on physicians' attitudes in Georgia toward family planning services, prescribing contraceptives, sex education, and therapeutic abortion," in *Advances in planned parenthood*, volume three. Edited by A. J. Sobrero and S. Lewit, 37–46. Excerpta Medica Foundation, International Congress Series 156. Amsterdam.

Legislation Influencing Fertility in Czechoslovakia

OLGA VIDLÁKOVÁ

Protection of marriage, maternity, the family, and the interests of all children, as well as increased care for families with more children, are effected in our country by society as a whole. The principles governing this protection and care are legally expressed in the Family Code (Act Number 94, effective April 1, 1964). To illustrate their character, we may quote:

The main social purpose of marriage is the founding of a family and the proper upbringing of children.

Family founded by marriage constitutes the basic element of our society, which provides comprehensive protection to family ties.

Both man and woman are equal in marriage.

Maternity is a woman's most honorable mission in life.

Parents are responsible to society for the overall mental and physical development of their children and, in particular, for their proper upbringing, so as to consolidate the unity of interests of the family and society.

All members of a family have the duty to help each other and ensure according to their ability and capacity the growth of the material and cultural standards of the family.

Society attends to the upbringing of children and to the satisfaction of their material and cultural needs, cares for them, and protects them through state organs, other public organizations, schools, and cultural, educational and health facilities.

LEGISLATION CONCERNING CONDITIONS OF MARRIAGE AND DIVORCE

Since January 1, 1950, the minimum age for marriage has been eighteen years for both sexes. In exceptional cases courts may give their consent to marriages concluded between minors under eighteen and older than sixteen provided there are important reasons and the marriage does comply with the social purposes of marriage. However, marriages are not valid in the case of a minor under the age of sixteen.

As a rule, marriage is concluded before a state authority. Religious marriage ceremonies may without exception take part only after the civil marriage procedure.

According to the Family Code, the conclusion of marriage establishes the mutual elementary obligation between husband and wife. This obligation may be enforced by a court if one of the partners fails to fulfill it. The criterion for fixing its extent is to achieve equality as regards the material and cultural level of both husband and wife. All property (including remuneration for work, income from social security, bonuses, etc.) acquired by one of the partners during the duration of the marriage, provided it can be the object of private ownership according to valid Czechoslovak law[1], is the so-called unapportioned joint ownership of both partners. Exceptions to this are only objects acquired by one of the partners by inheritance or as gifts, as well as objects which, according to their nature, serve the personal need or profession of only one of the partners. Husband and wife use their property held in unapportioned joint ownership jointly and jointly cover the costs involved by their use and maintenance.

The principle is upheld that the right to the joint use of a flat is established if both partners or one of them became eligible for using it. A further condition for establishing this right is the fact that both partners have been permanently living together. Similarly, the right is established to the joint use of land property by both marriage partners if during the marriage husband and wife or one of them make arrangements for the personal use of the land. The last important legal consequence of marriage concerning property is inheritance. According to the Civil Code, the surviving partner is the legal heir, i.e. the heir who in case no testament was affected, *ex lege entere* enters into inheritance.[2]

Apart from matrimonial union of man and wife we sometimes encounter their living together in the relationship of unmarried spouses. This relationship is not regulated specifically by valid Czechoslovak legislation. However, some branches of law take its existence into ac-

[1]   Objects of private ownership are above all income and savings from work and social security, objects for household and personal use, family houses and recreational cottages (Civil Code, Section 127).

[2]   At the time, however, the surviving marriage partner is not a so-called unconditional heir, e.g. an heir whom the testator cannot exclude from the inheritance by his own will. Such a position is reserved only to minor offspring of the deceased.

count and regulate certain specific questions connected with it, e.g. social security legislation.

Marriage is terminated by the death of one of the partners or by his being declared deceased. Marriage also may be terminated by divorce. Our law does not distinguish between separation and divorce. Above all, the Family Code imposes upon the state authorities the duty, in cooperating with the voluntary organizations and all citizens, to assist in fostering marriage and family, especially by forestalling the causes that may lead to a disruption of the close bonds and duration of marriage and family relations. The law also states that a frivolous attitude to marriage is in contradiction to the interest of society and that therefore the end of marriage by divorce may be considered only in societally relevant cases.

The court may dissolve the marriage on the application of one of the partners if the relationship between them has reached such a stage of disruption that the marriage can no longer fulfill its societal purpose. Thereby the court is obliged to ascertain the causes that led to the serious disruption of marriage and quote them in the motivation of its decision. The law regulates the alimony in support of the divorced husband and wife. This alimony may be claimed by divorced spouses incapable of supporting themselves. The obligation to pay alimony is limited by the law for a period of no longer than five years but may be extended, however, in cases where the divorced partner is incapable of supporting himself even after the lapse of this period. The court decides which of the divorced parents shall be given charge of a minor child and determines the form and rate of the contribution by each of the parents toward the maintenance of the child. In doing so the court is bound by the interest in securing optimal conditions for the further favorable development of the child. However, the law does not state the rate of the contribution, nor criteria for determining it, and it is for this reason that the practices of the district and regional courts are very diverse.

To diminish the divorce rate and to help husbands and wives to create a harmonious life, marriage advisory centers are being established which offer specialized advice to spouses on solving their marriage problems and on questions of family planning and adoption. At present, such centers are in nine towns of the Czech Socialist Republic and their further extension is under way. (See Table 1 for divorce rates 1964–1970.)

Table 1.   Marriages and divorces in Czechoslovakia

Year	Marriages Number	Per 1,000 inhabitants	Divorces Number	Per 1,000 inhabitants	Divorces in percent of marriages
1964	110,793	7.9	16,802	1.20	15.17
1965	112,269	7.9	18,702	1.32	16.65
1966	115,724	8.1	20,244	1.42	17.49
1967	119,896	8.4	19,889	1.39	16.50
1968	122,947	8.6	21,641	1.51	17.60
1969	125,197	8.7	23,936	1.66	19.12
1970	126,492	8.8	24,936	1.74	19.72

LEGISLATION CONCERNING PROCREATION AND CARE OF CHILDREN DURING INFANCY

There is no law regulating the dissemination and sale of contraceptives.[3]

Abortion is regulated by the Act Number 68 effective December 19, 1957, which gives the following basic conditions for abortions:

1.   Pregnancy may be interrupted only with the consent of the pregnant woman.

2.   Pregnancy may be interrupted by abortion only in an in-patient medical establishment.

3.   The application of a pregnant woman is decided by a special abortion committee.

4.   The committee may stipulate abortion for medical reasons or other reasons that merit special consideration.

Other reasons worthy of special consideration which with a certain degree of ambiguity may be called social reasons are listed in the Government Order Number 126/1962 O.G. They comprise the following:

1.   The advanced age of the pregnant woman.

2.   The presence of at least three living children.

3.   Loss of the husband or his disability.

4.   Disruption of the family.

5.   Jeopardizing the standard of living in cases where the responsibility for maintaining the family is exclusively in the hands of the woman.

6.   A difficult situation due to the pregnancy of an unmarried woman.

7.   A pregnancy due to assault or other criminal act.

[3]   The sale of condoms by machines is very rare owing to low demand. Other contraceptives are sold in pharmacies against medical prescriptions. As regards IUDs, these may be introduced solely by gynecologists in gynecological clinics or departments of the policlinics.

Abortions carried out without the proper professional knowledge in Czechoslovakia during the last years before the adoption of the Act on artificial termination of pregnancy caused the annual loss of life of about fifty women. During the first ten years of the application of the Act (1958–1967) 116 women died for this reason, twenty-five of whom died in 1958. During recent years, the number of deaths has ranged between three and six women for the whole country. Before the Act came into effect thirty thousand abortions were registered every year; during the first year of its application it was eighty-nine thousand and since 1959, the number of abortions regularly (with the exception of 1963 and 1964) surpassed the one hundred thousand mark. However, these facts do not warrant exact conclusions because up to 1957 only a small proportion of the abortions were registered, probably one-third, while the rest remained hidden.

Among the reasons for which women ask for abortions those of a social character prevail. Medical indications form only about one-fifth of all abortions. The majority of specialists and government authorities are of the opinion that it is necessary to make efforts toward reducing the abortion rate, both for medical considerations as well as for growth of the population. Reductions, however, cannot be achieved by administrative measures but only by a series of sociopolitical measures, above all of an economic and educational character.

In cases of pregnancy, birth and maternity benefits are given within the health insurance schemes. These are the supplementary benefit during pregnancy and maternity, the financial contribution during maternity, and the birth grant.

Pregnant working women enjoy special protection laid down by law. The Labor Code forbids a pregnant woman up to the ninth month after delivery to be employed at certain types of work. If for this reason the working woman must be transferred to lower-paid work she is eligible for this period for the supplementary benefit making up the difference between the old and new wage.

According to the last amendment in 1968 maternity leave is due for a period of twenty-six weeks (twenty-two weeks previously). Single women or women giving birth to twins are eligible for thirty-five weeks paid maternity leave. Beginning January 1, 1970, further unpaid maternity leave has been extended up to the second year of age of the child. The employer is bound to grant this further leave, to the extent demanded by the woman. Also eligible for this are women taking permanent care of a child in place of its parents. Returning from further maternity leave, the mother is entitled to be given employment corresponding to her working contract with the employer. If this is not possible because the job has been abolished the employer is compelled to offer her work corresponding to her skill. For the period of paid maternity leave (to the extent of twenty-six or thirty-five weeks) the mother is eligible for the financial contribution during maternity at the rate of 90 percent of her net daily wage.

On the birth of each child a grant is given in the form of a lump sum which since October 1, 1971 amounts to 2,000 Czechoslovak crowns per child (up to this date it amounted to half this sum). Mothers giving birth to triplets receive at the twenty-eighth day of their life a grant in the form of their layette and a savings account of 9,000 crowns.

The maternity grant was newly introduced by Czechoslovak legislation in 1969 and amended in 1971.

Conditions for eligibility are:
1.   All-day proper care of a child younger than two years of age,
2.   Apart from this the proper care of at least one other child before school-leaving age, and in the case of a disabled child requiring constant care younger than twenty-six years of age.

The rate of the maternity grant amounts to 500 crowns per month for the care of one child up to two years of age, 800 crowns for two, and 1,200 crowns for three or more children.

Since 1951 free medical care during pregnancy, delivery, and after it is due to all women. During pregnancy preventive and curative care is offered. For the entire period of pregnancy women receive, above all, outpatient care concentrated in special advisory centers for mother and child. It consists mainly of regular examinations and special tests. In the vast majority of cases delivery takes place in medical institutions; this, however, is not compulsory, for the woman also may deliver at home with the assistance of a specialized nurse or a doctor. After delivery the mother takes the child to the advisory center for regular preventive examinations of the health of the child. All medical services are given free of charge.

The Act on Medical Care for the People, effective July 1, 1966, distinguishes the following special establishments for children: infants' homes, children's homes, and nurseries, all of which are part of the unified health administration.

Infants' homes, as a rule, cater to children younger than one year if their development is handicapped or jeopardized for medical or social reasons or if the family surroundings do not offer suitable care.

Children's homes take in children from one to three years old if they cannot receive proper care in their families.

Nurseries cater to healthy children from four months to three years of age. Because their capacity is insufficient to meet the demand (due to the high female employment rate) children are admitted according to a priority list determined by the national committee[4] and in the case of factory nurseries by the trade union committee. There are day nurseries, weekly nurseries and full-time ones. The most common type are the day nurseries, which are open from 6 A.M. to 6 P.M. Mothers bring their children to the weekly nurseries on Monday morning and take them back home on Friday night or Saturday afternoon. These nurseries cater in particular to the children of mothers with alternating shifts and free Sundays, while full-time nurseries cater mainly to the children of mothers who have irregular working hours and irregular free days. The larger part of the cost of running the nurseries is borne by the state budget.

Nursery schools are the most widespread of preschool establishments in our country. They cater to children from three years of age up to the time they enter school at six or seven years of age. They are established and run by the locally responsible local or town national committees. In addition, they may be established by factories or farming cooperatives, in which case they are primarily reserved for the children of their workers. Attendance at a nursery school is free of charge and the parents pay only toward the meals provided.

During the last five years, the number of children attending nursery schools rose by 9 percent, from 50 to 59 percent. On the other hand, the number of children placed in nurseries as compared with the total number of children of the corresponding age group remained the same (7 percent), while the daily utilization of the nursery places has shown a consistent decline. This is probably due to the intermittent nature of illnesses of infants and smaller children.

LEGISLATION CONCERNING THE ECONOMIC STATUS OF THE FAMILY

Family allowances were introduced in Czechoslovakia in 1945 as a means of raising the overall income of families of employed workers. Gradually, however, they gained social significance through contribution towards the education of children graded according to the number of children and the income of the parents. This latter differentiation was suspended on June 30, 1968. Nowadays, family allowances are

[4] National committees are the local authorities, a type of local council.

obligatory benefits of health insurance for employed workers and of social security for cooperative farmers. As a result, the subject of the legal claim is the worker in employment or the cooperative farmer, not the child. However, the person receiving the allowance is obliged to use it exclusively in the interest of the child on whose behalf it is awarded. Rates of family allowances are ninety crowns for one child, 330 for two, 680 for three, 1,030 for four, and 240 for each additional child.

Special assistance may be given to families with a greater number of children interested in the proper maintenance and education of their children. In these cases the state awards regular monthly contributions paid by the national committees out of the funds of supplementary welfare, forming a part of social security.

The rate of the tax takes into consideration the rate of the income and the number of persons supported by the taxpayer. According to the number of persons supported, the basic tax rate is either increased or reduced.

The basic tax rate applies to a taxpayer supporting two persons. If he supports fewer the basic rate is increased, if more it is reduced. In applying the tax the principle is adhered to that supported persons can be counted only once, as a rule in the case of the man. Only in cases where the supported persons are children of a divorced couple, children whose parents live in permanent separation, or children who were born out of wedlock, is there an exception to this rule. Here the children are counted in taxing both the person caring for the child as well as the person paying contributions towards its maintenance. At the same time, the person directly caring for the child is regarded as supporting an additional person.

On behalf of children rent reductions also are being granted. These amount to 5 percent of the rent for one child, 15 percent for two, 30 percent for three, 50 percent for four or more.

LEGISLATION CONCERNING WOMEN'S EMPLOYMENT AND THE STATUS OF WOMEN

As was pointed out earlier, the law does not differentiate between men and women as regards access to education, property questions, etc. Similarly, men and women have the same duties and rights in educating and raising children.

The working conditions of women are regulated by the Labor Code in a separate chapter. Both working conditions of women in general as well as of pregnant women and mothers are regulated. The stipulations concern mainly the ban on certain work not suitable for women. Pregnant women and mothers caring for a child under one year of age (in case of a single woman, under three years of age) are protected against dismissal. However, this protection does not apply in cases of substantial organizational changes, such as liquidation or transfer of an enterprise or its partition or merger with another enterprise. But even here, single pregnant workers and women caring for children under the age of fifteen years are protected, the organization being bound to procure them new suitable employment.

The Labor Code has a special stipulation, in the regulation of working hours for women. According to this, the enterprise is obliged to respect the requirements of women caring for children when allocating them to work shifts. If pregnant women or mothers of children under fifteen years of age apply for shorter working hours or an adjustment of their weekly working hours, the establishments are obliged to accede to their applications provided there are no serious working reasons against this procedure.

Stipulations of the Labor Code also regulate intervals for breast-feeding. The establishment is obliged, in addition to regular work intervals, also to grant the feeding mother special feeding intervals.

According to the legislation, women are entitled to the same wage for the same work as men. Actually, however, the average wages of women are substantially lower than the average wages of men. This is due to the allocation of different wage rates to men and women, due to the fact that women as a rule are less skilled. Wage differences between men and women are, however, also conditioned by the social significance of the work performed. Physically demanding and difficult work, largely performed by men, according to its social significance is rated higher than other work. On the other hand, it cannot be denied that the feminization of certain branches was to some extent responsible for the lower social rating of these professions (e.g. education and health services).

EVALUATION OF THE IMPACT OF LEGISLATION ON THE REPRODUCTIVE BEHAVIOR OF THE POPULATION

The law, being a reflection of the political and economic situation, does not exist by itself. Therefore, its influence must not be seen in its isolated juridical aspects, but in wider political, economic, and social contexts.

The following classification of the relations between law and fertility is suggested:

1. Legislation is interrelated fairly directly with the protection of the basis of fertility, such as the physical health of the woman; it includes legislation on abortion, sterilization, and also those parts of the labor law banning certain jobs as unsuitable for women, in general, and for pregnant women or women after confinement, in particular.

2. Legislation creates social preconditions for the realization, protection and support of motherhood, such as family law, social welfare law, etc.

The legal means of the second category in connection with those of the first constitute the bulk of the population policy, which in our country has a pro-natalist character (two to three children per family).

Despite the abundant literature on demographic and population problems only scant attention has been given to legal aspects of population problems. In recent times, two significant steps were taken: one was the effort made by the International Union for the Scientific Study of Population (IUSSP) to constitute a study group on legislation and fertility in European countries under the chairmanship of Livi Bacci of Italy and Egon Szabady of Hungary; a comparative study is to be published this year and will serve as one of the preparatory scientific actions for the World Population Year 1974.

The other is an incentive study of the relations between population problems and law; it was prepared at Duke University and was sponsored by the Population Council. In the opinion of the editors:

Of the various components in a total attack of the world's population problem, the adjustment of a country's laws, regulations, appropriations, and administrative structures is increasingly coming to be seen as not only relevant, but at certain points of prime significance (Lee and Larson 1971).

For demonstrating the relations between the law and the reproductive behavior of the population in Czechoslovakia I have chosen three areas: abortion, divorce, and social welfare.

Abortion

As I have just pointed out, an evaluation of the influence of the law on fertility can hardly be undertaken if the causative effect of one act or other legal measure is isolated from economic, social, and political influences simultaneously at work. Where the law affects birth most directly, its impact is best seen. In this sense, the best example is the effect of legal abortions.

Czechoslovakian population policy since the end of the World War has endeavored quite unequivocally to support natality. Nevertheless, this country has rather liberal legislation on abortion. The 1957 Abortion Act has nothing to do with the regulation of natality, its only goal being the protection of women's health. As mentioned above, until 1957 about fifty deaths annually were caused by abortions carried out illegally. This has been eliminated entirely. However, such a positive effect of the abortion law has been overshadowed by a more visible effect which the high abortion rate has had on population growth in general and in particular on the future fertility of young women and girls. Despite these facts, our government is not inclined to adopt the way of the Rumanian Government, which prohibited legally carried-out abortions for other than strictly medical reasons. From the experience not only in our country but in all European countries it is well known that decreasing the number of abortions carried out on application results in an increase in the number of spontaneous abortions, the performance of which is incompetent and comprises a greater risk for the health of the pregnant woman.

The reduction of the abortion rate cannot be achieved by merely administrative measures. Therefore, the amended regulation to the Abortion Law, effective since 1973, postulates a more responsible consideration of social grounds for artificial termination of pregnancy, in particular the first pregnancy or the pregnancy of a woman with only a single child. The abortion committees[5] have been extended to include experts in social policy. The national committee (Local Authority) of which the abortion committee is an organ, is required to help the pregnant woman solve the social problems that stand in the way of the birth of a new child. Together with the improved population climate this new legislative measure has contributed to decreasing the number of abortions — both total and applied for (Table 2).

Divorce

Divorce is usually seen as a phenomenon upon which the law exercises

[5] The abortion committees are organs of the district or regional national committees, to which the pregnant woman must submit her application. In the composition of the abortion committee the lay element prevails: its chairman is a deputy of the national committee and only one member needs to be a gynecologist.

Table 2.   Abortions in Czechoslovakia 1963–1972

Year	Total	Applied for	Spontaneous	Other
1963	99,933	70,546	29,245	142
1964	99,211	70,698	28,414	99
1965	105,758	79,591	26,098	69
1966	115,807	90,263	25,494	50
1967	121,132	96,421	24,722	55
1968	124,132	99,886	24,214	32
1969	127,232	102,797	24,410	25
1970	125,074	99,766	25,288	20
1971	122,374	96,907	25,444	23
1972	118,390	90,697	27,675	18

an influence even though it may be indirect. In our classification it belongs to the second group of legislative measures.

The absolute number of divorces, like the divorce rate in the post-war decades, shows an unfavorable trend (see above). The Family Code regards divorce as a rather extraordinary termination of marriage, being possible only in socially relevant cases. Nevertheless, our legal arrangement may be considered to be a modern one, which does not force a couple to live together if the physical or psychic barriers against life in common are insurmountably strong.

The state intervenes through the services of a social worker who helps to solve problems of the children from divorced couples. The interests of minor children being first and foremost, our law refrains from preventing separation because the disintegration of the family life has a worse impact upon the children than has its final termination in the form of a judicial divorce.

In 1972, for the first time after many years, both the absolute number of divorces and the divorce rate were more favorable in comparison with the previous years. Even if we should like to interpret this as the influence of the legal and social arrangements taken up in the last two years, one year's change is too short a period to warrant any conclusion.

Social Welfare

Czechoslovakia is the only European country where since 1968 the live birth rate has been steadily growing (see Table 3).

Even more important are the changes in the age structure of the Czechoslovak population, in particular in quinquennial age groups. In 1972, population growth continued its previous favorable tendencies toward increase in marriage rate and live birth rate, natural increase,

Table 3. Birthrates in Czechoslovakia

Year	Live birth rate	Natural increase
1968	14.9	4.2
1969	15.5	4.3
1970	15.9	4.3
1971	16.5	5.0
1972	17.3	6.3

decrease in death rate and arrest of the increasing divorce rate of many years. Most Czechoslovak demographers and politicians see in these favorable trends of the last two or three years the result of the impact of a large number of new legal and socioeconomic arrangements. The aim of these measures is the stabilization of population development at a level which will answer the needs and requirements of our industrially developed socialist society. Among the new legal measures we find:
1.   The extension of paid maternity leave from twenty-two weeks up to twenty-six weeks, since July 1, 1968.
2.   The extension of additional unpaid maternity leave up to the second year of the child, since January 1, 1970.
3.   The raising of the birth grant received on the birth of each child from 1,000 crowns up to 2,000 crowns since October 1, 1971.
4.   The maternity grant, first introduced in 1969 and amended in 1971, which is given to mothers staying at home and taking care of a child under two years of age and an additional child (or children) under school-leaving age, or in case of an invalid child requiring constant care, up to twenty-six years of age.
5.   The introduction of exceptional scholarships for married university students, especially those with children, since October 1, 1971.
6.   The increased contributions which the national committees grant to minors who are not otherwise provided for, since October 1, 1971.
7.   The raising of family allowances since January 1, 1973.
8.   The introduction, since April 1, 1973, of loans on advantageous terms as aid to young married couples buying and furnishing their homes, loans which are partly written off when a child is born and attains the age of one year.[6]

[6]   The maximum loan is 30,000 crowns, repayable over ten years. The interest rate is 1 percent for acquiring a home, 2.5 percent for its furnishing. Loans are granted provided both husband and wife are under thirty years of age and the marriage has taken place on or after April 1, 1973 or not earlier than three years before that day. The total income of the married couple must not exceed 5,000 crowns a month. When a child is born and attains the age of one year, 2,000 crowns are written off the debt, and with each further child an additional 4,000 crowns is written off.

Among all these legal measures the maternity grant, which is being used by 90 percent of women who qualify for it, as well as the increase of family allowances upon the birth of the second and the third child, seem to affect the reproductive behavior of the population more than anything else. The raise in family allowances was prepared so that the families with two and three children would benefit from it, the growth index of two-child families being 142 percent and that of three-child families 129 percent.[7]

Immediately after their introduction, the loans to young married couples became widely used, which may also positively influence natality in coming years.

To evaluate the influence of these legal and socioeconomic measures the State Statistical Office of Czechoslovakia made a comparison between the level of natality and the indices of fertility in 1970 and 1972. At the level of age-specific fertility rates the total number of live births in 1972 — with regard to the age structure — should exceed that of 1970 by 6,005. But the actual absolute increase amounted to 22,707 live births. From this it follows that in 1972 the increase of 16,702 live births resulted from the new legal measures. Thus the proportion of these measures in the increase in live births in 1972 in comparison with 1970 amounted to 73.6 percent, whereas that of the improved age structure was only 26.4 percent (Srb 1973:13).

Concurrently with financial aid to families with children, the remaining areas of population policy also should be looked into, such as moral, ethical, and educational measures, housing policy, living and working conditions of female workers, etc. This shows that it is necessary to coordinate measures of population policy and social policy, as they are very closely linked.

The exact evaluation of the impact of legislation on fertility cannot possibly be undertaken at the existing stage of knowledge and experience. Not only family law, but civil, labor, criminal, and administrative law are involved, to mention only the chief ones. Experience has also shown that some of the measures adopted are not observed in practice. That means that the implementation of the law differs from the law itself. This is particularly true in the sphere of labor law. For example, the extent of women's night work is still excessive, and in some instances women are still employed on jobs which are banned for them.

---

[7] The relation between increased family allowances and the average monthly salary in the national economy, which at the end of 1972 amounted to approximately 2,100 crowns, is 4.3 percent of the salary for one child; 20.5 for two; 41.9 for three; 61.0 for four; and 72.4 for five or more.

Enterprises are very slow to adjust working hours for mothers with small children, including part-time jobs. The same is true in other countries as well. In Switzerland, although the same legal arrangement for artificial termination of pregnancy is valid in the whole country, there are great differences in the implementation of the law, thousands of abortions being registered in some cantons — as in Zürich — and not a single one in other cantons. Similar differences between the law and its implementation may be found in every country.

Great importance therefore is attached to a central supervision of the implementation of government regulations and to the procedures of individual central authorities in evaluating the effect of implemented measures as well as in tackling new problems that crop up and in submitting clearly conceived information and further proposals to the government. In order to deal with these tasks, the federal government of Czechoslovakia set up, in 1971, a Government Population Committee composed of representatives of ministries and other central authorities, leading research and university workers and other selected experts.

The above survey is an attempt to illustrate some of the influences exercised by the law on the reproductive behavior of the population. As has been pointed out, we cannot say that the law begins here and ends there because the law acts together with other social, economic, and political tools. Provided that law reacts flexibly to political, economic, and social conditions in relation to an effective support of larger families, it may be expected that the upward trend of the birth-rate begun in 1968 will continue and will lead to a more favorable development of the population structure, which is the first aim of the Czechoslovak population policy.

REFERENCES

LEE, LUKE T., ARTHUR LARSON, editors
1971 *Population and law.* Leiden: A. W. Sijthoff.
SRB, VLADÍMIR
1973 Populačí vývoj ČSSR v roce 1972 [The development of populations in the Czechoslovak Socialist Republic in 1972]. *Populčni zprávy* 3:13.

The Marginal Family in Chile: Social Change and Woman's Contraceptive Behavior

GERARDO GONZÁLES-CORTÉS and
MARGARITA MARÍA ERRÁZURIZ

INTRODUCTION

Social marginality has been one of the emergent processes of Latin American urban development during the last twenty years, and has been visible and evident particularly in the so-called belts of misery (*cinturones de miseria*) that have surrounded the large cities. Reproductive behavior in these social sectors has been characterized by a high level of fertility.

In Chile, the last two governments – of Eduardo Frei with the Christian Democrats, formed in 1964, and of Salvador Allende with the Unidad Popular, formed in 1970 set in motion specific policies directed toward these sectors. This interest was due partly to ideologically based policy objectives and partly to the strategic importance of attracting the marginal sectors in order to enlarge the power base of the political parties.

As a result of these policies and the action of other political agents (parties or movements), among other factors, marginal groups have experienced an intense process of social change, which includes among its principal characteristics a growing internal organization.

The objective of this paper is to discuss on a theoretical level the probable effects of the different political strategies which have been applied in marginal groups to the family structure and roles of women and, thus, to their reproductive behavior. We will confine the discus-

The authors wish to thank Luís Quirós, political scientist, member of the Population Policy Sector in CELADE, for his critical suggestions during the preparation of this article.

sion to the strategies and political activity of three parties, which vary in their positions from center-left to the extreme left and which have adopted specific policies toward the marginal sectors. The parties are the Christian Democrats, the Communist Party, and the Movement of the Revolutionary Left (MIR [*Movimiento de Izquierda Revolucionaria*]).

Our theoretical work is supported by empirical evidence obtained through a poll of marginal groups throughout Greater Santiago in 1966–1967 (DESAL–CELAP 1970; González 1969) and by information on political strategies obtained from official party documents and from recently published information in this field.

In the first section, we will describe the situation of marginal groups around 1966, when systematic political action toward them began, and their subsequent evolution. In the second section, we will discuss the strategies adopted by the political parties and the resultant operative changes in social organization. Finally, we will discuss the possible effects of the application of these strategies to the structure of family authority and women's roles on the assumption that changes in these factors can significantly influence reproductive behavior.

MARGINAL GROUPS

The Situation in 1966

About the end of 1966, when the study cited above was made, the estimated marginal population of Greater Santiago was 300,000 persons. The operational criterion adopted for the identification of this universe was housing, leading to the isolation of three types:

1.   Rundown sectors located in older neighborhoods of the central city.

2.   Spontaneous *poblaciones*[1] which include: (a) *poblaciones callampas* ("mushroom" *poblaciones*), so called because they sprang up quickly and without plan on vacant land, with crude or worn-out materials used to construct houses; and (b) *poblaciones de mejoras* which resulted from the occupation of sites through organized action, with small houses of light construction built by their owners.

3.   Planned *poblaciones,* constructed in large part by the state in order to provide a minimal housing solution.

[1]   The term *población* in this case designates a group of houses within more or less defined limits.

Here we will consider only the second type, spontaneous *poblaciones*, where the political activity that we will analyze has been concentrated. In 1966, these *poblaciones* encompassed a total of 34,300 dwellings on various points of the urban periphery of Santiago. They contained an estimated 46,700 women of child-bearing age.[2]

Migratory trends toward metropolitan centers appear to be one of the principal factors in the appearance and growth of these *poblaciones* (57 percent of the women and 59 percent of the men were immigrants). However, this migration should not be interpreted as a transplant of rural culture and life style to the marginal *poblaciones*. Results of the poll indicate in this respect that almost half the immigrants were born in other cities. Thus, the great majority of women (94 percent) either had lived in an urban environment since birth or had more than ten years' urban residence.

Urban residence explains, at least in part, why illiteracy was not very frequent (13 percent in women and 12 percent in men). Despite this, predominant educational levels were relatively low: 40 percent of the women and 32 percent of the men had not exceeded the third year of primary school.

Employment constitutes without a doubt one of the crucial elements of marginality. The data indicate in this respect that the great majority of the men were blue-collar workers (65 percent) or were "self-employed"[3] (18 percent). Unemployment levels were not very high, although job instability and high levels of underemployment were encountered.

On the part of women, a great majority did not carry out remunerative work away from the home (67 percent), and among those who worked the majority were employed in very low-level occupations such as service personnel, unskilled workers, or peddlers. It was verified that among the women who were not working at the time of the poll, many had worked in the past (72 percent). The principal causes of discontinuing employment were marriage (58 percent) and the birth of children (26 percent). This fact already indicates the prevalence of an authority structure in the marginal couple characterized by masculine dominance

[2] The data used come from the previously cited poll (see DESAL-CELAP 1970; González 1969). This poll was carried out at the end of 1966 and the beginning of 1967. It was applied to a stratified sample of women of child-bearing age (fifteen to fifty years old) and their husbands or companions. The total sample included 1,181 women and 757 men. The subsample for spontaneous *poblaciones* included 369 women and 213 men.

[3] This category includes peddlers, plumbers, carpenters, etc., who render services to private homes; shoemakers, newspaper vendors, etc.

and limitation of the woman's role to fulfillment of domestic functions. Through this observation we approach the nucleus of the analysis: reproductive behavior in relation to the family structure. In this respect the poll data establish the following attributes:

1.   High levels of fertility: The average number of pregnancies for women between twenty and fifty years of age was 5.26. The average number of live births, although high, was considerably less (4.12) due principally to a high mortality rate (0.10), spontaneous abortion (0.45), and induced abortion (0.49).

2.   The actual levels of fertility contradicted the attitudes of the women, WHO FOR THE MOST PART WERE ORIENTED TOWARD A SMALL FAMILY: The mean number of desired children was 3.32.

3.   For this reason, a great majority of the women were MOTIVATED NOT TO HAVE MORE CHILDREN: 74 percent declared that they desired no more children, and more than half of these would have preferred fewer children than they had.

4.   However, although these women were strongly motivated to avoid having more children, many WOULD NOT USE BIRTH CONTROL MEASURES to avoid new pregnancies: among those who desired no more children, 9 percent had been sterilized, and 20 percent were using highly effective methods (IUD, birth control pills); 35 percent had never used any contraceptive technique.

5.   A study of the factors associated with contraceptive practice showed that the ATTITUDE OF THE HUSBAND appeared to have an important influence on the behavior of the women in this respect: it was found that when the husband had a favorable attitude toward contraception, 74 percent of the women at some time had used a contraceptive method; in contrast, in those cases where the attitude of the husband or companion was unfavorable, only 40 percent of the women had practiced contraception. Thus, it can be assumed that an unfavorable attitude on the part of the husband constitutes an important obstacle to the regular use of contraceptive measures by women and that consequently the diminution of the husband's authority would facilitate their use.

6.   Moreover, it was found that MEN WERE IN GENERAL MORE TRADITIONAL THAN WOMEN in their attitudes toward the family: they desired more children (average 3.88) than the women (average 3.32), tended to be more conformist, and more frequently held a low opinion of the highly effective contraceptive techniques.

Based on the preceding evidence, we propose as a working hypothesis that ALL CHANGE IN THE FAMILY STRUCTURE THAT IMPLIES EMANCI-

PATION OF THE WOMAN FROM THE AUTHORITY OF HER HUSBAND AND, IN
GENERAL, REDEFINITION OF WOMEN'S ROLES ORIENTED TOWARD A
GROWING PARTICIPATION IN COMMUNITY ACTIVITIES OUTSIDE THE HOME
WILL FACILITATE THE GENERALIZED ADOPTION OF CONTRACEPTION AND
THUS WILL CONTRIBUTE TO A DECREASE IN FERTILITY. Using this
hypothesis, we will analyze the strategies that have guided political
action toward marginal groups and their probable effects on the family
structure.

Historical Evolution of Marginal Groups

We have described briefly several characteristics of the marginal sectors
around 1965, when specific policies toward these sectors were initiated.
However, 1965 is only a moment in an ongoing process which began
in the 1940's. The greatest expansion of the *poblaciones callampas* occurred between 1952 and 1959. In this period the number of families
in this situation grew from 16,500 to 32,300 (Duque and Pastrana
1972: 2).

Governmental action to solve this problem was limited initially to
housing programs. Between 1958 and 1961, the number of families in
poblaciones callampas was reduced to 16,400. Beginning in 1964, during
Frei's administration, given the urgent need to build houses and the
incapacity to provide definitively for all those who sought them, an
emergency solution called "operation site" was tried.[4]

In addition to government action, the *pobladores*[5] themselves acted
as a pressure group. Thus, already in 1964 the invasion of uncultivated
lands or state property with the objective of putting up houses had
begun.

This type of action, in a majority of cases under the control of the
Communist Party, became more frequent and better organized. One of
the most important was the takeover of La Feria in San Miguel, in
which 3,240 families participated. Only since the advent of the government of the Unidad Popular has the Christian Democratic Party participated in takeovers of land.

To assure success, the takeovers were organized by political leaders
well in advance. When the takeover actually occurred, legislators and

---

[4] It consisted of handing over small sites where each family could build a home
with light materials supplied by the state. The land has minimum urban services.
During Frei's government, 75,557 site operations were carried out in Greater
Santiago.

[5] Inhabitants of the *poblaciones*.

other politicians lent their support to defend the participants from police repression. As a result of the takeovers the *campamentos* were organized, often under strong political control. Between 1969 and May of 1971, there were 312 recorded takeovers of land in Greater Santiago, producing the formation of an equal number of *campamentos* with a total of 54,710 families. (Duque and Pastrana 1972: 7).

In 1972 the great majority of these *campamentos* were politically controlled, frequently with a single party in complete command. Data collected by the Communist Party acknowledge Socialist Party control over about 16,100 families; Communist Party control over 11,500; MIR 5,400 families; and the Christian Democrats, 3,100 families. These data are for Greater Santiago, and estimate that generally families belong to *campamentos* in accordance with their political affiliation.

In discussing the strategies of several political parties toward marginal sectors, we will present more background information on the internal organization of the *campamentos* and their relations with the government and other political agents.

POLITICAL PARTY STRATEGIES

For the past twenty years, various political coalitions with distinct strategies – Ibáñez and populism, Alessandri supported by the right, and the "Revolution in Freedom" of the Christian Democrats – have governed without achieving an economic growth in accord with the expectations and demands of the population. Because of the growing frustration of the majority of the social sectors as a result of this situation and the limits imposed by the system, its reform has been the central issue of political debate and electoral battles since 1952.

The reforms have affected political development through an increasing organization of all social sectors and a growing political participation, which has tripled during this period. Since November 1970, Chile has been trying a new political experiment, the peaceful transition to socialism, under the leadership of a coalition whose most important parties – the Socialist and Communist – are ideologically Marxist.

For the past five years, this process has been characterized as well by a polarization of political forces, with the appearance of political movements of both the extreme right and extreme left. MIR, which is one of the political groups whose strategy we will analyze, has assumed leadership among the latter. This movement, while not considered a political party, in the traditional sense, has a strong internal organization which permits it to carry out coordinated political action. It arose around 1965 with the unification of small extremist groups and dissident factions of the Socialist and Communist parties. MIR's political activity has concentrated on three fronts: among the peasants, an area of greatest conflict due to the agrarian reform; at the universities, where there is a small but highly militant minority; and among the marginal *poblaciones* of the great cities.

During Frei's government, MIR initiated urban guerrilla actions (assaults on armories, banks, supermarkets, etc.), which led to their going underground. Salvador Allende, on assuming power at the end of 1970, took means that permitted the movement to surface, putting it in a position of critical support of the government of the Unidad Popular. From this position the MIR abandoned urban guerrilla action and began a new style of political activity oriented toward the mobilization and cooption of the popular sectors.

In contrast to MIR, the Communist Party has a long history in Chilean politics. It was founded in 1922. Between 1949 and 1958 it suffered the effects of the Law for the Defense of Democracy, which forced it underground. The Communist Party is a party of *cadres* whose principal political base is among the urban industrial proletariat. Its percentage during recent elections gradually has increased from 11.4 percent of the vote in 1961 to 17 percent in 1971, which puts it in fourth place among the nation's political forces. In the world context of Marxist parties, the Chilean Communist Party clearly follows the pro-Soviet line. As we will see, this orientation is expressed in its political action toward the marginal sectors.

Whereas MIR and the Communist Party identify themselves ideologically as Marxist, the Christian Democrats reject both the Marxist model of development and the neocapitalist, proposing instead a reformist political plan which has as its goal communitarian socialism. From a multiclass political base, the Christian Democrats count on support from wide sectors of the urban middle class and peasantry, and a considerable part of the proletariat and urban subproletariat. Since 1965, they have been the strongest political force, attracting at the beginning of Frei's government 41 percent of the vote. Today, although still in first place, their electoral base has fallen to 28 percent.

The Strategy of the Christian Democratic Party

In accord with their humanist and Christian ideological base and their multiclass composition, the Christian Democrats tend toward a system of conciliation and through negotiation, the resolution of conflicts of interest among classes and social sectors. The greatest social justice, as a goal, is achieved through a growing participation by organized popular sectors in decision making. Thus, a more equal distribution of social benefits results not from a substantial change in the system but basically from a change in the correlation of forces within the system. Consequently, Christian Democratic politics is oriented toward minimizing class conflict and attempting to perfect traditional democratic mechanisms of participation through reformist politics.

Within this general conception lies its policy of social and economic incorporation of marginal sectors, *"promoción popular."* The basis for this program is the theory of social marginality developed by R. Vekemans and his Center for Latin American Economic and Social Development (DESAL). Marginality is defined as a lack of integration in the social organizational structure resulting from low or complete lack of participation. This is meant in a double sense:

1. as a lack of RECEPTIVE PARTICIPATION of goods and services (society is here conceived as the seat of social resources and benefits); and
2. as a lack of ACTIVE PARTICIPATION in the decision making process. The basis of the lack of participation, according to this theoretical framework, is another feature characteristic of marginal sectors: their INTERNAL DISINTEGRATION, whereby they take on more the character of aggregates than of social groups as such (DESAL 1967, volume one: 51–55).

The *promoción popular* strategy that emerges from this thesis is oriented primarily toward overcoming this internal disintegration through the creation and development of local organizations which, once institutionalized, fulfill the double function of channeling demands (active participation) and aiding in the distribution of social and economic benefits (receptive participation).

In practice, this policy was expressed during the Christian Democratic government through the creation of both "geographical" and "functional" community organizations. The former constituted an expression of internal solidarity and an attempt to aid the government in solving community problems defined geographically in terms of residence. Its most typical form is in the Neighborhood Councils (*Juntas de Vecinos*), created by law in 1968.

The functional organization attempted to promote specific values in the neighborhoods, and with this objective associations of mothers, sports clubs, youth organizations, and associations for parents of schoolchildren were created.

All of these organizations, both geographical and functional, are closely tied to the satisfaction of the needs and the fulfillment of the proper role of the family. Thus, the primary objective of the geographical organizations is to obtain family housing on private property. Once this is achieved, the solidarity thus generated is channeled toward the solution of problems of urban infrastructure (drinking water, sewage systems, transportation, etc.) and social services (health, police, children's recreation, etc.). In the same way, the functional organizations revolve around the family in their concern for children's education (parents' associations, youth clubs) and for preparing women for their domestic roles (associations of mothers).

The motif and form of the popular organizations promoted by the Christian Democrats lead to two important effects. First, communalities are organized around very concrete interests principally to the consumption of goods and services, which have no class basis. Second, because women are traditionally bound closer than men to the domestic and family sphere, they have taken a leading role in these organizations.

Last, it should be remembered that women historically have occupied an important position within the Christian Democratic Party and that they constitute its principal electoral base. (In the 1964 presidential election, Frei won 56 percent of the total vote. This wide margin was due principally to massive female support, which reached 63 percent). In this sense, the emphasis on women's participation within the popular organizations also implies as an objective cooption and political mobilization in support of the party.

In summary, one can trace the following characteristics of the Christian Democratic strategy toward marginal sectors:

1. The explicit final objective is to overcome marginality by dynamic incorporation of the currently marginal sectors into the existing system, with a view toward perfecting the democratic process.
2. The immediate political objective is to coopt marginal sectors to support the political action of the Christian Democratic Party.
3. This incorporation implies a growing participation, both active and receptive, as the hoped-for result of the institutionalized organization of the marginal population.
4. The organizations thus established are not allied with specific class interests but rather with problems related to housing and other necessities and functions of the family. In other words, anyone who participates does so not as a worker or subproletarian but as a community member or father or mother in a family.

5.   These organizations confer a prominent role on women.
6.   The socialization that results from participation in these organizations normally leads to an uncritical assimilation of the values and life style of the urban middle class.

Communist Party (PC) Strategy

The conquest of power in order to construct a communist society is the central objective of the PC. Following Marxist-Leninist principles, its general strategy adapts itself to the possibilities for total conquest of power offered by the political system and the correlation of social forces in their current state of development.

Analysis of these factors has led the PC to opt for a peaceful TRANSITION TO SOCIALISM, which implies the realization of revolutionary changes without an abrupt rupture of existing legality. The political viability of this strategy is based on the democratic character of the Chilean political system, in which the political awareness and mobilization of the population should make possible – via the electoral process – the substitution of "bourgeois legality" by a new "socialist legality" in order finally to establish the socialist system.

This transition to socialism involves a strategy with long-range goals and the acceptance of stages as much in the conquest of power as in the transformation of the social organization.

In a first stage, the political struggle centers exclusively on identifying and isolating the "principal enemies": imperialism, monopolies, and the oligarchy. This type of action pursues a double objective: in part it intends to direct and increase the militance of the proletariat, channeling it toward a single front; in part it intends to modify the correlation of forces by attracting all social forces that fall under the common denominator "progressive." Thus, it seeks a multiclass alliance of the peasantry and urban subproletariat to the petit bourgeoisie (including small and medium-sized entrepreneurs), maintaining the predominance of proletarian-based parties – the Communist Party and Socialist Party – in political leadership of the popular movement.[6]

---

[6]   "Chile needs an anti-imperialist and anti-oligarchical popular government that is supported by a national majority formed of all parties and currents that agree on a program of revolutionary transformation. It should include the workers, the peasants, white collar employees, women, youth, and small and medium-sized entrepreneurs, not only through their own parties but also through their representatives from the mass organizations in the corresponding institutions and echelons of state administration.

"Thus, we pronounce ourselves in favor of a popular government — multiparty,

It hopes that an alliance of this type will permit, if not an active mobilization of sectors of the middle class, at least their neutralization in the struggle with the "principal enemies."

This strategic option has made the PC the principal thrust behind the Unidad Popular – the current government coalition, which consists of a political alliance that unites the strength of the traditional Marxist parties (Socialist and Communist), the pro-Marxist left factions that split from the Christian Democrats (MAPU, the Christian Left), and the social democratic parties (API and the Radical Party).

Maintaining this broad base requires a politics of tolerance and moderation. As long as electoral processes continue to allow the conquest of formal power (Parliament, for example), they must satisfy the aspirations of their political base by raising the standard of living. Thus, the strategy of the Unidad Popular places special emphasis on a rapid redistribution of income and a full employment policy. Moreover, the growing state control of distribution of essential products has permitted it, in a situation of scarcity, to give preference to supplying the least wealthy sectors.

A second element that should be pointed out is the leading role assigned by the PC to the government of the Unidad Popular in the process of transition to socialism:

In this, a class war and a long one, the decisive weapon for the people is their government. To strengthen it and widen its sustaining base, surrounding it with greater mass support, and to use it to completely accomplish the Program, and then to strike at the principal enemies and increase the possibilities of isolating them, in that lies the guarantee of definitive victory, the consolidation of the revolutionary process (Cerda 1971: 191).

Communist Party political action toward marginal sectors is embraced within its general strategy. As for the other Marxist parties, the PC places the ultimate root of social marginality in the area of economic structure, it being the natural product of the dynamics of dependent

---

broad-based, strong, revolutionary, efficient — which will assure the nation democratic stability and increased social, economic, and political progress, and will give the people full liberty.

"A popular government that unites in its bosom a national majority will be capable of overcoming the internal and external obstacles which oppose transformation, will give rise to a display of all the revolutionary forces that exist in Chilean society, and will open the road to socialism. In the conditions of our country, the broader the government, the firmer, more revolutionary, and more capable it will be" (*Manifesto to the people*, published by the Communist Party during the parliamentary election campaign of 1969; Cerda 1971: 200).

capitalism. From this – in contrast to the Christian Democrats, who hope to overcome marginality through a more perfect democratic system with the growing participation of marginal groups in the mechanisms of pressure and representation – the PC maintains that replacing the capitalist system by a socialist one is the necessary and sufficient condition for the suppression of marginality.

Based on this analysis, the ideological action of the PC tends to subordinate the particular interests of marginal groups (housing, services, and employment) to the more general interests of the working class, thus allowing broad action on a wide popular front.

Historically, the political action of the PC was translated into support for housing requests, applying pressure to the point of resorting to "land takeovers" of either private or state property. In time, these were no longer aimed solely at acquiring housing but proceeded to be transformed into an instrument for electoral coopting and political indoctrination. Land takeovers were organized well in advance and only those considered suitable by the Party could participate. The entire social organization that would control the community afterward was organized with as much forethought as the land takeovers themselves. The rules were generally so strict that in extreme cases the entry or exit of all persons was controlled by a pass system.

The plan for land takeovers and political control was given impulse by the creation of organizations by the Christian Democrats. Once these organizations were created (especially the Neighborhood Councils), the Communist Party sought their control and called on *pobladores* to join them so that the Christian Democratic program would not prevail in the councils and they would become a "brake on the aspirations of the masses" (Giusti 1971: 32).

Little by little the Communist Party succeeded in transforming the demand for housing into a demand for power. Housing could be had only through the people's government. While this new situation was taking shape, there arose a complete system of internal relations for each *campamento* and a new type of relationship between the latter and the rest of society. The People's Courts (*Tribunales Populares*) were organized; great importance was given to the necessity for employment, and agreements were arranged with the government to invest in the infrastructure (schools, clinics, meeting places) of the *campamento* and to provide employment for its working-age members; Vigilance and Supply Committees were formed. The *campamentos* were converted into closed organizations where the units of housing served as well as units of work, as units of social assistance (justice, education, protection), and finally, through the Supply Committees, as units of consumption.

One can emphasize the following points of Communist Party strategy toward the marginal sectors:

1. The PC seeks political control of the *campamentos* – in competition with other leftist parties (the Socialist Party, MAPU, MIR) and with the Christian Democrats – as a form of widening its political base, which is primarily among industrial workers.

2. Ideological action toward the *campamentos* under their control tends to awaken class consciousness, incorporating basic demands for housing and services into a broader program of struggle for power via the government of the Unidad Popular. In this sense, it furthers political mobilization in support of government efforts.

3. Simultaneously, it pursues minimal immediate satisfaction of the most urgent necessities of the *pobladores* (housing, services, food supply, and especially employment) through concerted action of local organizations and organizations of the State.

4. Anticipating the relative anomy and lack of internal organization of these groups, it experiments with socialist forms of organization within the *campamentos* (People's Courts, Vigilance Committees, and Councils on Supplies and Prices), although without emphasizing the break with the life style and consumption patterns of bourgeois culture.

The Strategy of MIR

MIR struggles for the development of popular power. Its tactical objective is to strengthen the struggle of the people in their conquest of power.

MIR opposes the Communist Party strategy of gradual conquest of power and for this reason opposes the electoral process, while accepting the fact that it can be used tactically at certain moments.[7]

---

[7] "Whoever claims that by adding up electoral triumphs one can conquer 'pieces' of power within the state apparatus and thus live with the illusion of conquering 'power' by 'bits' within the framework of bourgeois institutions in order to carry out progressive 'reforms' of the State apparatus and the economy, not only will not be 'constructing' socialism but will be clumsily formulating what in the past other 'Marxists' (the brilliant reformists Bernstein, Kautsky, and Plekhanov) have already formulated; and in reality will be developing what Marx and Engels called 'parliamentary cretinism.'

"But on the other hand, as the theory and world-wide practice of the revolutionary struggle teach, even though the electoral struggle itself does not 'deliver Power,' revolutionaries cannot abstain from participating in it 'on principle,' and it is thus one of the means by which the political struggle of the proletariat develops" (MIR 1973: 2–4).

In its opinion, the conquest of power by the popular classes necessarily implies an armed confrontation of classes. However, in the present situation in which the government has been won over by leftist political forces, the MIR postpones all armed confrontation and directs its strategy toward "the duality of power, which is the only way by which alternative power can be constructed."[8]

The idea of creating a dual power is born from the "fundamental contradiction that exists between the mass movement and the State." MIR's position in this respect diverges from that of the Communist Party. For the former, the bureaucratic apparatus of the State, even though currently directed by a Marxist popular government, does not lose the quality of being a repressive instrument at the service of the dominant classes.[9] For this reason, it opposes all attempts by the government to guide or control the organized development of the popular forces.

Thus, it endeavors to construct autonomous class organs independent of the State and independent of the domination of classes, as fundamental tools that allow them to gather strength and move toward the conquest of power. Only thus

will it be possible to establish a new ratio of strength between the working class and the government, which through the strength of the working class and popular masses, based on their independence and ideological, programmatic, political, and organizational autonomy, will permit them to demand a specific course and content of government action (MIR 1973: 5).

In this sense MIR seeks to transcend the present confrontation between

---

[8] "This is not a task that is fixed permanently in whichever country, at whatever moment; but in a prerevolutionary period it is precisely one of the fundamental tasks and the fundamental tool — not the government — which would permit the gathering of strength and the real march toward the conquest of Power. It involved organizations independent of the dominant class, of the bourgeoisie. It involved mass organizations independent of the State apparatus and not subject to it. Without fear or timidity of any kind, we must build from the roots up the DUALITY OF POWER, the only way by which alternative power can be constructed" (Enríquez 1973).

[9] Through the Worker's Squadrons "we thought that the task of controlling the bureaucratic apparatus of the State could be begun, thereby raising the fundamental contradiction that existed and exists between the mass movement and the bureaucratic apparatus of the State. The antibureaucratic struggle that the people live minute by minute in health, housing, education ... is the only way to incorporate the forces of different sectors of the people. We thought that the generation of this type of organism should be based on these tasks. From there would spring the strength and conscience both to confront the bourgeoisie and to continue creating organs of power" (Enríquez 1973).

the Unidad Popular government (with a multiclass base) and the opposition, and generate in its place an unambiguous class confrontation between the alliance of workers, peasants, and urban poor (*pobres de la ciudad*) on one hand and the bourgeoisie on the other.

MIR's political action toward the marginal sectors is designed to plant the seeds of dual power, and it is precisely in the *campamentos* that they have concentrated their efforts. Using as a model the closed organizational structure of the Communist *campamentos*, MIR organizes theirs not in terms of support for the people's government but around the creation of new forms of social organization and the generation of popular power which can later be imposed on the rest of society.

In these terms, it dedicates itself especially to the marginal sectors organized into *campamentos*, with a clear intent of political awareness. The strength to create a new society centers on education, on cultural change. Toward this objective the state texbooks are reformed and great importance is put on cultural activity with clearly doctrinaire content. The formation of a new power is seen as supported by the creation of people's militias. Every *poblador* and *pobladora* is a militiaman, in accord with the basic MIR idea of conquest of power by armed revolution. The regulation of the militias rules the internal relations of the *campamento*, and its functioning is scrupulously observed.

Finally, one should note in line with our theme, that MIR explicitly proposed in its program "the establishment of women's rights and the immediate creation of conditions for the material liberation of women from the yoke and servitude of domestic work" (MIR 1973: 5).

The following points of MIR strategy should be noted:
1. Its general strategy is clearly distinct from that of the Communist Party in that:
a. It rejects the possibility of progressive conquest of power.
b. It seeks to polarize the struggle in terms of class, consequently rejecting all alliances with sectors of the bourgeoisie.
c. It poses the necessity of passing through armed confrontation in the conquest of power.
d. It does not believe that the bureaucratic apparatus of the bourgeois state can be converted into a prime instrument of the revolutionary process by the sole fact of having the government in the hands of the Unidad Popular. Consequently, it seeks to promote political organization of the masses with total autonomy from the government, thus creating the basis of an alternative power which springs from the people themselves.
2. Political action centers principally on the peasants and marginal

urban groups, tending to create an alliance between these sectors and the urban proletariat.

3. Institutional parallelism: with a view toward liquidating bourgeois institutions, it tests and advances socialist forms of organization within the *campamentos*.

4. It emphasizes ideological formation and cultural transformation, rejecting bourgeois values and life style.

5. Preparation for a future armed confrontation constitutes a pivot of the organization. From this arises the closed character of the *campamentos*, the strong internal discipline, the authority of the leaders, and paramilitary training with participation by men and women alike.

STRATEGY, LOCAL ORGANIZATIONS, AND FAMILY STRUCTURE

Finally, one can outline several hypotheses about the form in which the various types of social organization of the *campamentos*, resulting from the application of the political strategies described here, affect the structure of family authority.

Returning to the initial hypothesis, one can consider the changes in the structure of family authority in terms of emancipation of the woman from the authority of her husband. One assumes that this emancipation is directly associated with the redefinition of women's roles which orient her toward a growing participation in extradomestic activities, implying at the same time an elevation in her status in relation to men.

In the social groups being analyzed here this redefinition of roles and change of status will depend, in our opinion, on the degree of participation of the women in local organizations and the relationship that exists between the content of the socialization that the local organizations provide on one hand and the dominant values and behavior patterns in society on the other.

Regarding organizational participation, we accept as a working hypothesis that the greater the participation of women and the greater the importance of the functions they fulfill, compared with those to which men are assigned, the greater will be their emancipation.

Regarding the content of socialization, we propose the assumption that the dominant values and behavior patterns in the social context that we are analyzing are those of the urban middle class, which tend toward a growing emancipation of women. Their uncritical acceptance will lead, consequently, to greater emancipation. In contrast, their re-

Table 1. Relation of political groups to the emancipation of women

Strategies	Christian Democrats (DC)	Communist Party (PC)	MIR
Type of organization.	Geographical (neighborhood councils) and functional (mothers' centers, etc.) centered on housing and family interests. Open.	Same as DC, more organizations centered on class interests (committees for the jobless, people's courts, etc.). Closed.	Organizations centered on class interests. Paramilitary organization (militias). Closed.
Strategic functions of the organizations.	Attraction of political support. Dynamic incorporation into the system (integration).	Political mobilization in a broad alliance in support of the Unidad Popular government. Experiments in forms of social organization for the transition to socialism.	Consciousness-raising and political mobilization in a class alliance (peasants–workers–urban poor) to create an alternative power. Experiments in socialist forms of organization. Preparation for armed confrontation. Cultural change.
Degree of participation.	Dominant participation by women. (+)	Dominant participation by men. (−)	Equal participation of men and women. (+)
Relation to dominant cultural values and patterns.	Uncritical assimilation. (+)	A critical attitude, but without emphasis on changing the traditional family values. (−)	Critical rejection. Intention to re-socialize through education and ideological formation. (+)

(+), (−): Positive, negative effect on the emancipation of women.

jection and the intent to substitute a new cultural system will have a greater or lesser effect on their emancipation according to the values and patterns of the new system.

Table 1 summarizes schematically several characteristics of the organizations promoted by the Christian Democrats, the Communist Party, and MIR, emphasizing the degree of women's participation and its relationship with the dominant values and cultural patterns of Chilean society. The signs (+) or (—) indicate the probable effect of this factor on emancipation of women based on the hypothesis proposed here.

The organizations promoted by the Christian Democrats, by not involving class interests but rather interests specifically linked to housing and the family, confer a dominant participation on women, thus elevating their status. One would expect that this factor operates toward her growing emancipation from the authority of her husband. In addition, the open nature of these organizations and their orientation toward dynamic incorporation of marginal sectors in the system produces in fact an uncritical assimilation of the values and behavior patterns of the urban middle class, which equally favors emancipation.

The Communist Party, although it maintains several of the organizations initially promoted by the Christian Democrats, bases its action principally on a new type of organization which has as its objective the awareness of the class interests of the proletariat. Thus, the People's Courts arose as a rejection of bourgeois justice; the Committees for the Jobless deal with the problem of employment in a capitalist society; and the Councils on Supplies and Prices mobilize to compensate for the unequal distribution of consumer goods. The emphasis on class interests, which are defined in the economic and political spheres on a macrosocial level, leads to a predominant participation by men in these local organizations. One would expect that this masculine predominance would contribute to maintaining the traditional authority structure within the family.

On the other hand, the importance placed by the PC on maintaining a multiclass political alliance that includes important sectors of the middle class, and the transitional character of the process they are setting in motion, lets them leave aside at least temporarily the systematic critique of bourgeois values and behavior patterns that typify the life style of the middle classes.

Thus, within the *campamentos* controlled by the PC, although there exists a critical attitude toward the bourgeois life style, no emphasis is placed on producing cultural change with socialist content and, apparently, traditional family values with preeminence of the husband's authority within the family are maintained.

As was demonstrated in the preceding pages, MIR's political strategy differs in essential aspects from that of the Communist Party, which also expresses itself in the internal organization generated in the *campamentos* under its control. Its ultimate objective is the creation of an alternative power to that of the state, which arises from the people themselves and is cemented in an alliance of peasants, workers, and urban poor.

The political mobilization it promotes implies as a central element the increase in "combative capacity" through paramilitary organization and training. These organizations require the active participation of all, men as well as women, based on equal standing.

On the other hand, MIR in its stance as openly revolutionary critically rejects the values of bourgeois society and systematically attempts resocialization with socialist content. Liberation of women from the yoke of domestic labor is one of the values it inculcates and aims to translate into institutional terms. One would expect thus that in the *campamentos* controlled by MIR the degree and form of participation of women in local organizations as well as the value content of the new cultural system it attempts to implant will lead to their growing emancipation.

SUMMARY AND CONCLUSIONS

In the preceding sections we have discussed relationships among four levels of variables:
1. Political strategy.
2. Local organizations in *campamentos* or marginal communities.
3. Women's roles and the family structure.
4. Contraceptive practices and fertility.

We began by presenting the empirical background relating to levels 3 and 4. This formed the foundation of the hypothesis that the growing emancipation of women in respect to the husband's authority would facilitate contraceptive practices, thus modifying reproductive behavior.

The levels 1 and 2 were linked, showing how three different political strategies lead to distinct local organizations.

Last, and this time on strictly hypothetical grounds, we discussed the eventual relationship between the level of female participation in the organizations and the value content transmitted by them on one hand (level 2) and the emancipation of women on the other (level 3).

If the working hypotheses that we have adopted are valid, one can draw the following conclusions:

1. The political strategy of the Christian Democratic Party promotes local organizations, which in giving major participation to women and transmitting values and behavior patterns of the urban middle classes contributes to emancipation and by this means facilitates more extensive practice of contraception.

2. The Communist Party political strategy creates local organizations with predominant participation by men and without emphasis on a change in traditional family values. From this one would expect the maintenance of an authority structure with dominance by the husband, thereby perpetuating the resistance thus based to the practice of contraception.

3. MIR's political strategy creates local organizations with a high degree of participation by women which promotes a new value system in which emancipation is emphasized. One would thus expect a relative loss of authority on the part of the man, with a consequent increase in the practice of contraception provided that cultural factors not discussed here do not intervene.

4. In summary, the implementation of different political strategies toward the marginal sectors with a traditionally high level of fertility can produce differing effects on this variable (Christian Democrats and Communist Party, for example) or similar effects by means of differing intermediate factors (Christian Democrats and MIR).

REFERENCES

CERDA, CARLOS
1971   *El Leninismo y la victoria popular* [Leninism and the victory of the people]. Santiago: Quimantú.
DESAL
1967   *Marginalidad en América Latina* [Marginality in Latin America]. Santiago: DESAL-Herder.
DESAL-CELAP
1970   *Fecundidad y anticoncepción en poblaciones Marginales* [Fertility and Contraception in marginal sectors]. Buenos Aires: Troquel.
DUQUE, Y., E. PASTRANA
1972   *La movilización reinvicativa urbana de los sectores populares en Chile, 1964–1972* [Urban Mobilization of Popular Sectors in Chile, 1964–1972]. Latin American School of Sociology (ELAS).
ENRÍQUEZ, MIGUEL
1973   Comment in a forum on El Poder Popular y los Comandos Comunales de Trabajadores [Mass power and the workers' squadrons]. *Punto Final* 175:7–8.

GIUSTI, JORGE
1971   *Marginalidad y participación en las poblaciones marginales ur-banas chilenas* [Marginality and participation in Chilean urban marginal sectors]. International Institute of Labor Studies.
GONZÁLES, GERARDO
1969   "La limitation de naissances dans la population marginale de Santiago du Chile." Paris. (Mimeograph.)
MOVIMIENTO DE IZQUIERDA REVOLUCIONARIA (MIR), NATIONAL SECRETRIAT
1973   Letter to the Political Committee of the Socialist Party. *Punto Final* 176:2–5.

Kinship, Contraception and Family Planning in the Iranian City of Isfahan

JOHN GULICK and MARGARET E. GULICK

PROBLEMS AND PURPOSES

Iran has one of the most rapidly growing economies among the so-called "third world" countries. It also has a very rapidly growing population, its rate of increase being approximately 3 percent per year. The king of Iran, His Imperial Majesty Muhammad Reza Shah Pahlavi, has recognized that the future well-being of the Iranian people will depend, to an important extent, on reducing the rate of population

This is the second in a projected series of articles based on information which was gathered in Isfahan from November 1970 to January 1972. The project, "Cultural Influences on Human Fertility," was supported by a grant (GS-3108) from the National Science Foundation, with additional funding from the Carolina Population Center. The field research was carried out under the auspices of the University of Isfahan's Center for Population Studies whose director is Dr. Mahmoud Sarram. We are very grateful to Dr. Sarram for his many kinds of assistance. We also wish to thank Dr. Ghassem Motamedi, Chancellor of the University of Isfahan, for his support of our project.

We want to acknowledge the many kinds of assistance that were generously given us by Robert W. Gillespie of the Isfahan Communications Project, a joint endeavor of the Family Planning Division of the Iranian Ministry of Health and the Population Council, that was already in progress when we began our study.

We are most particularly grateful to those people without whose direct contributions this project would not have been carried out. Our special thanks go to Elaine Maleki. She helped us recruit and train our research team and was invaluable as our staff manager, assisted by Farideh Bassiri Malek and Fereshteh Sarram. From June 1971 to January 1972, Mrs. Maleki was in charge of the field operations in Isfahan. Farajollah Afrasiabi and Pauline Afrasiabi participated in the project in a wide variety of ways. The field interviewers were (in English alphabetical order): Naser Badami, Eshrat Darab, Mashid Emami, Ginous Hakimi, Sedigheh Karimpour, Asghar Kelishadi, Ali Langroudy, Mehdi Mansouri, Heshmatollah Nosrati, Parvaneh Rafe'i, Shaheen Shadzi, and Mahnaz Tashakkor.

growth while maintaining the country's economic development. Accordingly, the Iranian government inaugurated a family planning program in 1967. The organization and progress of this program have recently been systematically reviewed in a publication of the Population Council (Friesen and Moore 1972).

This article is based on some of the data gathered by a project whose background lay in urban anthropology, in the sociocultural anthropology of the Middle East, and in the applications of the anthropological approach to the population problem. The project was intended to explore the complexities of people's inclinations for and against the practice of family planning and contraception amid the complexities of urban family life and structure.

In presenting our findings, we intend to provide information that runs counter to some widely held notions, such as (1) there is a single, specific urban family type, (2) most families in countries like Iran and cities like Isfahan are inevitably turning into a particular kind of kinship group, namely the isolated, Western industrial nuclear family, and (3) urban living will directly cause people to have fewer children and so will directly mitigate the population problem. At best, such notions as these are over-simplifications that seriously distort reality.

Our project was originally conceived as a long-term longitudinal endeavor which would study the fertility behavior of the same people by means of repeated visits over time. It was hoped that by this means the factors influencing pregnancy or avoidance of pregnancy could be elucidated in process, rather than through the warped vision of hindsight. We also hoped that we could study the marriage and fertility behavior of the children of our primary respondents, who were husbands and wives, so that precise intergenerational comparisons could be made. (Eighty percent of the wives interviewed in our study were married between the ages of nine and sixteen, inclusive, and within the next two to three years following our initial study, approximately 80% of their daughters would be in the same age cohort, thus providing the basis for such comparisons.)

Because we were interested in the interaction of families with institutions, in the hope of eventually facilitating feedback between the two, we based our sample primarily on families whose wives had been registered at one of the city's family-planning clinics. This clinic was part of an outpatient clinic attached to a hospital administered by the University of Isfahan. This procedure obviously biased our sample in favor of those who had formally attempted to use the contraceptive methods emphasized by the national family planning program through the clinic (primarily the oral pill, secondarily the IUD, with condoms also made available).

The homes of these clinic-users were found to be scattered fairly generally throughout Isfahan except in strongly middle class and upper class residential areas (see Gulick and Gulick 1974). We therefore supplemented this part of the sample with additional families biased in favor of people who had not (as far as we knew) patronized family planning clinics and who lived in two contrasting clusters, one in a new squatter settlement near the airport, the other in one of the oldest parts of the city near the Friday Mosque. The families in this latter cluster had already been surveyed by the Isfahan Communications Project (Lieberman et al. 1973) and found to be primarily people who had not used family-planning clinics.

These two clusters as such were selected in the hope that in the long-term longitudinal extension of the project, neighborhood behavior could be studied directly. We did not further augment our sample by additional families from middle-class and upper-class areas of the city because we wished to keep it predominantly a working-class sample, just as Isfahan as a whole is predominantly a working-class city. There are, nevertheless, a few middle-class people in our sample.

While the aggregation of people we studied does not constitute a "representative sample" in the strict, statistical sense of the term, it does constitute a credible microcosm of the city. Comparing our sample with the Isfahan census of 1966, we found that the relative frequencies of certain household types are essentially the same in both populations, as are the levels of education of the husbands and wives in our sample as compared to men and women in generally the same age ranges of the population at large (Gulick and Gulick 1974: Tables 12, 15).

The research method was a series of interviews with each family, conducted by men and women students of the University of Isfahan whom we trained, and with whom we worked very closely. Every interview (husbands by men students and wives by women students) was reported to, and discussed with, us as soon as possible after it was done, and there were regular, frequent group conferences. The interviewers used both formalized open-end questions and free-style "anthropological" field notes. In all, four separate structured interviews were designed. In addition to several interviews with each wife, nearly every husband was also interviewed. (Also done was a special child-rearing interview with a subsample of mothers selected so as to replicate as nearly as possible Prothro's 1960 child-rearing interviews with mothers in Lebanon.) The first Interview (1) was conducted in November 1970, and the last Interview (4) was completed in January 1972. In all, 175 families were studied in sufficient depth so as to provide the data-base for our analysis of household composition (Gulick and Gulick 1974). For various reasons, there was some attrition in the sample, and consequently the data-base for analysis of materials gathered in Interviews 2 and 3 is about 150 families.

Interview 4 was done between September 1971 and January 1972. Like Interview 3, it monitored significant events and changes in vital behavior that had taken place since the previous visit, and it also probed further into the matter of perceived influences from important relatives and neighbors in regard to family planning and contraceptive practice. During the conducting of Interview 4, applications for the funding of the extension of the project were under review. By January 1972, however, our funds were exhausted, and refunding was not forthcoming, so the interviewing was terminated at a point where Interview 4 had been done with sixty-nine of the families.

This article is based on information that was gathered on these sixty-nine families in our sample. These are the families on whom we have the most complete information in terms of coverage by the maximum number of interviews and longitudinal span (at least one year). "Accidental" though this subsample of sixty-nine may be, it constitutes 40 percent of our total sample, and we have not detected in it any serious distortions of phenomena evident evident to us in the entire sample.

SOME IMPORTANT ISSUES

The next section of this article will present and discuss certain characteristics of our sample of sixty-nine families arranged into three categories based on lengths of time elapsed since the most recent pregnancy. First, however, we will discuss in more general terms some of the phenomena with which we are concerned in order to make general problems and our purposes more explicit.

Education

It has been rather widely observed that there seems to be a direct correlation between the number of years the husband and/or wife has spent in school and the readiness or ability of the couple to limit the number of their offspring. The corollary of this association is, of course, that the less schooling people have had, the less they are able or willing to practice family planning. However, as everyone knows, a correlation does not imply a direct causal relationship, and clear-cut causal relationships between number of years spent in school and effective contraceptive practice have, as far as we know, yet to be conclusively demonstrated.

As far as Iran is concerned, it is, at this juncture, difficult to see any features of the formal educational process itself that might be directly responsible for increased readiness to practice contraception and family planning. Teaching and learning methods, from first grade through university, rely heavily on rote memorization, a process which is not conducive to developing the skills of independent and innovative thinking. As to particularly relevant curricular material (however it may be learned), population awareness materials are presented to only some secondary school students in certain courses. This means that whatever effectiveness such materials may have, they reach only a tiny portion of the population. In 1968, only 21 percent of males and 14 percent of females of eligible age were attending secondary schools (Nortman 1972: 24), only some of whom (in 1970-1971) were exposed to these population awareness materials.

Rather than the schooling experience itself, we think it is probably more likely that the general attitude of those parents who get their children into primary school in the first place (often an accomplishment both in terms of effort and money), and encourage them to stay there, is part of a subculture of planning and control of one's own destiny (including family planning). Getting one's children into secondary school is even more of an accomplishment. There is not enough room for all the children of eligible age even in cities like Isfahan, and the cost (even in the public, let alone the private, schools) is a major consideration for working-class people.

This is a subject that is well worth further study. Meanwhile, it does not follow that those who have had little or no education (such as, for instance, a large proportion of working class Iranians) will necessarily be uninterested in family planning, or unable to practice contraception. We have evidence quite to the contrary which will be presented in the next section.

Dropouts

"The biggest problem in the whole family planning program . . . is that a significant portion of women who accept the pill give it up after a while. Why?" (Family Planning Division 1971: 20). We do not have a comprehensive answer to this question, but we have paid close attention to those women in our sample who are "pill dropouts." As will be seen, the circumstances are varied and complicated, but not very mysterious.

There were 17 women in our sample of 69 who were registered as pill users at the family planning clinic, were taking the pill at the beginning of our study, and were still taking it at the end of our study (although some had stopped and then started again during the period of our study). There were 8 women who were registered as IUD users at the beginning and were still using the IUD at the end. There were 16 women who were registered at the clinic as pill users at the beginning of our study who were no longer pill users by the end of it; and there were 2 registered IUD users in the same category. We will have more to say about these "dropouts."

Here our purpose is simply to indicate in our small sample the relative magnitude of a phenomenon which is more usually encountered in impersonal and abstract calculations based only on clinic records. In order to account here for the rest of our sample, we will simply say at this point that at the end of our study there were 7 more women in our sample who were using either the pill or the IUD but who were not registered at the particular clinic that we used as our base; there were 10 more women whose husbands were regularly practicing coitus interruptus as their main means of contraception (one of these wives also took the pill from time to time); there was one primarily condom-using husband; and lastly there were 15 women who were, variously, pregnant, nursing, practicing no contraception, or abstaining from intercourse.

Varied and Alternative Methods of Contraception

Looking at our sample somewhat differently from the above (taking into account what the "dropouts" were doing, certain changes that took place during the study, and multiple practices), we can enumerate various contraceptive practices by married couples as of Interview 4:

Pill users	18
IUD users	10
Nursing for spacing	7
Condom users	8
Coitus interruptors	15
Pregnant	6
No contraception (several very recently delivered)	8
Abstinence	1
	—
Total	73

The total comes to 73 instead of 69 because 4 of the couples are double-counted. Three of the coitus interruptors are also counted as condom users, and the wife of another coitus interruptor is counted as one of the 18 pill users.

Carrying this matter of multiple or alternative contraceptive methods a little further, twenty-six women listed above, but NOT as pill users, had tried the pill at one time or another previously. Six women not listed above as IUD users had once used the IUD. Sixteen men not listed above as condom users had used it previously, and at least nine additional men had previously tried coitus interruptus.

The point that needs to be made here is this: our sample illustrates very clearly an aggregation of men and women who have tried a variety of ways of contraception and keep on trying.

Why do they keep on trying? Because many have difficulties, such as side effects or failures, yet continue to want to space their children farther apart if not to stop having children. Considering only those six women who were pregnant at the end of our study, the magnitude of the problem is evident. Of these women, only one wanted to become pregnant at that time. The other five attributed the pregnancy to contraceptive failure. Four of these five wanted to have more children eventually, but not at that time, while one did not want any more children. Four of these unwanted pregnancies were attributed to failure of coitus interruptus and the other to condom failure. Three additional pregnancies reported in Interview 4, that were unwanted and had already been terminated by abortion or miscarriage, were attributed to IUD failure, pill failure (because of side effects, she stopped taking the pill for twenty days, thinking the protection against pregnancy would last), and reliance on lactation as a contraceptive. The freer talk engendered by such campaigns as that of the Isfahan Communications Project, if it becomes established in ordinary behavior, could facilitate well-informed experimentation that might lessen such failures.

The family planning program, however, does not seem to be oriented toward adapting the fullest possible variety of methods of contraception to the needs of the greatest number of people, but rather it seems to be oriented toward adapting people, willy-nilly, to the oral pill and the IUD. A more flexible and variegated approach could well result in a greater number of permanently effective contraceptors, and far less concern about pill and IUD "dropouts." As we will show, while the pill and the IUD may have the advantage of being coitus-independent and reportedly the most effective, many women have troubles with them that do not simply "go away" after a while, and there are husbands, too, who are troubled by their wives' difficulties with these methods.

There are men who find the condom uncomfortable, in addition to its tendency to decrease the intensity of pleasure. But other men apparently do not have these difficulties with it, or at any rate are satisfied with it, and with this in mind, condom use should be maximized in all feasible ways. This is particularly true in view of the improved condoms that are now available or may be developed (Harvey 1972: 29-30).

One of the most neglected contraceptive methods, seemingly, is coitus interruptus. Kantner, referring generally (not specifically to Iran) says it is "the most tried method of them all" and then proceeds to say hardly anything more about it in his review of conventional contraceptive methods (1966: 405). Misra appears to assume that coitus interruptus is unreliable on some absolute scale (1967: 184), and therefore does not seem to question the judgment of the Chicago men studied that it is unreliable (1967: 270). Some men, to be sure, are ineffective in its use and/or are dissatisfied with it. Others use it successfully and with satisfaction. Continued reinforcement of the idea of its unreliability can only promote more unreliable performance, whereas there are many men who are ready and able to use it satisfactorily if they are properly informed. According to two other authorities, the effectiveness of coitus interruptus "has been traditionally underestimated by the medical profession" (Segal and Tietze 1971: 2). Whether the medical profession is really the most appropriate one to have so dominant a voice in family planning programs in Iran, or anywhere else, is a question we will not argue here.

Coitus interruptus has a somewhat sanctified status among those Muslims who are aware that the famous theologian, al-Ghazālī (A.D. 1058-1111), viewed it with favor. Kirk (1966: 575) refers to this fact in his article on Muslim natality but says nothing further about the practice. However, many Muslims would appear to be unaware of, or oblivious to, al-Ghazālī's endorsement, and many of them appear to be ignorant of the practice. Only 48 percent of the Isfahan men and women surveyed by the Isfahan Communications Project indicated that they knew about it (Lieberman et al. 1973: Table 7), and certainly some of the people in our sample seemed to be ignorant of it. Nevertheless, the use and knowledge of it is not negligible, and it constitutes a potential that could, with appropriate procedures, be utilized far more than it is. Coitus interruptus is seen by some of our informants as being less of an interference with God's will than the pill and the IUD.

Husband-Wife and Other Communication

We are urging the encouragement of experimentation with various methods of contraception (effectiveness and satisfaction being the objectives) rather than fixation on one or two merely for want of knowledge or through failure of communication. Such experimentation would put a premium on communication between husband and wife. Little is known about this in Iran, where, as in the Middle East generally, public communication between husband and wife is inhibited by various rules of decorum. Vieille (1967: 119) vividly, but in wholly general terms, portrays the lack of communication in private that prevents effective family planning. We do not know how general this lack of private communication may be. In our sample, we have evidence of both the absence and the presence of husband-wife agreement concerning contraception and family planning.

We also have a suggestion of the amount of husband-wife communication in the form of comparison of wives' perceptions of what their husbands think with what the husbands themselves say. In regard to ideal number of children, husbands' statements agree with wives' perceptions of husbands' feelings in thirty-five cases and disagree in only ten cases. Some of the implied agreements may be accidental, but many or most of them may well be the result of communication between husband and wife.

We think that it is often overlooked that the very beginning of the marriage is a crucially important time for maximum communication and experimentation. A number of informants explained the lack of use of contraception by saying that the couple in question had not been married very long and therefore did not need to practice contraception.

By the time that such couples may begin contraception, they may well have had more than their desired number of children. Many of our informants have experienced contraceptive failure — notably with withdrawal and the condom, but also with the pill and IUD. Good instruction would probably lessen the frequency of such failure, help couples attain desired spacing, and increase the feeling of control over eventual family size.

Some details from a specific case will illustrate some of the kinds of communication and noncommunication, as well as some of the considerations that are involved in these matters. Ashraf[1] was the wife in a nuclear family household with rooms in the house rented to unrelated people. At the time of Interview 3, Ashraf's sister, Sedigheh, was staying with her. Sedigheh had come from her village to Isfahan in order to get oral pills because she felt that all the people in her village thought that contraception was sinful.

During the interview, Zahra, a relative of the two sisters, dropped in for a visit. Ashraf and Sedigheh signaled to the interviewer not to ask any questions in front of Zahra, but Zahra nevertheless asked if the interviewer were from the Health Department. Ashraf said (inaccurately) yes, she was, and then said to Zahra, "Sedigheh and I are taking the pill. We did not tell you before because we were afraid that if something happened to us, you would say it was because we were taking the pill." To their surprise, Zahra was very happy to hear this and proceeded to ask questions about the pill. Zahra added, "I asked a *mulla* [religious teacher and authority] 'Is it all right to prevent? Do you yourself prevent?' He said that it is not a sin and that he has himself been preventing for about seven years. When I have my period, I will go to get the pill for sure. I wanted first to ask about the pill from a person who takes it herself."

Early Marriage of Women

The average age at marriage of the women in our sample was about fifteen years. We have heard comments that, in effect, this finding is "impossible." Iranian census figures suggest a higher average age, it is said; fifteen is the minimum ordinarily legal age of marriage for women in Iran (true), and therefore fifteen cannot be the average age

[1] These and all ensuing personal names that are used in this article for purposes of presentation are not the names of the people discussed, but they are common names among the people we studied.

of actual marriage, it is asserted. The latter reasoning is faulty because special permission to marry may be legally granted for girls of thirteen and fourteen; and, furthermore, it is known that the ages of engaged girls commonly are presented to the authorities as being higher than they actually are.

The reasons for this pressure for early marriage are not far to seek. Marriage as soon as possible after puberty relieves the girl's parents of their responsibilities for safeguarding her chastity and at the same time provides them either with the cash of the *mehriye* 'bridewealth' or the groom's family's obligation to pay it under certain conditions, which obligation in itself can be used advantageously in various ways. The longer a girl remains unmarried, the more intense become the parents' anxieties concerning the nonfulfillment of these matters.

Furthermore, in a culture where education is relatively expensive for most people, and where the meager educational and occupational opportunities, even though greater than they have been in the past (cf. Touba 1972), are still not sufficient to serve most of the girls and young women (18 percent of total female population literate; 44 percent of female population of primary school age in primary school [Nortman 1972: 24]), there is little else for them to do except either to get married as soon possible or to continue to incur expense for their parents by living at home, even though they may earn a little money sewing or carpet weaving.

We make this statement in full awareness that there are, for example, Iranian physicians and laboratory technicians who are women and many more highly educated Iranian women who hold professional positions. The fact remains, though, that such accomplshments are unusual except among young women who have the initial advantage of belonging to middle-class or upper-class families. These are relatively few. Consequently, the pressures for early marriage remain widespread and intense.

In regard to girls' marriages at the age of nine, and slightly older, a few of which will be enumerated later, only these are unusual, but not "impossible." The Shia Muslim wedding consists of two main parts which may be performed simultaneously or with a considerable interval between them. The first part is the closing of the marriage contract. This legally marries the couple and so enables, for example, a child-bride-designate of nine to move into the home of her husband-designate — or, by contrast, a woman medical student bride-designate to go out on dates *à deux* with her husband-designate — with no question asked. In neither case can the relationship be broken except by divorce, but in neither case, supposedly, is the marriage consummated until the second part of the wedding. This is the *arusi*, a party to which the bride is traditionally conveyed privately (while the guests and groom revel in feasting, music and dance) and thence to the bridal chamber where the marriage is consummated and close relatives are then reassured that the bride was a virgin. (Among some "Westernized" middle-or upper-class people, the two phases of the wedding may be combined into one affair which resembles a Western wedding ceremony in the home, immediately followed by the reception.) While forced intercourse, immediate flight, and subsequent divorce were recalled by one woman in our sample who had initially been married at nine, the traditional system does not automatically legitimize the bride's pre-pubertal involvement in sexual intercourse. Nor, on the other hand, do more recent laws prevent families from entering into marriage commitments well before the bride has attained the age of fifteen.

It is obvious that the earlier a woman marries, the longer she is exposed to pregnancy, and the more pregnancies she is likely to have. Early marriage is therefore generally acknowledged to be a contributory factor in the population problem. Our impression is that there is a tendency among observers of the Iranian population scene unduly to minimize early marriage. We have already touched upon some indications of this. We should now add our impression that there is a general assumption that early marriage is one of those archaic elements in the culture which "modernization" is steadily and rapidly eliminating, particularly in urban areas. In other words, there seems to be an idea that early marriage is no longer a problem to be reckoned with because it is somehow or other already well on the way to "correction."

Our findings suggest otherwise: that even among urban people, early marriage continues to be important because it continues to be linked to other aspects of the functioning value system of the people concerned. What the effects of raising the minimum legal age and attempting systematically to enforce the new rule would be, we do not precisely know, but it seems reasonable to guess that acute difficulties would ensue for many people, particularly if educational and occupational opportunities for teenage females were not greatly expanded at the same time.

Old-Age Support and Sex Preference

Desire for large numbers of children, in the hope that some will survive and be able to support their parents in their old age, is widely assumed, with good reason, to be a pro-natalistic factor in such countries as Iran. With decreased infant and child mortality, and perhaps with more opportunities for more lucrative occupations, the hope is that the pressure to produce large numbers of children will be reduced, at least in terms of this factor. Nevertheless, the desire for, or expectation of, support in old age by children has been shown in one study to be held by the vast majority of a sample of Isfahan men and women (Lieberman et al. 1973: Table 7). Our findings are more complex and not so one-sided, revealing as they do, the ambivalent feelings many people have, not only about the government (an alternative source of old-age support), but also about what they can expect from their closest relatives.

While our findings are consistent with the common generalization that Iranian parents say they prefer boys, the social and emotional pressures on them to produce a maximum number of boys in order to insure support in old age, does not seem to be quite so clear-cut as might be expected. Wives mention the expectation of support by sons more often than do husbands. Husbands are more likely than wives to mention the government as a preferred source of old-age support, possibly because it is on themselves as sons, traditionally, that the expected obligation has fallen more heavily. The prospect of government support is something entirely new, the prospect at present being considerably more than the reality.

The Web of Kinship

One of the posters that has been used by the Family Planning Division of Iranian Ministry of Health shows two vivid scenes. The caption for one of them says, in effect, more well-being through family planning, and the picture is of a happy mother, father, and two children (boy and girl), all dressed in completely Western clothes in a completely Western living room (upholstered chair and sofa, television, picture on the wall, coffee table, book, and magazine). The other scene's caption says, "the more children, the less well-being," and it shows a husband and wife and seven children (plus baby in cradle), all with expressions of agonized rage or despair, the furniture (bedding rolled against the wall) and the patched clothing all being completely traditional in style. Doubtless many clinic patients seeing this poster could identify their aspirations with the first picture and their reality, at least at times, with the second. But a further reality of Iranian family life is missing from both scenes, and it is important. Another poster shows happy mother, father, and young son bending lovingly over a happy baby of indeterminate sex. "Fewer children, more well-being," says the caption. Here, too, something is missing.

A third poster was designed, after having been pre-tested, by the Isfahan Communications Project (Lieberman et al. 1973: 86–87). It was printed on paper and cardboard and posted all over the city of Isfahan, and it was printed on cloth banners that were hung from the lamp posts along the great Chahar Bagh Avenue and in all the major traffic intersections of the city — all of this during the period of our study. The caption, which is a rhyming and metered couplet, says, "Two or three children are better. The loop and the pill are harmless." The picture shows a woman physician (holding aloft in one hand a cycle of pills and in the other a Lippe's loop) smiling at a father, mother, son and daughter, all in Western-style clothes except that the wife is also wearing a *chador* (the head-to-heels open-fronted traditional gown that is worn in public by most women in Isfahan). Again, something is still missing.

What is missing from all these posters is any indication that "the family" consists of anything more than husband, wife, and immature children — the "independent nuclear family." Contrary to such an image as this, we have abundant evidence that though a majority of families live in nuclear family households, most of them are at the same time in constant and complex interaction with their extended families. The influences of these relatives in regard to family planning and contraception will be discussed later.

In analyzing the household types in which the people in our total sample lived, we were able to divide them into eight different domestic arrangements. These were:

1. Single nuclear family alone in its own house-compound.

2. Single nuclear family in same house-compound with unrelated individuals and/or families. The single nuclear families in these circumstances we call "simple households."

3. Simple household plus noncommensal relatives (relatives who do not regularly eat with the referent family) in the same house-compound.

4. Simple household plus noncommensal relatives and unrelated persons in the same house-compound.

5. Complex household alone (at least one nuclear family plus other related individuals or related nuclear families all eating together).

6. Complex household with no other related persons but with other unrelated persons in the same house-compound.

7. Complex household with other related (but noncommensal) persons in the same house-compound.

8. Complex household with other related and unrelated individuals or families in the same house-compound.

Table 1 collapses these eight arrangements into three household/compound types: I (1-2) Simple household alone and with unrelated persons in the same compound; II (3-4) Simple household and noncommensal relatives, with and without unrelated persons in the same household compound; and III (5-8) Complex household with and without relatives and/or unrelated persons in the same compound. Household/compound Type I obviously most closely resembles the "independent nuclear family." Household/compound Types II and III obviously involve various arrangements of nuclear families in very close domestic quarters with other relatives and, in many cases, with unrelated persons, too.

Table 1. Household/compound type by years married

Years married (beginning of study)	Household/compound type						
	I		II		III		
	N	Percent	N	Percent	N	Percent	Total
1– 2	2	25.00	4	50.00	2	25.00	8
3– 4	1	25.00	1	25.00	2	50.00	4
5– 6	1	33.33	0	0.00	2	66.67	3
7– 8	1	14.29	4	57.14	2	28.57	7
9–10	8	57.14	6	42.86	0	0.00	14
11–13	4	50.00	3	37.50	1	12.50	8
14–16	3	50.00	3	50.00	0	0.00	6
17–19	5	55.55	1	11.11	3	33.33	9
20–22	1	33.33	2	66.67	0	0.00	3
23–31	4	57.14	0	0.00	3	42.86	7
Total	30	43.48	24	34.78	15	21.74	69

Note: The frequencies and percentages of these three types in our larger sample are: I (77, 44.51 percent); II (60, 34.68 percent); III (36, 20.74 percent). The total of these frequencies is 173 instead of 175 because we could not get length-of-marriage information from two families.

Table 1 arranges the sixty-nine married couples in our sample according to their length of marriage and the household/compound type to which they belong. It can be seen from this table that, regardless of length of marriage, the married couples in our sample to a very considerable extent live closely and constantly in touch with other relatives. These other relatives are, particularly, husband's sister, husband's mother and/or father, husband's brothers with or without wives and

children; less often wife's parents and/or siblings; or, as they grow older, their own married daughters or sons and spouses. There seems to
be a slight tendency for relatively recently married couples to live with
relatives somewhat more frequently than do longer married couples,
but the tendency is only moderate. The important point is that these are
people who, for the most part, are immersed in relatives, people whose
"typical family" situation is very different from the "independent nuclear family" of the industrial West or of the family-planning program's
posters. Not only are the Type II and III household/compounds very numerous, but the members of the Type I household/compounds, too, are
immersed in relatives even if they may not be living in quite such close
quarters. All but two of the sixty-nine families in our sample see at least
one relative at daily to weekly frequencies. The exceptions are two
simple households one of which denied seeing any relatives because
of their poverty, and the other in which both the husband and wife
came from the city of Yazd where all their relatives still live.

ANALYSIS

Recency of Pregnancy

For the purpose of analyzing our sample, we have divided the families
into three categories defined in terms of amount of elapsed time since
the most recent pregnancy. It seems to us that this categorization has
saliency, since ultimately, if not in this study, the effectiveness of family planning will be measured by the numbers of offspring that are produced over given periods of time. The categories are as follows:
CATEGORY A (24 cases)   The wife was pregnant at some point during
the year immediately preceding the END of our field research. In other
words Category A includes women who gave birth, miscarried or
aborted, or became pregnant, during the period of our field research.
It happens that women in our sample who became pregnant during
this period, did so during the family planning mass media campaign
of the Isfahan Communications Project.
CATEGORY B (27 cases)   The wife was not pregnant for one year preceding the end of our field research, but she had been pregnant at
some point during the period of anything more than one full year to
anything less than three full years before the end of our field research.
CATEGORY C (18 cases)   The wife had not been pregnant for at least
three full years since before the end of our field work. However, seven-

teen of these wives had been pregnant during the period of anything more than three years to anything less than six full years before the end of our field work. One wife had not been pregnant for sixteen to seventeen years, her husband having successfully used the condom for fifteen years before she decided to try the oral pill. The Category C wives had not been pregnant since the national family planning program had come into effect.

We shall devote most of our detailed analyses to Categories A and C. First, however, we will present some tables that exhibit various kinds of easily quantifiable information on each category. These tables will, within the limits of their data, describe the people in the categories in comparison. We will discuss only a few of the data in the tables and will certainly not attempt to explain or account for all of them. Readers are, of course, most welcome to draw their own conclusions or raise their own questions.

Marriage Age and Duration

The age at marriage and length of marriage averages shown in Table 2 do not convey any idea of certain extremes of difference in age between husband and wife or of the fact that Category A includes five couples who have been married only two to three years (in contrast to three in B and none in C), which tends to pull down A's overall average. Three Category B wives were married at nine to eleven years of age, as opposed to none in A and two in C. With only three exceptions, the maximum husband's age at marriage was thirty-one to thirty-two years in all three categories.

Table 2. Mean ages at marriage and lengths of marriage, by recency of last pregnancy

| | Category A | | Category B | | Category C | |
	Mean	Range	Mean	Range	Mean	Range
Age at marriage (in years)						
Wife	15.42	12–20	13.85	9–17	15.67	10–25
Husband	22.96	20–31	23.46	17–32	24.44	20–32
Length of marriage (end of study)	10.13	2–25	13.63	2–28	15.50	4–27

Note: We excluded from our calculations one man in B and two in C who had been married at forty-three to forty-five. We excluded from our calculations one woman in B whose current marriage is her second, which she entered into at the age of thirty-two.

Ideal and Actual Numbers of Boys and Girls

The excess of boys over girls in Categories A and B, shown in Table 3, both real and ideal, is consistent with general demographic findings in Iran, as well as with our own findings from our total sample. Unfortunately, we are not able to elucidate it, although we might just mention that thirteen babies were born to the sixty-nine couples during the period of our study, nine of them girls and four of them boys.

However, there is one very important point that will be detailed later on, and this is that desire for girls IS a factor in motivation for pregnancy, despite what general figures (ours included) seem to show, and despite the widely held assumption that desire for boys is the only sex-preference that has to be taken into account as far as the population problem is concerned.

Table 3. Mean number of outcomes of pregnancy per couple and ideal number of children, by recency of last pregnancy

	Category A	Category B	Category C
Total pregnancies	5.29	6.08	5.56
Total prenatal deaths	1.38	1.12	0.39
Total child deaths	0.75	0.65	1.00
Living children			
Boys	1.88	2.50	2.06
Girls	1.29	1.81	2.11
Total living children	3.17	4.31	4.17
Wives' ideal number of children			
Boys	2.22	2.20	1.81
Girls	1.61	1.56	1.88
Total	3.83	3.76	3.69
Husbands' ideal number of children			
Boys	1.92	1.86	1.69
Girls	1.54	1.43	1.38
Total	3.46	3.29	3.07

The husbands consistently expressed a lower ideal number of boys and girls than the wives. In their comments, they more often than the wives mentioned the financial problems of supporting children as a reason for not having too many, or for saying they had enough already. More husbands than wives would not express any SEX preference, but rather simply gave a total desired number (about the same as the calculated averages shown in the table). Several said that the sexes of their children did not matter or that whatever happened was "up to God." Two husbands said that if they had enough money, they would

like ten or twenty children, but otherwise there was very little reproductive braggadocio in the husbands' remarks.

It is possible that the wives' consistently higher ideal numbers of
children are a reflection of the women's heavy dependence on child
bearing for social prestige.

Both husbands and wives mention the difficulty of disciplining large
numbers of children as being a reason for having relatively few. However, it is clear that four or five children, or putting the limit at four
is seen as "few" rather than "many."

Our average figures on ideal number of children mask an apparent
rationale which could have considerable importance for family planning. Very frequently, both husbands and wives said that they wanted
two boys and two girls, the reason being that a child of one sex should
have a companion sibling of the same sex. In Middle Eastern cultures,
including Iran's, intra-sex companionship and support is particularly
important for both sexes.

The adjustments that people make in their thinking about ideal
number of children in the face of real outcomes is illustrated by five
cases from Category A. Mrs. 202 had two sons and no daughters and
said she did not want any more children, though her husband said he
would like to have a daughter.[2] Mrs. 213 had two sons and no
daughters and said her ideal number was two sons and one daughter.
The same was true of Mrs. 214 whose husband said that it would be
nice to have a daughter but that two children were enough. Mr. and
Mrs. 501 had five sons and no daughters. They both gave their ideal
as five sons and one daughter.

Mrs. 319 had one five-year-old son and was pregnant at Interview
2. Her mother-in-law (who had had eleven pregnancies but had only
two living children) was urging her to have more for fear of losing
some. However, the mother-in-law was ambivalent about large numbers of children. Her other living child, a daughter, she married off at
the age of nine; this daughter first became pregnant at twelve and had
given birth every year for five years owing to the fact that her husband
was reported to be too selfish to use the condom or other contraceptive
method.

Mrs. 319's father-in-law recommended two boys and two girls so
that each sex would have a sibling of the same sex. Mrs. 319's ideal
number at Interview 2 was four children, two boys and two girls. She

[2] This and all ensuing case numbers are code numbers assigned for the purpose
of analysis. They are not the same as the code numbers that many of the women
in our sample had been given by the family planning clinic.

said that if she should have three sons in a row, she would not get pregnant any more because the fourth child might be a girl, and if that happened, she would have to get pregnant a fifth time in the hopes of providing the girl with a sister. Mrs. 319 had four married sisters, all with children and all using some kind of contraception.

By Interview 3, Mrs. 319 had given birth to a girl. With a boy and a girl, she now had mixed feelings. Her husband would like another boy and another girl (for the reasons already mentioned), but she felt two children were enough. By Interview 4, (five months later), Mrs. 319 said that her husband still wanted a male sibling for his son but was not insisting on a sister for his daughter.

Table 4.   Spacing of children in mean number of years between each event, by recency of last pregnancy

	Category A	Category B	Category C
Ideal spacing			
Wife's minimum	4.86	5.44	4.79
Wife's maximum	6.48	5.96	6.71
Husband's minimum	3.64	3.81	5.56
Husband's maximum	4.29	4.00	6.11
Actual spacing			
Pregnancy	1.91	2.31	2.79
Live Birth	2.59	2.83	3.00

Spacing

In Table 4, a crucial question obviously is why the ideal spacing diverges so much from the actual. If the ideal of the women, especially, were to be realized, the population problem would eventually be greatly mitigated. A frequent type of comment on our inquiries was that a good time for the next child would be when the existing youngest one was old enough to go to school. In Iran, those children who enter first grade do so usually at the age of seven, and ideal spacings of five, six, and seven years were very frequently mentioned. This is another rationale, rooted in the culture, that might be capitalized upon in motivational efforts. A major difficulty, of course, that has already been alluded to, is the doubtful prospect for even primary school education for the children of many of the people we studied.

Two-year spacing because of the mother's nursing for two years was another repeated response. Expressions both of faith and of doubt in the efficacy of lactation in preventing pregnancy were forthcoming from our sample. The subject should not be brushed aside by those professionals in family planning programs who know that "OF COURSE lactation is not a certain preventer of conception." Rather, the problem and the probabilities should be discussed as such. One wife said she knew it didn't work for everyone, but that it had so far been effective for her.

Education

Table 5 shows the educational level of the husbands and wives in each of the categories. Most of the husbands and wives in our sample are uneducated, or educated only a little, and most of them are practicing some sort of contraception (chiefly pill, coitus interruptus, IUD, and condom). The exceptionally well-educated people among them (twenty-one men and women representing fifteen different married couples) exhibit the full variety of contraceptive behavior except for nursing-for-spacing. Three of the wives were pregnant (one an unwanted pregnancy because it occurred too soon for the parents' liking). Two couples were not practicing contraception at Interview 4, including one case in which the wife had given birth only twenty days before the interview. Two husbands were using the condom, and two others were interruptors; four wives were using the IUD, and two were taking the oral pill.

Table 5. Wives' and husbands' schooling, by recency of last pregnancy

	Category A		Category B		Category C	
	N	Percent	N	Percent	N	Percent
Wives
Uneducated	10	41.67	21	77.78	11	61.11
A little	4	16.67	3	11.11	2	11.11
Completed primary	6	25.00	2	7.41	1	5.56
Secondary	4	16.67	1	3.70	3	16.67
University	0	0.00	0	0.00	1	5.56
	24	100.00	27	100.00	18	100.00
Husbands
Uneducated	7	29.17	12	44.44	7	38.89
A little	5	20.83	6	22.22	6	33.33
Completed primary	6	25.00	6	22.22	2	11.11
Secondary	6	25.00	2	7.41	1	5.56
University	0	0.00	1	3.70	2	11.11
	24	100.00	27	100.00	18	100.00

Middle-class people in our sample, indicated by secondary or university education and types of occupation (not discussed here), seem to be somewhat more successful than many working class people in spacing, but their reproductive goals (expressed in terms of ideal number of children) do not appear to be any less than those of working class people.

Household/Compounds and Fertility

Table 6 shows the couples, by category, divided according to the type of household/compound in which they live. Not only were most of the couples (except in Category C) living in very close quarters with other relatives (Types II and III), but data not shown in Table 6 show that most of those living in simple households are also in very frequent contact with relatives.

Table 6. Household/compound types, by recency of last pregnancy

Types		Category A		Category B		Category C	
		N	Percent	N	Percent	N	Percent
IA	Simple alone	4	16.67	6	22.22	7	38.89
IB	Simple with unrelated	5	20.83	5	18.52	3	16.67
II	Simple plus related non-commensal	9	37.50	11	40.74	4	22.22
III	Complex	6	25.00	5	18.52	4	22.22
		24	100.00	27	100.00	18	100.00

The apparent differences among Categories A, B, and C suggest the slight tendency (already mentioned earlier) for simple households to be more frequent among people who have been married longer, but this should not be overemphasized. Among the longer-married couples in our sample, there are several cases of newly-married children moving into the homes of their parents, resulting in new Type II or Type III household/compounds.

Furthermore, there were numerous other structural changes in household/compound composition during the period of our field research, which either directly changed the "type" (according to our definitions) or potentially did so. Some examples: newly-married child either moving out (simple household tendency) of bringing his/her spouse in (complex household tendency); erstwhile Type I household moving back into the household of the husband's parents — an incompatible husband's sister having moved out of the parents' household; husband's mother moving in with her son and daughter-in-law; and others.

In all, there were, during the one short year of our study, three households in Category A, eight in Category B, and five in Category C that experienced such structural changes. There is obviously a continuous process of shifts and moves. Whether there is more intentional steadiness in some families than in others, we do not know as far as our sample is concerned. One element in what we are dealing with is the domestic "developmental cycle" that has been given some attention by Goody (1962) and others. The subject is intrinsically difficult to study, and it needs much more investigation. We wish to take it as much as possible into account but at the same time be cautious about drawing unwarranted conclusions.

Nag's (1967) pioneering work on fertility rates and household composition has raised some intriguing questions, as have other studies on the same general subject yielding somewhat different results (Burch and Gendell 1971). In this connection, we will examine the households in Category A in more detail. We feel that this category is more appropriate for such examination than the other two. The people in Category A were currently begetting and giving birth at the time of study and in the household arrangements observed. Owing to greater elapsed time since last pregnancy, and owing to structural changes whose actual magnitude through time has surely been far greater than the number that occurred during the course of our study, examination of categories B and C would, we feel, only yield frustrating ambiguities.

We do not, as Nag did, have information on frequency of coitus. For various reasons, we did not think that asking questions about it would be appropriate, and we were not confident of getting reliable answers if we did ask. (A woman physician, who undertook such an investigation among Isfahan women clinic patients in a project under John Gulick's direction, felt that she could not correct for the women's misrepresenting the facts, there being reasons, compatible with Iranian cultural patterns, for both their exaggerating and minimizing frequency.) In this connection, we need to mention a surmise which might be worth investigating in some other studies.

Discussions such as Kirk's leave the reader with a plausible but wholly unsubstantiated impression that Muslim husbands and wives are very active sexually (1966: 570, 574). Perhaps this should be examined a little more critically. We have in our total sample several instances in which the wife said that her current means of contraception was "sleeping apart" from her husband. Suggestions that intercourse may be distasteful to some wives — possibly because of having been traumatized by too early experience — occur here and there. Our surmise is that maybe one element in the pill and IUD dropout rate is that use of these methods deprives the wife of the opportunity to avoid intercourse on the grounds of fear of becoming pregnant.

Crowdedness, Privacy, and Desire for Children

Table 7 presents another type of information that is pertinent to the general subject of household composition and fertility behavior.

Table 7. Category A: Space perception, by household/compound type, and by number of pregnancies

N	Household/compound type							
	IA		IB		II		III	
Preg-nancies	Husband	Wife	Husband	Wife	Husband	Wife	Husband	Wife
1					C*	C*		
2			S	S	C*	C*	C*	S*, C*, S*
3			S	C	C*, C	S*, S	–	C*
4	S	C			–	S*	S	S
5	S	S			C*	C*		
6	S	C	S	S				
7					C	C		
8	C	C						
11			–	C				
12			S	–				
13					–	S*		
14							–	C

Note: C = perceived as being crowded
 S = perceived as having enough space
 * = parents living in same compound

The husbands, who generally spend little time at home, tend to be satisfied with the amount of living space if they are not living in the same compound with relatives. Their wives, who spend a very large amount of their time in the compound, in more cases do feel crowded (spatially crowded or emotionally enclosed?). When we look at household/compound Type II in Table 7, the perception of crowdedness appears to be considerably more frequent among the husbands. How much of the perception of crowding is due to what is felt to be insufficient physical space and how much of it is due to what is felt to be intrusive personalities? We do not know, but the two factors, often intertwined, are crucial in the whole question of crowdedness and density.

Only one of the couples living in Type IA wants more children, this being the couple that has both the fewest children and the fewest pregnancies. Three of the five wives living in Type IB want more children. One of these feels crowded with one son and one daughter but says she wants five of each. Her husband, who does not feel crowded, says a total of three children would suit him. One of the other two wives says she and her husband want a daughter; they have five sons. The other wife has two daughters and wants to try for a son. Her husband says two are enough. Neither of these two couples feels crowded.

Of the five couples living in Type II who want more children, all of the husbands and three of the wives feel crowded. Each of these five couples has only one or two children (although one wife has had seven pregnancies). Three of the couples live with the husband's parents, and two of these wives feel crowded. Although she feels crowded, one pregnant wife, who has one son, wants to have two sons and two daughters. She reports that her mother-in-law wants her to stop at one of each, so perhaps this mother-in-law feels more crowded than she does. The other two mothers-in-law are reported as wanting many grandchildren. This could be one of the influences that may override whatever inhibition feeling crowded in the same house with relatives may have on the desire for more children.

Four of the six wives living in Type III, and all with husbands' parents, say they want more children, although one is not so sure after the birth of a daughter which gave her one of each sex. She does not feel crowded in regard to living space and reports that her mother-in-law wants her to have seven boys and three girls. Her own mother, on the other hand, reportedly thinks her present two children are enough. Only one of these four wives has a mother-in-law who prefers only a few children. (In fact, this mother-in-law takes the pill herself.) In this case, the situation is felt to be so crowded that they want an elderly relative living with them to move out and live with her son. However, during the course of our study, they could not bring themselves to push her out. The wife in this couple was pregnant (condom failure) at Interview 4 and had tried unsuccessfully to get an abortion because, though she wants a daughter, she had wanted to wait until her two young sons were of school age.

Feeling crowded in the presence of relatives may or may not be connected with a feeling of lack of privacy. Families in our sample living in multiple-household compounds generally share the courtyard, the toilet, the water tap or pool, and one door opening on the street, but they generally sleep in separate rooms per nuclear family. Under such conditions, couples must have sexual intercourse in the presence of their children. We do not know anything about what inhibiting influence this may have. However, even if it has little, the presence of other relatives in the compound — where there is constant, unavoidable interaction — may have an inhibiting influence. For example, since it is obligatory for Shia Muslim men and women to perform ablutions after (usually the morning after) having had intercourse, any suspect drawing of water or leaving the house in order to go to the public bath (*hamman*) may invite questions or comments. In fact, we were told that "I am going to the bath this morning" is often intended and understood as a euphemism for "I had intercourse last night," and that the frequency of such statements, exchanged, for example, by the wives of brothers living in the same house, may be an element in their competition in asserting their attractiveness and security in relation to their husbands.

Details from another particular case will illustrate some of the points we have been making. Masumeh, who had been pregnant fourteen times and has nine living children, was interviewed one day in the presence of her eldest child, a daughter, Soghra. Soghra, aged sixteen, had been married at the age of twelve to a cousin whose family had been insistent, and she had not tried contraception because it was felt by various relatives to be unnecessary since she was so young and newly married. At fifteen, Soghra found herself pregnant. Masumeh and her husband had tried "sleeping apart" as a means of prevention after their fifth child, and at one point, she decided she did not need to take the pill because she was nursing. She was reluctant to use the IUD and feared that the sutures resulting from tubal ligation would open up when she was working. At Interview 2, Masumeh had been asked if she wanted any more children. She said no, definitely not. However, she added a comment about Batoul, her husband's brother's wife who lived nearby and had seven children: "Batoul SAYS she does not want any more children, but she and her husband really do, and they go to the bath every morning." At Interview 4, Soghra, who had had a stillbirth in the interim, was present. Masumeh mentioned her fear of tubal ligation and said that she and her husband were now sleeping apart; and Soghra said, teasingly, "She is lying."

Whether the presence of unrelated neighbors in the same house has the same impact as the presence of relatives in regard to the sense of crowdedness or lack of privacy, we do not know. We do know that there is considerable knowledge of what contraceptive practices these neighbors may or may not be using, of whether they are pregnant or not, and so on. One woman, asked at Interview 4 whether any of the neighbors had become pregnant, said, "I don't know. I've had a fight with them, and we have not been speaking to one another for a week." The implication is that ordinarily she would be keeping up with their condition on a day-to-day basis.

Another case is from Category B, illustrating a concatenation of factors related to crowdedness, relatives, household/compound type, and fertility behavior. Mrs. 129 has four boys but no girls, yet her ideal is two boys and two girls. Her mother-in-law is a pro-natalist, "the more boys the better." Mrs. 129 says that if she were to have more children, it would be troublesome for neighbors living in the same house, although if those neighbors are relatives they will not say so. Her neighbors in the same house are in fact her parents-in-law and two brothers-in-law and their wives and children. Asked if she would want to have more children if she and her husband moved out and set themselves up as a simple household, Mrs. 129 said no.

Commenting generally on Categories B and C, the data are similar to those in Category A in that those who say they want more children are primarily living in the same house with other relatives (rather than in simple households) and are primarily people who have relatively few children. Their perceptions of crowdedness are varied and, over all, inconclusive.

The last three tables in this article enumerate the contraceptive practices at Interview 4 of wives who want to have more children (Table 8), wives who do not want to have more children (Table 9), and wives about whom it is particularly questionable whether they want more children or not (Table 10).

First we will discuss Table 8. This discussion will be followed by a more detailed discussion of the five families in Category C who appear in Table 8. These are possibly the most effective family planners in our sample. The wives say that they do want more children, but they have avoided pregnancy for several years.

Then we will discuss Table 9. Our discussion will include detailed consideration of a number of couples, with particular emphasis on those factors that may influence the wives (all of whom say they do not want any more children) one way or the other as far as any future pregnancies are concerned. The range of number of actual children is from exactly the same as the stated ideal (usually no more than four) to six children more than the stated "good number of children to have." Among some of these couples, our judgment is that the chances look good for no future pregnancies. In other cases, they do not. We will elucidate as best we can what we consider to be the influences which may tip the balance one way or the other.

Table 10 will be discussed briefly at the end of this section of the article.

Women Who Want More Children

There are ten couples indicated in Table 8 who have no daughters. They all have from one to five sons each, mostly one or two sons. All of these wives say that they want a daughter, eight of them saying that they want only a daughter, but two of them saying they want a son also. These two wives have one son each, and the stated ideal of both is two sons and two daughters.

Four of the wives who have no daughters are pregnant, and two of these volunteered the information that they had considered abortion because they do not want pregnancy at this time. Both had earlier stopped taking the pill because of side effects.

One of the wives who have no daughters is nursing and believes that lactation has contraceptive effectiveness; one is using no contraceptive at all; and the husband of one is practicing coitus interruptus.

Only three of these wives are using what are currently widely considered the most effective contraceptives, namely the pill and the IUD. Two of these wives are among the very few highly educated people in our sample. Mrs. 227 uses the IUD. Although her mother fears that the IUD may be harmful, Mrs. 227 brushes these fears aside. The IUD has not troubled her. She reports that her husband wants no more children at all, and she herself does not want a daughter for ten or fifteen years. She says that she does not like girls at all but wants one so as to be able to dress her up nicely and make her pretty. Otherwise, she says, girls are too much of a headache. "If my daughter doesn't obey, I will become angry. If a son does not obey, it is all right because he will become a man and men are selfish and don't listen to anybody and should not be meek." (Elsewhere in the same interview she said that her husband had been brought up very well and that he was wonderful.) One of the pill users believes in close spacing of children, but says that she wants to finish her undergraduate studies at the university before having a second child. The other pill user has three sons already. Neither pill user reports discomfort from side effects.

Five of the couples indicated in Table 8 have no sons, and all of the wives say they want sons, two of them saying that they want daughters also (the ideal of these two being two boys and two girls). One of these wives is nursing, one is using no contraception, one husband is using the condom, and two husbands are practicing coitus interruptus.

Eight of the couples indicated in Table 8 have, in various ways, not reached the goals stated by the wives as being their ideal number of children. Mrs. 402 says she wants five boys and five girls; she has one of each, and is nursing. Her husband says he thinks two children are sufficient, and he certainly wants no more than three. Mrs. 430 wants two boys and one girl, has one of each, and is pregnant.

Table 8. Wives who want more children: category and type of desire for more children, by type of contraceptive practice

	Pregnant	Nursing	None	Coitus interruptus	Condom	IUD	Pill	Total
Category A								
Has no daughter	4		1					5
Has no son		1	1		1			3
Ideal not reached	1	1			1			3
Category B								
Has no daughter		1				1	1	3
Has no son				1				1
Ideal not reached		1		2			1	4
Category C								
Has no daughter				1			1	2
Has no son				1				1
Pro-children							1	1
Ideal not reached							1	1
Total	5	4	2	5	2	1	5	24

Mrs. 112 originally said she wanted one of each, that being exactly what she had at the time, having recently given birth. Her mother and father do not want her to have more children, fearing for her health, as she had previously had several pregnancies that ended in miscarriage or child death. However, Mr. 112 wants two boys and two girls (so that each sex will have a sibling of the same sex), but he believes in spacing, and is using the condom. (He also said at one point that twenty children would be all right provided there were enough money to support them). Mrs. 112's father once argued with Mr.

112 that he had only one daughter and did not want to lose her. Toward the end of the study period, Mrs. 112 said that she wanted two boys and two girls, evidently having brought her own goals into line with her husband's.

Mrs. 407 wants eight boys and two girls; she has three boys and one girl and is nursing. Mr. 407 thinks six children a good total, but his wife reports that he is worried about the expense and told her to marry another husband if she wants six more. Mrs. 418 wants two boys and two girls, has one of each, and her husband is a coitus interruptor. Mrs. 255 wants two boys and two girls, has one boy and two girls, and is taking the pill. Mrs. 401's ideal is two boys and two girls, but she actually has three boys and one girl. She has her ideal total number of four children but has not provided a sister for her daughter; Mr. 401 is practicing coitus interruptus. Mrs. 204 wants two boys and two girls; she has one of each and is taking the pill.

Mrs. 200 is indicated in Table 8 as being "pro-children." She does not state an ideal number of children but simply says that she wants two or three more than what she has, which is three boys and one girl. Mr. 200 says that his ideal is one boy and one girl. Mrs. 200 is taking the pill.

Of the five families in Category C who appear in Table 8, three are using the pill, and two are practicing coitus interruptus. The wives of the latter two had tried the pill but stopped because of side effects. All five couples had tried at least two methods of contraception. Two of the husbands want no more children at all. Two wives reported four abortions of unintended pregnancies, one due to nursing failure and the others to condom failure. These were two of the three highly educated women in this group of five. (Although the cost of a safe abortion was not mentioned by them, it was by others in our sample for whom the expense probably was proportionately much greater.)

All five of these cases in Category C are borderline between being placed in Category C or in Category B, and it might be useful to look at each case closely for the factors which might or might not tip the balance toward pregnancy in the near future. Mrs. 110 and Mrs. 226 stated seven years and five years, respectively, to be a good (minimum) space between children. Mrs. 132, Mrs. 200, and Mrs. 204 all spoke of two years between children but have avoided pregnancy for longer than that.

Mrs. 132 is the university student mentioned earlier. Her reason for delaying a second pregnancy has already been mentioned as being her desire to finish college first. Her eventual goal is a daughter as well as a son; Mr. 132 thinks four children a good number but prefers to stop at three. Mrs. 132 reports agreement with her parents on the use of contraception and the limiting of her children to two. She has not discussed contraception with her parents-in-law, but she says they want her to limit to three children. No contraception was tried before her first pregnancy, which occurred immediately after her marriage at age twenty, but they have since tried condom, rhythm, coitus interruptus, and pill. On the pill for about two years, Mrs. 132 has not found side effects to be a problem. Mrs. 132 reported at an early interview that she felt crowded (in five rooms); Mr. 132, at the next interview, reported enough space in the house into which they had recently moved.

Mr. and Mrs. 200 also moved during the course of our study from the house of Mrs. 200's incompatible cousin (who was taking the pill also) to a house with unrelated neighbors. However, they continued to feel crowded because in each house they had only one room for themselves and their three sons and one daughter, ages fourteen to four. They had trouble renting a room (they cannot afford more) because of the number of their children, but Mrs. 200 hopes (unrealistically in view of their poverty) for a house to themselves so that they can have more space and two or three more children. Mr. 200 wants no more children, began practicing coitus interruptus after their second child, and continued for eleven years with that and sometimes the condom. Married at the late age of twenty-five, Mrs. 200 reported six pregnancies, six live births, and two infant deaths in fourteen years of marriage. While at the clinic for other treatment, she was told about the pill and, with encouragement from her husband, began taking it when her youngest (her daughter) was about two and a half years old. Mrs. 200 has various physical complaints, some of which she attributes to the pill. She says that the new neighbors tell her the pill causes sickness. At least twice during our study, Mrs. 200 spoke of not taking the pill for one month. Mr. 200 tells her to get an IUD if she stops taking the pill. Throughout the interviews, Mrs. 200 speaks of getting well and then getting pregnant again.

Both Mrs. 200's parents and her parents-in-law are dead. Mrs. 200 was orphaned at five years, at which time all of the many children her mother had borne were also dead. She was raised by an aunt until she was considered old enough to work in people's houses. Uneducated themselves, Mr. and Mrs. 200 have hopes for the education of at least the two younger children. The fifteen- and eleven-year-old sons are already out of school, after fourth and second grades, earning a little money to pay for some of their expenses. With all of the reasons Mrs. 200 has for not becoming pregnant again (ill health, poverty, crowdedness, her husband's wishes), it is difficult to guess her motivation for wanting more children. Loneliness in her childhood? Bearing children as the justification for a woman's existence? Future help? She hopes sons will help if they can, but foresees the possibility of daughters-in-law refusing to welcome Mr. and Mrs. 200, in their old age, living with them.

Mr. and Mrs. 204 have one daughter and one son, and both want two and two. Mrs. 204 is living with her husband's mother, his divorced sister, his married brother and family, none of whom has much (if any) education. Living with relatives probably enabled Mrs. 204 to leave her young daughter and son at home while she continued her studies in order to complete her secondary school education. Married seven years previously at eighteen while her older sister was in college, Mrs. 204 is ambitious to train herself for the kind of work which, among other things, will enable her to be independent of help from her children in later years. By Interview 4, she had her diploma and was working with the Education Corps six hours a day. She was worried that there might be some new law that would prevent her from becoming a teacher after serving her two years with the Corps. A year or so before our study, Mrs. 204's sister persuaded her to take the pill. However, at Interview 3, Mr. 204 had used the condom for two months. At Interview 4, Mrs. 204 was using the pill again. Mrs. 204 originally thought that ten years would not be enough between children, but she changed her mind when she saw how well her children, two and a half years apart, played together. However, she does not want the next pair for ten years. Mrs. 204 says that her parents want her to have however many children she herself wants. Of her mother-in-law, who lives in the same house and is supported by Mr. 204, Mrs. 204 says, "Mothers-in-law like their daughters-in-law to have twenty children." Mr. 204's brother and his wife, living in the same house, also have one son and one daughter and have apparently been successful in preventing pregnancy for six years with the condom.

Mr. and Mrs. 226 and their two daughters live with Mr. 226's mother in a small house which belongs to Mr. 226, his mother, and also to his four grown brothers and sister who live nearby. Mrs. 226 feels crowded, and there is clear indication that some of this feeling is due to psychological crowding from the ill temper of her husband and mother-in-law. Mr. and Mrs. 226 were married about nine years ago; he was thirty and she was fifteen. Both were uneducated. He practiced coitus interruptus for about three years before her first pregnancy, and again before and after her second pregnancy. Both pregnancies resulted in daughters. They have no sons, and Mrs. 226 says they both want sons. She is willing to have two more daughters in trying for a son. She says five to seven years is a good space between children, and her younger one is about three years old.

Mr. 226 has occasionally tried the condom, and Mrs. 226, responding to the influence of Health Corps girls who came to their house, had tried the pill for two months in the spring before our study began. The side effects bothered her and, besides, she never told her husband that she tried the pill, and she did not like to see a male doctor in order to get the pills at the clinic. Both she and her husband's sister, present on one occasion, are afraid he will get angry if he learns about it. Mrs. 226's mother-in-law interrupted one interview to imply that the *mullah* had been very critical of contraceptives in his sermon the night before. Mr. 226 and his mother both disapprove of pill and IUD (apparently for religious reasons), although Mr. 226 obviously approves of coitus interruptus. Mrs. 226 would not give her permission for her husband to be interviewed despite assurances that her secret taking of the pill would not be disclosed. Mrs. 226 sees her own parents and siblings frequently but less often than the daily contact with her husband's family. She says that her father urges her to limit her children to the two daughters she already has, so as to be able to discipline and educate them properly. She says her mother wants her to have two sons as well as two daughters, but her mother-in-law doesn't want her to have any more children.

Mr. and Mrs. 110 are both educated and working at middle-class jobs. They married ten years ago at the ages of twenty-five and fifteen, after college and eighth grade, respectively. They have two sons, three years apart, and Mr. 110 wants no more children, mentioning as reasons the expense and the need to discipline children well. Mrs. 110 wants only one daughter in about ten years, even though her ideal is two sons and two daughters. They did not achieve the seven-to-ten-years' space between children which both think desirable. Condom failure led Mrs. 110 to try both the IUD and the pill. She was using the latter at an early interview, but by Interview 4, Mr. 110 had been practicing coitus interruptus for four months. Mrs. 110 said the discomfort she experienced with the IUD and the pill made her give them up. She said they had tried all the methods and were satisfied with none.

Mr. and Mrs. 110 live by themselves where they feel uncrowded. They see his parents and siblings frequently, hers less often. However, because Mr. and Mrs. 110 are relatives, his parents and siblings are her relatives as well as in-laws. Mrs. 110 says her parents-in-law both think two children enough, and her mother-in-law approves of contraception. Mrs. 110's own mother (her father is dead) is also apparently encouraging her to stop at two although each of Mrs. 110's two married sisters has three children.

Women Who Do Not Want More Children

Table 9 enumerates the wives who do not any more children, by certain circumstances that may be salient in their desire for no more children, and by their contraceptive practices. Those whose "ideal has been reached" have the same number of boys and of girls that they say are good numbers of boys and girls to have. In most cases, the ideal and actual numbers are either the same for both sexes or more boys than girls. However, in one case, the wife (Mrs. 237) has two girls and one boy and gives these figures as her ideal. There seem to be pressures on her to change her mind, however, because Mrs. 237 says that her parents and parents-in-law think that two boys and one girl are

Table 9.   Wives who do not want more children: Category and circumstances, by type of contraceptive practice

	Pregnant	Nursing	None	Coitus interruptus	Condom	IUD	Pill	Total
Category A								
Ideal reached	1					1	1	3
Ideal passed		2*	1		2**			5
Total enough			2					2
Category B								
Ideal reached				1	1	2	2	6
Ideal passed		1			1	2	2	6
Total enough				3			2	5
Category C								
Ideal reached					1	2		3
Ideal passed			1	1	1	1	1	5
Total enough			1***				3	4
Total	1	3	5	5	6	8	11	39

*   abstinence also mentioned
**   abstinence and coitus interruptus also mentioned
*** sexually inactive (ill and elderly husband)

ideal. Mr. 237 is using the condom, having failed as a coitus interruptor; Mrs. 237 is a pill dropout.

Those wives who have passed their ideal number of children have at least as many boys and girls, and more of one sex or the other, or both sexes, than the wife says is her ideal. Those enumerated in terms of "total enough" have apparently decided that the total number of children that they have is enough, even though the number of boys and girls they have is not the same as their ideal number of boys and girls.

Thirty of these wives gave four or fewer children as their ideal, sixteen of them specifying two boys and two girls, and the range being from one and one to four and one. Nineteen of them actually had no more than four children, the 20 others having anywhere from five to nine inclusive.

Further consideration of seven cases in Categories B and C along the range of actual numbers of children may be instructive.

Two couples (both in Category B), each of whom has one boy and one girl, are Mr. and Mrs. 104 and Mr. and Mrs. 428. Both couples have reached their ideal number of children. Mr. and Mrs. 104 are from another city, and Mrs. 104 does not like Isfahan, where she has no friends or relatives except her unmarried brother-in-law who lives with them. She is looking forward to the time when her husband finishes his professional studies (for which purpose he is in Isfahan) and they can move away. Mrs. 104 finished primary school. They practiced no contraception after their first child, and the second was born after a year. Mrs. 104 then tried the pill but gave it up because jaundice ensued. She was fitted with an IUD but had it removed because of bleeding. Her husband tried coitus interruptus. She is again fitted with an IUD and seems to be having less trouble with it. Mrs. 104's mother, whom she sees yearly, is very positive in regard to contraception, herself having an IUD. Mr. 104's parents are described as being generally pro-children, but contraception has not been discussed with them. They are seen yearly. Mr. 104 is positive toward contraception and says they should limit to two. Mrs. 104 herself says they have enough now. It would be interesting to know if their reproductive goals change once Mr. 104 is set up in his profession in a place that Mrs. 104 finds more congenial.

Mr. and Mrs. 428, by contrast, are both uneducated. He is a shoemaker's assistant; she does some carpet weaving. She had three pregnancies that ended in two miscarriages and an infant death, prior to her two living children. She has been taking the pill for a year and has had no problems with it. In addition to having no side effects, she is strongly supported by her relatives. Her parents, whom she sees every day, are in favor of her limiting the number of her children and her use of the pill provided it does not make her sick. Her husband is supportive and agrees with the goal of one boy and one girl; and his parents, seen frequently, are similarly positive.

Mr. and Mrs. 302 (Category C) have three children — a daughter and two sons (her stated ideal being two of each). However, she has remained unpregnant for sixteen to seventeen years. This is the couple marked by a triple asterisk in Table 9. It seems quite clear that Mr. and Mrs. 302 have stopped having intercourse because he is ill and at least seventy years old. Mrs. 302 is about forty-five. Mr. and Mrs. 302 appear to have been successful family planners with a purpose: the education of their children. Mrs. 302 was herself uneducated and regrets it, saying that girls were just prisoners in their homes in those days and that things are better now. Mr. 302 learned to read and write — the present school system did not exist when he was of school age — and was a cloth dealer before he retired. He used the condom successfully for about fourteen years, after which his wife took the pill for about two years. Their daughter had some secondary school education, married at twenty-two and is now twenty-five. Their twenty-four-year-old son has a secondary school diploma and hopes to go to the university when his military service is finished. Their younger son is now in the ninth grade.

Mrs. 219 is noted in Table 9 as the other case in Category C of not practicing contraception, but the circumstances are very different from those of Mrs. 302. Mrs. 261 is the one case in Category B noted as nursing for contraceptive purposes. The circumstances of Mrs. 219 and Mrs. 261, though different from each other in many ways, pose similar problems and raise similar questions. In the first place, both have seven living children, three sons and four daughters, and both have far exceeded their ideals of two and two, and two and one.

Mrs. 261 has been married twenty-eight years and has had ten pregnancies (three of which ended with two child deaths and one miscarriage). Both she and her husband, who is her patrilateral cross-cousin, are uneducated. Mrs. 261 has never used any contraception except nursing (in whose efficacy she believes), and has not discussed the subject with her husband. She fears the IUD for health reasons. Her mother-in-law and her own mother (related to each other through marriage) both live in the house (both being supported by Mr. 261). Mrs. 261's mother reportedly thinks Mrs. 261 has enough children now. Mrs. 261's mother-in-law also thinks she should have no more, but she is very negative in regard to contraception, objecting to it for religious reasons. Mrs. 261 says that when she stops nursing, she will go to the clinic and get contraceptive pills. If she does start taking the pill, it will be a major change because she has a long-established pattern of pregnancy, nursing, pregnancy, etc. There are others in our sample who have had more children beyond their ideal than Mrs. 261 before resorting to more effective contraception.

Mrs. 219 has been married for twenty-two years, during which she has been pregnant eight times. She and her husband and children live in a house without other relatives and without unrelated neighbors. Mr. 219 had some primary school education, and Mrs. 219 has had one year of adult literacy classes. Mrs. 219 is supported in her desire for no more children by her husband, her parents, and her husband's parents, all four parents being seen weekly. The contraceptive problem was that Mrs. 219 sometimes stopped taking the pill because of side effects, being supported in this by her mother; sometimes her husband practiced coitus interruptus; and sometimes they abstained from intercourse. At Interview 4, Mrs. 219 said she had not taken the pill for the previous month because she was kept waiting for three hours at the clinic and then sent home without her monthly supply of pills. She was uncertain whether or not she was pregnant. We assigned Mrs. 219 to Category C because her last pregnancy ended with the birth of her youngest, four-year-old, child.

What will prevent Mrs. 261 and Mrs. 219 from going on to become like Mrs. 120 and Mrs. 134 who have nine children (six boys and three girls) apiece? More informed communication and more experimentation with a variety of contraceptives (rather than fixation on one) would certainly seem to be part of the answer.

As to Mrs. 120 and Mrs. 134, each is a pill user included in Categories B and C, respectively, in Table 9. What is the likelihood that they really will continue to avoid pregnancy and stop having children altogether? Mrs. 120 has been taking the pill for two and a half years despite the discomfort she suffers from it and despite generally negative influences from relatives and neighbors. Her mother is against the pill for health reasons, as is her mother-in-law, who lives in the same house. Her husband is for contraception but says the pill is dangerous; her neighbors comment on how many children she has but also say the pill is harmful. As in many other cases, her relatives are negative about the method she is using but are unwilling or unable to suggest adequate substitutes. She is experimenting with different kinds of pills and finds one less disagreeable than others.

Mrs. 134 has been taking the pill for two years, though she has had some problems with it. Her parents and parents-in-law are all dead. Her mother, who was afraid of the pill, died fairly recently after childbirth. Mrs. 120 and Mrs. 134 have at last become sufficiently motivated to try a contraceptive method and to persist in its use despite the problems that they have had with it. But whatever may have tipped the balance for them, it did not do so until they each had nine living children.

We will now consider seven cases in which the wife was pregnant at some point or other during the period of study (Category A). In each case, the wife indicated that she did not want any more children. In three cases the ideal had been reached; in three cases it had been passed; and in one case the total was felt to be enough. These cases also represent the full range of ideal numbers of children (from one and one to four and one), and from two to nine actual children.

Farangis (Mrs. 202) married her patrilineal parallel cousin, Faridoun, when she was twelve and he was twenty. They have been married seven years, and she has been pregnant four times during those years. Her first two pregnancies were condom failures and resulted in her two sons. She has no daughters. Her two latest pregnancies ended in miscarriage. One of these pregnancies was due to IUD failure. Then she took the pill, but not regularly, and got pregnant again. Faridoun has also used the condom occasionally.

Farangis and Faridoun do not seem to be getting along well together. Farangis says that her most recent miscarriage was caused by his striking her very hard when he was angry and that he strikes the little boys when he is angry. She is not having difficulties with the pill, and she does not want any more children especially because she feels ill and weak. Faridoun thinks that her illness is due to her taking the pill, and he does want more children. (Actually, it is quite likely that Farangis' illness is *brucellosis*, undulant fever, an enervating disease transmitted through the milk of cows infected with Bang's disease, a serious public-health problem in the Isfahan area).

Farangis' mother, whom she sees daily, supports her in her use of the pill, but she and Farangis' father would like it if she had a girl. Faridoun thinks that two boys and two girls is a good goal, but he says that if her next child is a boy, three boys will be enough. Farangis says that her parents-in-law (her father-in-law is her own father's brother) are against contraception (for religious reasons) and want her to have more children (specifically four boys and one girl).

Farangis and Faridoun live in two rooms with their sons and a seventeen-year-old brother of Faridoun. They rent the rooms from the owner of the house (unrelated) who also lives there. They say they have enough space. Farangis is uneducated, while Faridoun can read and write.

It seems likely that unless her bad health itself prevents it, Farangis will probably become pregnant again despite her stated preference for having no more children. The influences from her husband and relatives are all in the direction of having more children. If her' disease is demonstrated to herself and her relatives and husband to be *brucellosis* and not due to the pill, Faridoun may become more positive toward his wife's use of it after a limited number of additional pregnancies — and provided there is more good will and communication between him and Farangis.

Aghdas (Mrs. 508) gave two sons and one daughter as her ideal at an early interview when that was the number she actually had. At Interview 4, she was eight months pregnant against her wishes. Why? Married at fifteen years of age, nine years earlier, she had borne five children, of whom the first two died in infancy. When her third living child (her daughter) was a little more than one year old, Aghdas, encouraged by her sister who was using the pill, and another relative who was using the IUD, began to use the pill. She and her husband, Ali Muhammad, had not tried contraception before then. At Interview 1, Aghdas had been using the pill for five months despite problems. One incentive was that she and Ali Muhammad felt they could not take proper care even of those children they had, since he was often out of work. At Interview 2, Aghdas spoke of the rash on her face and the headaches the pill gave her despite changes from one kind to another. She also spoke of how difficult it was for her to have to see a male doctor. She had stopped using the pill one month earlier, and Ali Muhammad was uncomfortably trying to practice coitus interruptus.

At mention of the IUD she said she was afraid one would not stay in her uterus. She spoke of reading about family planning in her adult literacy class and her hope of studying through sixth grade at the rate of two grades a year. By the next interview, Aghdas was four months pregnant. She was very unhappy about it and had wanted to get an abortion, but Ali Muhammad refused to allow it for religious reasons. He commented that although ten was a good number of children to have if one had money, he himself could not afford more.

Aghdas has relatives in Isfahan using, and presumably satisfied with, the pill and the IUD. She also has a mother-in-law, who lives in a village and is visited monthly, who is against any kind of contraception and in favor of as many children as possible. Ali Muhammad disagrees with his mother about having many children because of his inability to support them, but, for more than eight years, he made no attempt to achieve the three years he thought a good interval between children by practicing contraception. Ali Muhammad said he would not agree to his wife being seen by a male doctor, and Aghdas did not tell him that she had been to a male doctor at the clinic. If there had been a female doctor, would Aghdas have asked more questions about her problems with the pill? Would she perhaps have been willing to try the IUD before this unwanted pregnancy? She tentatively indicated that it will be the IUD that she will try next. She will probably still need to be carefully and patiently reassured by a female physician in order to counterbalance what her friends and neighbors tell her: that the pill and the IUD are dangerous.

Of the four cases in Categories B and C in which the wife has reached her ideal of two sons and two daughters, three are using the IUD. One of these has used it for five years. The other two have used the IUD for shorter periods, having first tried the pill and stopped because of side effects. The fourth wife tried both the pill and the IUD, was bothered by each in turn, and reinforced in giving them up by both her mother and her husband. Her husband had, at Interview 4, used the condom for two months.

Fatimeh (Mrs. 228), in Category A, also tried the pill before the IUD, and she also has reached her ideal of two sons and two daughters. Her second son was born forty days before Interview 4, and Fatimeh would have aborted the pregnancy if the woman doctor to whom her husband, Siavosh, always sends her had agreed to perform an abortion. Fatimeh, at our first interview, had been married nine years and had had four pregnancies during that time, resulting in one son and three daughters. Her third daughter had died at the age of four months, only a few months earlier. Fatimeh and Siavosh said they had as many children as they wanted (one son and two daughters) and that a neighbor who was a nurse had influenced Fatimeh to go to the clinic to get the pill. She had not taken any yet because of a "heart problem." At the second interview four months later, Fatimeh said she had taken the pill only for a short time after our earlier interview. She stopped because of discomfort, and had become pregnant again. Since she was denied an abortion, she hoped it would be a boy because two sons and two daughters was a good number of children to have. Siavosh said that after this baby was born, they were ready to have an operation so as not to have more children, presumably tubal ligation for his wife since vasectomy is very rare in Iran.

At Interview 4, Fatimeh had had the IUD only ten days and had already had some problems. However, she reported that they took good care of her at the clinic and told her to come whenever she was uncomfortable. She said she expects to continue to use the IUD, and it seems to us that the chances for this are good. Her husband and her sister, with whom they live, are both supportive. Her sister, with one son and one daughter, has herself now been using the pill for four months. Fatimeh says her parents-in-law and her father think that one son and one daughter would have been enough. She says that her mother would like her to have three sons and three daughters and does not approve of any contraception except coitus interruptus which is better and less harmful than the pill and the IUD. Fatimeh and Siavosh, who are relatives, were married at ages sixteen and twenty-five (he with primary school education, she with three grades). They seem to get along very well with each other and seem to be thoroughly in agreement about having no more children. One reason is that, for their sons especially, they hope for considerably more education than Siavosh had, and they understand the financial problems.

Mrs. 231, Khadijeh, lives in a house with her husband, Ahmed, and their three sons and one daughter. (This is the case marked by a double asterisk in Table 9). No other people, related or unrelated, live in the house, which has three small rooms in which they feel crowded. Khadijeh is uneducated, but Ahmed finished sixth grade. She was fifteen and he was twenty-three when they were married nineteen years ago. Their oldest child, their daughter Puran, is seventeen and finished ninth grade during the period of study. Puran had been interested in going into nursing, but her friends told her it was dirty work. At the end of the study she was studying typing. Khadijeh had originally said she would like Puran to go to the university but that Puran was more interested in training herself for a good job. (By Iranian standards, a woman with a ninth grade education and typing skills is an unusually well-trained woman who is eligible for a good job in some kind of modern organization, where more jobs for women are beginning to open up.)

Khadijeh expects the last of her children who remains at home to be the one to support her and Ahmed in their old age, because the older ones will have gone away. If she were to find a GOOD husband for Puran, she would like her to marry as soon as possible, but there is apparently no immediate prospect of that.

Khadijeh has been pregnant eight times, and her history has been one of repeated contraceptive failures and mostly unwanted pregnancies. She cites her brother's wife, who has nine children, as being an example of the bad results of not practicing contraception. Her own ideal number of children is one boy and one girl, and Ahmed's is two and two. Their first two children were a girl and a boy, and she says all her pregnancies since then have been unwanted. Her last two pregnancies ended in induced abortion, one having been done a month before Interview 4.

Khadijeh and Ahmed have abstained from intercourse at various periods in their marriage, including the period following her last abortion. He has used the condom and tried coitus interruptus, both unsuccessfully. Recently he urged her to go the clinic to get the pill; she did, but the pill made her stomach upset. Khadijeh is full of fears about various contraceptives. She has heard that the IUD will cause the husband and wife to stick together and be unable to separate after intercourse. She has heard, and believes despite reassurances, that tubal ligation will cause menstrual blood to be retained in the abdomen and become poisonous.

Neither Khadijeh nor Ahmed wants any more children, and Khadijeh's mother (whom she sees weekly) is entirely supportive in this. However, their contraceptive failures, her fears that result in rejection of all methods, and her unpleasant experiences with clinic staff do not augur well for successful contraception in the future. There is evidence in her comments that abstinence may be as much motivated by incompatibility with her husband as it is by the desire to have no more pregnancies. Adequate instruction in condom use (there is evidence of either bad luck or ineptitude in the past) or really effective persuasion by able clinic staff in regard to tubal ligation might tip the balance favorably for this couple who obviously want no more children. Otherwise, she will probably continue to depend on abortion, although the cost would be an additional financial burden.

In contrast to the four preceding couples, none of whom has more than four children, Mrs. 262 (Masumeh) has nine children, which is the maximum number of living children in our sample. (It will be remembered that two other cases with nine children have already been discussed, as have Masumeh herself and her married daughter, Soghra).

Masumeh and her husband, Hosayn, are patrilateral cross-cousins. They were married when she was twenty and he was twenty-four, and they have been married for twenty-four years. They live in a house in the squatter settlement near the airport with their eight unmarried children (six sons and two daughters) and two of Masumeh's nephews (cousins to each other, not brothers) who are living in Isfahan during the school year to go to school but return to their village in the summer. The nephews are in the ninth and seventh grades and have had more schooling than any of Masumeh's and Hosayn's children. Masumeh and Hosayn themselves are uneducated, and Hosayn works in a quarry. He is away from home much of the time. An unrelated woman, with a son, rents living space in the house, and Masumeh feels crowded there.

Masumeh has had fourteen pregnancies. There were three child deaths, one of which occurred soon after difficult delivery and was attributed to the "Evil Eye." There was also a miscarriage after the third child. During the period of our study, Masumeh had an abortion, induced by an injection given at a clinic. She was, at the time, nursing her youngest child (about a year old).

Masumeh and her husband have never used any contraceptive method, although they have abstained from intercourse from time to time for contraceptive purposes. During the early years of the marriage, she was pregnant every year. She is convinced that nursing prevents conception, in spite of all the evidence to the contrary in her own experience, and she gives this as the reason for not trying the IUD or the pill. Her mother-in-law, whom she sees frequently, is wholly opposed to contraception, viewing it as a defiance of God's will, and says, in effect, the more children the better. As mentioned earlier, Masumeh feels that her husband's brother and his wife — also seen very frequently — want to have more children (even though they deny it) because she believes they have intercourse very frequently. It would seem that Masumeh and Hosayn think that abstinence is the only way of preventing conception, but they obviously cannot persist in it, and they are unable or unwilling to try alternatives. There is apparently litle communcation between them on the subject, and it will be recalled that Soghra, their sixteen-year-old married daughter, said that Masumeh was lying when she said that she and Hosayn were "sleeping apart."

Masumeh says that she might take the pill after she stops nursing this time, but she relies on nursing and thinks the pill will dry up her milk. She is unwilling for Hosayn to use the condom because it might rupture. (She once found a condom floating in one of the streams that flow through the city and took it home to her children to play with as a balloon. She claims she did not know what it was at the time, but that her neighbors did and made jokes about it. There are other instances in our sample of ribald humor on the subject of encounters with condoms.) In short, Masumeh gives many reasons for not practicing any contraception except for highly ineffective abstention and nursing.

Soghra herself presents an interesting contrast to Puran, discussed in the previous case. Masumeh says she wishes Soghra had had more education (she did send her to adult school for one year before her marriage) and that she had not married so young. She blames Soghra's early marriage on the insistence and interference of Soghra's husband's father's sister, Sekineh, who was present at one of the interviews and was treated rudely on this account by Masumeh. The interviewer visited Soghra in her own house nearby, together with Sekineh. Soghra said she would have liked to have gone to school longer and that two children was a good number. Sekineh said, "Two is not enough." Soghra has no opinion about spacing and no knowledge of any contraceptive methods, and Sekineh commented that it was "too soon" for pregnant Soghra to have any knowledge of such matters. Soghra weaves carpets at home and says she has too much to do to resume adult school classes.

The last two cases of these seven in Category A who want no more children have a number of similarities. Both wives had just given birth shortly before Interview 4. Both said they were not practicing contraception. (They were presumably nursing their newborns, but neither believes in the contraceptive efficacy of nursing. Neither was probably risking pregnancy yet, either.) Both spoke of possibly trying the IUD soon. Both have more sons than daughters. Both gave two sons and two daughters as their ideal. Both refused to arrange for male interviewers to talk with their husbands. However, that is where the similarities end.

Mrs. 233 (Ezat) married Bahram eleven years previously when she was fifteen and he was twenty-four. She had finished primary school, and he had finished ninth grade. They live with his uneducated parents, his twenty-two-year-old unmarried sister who is a nurse, his unmarried brother who is in secondary school, a married brother, his wife, and two sons. (It is important to note that Bahram's parents, though uneducated themselves, valued education sufficiently to see that all four of their children received secondary school education.) Ezat does not feel crowded and seems to get along well with her mother-in-law and two sisters-in-law. She has had four pregnancies and four children (three sons and a newborn daughter). After the first delivery, Bahram used the condom to space, and there were nearly three years between their first two children. Apparently, the third came before Ezat wanted it. Bahram was more careful after the third child who was five years old when Ezat became pregnant the next and most recent time. Considering Bahram's successful use of condoms, it is unclear why Ezat decided to try the pill, but both she and Bahram's brother's wife decided to do so. Both became pregnant sooner than they wanted to when they stopped taking the pill, which Ezat did because of side effects. Ezat now has the daughter she said at Interview 2 that she wanted to have after a few years. Her parents, seen weekly, and her parents-in-law, with whom she lives, all tell her not to have more children. She does not discuss contraception with them. She says Bahram does not want any more children either, and that he would rather use the condom than have her take the pill with its bad effect on her health. Ezat said Bahram had not said anything about the IUD. It seems to us that all these factors — their past successful condom use, their high educational aspirations for their children, Ezat's satisfied desire for a daughter, the influence from all relatives in favor of limitation, and Ezat's statement that women who want abortions should go to a doctor for a safe one — point to probable success in limiting to four children, whether by condom, IUD, or, if necessary, abortion.

The picture does not look so hopeful for Mrs. 113 (Shaheen). Married eighteen years ago at the age of fourteen to a man of thirty, Shaheen has had eleven pregnancies: three miscarriages, one abortion, one infant death, and six living children, four of whom are boys. Shaheen said that, when she had four children, her father, whom she sees annually when she visits the village from which she and her husband came, told her not to get pregnant again. Her brother in Isfahan also strongly advised her to practice contraception. (Her mother is dead.) However, her husband, Daryoush, has always thought contraception a sin. Daryoush and Shaheen live with their children in one room of a house where there are three other families not related to them. When Daryoush, an uneducated day laborer, has no work, he is apt to be at home where he treats his and others' children badly. Shaheen, understandably, says she feels crowded. Uneducated herself, she says that she wants primary school education for her children, but none of the three who are of school age has been sent to school. Shaheen's efforts at contraception have included injections which she said she was told would keep her from getting pregnant for two years. She had two sons and two daughters (and had had eight pregnancies) at that time, and the doctor told her it would be risky for her to become pregnant again. Later, though believing it a sin to do so, she aborted her tenth pregnancy at home and had severe bleedings afterwards. Then she made a pilgrimage to the tomb of Fatimeh the Immaculate in the shrine city of Qom, where she prayed that she would not become pregnant again, only to discover that she was already several months into her eleventh pregnancy.

With the recent birth of a fourth son, Shaheen says that Daryoush has finally realized that he cannot afford more children and has agreed that she should have a tubal ligation. (This may or may not be what Shaheen's brother's wife has done, who has reportedly had her uterus "twisted.") Shaheen, however, at Interview 4, says that she is afraid that if she has a tubal ligation, her stitches will open when she weaves carpets. (She pays the rent with what she earns from weaving.) She says that a doctor has told her she cannot take the pill because she is nervous. Therefore, she says, she will try the IUD.

We are extremely doubtful whether Shaheen, with all her fears and misinformation, is likely to get an IUD in the near future. Daryoush may allow her to do so, but, as angry and uncommunicative as he seems to be, he is not likely to encourage her. We think it more likely that Shaheen will become pregnant again, perhaps causing irreparable damage to her health.

Women Who Do Not Know If They Want More Children

Table 10 enumerates the six remaining cases in our sample, those not enumerated in Table 8 and Table 9. These are cases in which the wife's wishes for, or not for, more children seemed to us to be so ambiguous that we could not include them either in Table 8 or Table 9. We recognize that the extent of ambiguity is often a matter of degree, not of absolutes.

Table 10.   Wives about whom it is not clear whether or not they want more children: by category and contraceptive practice

	None	Coitus interruptus	IUD	Pill	Total
Category A	1		1	1	3
Category B	1	1			2
Category C				1*	1
Total	2	1	1	2	6

* Coitus interruptus reported as being used in alternate months instead of the pill.

Of the cases in Category A, Mrs. 319 (who uses the IUD) has already been discussed at some length earlier in this article. Mrs. 416, using the pill since the birth of a second girl, first talked about two children as being a good number to have, but later on was talking about having a boy after seven or eight years. Her husband's ideal was two boys and two girls. Mrs. 400 uses no contraceptives. She does not really want the burden of more children; her husband says he does not want any more, and his mother feels the same way. However, Mrs. 400's own mother says "the more the better," and Mrs. 400 herself is afraid that she may lose her husband if she is not always either pregnant or nursing. This fear is due to the fact that Mr. 400 divorced his first wife only because she had no children. Ambivalent or negative feelings about contraceptives as such do not seem to be the most crucial factors in these cases.

The two cases in Category B changed their minds (in opposite ways) during the period of study. Mrs. 216, who does not use contraceptives, said at Interview 4 that she wanted to get pregnant again, having earlier indicated differently. Mrs. 414, whose husband was practicing coitus interruptus, first said she wanted more than her four boys and three girls, but at Interview 4 she said she had enough. Her youngest, an infant becoming a toddler, may inadvertently have effected this change.

Mrs. 510 (Category C), who has two sons and one daughter, says that she would like a second daughter in seven or eight years. But she also said, on another occasion, that three children were enough to care for. Her mother says three are enough, and her husband says they cannot afford any more, though three boys and three girls would be nice if they could afford to support them. They live with Mrs. 510's sister (who is also Mr. 510's cousin); she has four daughters. Mr. and Mrs. 510's daughter therefore has female cousins for companionship even though she does not have a sister. Mr. and Mrs. 510 use the pill and coitus interruptus in alternate months (so as, they believe, to lessen any undesirable effects of the pill), and Mrs. 510 has avoided pregnancy for three years.

CONCLUSION

Throughout this article, we have made numerous comments and suggestions which grew out of our data but were aimed at wider horizons and intended for wider applications. We will not repeat or summarize these comments and suggestions here. Instead, we will make three major points that are related, respectively, to kinship, contraception, and family planning. While all of these points have already been mentioned, we think that they need particular emphasis.

Kinship

We have in a variety of ways enumerated and illustrated the immersion of the lives of the husbands and wives we studied in their relationships with many other relatives. Here we will consider only two of these relatives in particular, whose influences should be taken into account: the wife's mother and the husband's mother. Fifty-eight mothers of the sixty-nine wives, and fifty mothers of the sixty-nine husbands were alive during the period of our study. Fourteen of the wives' mothers were in daily contact with their daughters, five of them living in the same house with their daughter and son-in-law. Most of the other wives' mothers were in very frequent contact with their daughters. Twenty-six of the husbands' mothers were in daily contact, twenty-one of whom lived in the same house with their sons and daughters-in-law.

The opinions of these mothers regarding contraception and limiting the number of children run the gamut from definitely positive to categorically negative. However, to a substantial degree their opinions are less frequently positive than their daughters' and sons' opinions. Twelve of the wives' mothers are seen by their daughters to be positive toward contraception and three to be definitely negative for religious reasons. Twenty-six others are ambivalently positive, that is to say, while they are generally in favor of limiting the number of children, they are dubious about, or opposed to the use of, contraceptives like the pill or the IUD, mostly for health reasons.

Negative opinions are more pronounced among the husbands' mothers. Eleven of them are reported by their daughters-in-law to be positive toward contraception, but thirteen of them are reported to be definitely negative for religious or pronatalist reasons. Three are ambivalently positive, and a number of others, with whom contraception has not been discussed, are reported to be in favor of large numbers of children.

The family planning program appears to ignore or disregard the massive presence of these mothers, not to mention many other relatives. The influence of a mother or a mother-in-law, felt very frequently, can either support or undercut the counsels of a clinician seen by a woman only occasionally. The most appropriate behavior of that clinician would at the very least include finding out who the other significant relatives of the wife are and what their opinions are about family planning and contraception. Having done that, the clinician should be trained and enabled to undertake procedures of the "family medicine" variety, in which significant other relatives are not only taken into account but also directly reached.

Our concentration on wives' mothers and husbands' mothers is not intended to suggest in any way that the influence of other relatives need not be considered. For instance, though the influence of fathers and fathers-in-law may often be felt indirectly, through their influence on mothers and mothers-in-law, there were several cases in which it was much more direct. Mrs. 203, who has nine children and feels that four of them are "extra" and that two or three would have been enough, has used the IUD for a year and a half but has not told her parents. She said at Interview 4 that her father had come to the house two days before and asked why she had not had a baby for two years. He told her that if she was using contraception, she was interfering with God's will.

Contraception Versus Pregnancy

While almost all of the wives in our sample are positive in principle about the idea of limiting the number of their children (and perceive most of their husbands in similar terms), the problems and the doubts that they have concerning the supposedly most effective contraceptives (pill and IUD) are very important factors in their motives. Thirty-nine of the wives, in fact, express very serious doubts and fears in regard to the pill and the IUD, doubts and fears that are reinforced in many cases by their own experiences with side effects and the talk of relatives, friends, and neighbors. Some of the wives persist in the use of these methods despite problems and fears, because of the intensity of their desire not to have any more children. However, many of them, for the same reasons, have not persisted and so become pregnant again if they fail to find a satisfactory and effective alternative soon enough.

This massive ambivalence about contraception itself, together with a number of influences and counterinfluences, lies at the root of the "dropout problem."

Two sets of choices are entwined with each other. One is whether or not to have more children. The other is whether to try to prevent pregnancy with the pill or the IUD which are supposedly the most certain methods but also the most troublesome and the most fear-ridden both for religious and health reasons.

In addition to problems and fears concerning, or ineptitude in the practice of, various contraceptive methods, the pressures which incline wives towards more children and less effective contraception include short-term rewards, such as the widespread hope that pregnancy will cure many ills, and the great attention that new mothers can expect to receive (reported to us by our research staff). Affecting both husbands and wives is the desire for a certain sex balance among their children.

Also a pressure for more pregnancies is the idea that "children are poor people's only fortune," a tangible expression of hope for a better future. This is more deep-seated than the specific hope that one's children will support one in old age, a hope that is often tinged with bitter doubts that they will, in fact, do so.

There is the woman's rivalry with other women (most especially her *jari*, her husband's brother's wife) in child production, which is at once an assertion and a way of insuring, her husband's attention and devotion. It is also an essential expression of the fact that child bearing is still the major woman's occupation in the culture, and the only one through which most women can hope to earn any social recognition or prestige. Although many of the wives and husbands in our sample hope, often unrealistically, to give their daughters more education and marry them at an older age (but still in their teens) than was true of the wives themselves, very few have any expectation for their daughters other than marriage and child bearing.

On the side of having fewer children and practicing more effective contraception is the feeling, widespread among both husbands and wives, of being overburdened by too many children. The wives are worn out by the work of caring for the children. The difficulty, if not impossibility, of disciplining them properly if there are too many of them is widely recognized. Also widespread is the recognition of not having enough money to care for them. Parents' hopes for vicarious achievement through the worldly success of their children — that success being very much dependent on protracted and expensive education — are definitely present. However, the extent to which this "my son the doctor" syndrome is logically connected with the need to have fewer children so as to have more money to spend on each is another matter. We are doubtful that there is very much "cost-benefit analysis" on this subject.

There is a large element of hope in these "counter-natalistic" influences, much of that hope depending on the present and future performance of the government in providing various new social services, and encouraging new social orientations and employment opportunities. Wary and cynical, the people are still inclined to continue in older ways where there are at least the securities of the familiar. On the other hand, the lucky chance of successful EARLY limitation of children through satisfactory and effective contraception (such as that achieved by a few of the husbands and wives in our sample) can, by increasing their feeling of control over their lives, set a new pattern (and example) of having only a small number of children.

Family Planning Clinics

In any particular case, any one of the above factors can tip the balance one way or the other as far as getting pregnant again is concerned. It is very likely that over the course of a marriage, one factor can tip the balance one way on one occasion and another factor can tip it the other way on another occasion. (We were planning to try to document such sequences of events in our hoped-for long-term longitudinal study.)

At this juncture, there is one set of factors that can at least be controlled, to some extent, for large numbers of people, even though its effects may not be predictable. This set of factors is the activities and services of the family planning program. We shall limit our remarks to just one: the basic behavior and attitudes of family planning clinic personnel. Given the delicate balance between the pro-natalistic and counter-natalistic factors in many married couples' reproductive behavior, the effect of the clinic experience may well be an important tipper of the balance.

We will not argue the question of whether Iran's family planning clinics should or should not continue to be incorporated into medical outpatient clinics. The fact is that at present most of them are, and therefore most of them are subject to the same defects as the outpatient clinics.

Outpatient clinics are notorious everywhere, in the United States no less than in Iran, for their inconsiderate treatment of their patients. This is apparently due in part to the disdain in which the staff hold the patients who are mostly poor and uneducated. And the callous treatment can only be reinforced by the fact that most patients will endure long waiting and rudeness because of their overriding need for relief from anxiety and pain.

Clinic personnel accustomed to this situation may be likely to assume that family planning clients will endure the same indignities as medical patients, and that therefore there is no need to change the situation. We would disagree with such an assumption. Family planning patients are not likely to be "hurting" in the same way or to the same degree, literally and figuratively, as medical patients are. This is probably a major cause of the high "dropout" rate which is calculated in terms of the number of pill users who stop returning to the clinic for pills.

Therefore, in addition to such widely recommended reforms as providing more women physicians and women paramedical personnel (to lessen the dependence on male physicians whom many family planning patients are reluctant, or refuse, to consult), we suggest a fundamental reorientation. Family planning clinic personnel must be trained to recognize that in order to succeed, they must reinforce the counternatalistic forces in their patients' lives and help their patients cope with the pro-natalistic influences. This will best be achieved if they can learn to think of themselves not as dispensers of "treatment," but as teachers, and indeed salespeople, of innovative behavior. Who is to teach them? Social work and family medicine are existing fields which can be drawn upon for models, to mention just two specific examples.

Such reorientation of attitudes might well involve extensive sociocultural restructuring within the clinical domain. Perhaps this restructuring would seem less fearful and would be less resisted if it could be perceived as being just one aspect of far more extensive sociocultural restructurings — in sex-role definitions and expectations, occupational roles, husband-wife relationships, and economic goals. Such restructurings as these will probably be necessary for the permanent maintenance of a relatively stable, rather than a dangerously expanding, population.

REFERENCES

BURCH, THOMAS K., MURRAY GENDELL
  1971   "Extended family structure and fertility: some conceptual and methodological issues," in *Culture and population: a collection of current studies*. Edited by S. Polgar, 87–104. Carolina Population Center, Monograph 9. Chapel Hill, North Carolina.
FAMILY PLANNING DIVISION
  1971   *Family planning in Iran: four years of progress.* Iran Family Planning Bulletin 9.
FRIESEN, JOHN K., RICHARD V. MOORE
  1972   "Iran," in *Country profiles.* New York: The Population Council.
GILLESPIE, ROBERT, S. LIEBERMAN, M. LOGHMANI
  1972   "The Esfahan Communication Project." Mineographed manuscript. Isfahan, Iran.
GOODY, JACK, *editor*
  1962   *The developmental cycle in domestic groups.* Cambridge: Cambridge University Press.
GULICK, JOHN, MARGARET E. GULICK
  1974   "Varieties of domestic social organization in the Iranian city of Isfahan," in *City and peasant: a study in sociocultural dynamics.* Edited by A. L. La Ruffa, et al., 441–469. New York: Annals of the New York Academy of Sciences.
HARVEY, PHILIP D.
  1972   "Condoms — a new look." *Family Planning Perspectives* 4(4): 27–30.

KANTNER, JOHN F.
1966 "The place of conventional methods in family planning programs," in *Family planning and population programs: a review of world developments.* Edited by B. Berelson, 403–409. Chicago: University of Chicago Press.

KIRK, DUDLEY
1966 "Factors affecting Moslem natality," in *Family planning and population programs: a review of world developments.* Edited by B. Berelson, 561–580. Chicago: University of Chicago Press.

LIEBERMAN, S. S., ROBERT GILLESPIE, M. LOGHMANI
1973 *The Isfahan communications project.* The Population Council, Studies in Family Planning (4). New York.

MISRA, B. D.
1967 "Correlates of males' attitudes toward family planning," in *Sociological contributions to family planning research.* Edited by D. J. Bogue, 161–271. Chicago: Community and Family Study Center, University of Chicago.

NAG, MONI
1967 "Family type and fertility," in *Proceedings of World Population Conference, 1965,* 160–163. New York: United Nations.

NORTMAN, DOROTHY
1972 *Population and family planning programs: a fact book* (fourth edition). Reports on Population/Family Planning 2. New York: The Population Council.

SEGAL, SHELDON J., CHRISTOPHER TIETZE
1971 *Contraceptive technology: current and prospective methods.* Reports on Population/Family Planning 1. New York: The Population Council.

TOUBA, JACQUELINE RUDOLPH
1972 The relationship between urbanization and the changing status of women in Iran, 1956–1966. *Iranian Studies* 5(1):25–36.

VIEILLE, PAUL
1967 Birth and death in an Islamic society. *Diogenes* 57:101–127.

Mass Acceptance of Vasectomy: The Role of Social Interaction and Incentives in Social Change

D. C. DUBEY and A. BARDHAN

This is largely a descriptive field report of a situation of social change which overtook its promotors by surprise in several ways. This surprise was born out of unexpected success in bringing about social change in an area which had hardly known any substantial success in the past in spite of huge financial and technological investments. It deals with family planning, which is one of the most intimate, emotional, and personal areas of life. It is concerned with values of sex behavior and the processes of family formation. It involves children and, through them, such primary institutions as kinship and clan groups. This complex has been recognized by social scientists as the hard core of any given value system. It is hard core primarily because it is most difficult to change. It is even more so when the change is manipulated under democratic situations fully respecting the freedom of the individual and having faith in his ability to choose for his development.

Given these constraints if change takes place, change which overshoots all expectations and assumes proportions of a mass movement, it presents a situation of great significance to social scientists and particularly for the students of social change. Even a systematic description of the situation has scientific value, particularly because it is likely to happen so rarely.

THE PRIOR SITUATION

Family planning in India started as one of the programs included in the Five-Year Plans of the country. Over the years it has assumed greater and greater importance. Today it is a program of highest priority. Practically all expenditure by the state governments for this program is fully met by the central government. Both in the Center as well as in the states the program operates as a part of the Ministry of Health.

At first, the main emphasis of the program was on the opening of family planning clinics. The assumption was that the people would accept the new concept, go to the clinics themselves, and ask for family planning services. It was soon learned that mere availability of services, or technology alone, does not prove enough to bring about change in the lives of people.

In 1963, this approach was given up in favor of the extension education approach. The emphasis was now on informing and motivating couples by using different extension education approaches to bring about the desired change. Simultaneously, the financial and manpower resources of the program were increased many times to ensure easy availability of services and educational contact with couples. This did make some increase in the acceptance of family planning.

However, the increase was below the expectations of the program workers and definitely far below the demands of the program situation. The attractiveness of new contraceptive technology like IUD and the pill did make an impact but it was limited. Soon it was found that people retraced their steps to find solace and satisfaction in the status quo. Any additional amount of input did not bring corresponding returns in terms of people accepting this new way of life. The situation remained more or less stagnant. Very soon it was realized that even the forceful and heavy doses of the three factors of technology, information, and inputs did not create situations sufficiently conducive to bring about planned and desired social change on a mass scale.

SUDDENLY HOPES ARE RAISED

At this stage of the program, something very unique happened in Kerala, one of the states in the extreme south of India. The headlines in national newspapers announced the astounding number of 63,418 people accepting vasectomy in a mass camp of one month's duration organized at Ernakulam. Some papers had pictures showing long queues of people holding umbrellas over their heads to protect themselves from rains to ensure that they could undergo the operation before the day's work at the camp was closed. A few days later, it was announced that the encampment had been extended because of the enthusiastic response of the people.

Similar stories from other states started appearing. In Gujarat 223,060 operations were performed in a period of two months. The states of Uttar Pradesh, Bihar, and Madras reported similar enthusiasm of people in accepting this innovation and change. All of a sudden, the overall picture started looking bright. It appeared as if a mass movement of social change had started.

WHAT HAD CHANGED?

While the success drew applause it also raised several questions. What did the trick? Was there any coercion? Were the people accepting it with the full knowledge of what they are doing? Why did these people reject the innovation all these years? What had happened to fears, doubts, and suspicions they had been voicing against vasectomy in the past?

As social scientists involved in this program it became our responsibility to systematically study and analyze the phenomenon so that such questions could be answered and a more appropriate and informed policy decision be taken to incorporate the success into the program.

For collecting this information, the authors made field trips to the states of Kerala, Haryana, Delhi, Uttar Pradesh, and Bihar. The states were visited when the camps were in full swing. We stayed in each camp for several days. We observed as well as interviewed acceptors, administrators, technicians (doctors), local leaders, nonofficial motivators, and workers involved in the camp. An in-depth-interviewing technique, with the help of a schedule, was adopted for collecting information. All the interviews were held in conditions ensuring the maximum privacy and after establishing a relation of confidence and rapport with the informants.

Some interviews were done before the operation, some immediately after it, and others several days after the operation. The interviews were held in the camp as well as in the villages of the respondents. On an average, each interview took about an hour and a half. None took less than an hour. Tape recorders were used for verbatim recording of the whole conversation in such a way as not to make the respondent conscious of this.

Our emphasis was more on getting as true a picture as possible of people's feeling, thinking, and behavior involved in the process of accepting vasectomy. Following this method, two interviewers together could conduct 619 in-depth interviews (of all types) in the five states in the country over a period of two months. Of these 619 interviews, 410 related to acceptors of vasectomy in the mass camps. Before we analyze the processes of decision making and change, we give in brief the socioeconomic and demographic characteristics of the acceptors of vasectomy in these mass camps.

About 97 percent of the cases were married while 3 percent were widowers. About 88 percent of the respondents were illiterate or just barely literate. Nine percent had education of high school or more. One-third of the respondents belonged to the service and business class and the remaining two-thirds were farmers and agricultural laborers. Only 7 percent of the respondents had monthly incomes of at least 300 rupees per month. The remainder earned 150 rupees or less. The average age of respondents and that of their wives was thirty-eight and thirty-two years respectively.

What moved our respondents and several thousands of others like them to accept social change on a mass scale is the factor to be examined. Our analysis indicates that given the factors of services and adequate inputs, the factors of (1) social interaction and (2) motivation and decision making proved to be the key variables responsible for initiating change on a mass scale.

SOCIAL INTERACTION

Mass acceptance of vasectomy resulted from a strategy that emphasized promoting people's participation to the maximum. Ad hoc vasectomy camps were organized. Each encampment was preceded by one month of an intensive educating and informing campaign. All the local institutions such as the village panchayats, cooperatives, library clubs, trade unions, cultural song and drama clubs, political parties, and women's clubs were involved by offering them a certain amount of diffusor incentives for each case promoted by them for vasectomy.

To strengthen their participation, workers of all the developmental agencies such as Community Development, Health and Family Planning, Education and Social Welfare, and General Administration were encouraged to promote small squads of influential leaders at the village level to personally reach and visit the homes of potential acceptors in a systematic way. This personal soliciting of the cases by mixed teams of local and official leaders was responsible for creating a social climate of confidence in favor of change through the acceptance of the innovation of vasectomy.

Each case was individually approached and solicited. Our respondents were asked how many times such local squads promoting the change had visited them. Table 1 gives this information. We found

Table 1. Number of times cases were contacted by promotors of change

Number of cases	Frequency	Percent
110	1–2 times	26.83
158	3–4 times	38.54
26	5–6 times	6.37
54	7–8 times	13.16
38	9–10 times	9.26
24	No response	5.84
410		100.00

that, on an average, each of our respondents was contacted a little over four times at his home before he agreed to accept a vasectomy operation.

In the course of our intensive observation and discussion, very frequently we came across evidence which made us believe that this interaction brought into play the influence of groups in accepting change. The situation is best illustrated by a respondent who said,

On my return home after working outside the village for fifteen days I felt as the one who has been left out because most of my friends had already undergone the operation in the camp. This is the main reason I have come for the operation to the camp today.

This sense of being left out created a psychological atmosphere most conducive for mass-scale acceptance of change. Bringing people in groups to the camp and taking them back in groups after the operation also provided opportunity for mutual group reassurance in favor of change. This acceptance in groups and the camp approach which created an impression of collective acceptance can be credited with making possible the phenomenon of large-scale social change.

MOTIVATION AND DECISION MAKING

We have noted above how the camp approach promoted interaction and created a facilitating social climate that constituted the general context within which individual couples were to behave in the direction of desired change. To promote this behavior there must be some motivating force. In this case this motivating force was provided by giving incentives to would-be acceptors and diffusors of the innovation.

In the past, the approach to incentive in the program has been somewhat uncertain although one of the state governments in the Union tried it and was successful, particularly in the form of diffusor incentives. In spite of the success some argued that it ran counter to the announced goal of voluntary acceptance of family planning. Further, it was claimed that it goes against the accepted approach of extension education based upon self-conviction and self-help. As a result, this solitary experiment was discontinued.

After a lapse of a few years these mass vasectomy camps with both the adoptor incentives and diffusor incentives were reinstated on a trial basis. Those who accepted vasectomy during the encampment were paid between 80 and 100 rupees, mostly in cash. The promotor of each case was also paid about 10 rupees in cash.

As these large incentives were followed by mass acceptance it became of interest to investigate how acceptors perceived incentives. When respondents were asked about this, very often they said things that implied that for them incentives were means to several additional advantages. One person replied, "It is a help to enable people to purchase food or help to enable acceptors to take rest for five or six days or help to eat nutritive food to overcome the general weakness caused by the operation." This was a typical response. The important thing to note is that these were additional advantages to their basic need for limiting the number of children through vasectomy. In other words, payment of adopter incentives created a higher degree of relative advantage in the minds of the people.

It has been indicated previously that incentives were given up in the Indian program because they were thought to be contrary to the accepted approach of the program, that is promoting voluntary acceptance though extension education. Our study also inquired in detail into this aspect of the problem.

It was postulated that in essence, extension education involves promoting information-getting behavior among the people, encouraging evaluation of the recommended practice by the acceptors themselves through consultations to remove doubts, fears, and misapprehensions, and making use of already available experience in the group, with a view to getting social support and thus achieving self-education for desired change.

As opposed to this, it was thought that indications of "instantaneous decisions" might reveal an absence of these processes (though there is by no means conclusive evidence) and a possibility of high incentives undercutting the extension education approach, which has been the officially accepted methodology for propagating family planning programs in the country since 1953.

With this in view, several questions were especially devised, after extensive pretesting, to collect information on the decision-making process. Answers were sought to these questions: How long, in months or years, had the respondent known about vasectomy? What did he do after he first learned about it? Why did he not accept vasectomy then? When did he come to know about the camp? Through whom? What did he do on hearing that? Why did he accept the operation now? When did he have more discussion and consultation and why? Did he consult his wife? What did she say? What was her opinion? There were questions on his consultations with cases who had had the operation and with other people in the community. What did he talk about with these people and what was the result of the talks?

The information we gathered led us to believe that only 33 percent of the cases learned about the vasectomy operation for the first time during the camp. The rest of the respondents (67 percent) knew about it several years before the organization of the camp. The first knowledge somehow did not evoke sufficient interest in the proposition. It appeared that over a period of time they came to know of people who had accepted vasectomy and were suffering from various ailments. This raised some fears and doubts in their minds. The data reveal the following main reasons for their indecision:
1.   Fears of physical pain, weakness, complications, and lack of risk-taking capacity (35.14 percent of the cases)
2.   Fear about the comments and reaction of others (27.84 percent of the cases)
3.   Other reasons for indecision or non-acceptance: small family, wanted a son, using family planning methods, sickness in family, pregnancy of wife, etc. (34.59 percent of the cases).

In brief, the situation in most of the cases, at the time of receiving first information, can be described as follows:

People had heard of vasectomy for limiting family size about three to four years before the camp. Most probably this aroused a sort of cognitive dissonance and anxiety among them. How would vasectomy affect their lives? Would it fit into their routine day-to-day activity? Would it cause variations and therefore possible dislocations? The three reasons given above are indicative of these and several other similar concerns.

In the absence of any planned diffusion attempts (both by official and private agencies), the negative after-effects were uncontrolled and unchallenged. When such after-effects came to the knowledge of those who were feeling uneasy and anxious upon first learning of vasectomy, they achieved consonance by freezing the issue and relegating it to the back of their minds.

The mass vasectomy camp along with incentives then came into the program. In those sections of population where the incentives appeared to be high or very high, it had the effect of making the issue live again. To them the incentive proved significant enough and could not be ignored easily. This reopened the whole question and the proposition had to be reconsidered once again. Thus it recreated a stage of cognitive dissonance.

Uneasiness and anxiety were once more created, depending upon how the incentive appeared to different sections of the society. The knowledge about the limited duration of the camp introduced an element of urgency in resolving the dissonance. The result was the initiation of frantic attempts on the part of such people to collect new evidence.

Invariably, the cases were found to have talked to others operated on earlier in these camps regarding their fears and apprehensions. The decision to involve the entire governmental machinery, the *panchayats*, and the village leaders proved helpful as is seen in Table 2.

Table 2.   Response to the question, "Who convinced you most about coming to the camp?"

Category of persons	Number	Percent
Officials (workers of all government agencies)	208	50.73
Operated cases and other local nonofficials	202	49.27

The cases indicated that many people never talked about it so freely and frequently as they did during this month of the mass camp. They gave enough evidence to indicate that they had the maximum amount of interpersonal communication during this period. They had never before talked about it so often, although they had already known of vasectomy three to four years earlier. About 75 percent of the respondents said that they talked to others about vasectomy only during the camp, while only 21 percent said that they discussed vasectomy both during and before the camp.

Similarly, during the camp, the extent of interspouse communication was also evident from the data. About 79 percent of the cases discussed the operation with their wives while 17 percent did not care to consult their wives. This situation can be best described in the words of the respondent:

Everybody is saying that vasectomy is good and people are crowding at the camps.
When everybody is accepting it I thought why should I also not accept it?

It must be something good.

It must be good for people, and that is why government is spending so much.

I decided to have it because several other people in the villlage have got it done at the camp.

I came along on seeing a few others of my group who were coming in the jeep.

When I talked to a case from this camp he said there was no pain and the doctors were very good.

Some interpreted the huge arrangements and the high expenditure on the camp to be indicative of the availability of good services in terms of doctors, medicines, etc. In other words, in the case of respondents to whom the incentive offered proved so important that they could not ignore it easily, the issue became live again and there was intense activity to gather additional information and new evidence, as well as a search for social and group assurance. As was already explained, the camp approach created situations that induced these activities which are the hallmarks of extension education. As a result, most of the affected people went from the stage of dissonance caused by incentives, to the stage of consonance by taking a positive decision to accept vasectomy this time.

Thus, all the evidence shows that the incentive actually created situations favorable for more intense and fruitful extension education. Also, the contention that incentive undercuts or is opposed to the extension-education approach does not seem to be true. If anything, the high incentives and mass camps together can be credited with having made the theoretical concept of extension education practical and a reality. These two are by no means either-or propositions and it would be wrong to view them as contradictory approaches and as such mutually exclusive.

In short, the organization of the mass vasectomy presented a challenging strategy to bring about social change on a mass scale to those who had been unaffected earlier. The family planning program functioned in a most democratic way, respecting fully the freedom of the individual and faith in his ability.

The challenge was successfully met. The main ingredients of this tremendous success were based on two main factors. First, the involvement of local institutions like the village *panchayats*, cooperatives, library clubs, trade unions, and women's clubs was achieved by offering a certain amount of diffusor incentives for each case promoted by them for vasectomy. Their participation was further strengthened with the involvement of all the developmental agencies such as Community

Development, Health and Family Planning, etc.

At the village level small squads of influential leaders were promoted for personally reaching and visiting homes of each of the potential acceptors. This enabled each case to be approached and solicited individually. Close observation of the situation revealed that the strategy had a great impact in making vasectomy acceptable to a large number of the people.

Secondly, the role of incentive proved crucial in promoting social interaction and decision-making processes insofar as individual cases were concerned.

The people were aware of vasectomy long before the mass vasectomy camps. But somehow they did not accept it. The introduction of large incentives was seen as an additional advantage over the past situation. This made this issue live again for a vast number of people for whom incentives looked attractive. It thus created a stage of cognitive dissonance. The news regarding the limited duration of the encampment introduced an element of urgency in resolving the dissonance.

As a result, people made frantic attempts to collect new evidence. Discussions with several persons who had been operated on were held to remove their fears and doubts. This intense activity was continued to collect additional information and new evidence for social and group assurance and thus achieve self-education for the desired change. The payment of adopter incentive created a higher degree of relative advantage in the minds of the people.

In brief, we have seen that in spite of the huge amount of financial and technical investment in the program, substantial success in the past could not be achieved. The real difference came when the two additional elements of people's participation and incentives were introduced into the situation.

REFERENCES

ENKE, STEPHEN
    1960   The gains to India from population control: some money measures and incentive schemes. *Review of Economics and Statistics* 42: 175–181.
FESTINGER, LEON
    1957   *A theory of cognitive dissonance.* Evanston, Illinois: Row, Peterson.
FINNIGAN, OLIVER D. III, T. H. SUN
    1972   Planning, starting and operating an educational incentives project. *Studies in Family Planning* 3(1):1–7.

INTERNATIONAL PLANNED PARENTHOOD FEDERATION
n.d.   *Incentive payments in family planning programmes.* London, IPPF, Working Paper 4.

KRISHNAKUMAR, S.
1971   *The story of the Ernakulum experiment in family planning, Trivandrum, India.* Report, Government of the State of Kerala.

REPETTO, ROBERT
1969   India: a case study of the Madras vasectomy programme. *Studies in Family Planning* 31:8-16.

RIDKER, RONALD G.
1969   Synopsis of a proposal for a family planning bond. *Studies in Family Planning* 1(43):11–16.

ROGERS, EVERETT M.
1971   Incentives in the diffusion of family planning innovation. *Studies in Family Planning* 2(12):241–248.
1972   *Communication strategies for family planning.* East Lansing: Michigan State University.

ROGERS, EVERETT M., DILIP K. BHOWIK
1971   Homophily and heterophily: relational concepts for communication research. *Public Opinion Quarterly* 34:523–538.

ROGERS, EVERETT M., et al.
1970   *Diffusion of innovations in Brazil, Nigeria and India.* Diffusion of Innovations Research Report 24. East Lansing: Michigan State University.

ROGERS, EVERETT M., F. FLOYD SHOEMAKER
1971   *Communication of innovations: a cross cultural approach.* New York: Free Press.

SCHRAMM, WILBUR
1971   *Communication in family planning.* Occasional Reports in Population/Family Planning. New York: Population Council.

THAKOR, V. H., VINOD M. PATEL
1972   *A report on the Gujarat state massive vasectomy campaign.* Directorate of Health Services, Gujarat State.

PART THREE

Migration

Families to the City:
A Study of Changing Values, Fertility,
and Socioeconomic Status
among Urban In-migrants

SUSAN C. SCRIMSHAW

Since urbanization is traditionally considered a prime force leading toward lower fertility, it is of theoretical interest to
study closely the prospect of fertility
decline among recent migrants in the
developing nations.

MACISCO, WELLER, AND BOUVIER[1]

INTRODUCTION

The explosive growth in the rate of rural-urban migration in Latin
America in the years since World War II has stimulated questions
about the effects of urbanization on the fertility behavior of migrants
(Kiser 1971: 381; Stycos 1965: 205). Urban in-migrants swell the
cities as they pour in, but do they also contribute proportionately
more children to the next generation than their urban-born neighbors?
While the validity of the widely accepted belief that rural fertility
generally is higher than urban fertility has been questioned (Robinson

This paper is based on a study supported by USAID (Contract Number 0113-26332-
00, AID'csd-2479 Task Order Number 3B) and by the Ford Foundation. The research and findings are fully described in a report by Susan C. Scrimshaw entitled
*Migration, urban living and the family: a study among residents in the suburbios
and tugurios of Guayaquil, Equador* prepared for Division of Social and Administrative Sciences, International Institute for the Study of Human Reproduction,
Columbia University.
    While many people participated in the project, I would particularly like to
acknowledge the contributions made by my colleagues at the Institute, most notably
Dr. Samuel M. Wishik, Dr. Mario Jaramillo Gómez, and Dr. Moni Nag.
[1] In: *The family in transition* (1969), page 285.

1963: 292), many researchers present strong cases for the existence of such a differential under most conditions (Carleton 1965: 20; Davis and Casis 1946: 199; United Nations 1961: 91; Micklin 1969: 461; Weller and Macisco 1970: 3; Pool 1969: 1; Mertens and Miro 1969: 7).

Given a rural-urban fertility differential, do rural immigrants to cities reproduce at higher "rural" rates, or do they adopt some or all of the urban attitudes and behavior which are related to the relatively lower urban fertility patterns? If the exposure to the urbanization process does affect the fertility of urban in-migrants, how soon after immigration is fertility behavior modified? Both Hawley (1969: 25) and Goldberg (1959: 214) indicate that while no precise knowledge is available, lowered fertility as a result of acculturation to the urban milieu occurs after about two generations.

Zarate (1967: 1), however, found that fertility does not always correlate with length of urban residence. Speare, Speare, and Lin found the same situation in Taiwan after controlling for education (1972: 10). For Thailand, Goldstein (1971: 45) reports no "substantial difference in fertility levels between the migrant and non-migrant segments of the Thai population." Macisco, Weller, and Bouvier (1969: 287) report that in Puerto Rico, migrants have *lower* fertility than nonmigrants. They state "following available evidence, there is no clear-cut answer to this question of possible fertility differentials between migrants and non-migrants."

In a 1970 article, Weller and Macisco suggest that selective migration may provide an explanation for the relatively low fertility of urban in-migrants in some countries. "Perhaps migration itself is selective of low fertility." Similarly, Goldstein writes " . . . urban places either attract those with much lower fertility levels, or migrants fairly rapidly assimilate the general patterns of fertility behavior in the place of destination" (1971: 35).

It is obvious that there is no answer applicable to all migrants to cities everywhere. It also is clear that research on the subject barely has begun. We need to understand a great deal more about the factors affecting fertility in rural and urban areas. Some apparent contradictions, such as evidence that some migrants have lower fertility than long-term urban dwellers, may be understood by looking at the values held by migrants and the values associated with low fertility. In the following pages we will summarize the findings of a study of urban in-migration and urban living in Guayaquil, Ecuador, which examined the questions raised in the preceding paragraphs:

1. What values are involved in the relatively lower urban fertility as compared with the relatively higher rural fertility?
2. What is the process of acquiring these values?
3. How long does it take migrants to Guayaquil to acquire them?

METHODOLOGY

The data presented here were collected by a combination of methods: intensive anthropological research followed by a randomly sampled survey of two thousand households in the squatter settlements (called *suburbios*) and central-city slums (called *tugurios*) of Guayaquil. In each household, all women between the ages of fifteen and forty-five and all men currently in a sexual union with women in that age range were interviewed on such subjects as housing; job histories; economic factors; union and fertility histories; knowledge, attitudes, and practice of contraception; and migration (if migrants). One hundred househoulds in each of two rural villages (one coastal and one in the Ecuadorian Andes) also were interviewed.

This intensive-extensive methodology was designed to help the anthropologist cope with some of the problems of studying a large city, which cannot be approached in the same way as a small village, where every individual can become an acquaintance of the researcher. At the same time, it was believed that the usefulness and accuracy of survey research could be increased by designing and testing questions during the anthropological phase and combining the findings from both phases for a breadth and depth of understanding not available through either method alone. [2]

MIGRATION AND ADAPTATION TO THE CITY

Migrants [3] to Guayaquil come from the *sierra* (the Ecuadorian Andes) and the coast, and from cities over 10,000 and tiny villages (see Table 1). They are young (see Figure 1) and tend to be positively selected. Most men (65 percent) are single when they migrate, as are nearly half the women (48 percent). About a third of the women (36

[2] See Appendix A for a more detailed description of the methodology.
[3] For the purposes of the study of adaptation of migrants only individuals who were fifteen or older at the time of migration were interviewed. There were 381 men and 850 women who fitted into this category.

Figure 1. Age of migration to Guayaquil for men and women

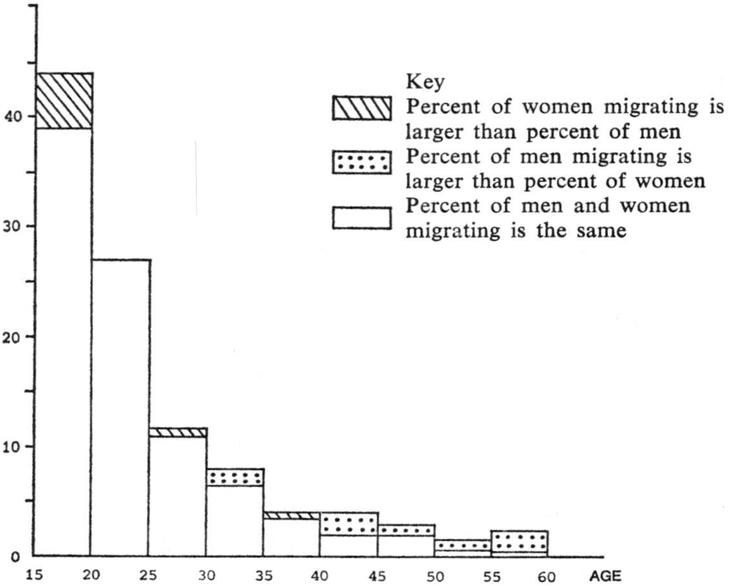

Key

⬛ Percent of women migrating is larger than percent of men

▦ Percent of men migrating is larger than percent of women

▢ Percent of men and women migrating is the same

Table 1. Size of place of birth for migrants

	Men Sierra		Coast		Oriente		Women Sierra		Coast		Oriente		Row total
	Number	Percent	Number	Percent	Number	Percent	Number	Percent	Number	Percent	Number	Percent	Number
Cities over 10,000	77	20	70	18	–	–	115	14	230	27	–	–	492
Towns under 10,000	26	7	49	13	7	2	39	5	136	16	8	1	265
Rural	47	12	104	27	–	–	66	8	254	30	–	–	471
Column totals	150	39	223	59	7	2	220	26	620	73	8	1	1,231
Total	Men — 381 — 100 Percent						Women — 850 — 100 Percent						

percent) bring children with them, but most of those who do bring only one or two. They are motivated primarily by what are called "pull" factors: the perceived opportunities in the city for jobs, education, and "a better life." Significantly more men are motivated by jobs and the opportunity to advance, while women seek education and a better life (P<.01).

Beyond these obvious reasons emerging from the survey data, the migrants I knew, and especially the men, had a deep concern with making a better life for their children. Because schools in the rural areas may not even go through the primary grades, migrating to the city has definite advantages. Women who migrated alone often were motivated by boredom and restriction on their activities in the villages, and the complementary attractions of independence and excitement in the city. Both men and women expected better health care in the cities.

Migration in Latin America sometimes involves several steps, where migrants move first to a town or small nearby city before moving to a major city (Macisco n.d.: 3). In the current study, 46 percent of the men and 32 percent of the women who came to Guayaquil had lived in a town or city other than their birthplace before migrating. Thus, less than half of all migrants had participated in step migration. This does not mean necessarily that most migrants came straight from their birthplace to reside in Guayaquil, with no previous experience beyond their home town. More than half of the men and women (69 and 56 percent respectively) had visited Guayaquil before migrating there. This finding bears out an impression gained during the intensive study that a great deal of visiting goes on between relatives in the city and the country.

These relatives also provided vital help for migrants during the adaptation process. Three-fourths (76) percent of the men and two-thirds (66 percent) of the women knew someone in Guayaquil before migrating, and over half stayed with friends or relatives after arrival. This type of help appears to have produced a different migration pattern for some migrants to Guayaquil. In the classic pattern migrants usually move first to the central city slums and only later to the squatter settlements, where they can build a home and hope to eventually own the land (Mangin 1967: 68). While more than half of the migrants now living in the *suburbios* originally came by way of the *tugurios*, staying there from a few days to over eight years, as many as a third migrated directly to the *suburbios*, their adaptation facilitated by friends and relatives there to welcome them.

Adaptation to the city seemed rapid. New migrants were defined as having arrived during the past year or so and were pointed at because they "went out" less often. Before too long, however, they would demonstrate greater familiarity with the city life and move about more freely. The "country bumpkin" was a well-developed concept and no one liked to remain one for long.

The real evidence of adaptation lies in the comparison of migrants with long-term urban dwellers. Male migrants and long-term urban dwellers were similar in many characteristics related to economic status. There was no statistically significant difference between the types of jobs held by the two groups, nor for most of the variables used in constructing a socioeconomic scale. The three exceptions were related to housing. Significantly more migrants than nonmigrants had poorer housing (usually bamboo), slightly more living space, and no electricity ($P < .05$, $P < .01$, $P < .05$). Also fewer migrants had television sets than did nonmigrants.

The likely explanation for these differences is that significantly more migrants live in the recently settled areas of the *suburbios* ($P < .05$), where most of the houses are still bamboo, and electricity has not yet reached all homes. However, there is more space per family because the squatters have established as much space as possible for themselves. Thus, the recently built house of cheap materials (which later will be replaced by a better one) is correlated with more living space. The difference in television-set ownership could be due to the scarcity of electricity rather than to economic factors, as migrants and nonmigrants do not differ significantly in their overall economic situation. The newly settled *suburbio* areas may lack some amenities, but they usually represent a step up for those who move there because they have a chance to claim a piece of the swamp and build their own homes.

While there are few economic differences between migrants and nonmigrants, the two hundred rural dwellers were not as well off. The people in the coastal village appeared to be better off economically than the people in the sierra village, but both villages ranked below all the urban sample areas in terms of the variables used to estimate economic status. Nor did the migrants feel they had all come from the top economic strata in their villages or towns. A third felt they had been better off than their neighbors, 24 percent felt they had been "worse off," while the remainder felt their situation had been about average.

Migrants appear to be positively selected in terms of education. While the rural school system is reportedly far less complete and extensive than the urban (Erickson 1966: 157), there is no statistically significant difference between the years of schooling for migrant and nonmigrant males ($P > .05$).

The data on education from the two rural villages support the idea that migrants, especially male migrants, as a group are more highly educated than the rural residents left behind. In both rural villages, 9 percent of the adults had received no formal schooling as compared with 5 percent of long-term urban dwellers and 7 percent of urban in-migrants. Ninety-seven percent of the sierra village residents and 98 percent of the coastal village residents had stopped their education after six grades or less, as compared with 67 percent of long-term urban dwellers and 91 percent of urban in-migrants. Because migrant and nonmigrant urban men showed no statistically significant difference, the figures on adult migrants influenced are strongly by the relatively lower educational status of migrant women. Three percent of the sierra village adults and 2 percent of the coastal village adults continued beyond the six primary grades, while 33 percent of urban nonmigrants and 9 percent of urban in-migrants continued their education. Less than one percent in both villages completed secondary school, while 6 percent of urban nonmigrants and 3 percent of migrants did. It is worth noting that a third of the migrants who entered secondary school completed it while only about a fifth of urban nonmigrants completed secondary school. Thus migrants clearly have more education than the rural norm.

There is a significant difference in reported educational levels for migrant and nonmigrant females (P<.01). This is not surprising in view of the relatively greater differences between male and female roles in the urban areas. The differences in educational levels of migrant males and females are statistically significant (P<.02), but the same is true for urban men and women (P<.05). This means that women in both the rural and urban settings have different (usually lower) educational levels than men, but that urban women have received significantly more education than migrant women, while men in both groups are roughly on a par. Given the low levels of education in rural areas, male migrants probably come from the more educated portion of the rural population. While some individuals acquire additional education after migrating (mostly on the secondary school level), comparisons with their reported years of schooling at time of migration reveal that most did not. However, of those who pursue further education in the city, proportionately more migrants persevere than among their long-term urban dweller counterparts.

Migrant and nonmigrant men's feelings about their current situation were also very similar. The majority of both groups described their current situation as "so-so," while 25 percent said it was "bad" and 13 percent said it was "good." Roughly two-thirds of both groups focused on the same reason for their "bad" or "so-so" current situations: "no money." Most, however, were optimists. Sixty-eight percent of both groups combined felt their situation would improve in the future.

Most of the remainder felt things would remain the same (15 percent).
A few felt things would get worse and the rest "didn't know."

The two groups of men also showed similar distribution in their
assessment of what "a better life" meant. To most it was "everything
one needs." To 14 percent it was "money," and to another 14 percent
it was "having a job."

Male migrants and nonmigrants did have different answers to the
question: "What is the problem which preoccupies you most at the
moment?" ($P < .02$). While portions of both groups were concerned
about their economic situations, proportionately more of the migrants
were concerned with debts, while more of the nonmigrants had
"family" problems.

There were no statistically significant differences between migrant
men and urban nonmigrant men for the variables probably related to
aspiration such as desire for change in their own lives and hopes for
children.

As rural aspirations are similar to those held by migrant and nonmigrant men in the city, it appears that all the men studied had aspirations in common. However, the migrant men were probably in a
better position to have a chance at attaining their aspirations than
were rural men. By migrating, they had done something concrete to
improve their lives.

It is, of course, difficult to predict the eventual success of migrants
in attaining the upward mobility they desire. Looking retrospectively,
the very fact that they do not differ economically from their nonmigrant urban neighbors means they have attained some degree of
success. Both the data and the people themselves indicate that life is
better in the city than in rural areas. The success of the migrants is
evident by their rapid assimilation.

However, the nonmigrant urban dwellers to whom in-migrants are
compared are themselves at or near the bottom, with little mobility.
While the migrants have moved up on the socioeconomic scale simply
by moving to the city, it is difficult to predict their success beyond
that initial move upward. It may be that, in studying the slums of
Guayaquil, we have caught them during one stage in their progress
toward a higher socioeconomic status than their nonmigrant counterparts will attain — but it would take another large study to find out.
Nevertheless, my feeling after a year of living and working in Ecuador
is that the migrants will be more upwardly mobile than their nonmigrant neighbors in the *tugurios* and *suburbios*.

FERTILITY

Sexual Unions

Types of sexual union in Ecuador fall primarily into two categories: those formalized by both church and state (formal marriages) and *compromisos*, sexual unions recognized by family and neighbors in which a man is expected to take responsibility for his partner and their children. In a *compromiso* as in a formal marriage, the family unit is known by a composite name composed of the last names of both partners. Partners in a *compromiso* do not always live together. If the man already has another union he will divide his time (not always equally) between the two households. Where he can, he will set up each woman in a separate household. If that is impossible (usually for financial reasons) there are nearly always relatives for one of the women to live with.

In addition to *compromisos*, there are more casual alliances or affairs which may or may not later become *compromisos*. As almost anywhere in the world, there are also "one-night stands" and prostitution.

Women begin to enter sexual unions as early as ages twelve and thirteen. Nonmigrant women are significantly younger when they first enter a union than are migrant women (P<.01). The mean age at first union is 18.4 for nonmigrants and 19.6 for migrants. Since around half of the migrant women were single at migration, the process of migrating probably delayed their first union.

Men have early sexual experience but start unions at later ages than women.[4] While over half the men had had sexual experience by age fourteen, most were in their late teens or in their twenties when they began their first union.

One third of all first unions had ended by the time the woman was interviewed. Nearly half of all first unions were legal marriages, but most of those that ended (83 percent), ended in separation rather than divorce or widowhood. Over two-thirds of women whose first union had ended went on to form a second union. A smaller proportion (23 percent) of these second unions also ended, again mainly through separation.

---

[4] It must be kept in mind that the sample consisted of all women between the ages of fifteen and forty-five but was limited to men currently in unions with women in those ages. Thus the two groups are only roughly comparable when union patterns are examined.

Forty-one percent of those women ending their second union initiated another one. Forty-three percent of these unions ended, with separation once more the principal reason. Over half of these women went on to a fourth union, but the number is very small at that point, so that out of 2,522 women who had sexual unions, only 14 (0.6 percent) had as many as four. Of the total number of women between the ages of fifteen and forty-five studied, 18.6 percent had never entered a union.

Another way to look at union histories is to compare women by the length of time since the start of the first union. Fertility behavior among women with different lengths of time since the first union then can be compared. However, this measure does not take into account interruptions in unions. For example, if two women start their first unions at the same time, and one is later divorced but initiates a new union after two more years, then she will have been exposed to preg-

Figure 2. Years in alliance and alliance span for men and women surveyed in Guayaquil

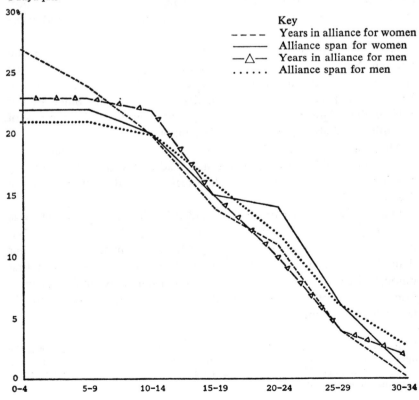

nancy two years less than the other woman who started her first union at the same time.

Dr. Samuel Wishik and three staff members of the International Institute for the Study of Human Reproduction have developed some alternative ways of analyzing union histories for polygynous men which can also be applied to women (Wishik et al. 1972). We call the measure of years since the start of the first union to the present the ALLIANCE SPAN. To deal with the problem of separations during the alliance span we developed a measure called YEARS IN ALLIANCE. Years in alliance is defined as "The number of years . . . engaged in any alliance . . . alliance span minus the total time periods spent in no alliance at all." (Wishik et al. 1972: 12). Figure 2 shows years in alliance and alliance span for the women studied. It is clear that years in alliance is a more accurate measure of exposure to pregnancy, greatly facilitating comparisons of groups of women.

Years in alliance does differ for migrant and nonmigrant women. The mean for migrants is 11.31 years in alliance and for nonmigrants it is 10.08 years. Thus, while migrant women married later than nonmigrant women, they are also older. The mean age for migrant women is 31.6, while the mean for nonmigrant women is 27.3. The difference is statistically significant ($P<.01$).

The male sample cannot be treated in precisely the same manner as the female sample because only men who were in unions with women between the ages of fifteen and forty-five were interviewed in the first place. This was done in order to concentrate the effort on the study of fertility. Thus, men who never started unions or were not currently in unions were not interviewed. Of the men who were studied, 29 percent had ended their first union, primarily through separation. More men began a second union than had ended their first one. Obviously, some of these men were polygynous. As can be seen in Figure 2, years in alliance is a more accurate measure of years during which responsibility for pregnancy was possible for men, just as for women (at least within formal unions). However, in order to take polygyny into account, another measure is necessary, which we have called ALLIANCE YEARS. Alliance years is defined as: "Sum of woman-years of relationships a man has spent in all his alliances separately or concurrently. A man who maintains two wives concurrently for ten years would have twenty alliance years at the end of the tenth year." (Wishik et al 1972: 12). This is clearly a more accurate measure of potential "child-producing" time for men in societies where polygyny occurs.

When the union histories of men and women are compared, it is evident that men have more unions than women. When ever-married women (in order to make the two groups roughly comparable because only men who were currently in unions were interviewed) are compared with the men, only 24 percent of the women have had two unions, compared to 31 percent of the men. Proportionately fewer women have had three unions — 2 percent as compared with 8 percent for men. Only 1 percent of the women had had four unions, compared to 2 percent of the men. No women had had more than four unions, while a few men (1 percent) had.

Family Size and Fertility

Table 2 reports the incidence and outcome of first and subsequent pregnancies for the women studied in Guayaquil. For first pregnancies, admitted induced and spontaneous abortions are relatively low, as are stillbirths. Total pregnancy wastage is only 103 per 1000 live births. It is possible that some pregnancies were missed. As the data were collected with great care, it is doubtful, however, that more could have been obtained retrospectively, i.e. some women had forgotten completely one or more pregnancies. The only concealment I suspect is of some induced abortions. It is likely that some of the "spontaneous" abortions were actually induced. About 89 percent of all firstborn survived at time of interview. Subsequent pregnancies show a rise in the proportions of both admitted induced abortions and spontaneous abortions, while stillbirths and infant and child deaths remain fairly constant. It is clear that with each succeeding pregnancy, the chance that another child will not be a welcome addition to the family increases. The rising proportions of admitted induced and spontaneous abortions probably reflect this. After about the tenth pregnancy, the numbers become too small to permit reliable interpretation.

Table 3 is a summary table of mean pregnancies and mean living children by age for migrants and nonmigrants. It would appear at first that migrants have higher fertility than nonmigrants. While the mean pregnancies and living children for both groups as a whole differ by about one child (3.4 pregnancies and 2.6 living children for nonmigrants as opposed to 4.2 pregnancies and 3.6 living children for migrants), when the means are compared age group by age group the differences are slight. The apparent difference in overall fertility is thus created by the significant difference in the age distributions of

Table 2. Frequency and outcome of first and subsequent pregnancies for urban women

Pregnancy number	Total Number	Total Percent[a]	Induced abortion Number	Induced abortion Percent[b]	Spontaneous abortion Number	Spontaneous abortion Percent[b]	Stillbirth Number	Stillbirth Percent[b]	Live birth Number	Live birth Percent[b]	Children dead since birth Number	Children dead since birth Percent[c]
	2,268	20.7	6	0.3	169	7.4	26	1.1	2,067	91.1	225	10.9
	1,978	18.1	19	0.9	197	9.9	31	1.5	1,731	87.5	194	11.2
	1,649	15.0	26	1.5	180	10.9	21	1.2	1,422	86.2	154	11.8
	1,322	12.1	19	1.4	146	11.0	12	0.9	1,145	86.6	125	10.9
	1,034	9.4	27	2.6	117	11.3	10	0.9	880	85.1	83	9.4
	794	7.2	21	2.6	83	10.4	10	1.2	680	85.6	61	8.9
	594	5.4	23	3.8	94	15.8	11	1.8	466	78.5	48	10.3
	429	3.9	17	3.9	58	13.5	5	1.1	349	81.4	33	9.5
	302	2.7	19	6.2	52	17.2	4	1.3	227	75.2	28	12.3
	207	1.8	12	5.7	35	16.9	5	2.4	155	74.9	24	15.4
	136	1.2	6	4.4	24	17.6	3	2.2	103	75.7	11	10.7
	86	0.7	4	4.6	12	13.9	0	0.0	70	81.4	10	14.3
	56	0.5	3	5.3	12	21.4	1	1.7	40	71.4	8	20.0
	32	0.2	2	6.2	4	12.5	1	3.1	25	78.1	3	12.0
	19	0.1	2	10.5	7	36.8	0	0.0	10	52.6	1	10.0
	8	<0.1	1	12.5	3	37.5	1	12.5	3	37.5	0	0.0
	5	<0.1	0	0.0	2	40.0	0	0.0	3	60.0	0	0.0
	3	<0.1	1	33.3	2	66.6	0	0.0	0	0.0	0	0.0
	3	<0.1	1	33.3	1	33.3	0	0.0	1	33.3	0	0.0
Total	10,925		209		1,198		141		9,377		1,008	
Percent[a]		99.8		1.9		10.9		1.2		85.8		10.7
Mean (N=2,936) 3.7										3.2		

a = Percent of total pregnancies.
b = Percent of row total (i.e. percent of 1st pregnancy, etc.).
c = Percent of live births.

Table 3. Mean number of pregnancies and of living children for migrant and nonmigrant women by age

Age	Nonmigrant Mean pregnancy	Nonmigrant Mean living children	Migrant Mean pregnancy	Migrant Mean living children
Lowest –19	0.4	0.3	0.5	0.5
20–24	1.7	1.4	1.9	1.6
25–29	3.7	2.9	3.6	2.8
30–34	5.2	3.9	4.6	3.7
35–39	6.5	4.8	6.6	4.9
40–+	6.9	5.1	7.1	5.4
Total	3.4	2.6	4.2	3.6

the two groups of women discussed previously. The larger proportion of older migrants thus weights the means for pregnancies and living children when age is not considered. When analysis of covariance is performed with age at marriage and current age held constant, there is no statistically significant difference between migrants and non-migrants in either the number of pregnancies or the current family size. While migrants marry slightly later, they average more years in alliance because they tend to be older. Again, when years in alliance are held constant, no significant differences in the numbers of pregnancies or family size are apparent.

Completed fertility for the population studied was about seven pregnancies, with about five children still alive. This turns out to be about two children more than the expressed ideal family size, discussed further on.

Table 4 summarizes number of "children ever fathered" reported by men, by alliance years and by age. The mean number of children ever fathered is slightly lower than the mean pregnancies for women

Table 4.   Children ever fathered by age of men and alliance years

Age	0–4	5–9	10–14	15–19	20–24	25–29	30–34	35–39	40–44	Tot
–19	0.53	–	–	–	–	–	–	–	–	0.53
20–24	1.30	2.23	–	–	–	–	–	–	–	1.47
25–29	1.53	3.04	4.79	–	–	–	–	–	–	2.59
30–34	2.03	3.54	4.93	6.18	7.00	10.25	–	–	–	4.20
35–39	1.33	3.84	5.52	5.98	11.88	9.00	–	–	–	5.77
40–44	2.60	4.93	5.24	6.65	7.27	10.43	8.00	–	11.50	6.51
45–49	2.00	5.00	5.78	6.67	8.00	8.95	8.25	15.00	15.00	7.72
50–54	–	6.00	7.67	6.50	7.14	9.70	8.82	13.00	–	8.49
55–59	–	4.00	6.00	6.00	9.20	10.14	11.25	–	–	9.70
Total	1.46	3.37	5.26	6.34	8.24	9.56	9.50	13.67	12.67	4.76

in each age group. However, comparisons are difficult because it is doubtful that men can provide the details on pregnancy wastage and dead children that women can supply. In fact, the means for men more closely resemble the mean number of living children for women than they do the mean number of pregnancies.

Women's fertility has a definite age limit, while men's does not. Men go on to produce children so that men between the ages of fifty-five and fifty-nine have an average of 9.7 children (the few cases of men over fifty-nine were dropped). Thus, men apparently have more children on the average than do women. Statistically, this can happen only if some men never marry, and if other men have more than one spouse (simultaneously or sequentially). This is indeed the case in the population studied.

The fertility behavior of migrant and nonmigrant women has been discussed, but in a study of adaptation to urban values, the migrant or nonmigrant origin of the spouse is also potentially of significance. In order to explore this further, the men and women interviewed were matched with their respective spouses and four types of couples designated: migrant men married to migrant women, migrant men married to nonmigrant women, nonmigrant men married to migrant women, and nonmigrant men married to nonmigrant women. After establishing that there were no significant differences in the number of pregnancies and living children among families in the various sample areas ($p > .05$), multiple stepwise regression[5] was performed, using the combined data from all sample areas for the four types of couples. The number of pregnancies and the number of living children in the CURRENT union were considered the dependent variables (each in a separate run). The independent variables included the four marriage types already described: the duration of the current union; economic status; aspirations; education; and knowledge, attitudes and use of contraception. Except for a very slight negative correlation between economic status and the dependent variables (.037), none of the variables affected pregnancies or living children except the duration of the current union. This varied among the four marriage types (see Table 5). Migrants married to migrants had current unions about two years longer than the other three marriage types, which resembled each other very closely. They also had about one more child than the other three groups.

Analyses of covariance were performed to see if the differences in the number of pregnancies were significant when the duration of the current union was controlled for. In one case, the dependent variable was the number of pregnancies; in the second run, it was the number of living children. The covariates were duration of current union. As Table 5 shows, controlling for the duration of union eliminates any significant difference in the number of pregnancies among the four groups. The same held true when number of living children was considered.

Migrants "married" to migrants have probably been in their unions longer because three-fourths of them started their unions before migra-

---

[5] All multivariate analyses were run by using the computer programs available in the Statistical Package for the Social Sciences (SPSS) and by the Biomedical Division of University of California at Los Angeles (BMD).

Table 5. Table of adjusted means and standard errors for analysis of covariance using pregnancies in current union as the dependent variable

Treatment group[a]	Mean duration of union	Treatment mean[b]	Adjusted mean	SE adjusted
1	11.96	5.2086	4.5540	0.1899
2	9.92	4.1094	4.1279	0.1970
3	9.59	4.0814	4.2087	0.1700
4	9.69	4.0766	4.1730	0.0848

[a] 1 = Migrants "married" to migrants.
   2 = Migrant men "married" to nonmigrant women.
   3 = Nonmigrant men "married" to migrant women.
   4 = Nonmigrants "married" to nonmigrants.
[b] Mean number of pregnancies.

tion. Migration evidently delayed the age of first union for those who migrated single. What is so surprising is that even those migrants who married while in their villages show no significant differences ($p > .05$) in fertility from the other three groups including long-term urban dwellers when the differences in length of union are adjusted for. That is very fast adaptation indeed, particularly because the data from the rural villages shows a mean family size of several children more than the urban family-size mean.

Similar analyses also were performed on the women alone, looking at their complete fertility histories. The regressions on the data for the women showed the same result as those for the couples: only duration (in this case years in alliance) had any effect on fertility.

The analysis of covariance again told the same story. Alternately using the number of pregnancies and the number of living children as dependent variables, and years in alliance as the covariate, no significant fertility differences between migrant and nonmigrant women existed. Aware that the age of onset of first union and the current ages varied for the two groups, we also ran the analysis using those variables as covariates. Again, there were no significant differences in the number of pregnancies or in family size.

SUMMARY AND CONCLUSIONS

Migrants from rural areas to Guayaquil in Ecuador appear to be a highly selected group. Most are young, and migrate single or before starting their families. They accommodate rapidly to the city, assisted by friends and relatives, so that as a group statistically they resemble long-term urban dwellers. For many accommodation appears to be a matter of a few years rather than a generation.

Their fertility is statistically equal to that of long-term urban dwellers when age and duration of union are held constant. This may be influenced by the intermarriage of migrants and nonmigrants, but as migrants married to each other show the same pattern it is doubtful. It appears more likely that migrants are an aspiring group who see the potential for the realization of some of their aspirations in urban values as probably related to comparatively low fertility. [6] The foremost such value mentioned in this study was aspiration for children's education. People felt their own lives would not change very much, but that their children had a chance for improvement through education. They also made a direct connection between the number of children they had and the extent to which they could educate them; fewer children could be sent farther through school. The economic advantages of fewer children were also perceived.

In the two rural villages studied, aspiration levels were high, but economic and educational levels were low, and possibilities for improving the situation were poor. Also low were the levels of knowledge of ways to prevent the occurrence of pregnancy within a union and acceptance of the concept of pregnancy prevention.

In the city, the available means of improving their situation were quickly perceived and utilized by migrants. Not only was this true for employment and educational opportunities, but migrants did not differ significantly from nonmigrants in their knowledge and use of contraception. Overall knowledge and use levels were relatively high (44 percent of the women used some form of contraception at some time, and 22 percent of the women are current users). Unfortunately, many of the methods used are fairly ineffective (such as rhythm and withdrawal), and the demand for acceptable means of preventing pregnancy is high (three-fourths of the women interviewed want no additional children). Nevertheless, urban dwellers manage to have fewer pregnancies than their rural counterparts.

On the basis of the evidence presented here, some answers to the questions posed in the beginning of this paper emerge. Some of the values leading to lower fertility are aspirations for children and improved economic status of the family. The city provides at least the

---

[6] Urban fertility in Guayaquil is not low, at a complete fertility of about seven pregnancies with an average of five living children. However, rural fertility is at least two pregnancies higher, so that urban immigrants have altered their fertility behavior.

hope of realizing these aspirations, as well as the means to limit fertility. Migrants adapt to the city rapidly, and have fertility patterns similar to the urban ones within the same generation.

APPENDIX: METHODOLOGY

Guayaquil is a tropical port city of approximately one million people located where the Daule and Babahoyo Rivers meet to form the Guayas River, which empties into the Pacific Ocean 100 miles downstream.

The two areas that receive most of the migrants are shown on Map 1. The *tugurios*, or central-city slums, are in the heart of the business district, which extends westward from the river. There is a small transitional zone to the west of the *tugurios* containing some slum dwellings, and then the vast *suburbio* begins, crawling visibly further into the swamps and estuaries each year. The area in downtown Guayaquil between the *tugurios* and *suburbio* is mostly middle and lower upper-class housing. The very wealthy live in suburbs to the north.

The intensive phase of the project focused on the *suburbios*. I located a house in an area which is solid ground in the dry season, but within walking distance of the swamps still being settled. It was intermediate between the best and worst dwellings in the area.

In this setting, I conducted traditional ethnographic research through participant-observation, interviews, and conversation. Many questions were tested for possible use in the survey. A total of sixty-five households were studied in January through May 1971.

On the basis of the intensive work, five questionnaires were designed and pretested:

1. Household: Basic questions on household composition, ages, occupations and education of household members, house type and ownership, household inventory and exposure to mass media.

2. Migration (urban questionnaire): Administered to any individual who had arrived in Guayaquil at or after age fifteen. It included questions on situation at place of origin, reasons for, and circumstances of migration, expectation of changes the city would bring to his or her life, accommodation to the city, and current expectations and aspirations.

3. Male: Administered to males involved in a sexual union with a woman (or women) in the fifteen to forty-five-year age group. Questions were asked on job history, working hours, aspirations for self and for children, knowledge, attitudes and practice of contraception, fertility and sexual union histories, attitudes toward induced abortion, ideal family size, and feelings about children and *machismo*.

4. Female: For women between the ages of fifteen and forty-five. If, however, there was a girl under fifteen in a sexual union she also was interviewed. This questionnaire elicited information on nutrition and beliefs about food, food-buying habits, employment history, sexual union history, a detailed fertility history, knowledge, attitudes and practice of contraception, knowledge, attitudes, and use of family planning clinics, female

Plan of Guayaquil

sterilization, induced abortion, and ideal family size.

5. Migration (rural questionnaire): Administered to household heads and teenagers in the villages in order to learn the extent of knowledge about Guayaquil, and to measure the feelings about migrating there.

The sample was drawn by Professor Albino Bocaz of Centro Latino Americano de Demografía (CELADE), Santiago, Chile, with the assistance of Ernesto Pinto Rojas. It did not involve the entire city of Guayaquil, as the upper and upper-middle classes were not part of the study population. The upper classes live mainly in a few exclusive neighborhoods, which were eliminated. The sample then was drawn in four areas:

1. The central city slums (*tugurios*)
2. The *suburbios* settled at the time of the 1962 census
3. The *suburbios* settled since the 1962 census
4. An intermediate zone between the *tugurios* and *suburbios*, which contained a few *tugurio* type buildings.

The sixty-five families studied intensively also were interviewed as a special sample in order to see how they compared to a random sample and to compare what they would tell an interviewer with what I already knew about them. They "fit" well when compared to the large sample. The report on which this paper is based contains a comparison of data obtained intensively and extensively.

The number interviewed in each area was in proportion to the estimated population of the area. Households were revisited two times if eligible individuals were not at home when the first visit was made. The refusal rate for households was a low 1.65 percent. In all, 2,294 families were interviewed in the city. Slightly under a hundred families, also selected randomly, were interviewed in each village.

Interviewing began on September 13, 1971. There were six teams of five girls each, three full-time teams and three part-time teams. All of the blocks selected for the survey had been canvassed by November 14. Coding, keypunching, and verifying were completed by December 15.

REFERENCES

CARLETON, R. O.
1965   Fertility trends and differentials in Latin America. *Milbank Memorial Fund Quarterly* 43:27–29.
DAVIS, K., A. CASIS
1946   Urbanization in Latin America. *Milbank Memorial Fund Quarterly* 24(3):186–207.
ERICKSON, E. E.
1966   *Area handbook for Ecuador.* Washington, D.C.: U.S. Superintendent of Documents.
GOLDBERG, D.
1959   The fertility of two-generation urbanites. *Population Studies* 12 (3):214–222.
GOLDSTEIN, S.
1971   *Interrelations between migration and fertility in population re-*

distribution in Thailand. Institute of Population Studies Research Report 5. Bangkok, Thailand: Chulanlongkorn University.

HAWLEY, A. H.
1969 "Population growth and urbanization in developing countries." Paper presented at the National Academy of Sciences. Woods Hole Conference, July 27-August 8, 1969.

KISER, C. V.
1971 Unresolved issues in research on fertility in Latin America. *Milbank Memorial Fund Quarterly* 49(3, part 1):379–388.

MACISCO, J. J., JR.
n.d. "Some thoughts on an analytical framework for rural to urban migration." Paper prepared for Centro Latino Americano de Demografia (CELADE), Santiago, Chile.

MACISCO, J. J., JR., R. H. WELLER, L. F. BOUVIER
1969 "Some general considerations on migration, urbanization, and fertility in Latin America," in *The family in transition: a round table conference sponsored by the John E. Fogarty International Center for Advanced Study in the Health Sciences, National Institutes of Health, Bethesda, Maryland, November 3–6, 1969. Fogarty International Center Proceedings* 3:285—297.

MANGIN, W.
1967 Latin American squatter settlements: a problem and a solution. *Latin American Research Review* 2(3):65–98.

MERTENS, W., C. A. MIRO
1969 *Influencia de algunas variables intermedias en el vivel y en las differenciales de fecundidad urbana y rural de America Latina.* Santiago, Chile: Centro Latino Americano de Demografia (CELADE).

MICKLIN, M.
1969 Urban life and differential fertility: specification of an aspect of the theory of the demographic transition. *Sociological Quarterly* 10(4):480–500.

POOL, D. I.
1969 "The rural-urban fertility differential in Ghana." Paper presented at the General Conference of the International Union for the Scientific Study of Population, London, September 1969.

ROBINSON, W. C.
1963 Urbanization and fertility: the non-Western experience. *Milbank Memorial Fund Quarterly* 41:291—308.

SPEARE, A., JR., M. C. SPEARE, H.-S. LIN
1972 "Urbanization, nonfamilial work, and fertility in Taiwan." Paper presented at the Annual Meeting of the Population Association of America, Toronto, April 1972.

STYCOS, J. M.
1965 Needed research in Latin American fertility: urbanization and fertility. *Milbank Memorial Fund Quarterly* 43(2):255–273.

UNITED NATIONS
1961 "Demographic aspects of urbanization in Latin America," in *Urbanization in Latin America.* Edited by P. Hauser, 91–115.

Population Branch, United Nations. New York: International Documents Service.

WELLER, R. H., J. MACISCO

1970   *Migration, aspirations for social mobility, and fertility in developing countries: suggestions for further research.* Providence, Rhode Island: Population Research and Training Center, Department of Sociology, Brown University.

WISHIK, S. M., K. H. CHEN, S. KLEIN, S. SCRIMSHAW

1972   "The definition and measurement of male fertility." Paper presented at the Annual Meeting of the Population Association of America, Toronto, April 1972.

ZARATE, A. O.

1967   "Community of origin, migration and completed marital fertility in metropolitan Monterrey." Paper presented at the Annual Meeting of the Population Association of America, Cincinnati, Ohio, April 1967.

Residential Patterns and Population Movement into the Farmlands of Yorubaland

PHILIP O. OLUSANYA

Since the early years after World War II when the tempo of rural-urban migration in Nigeria began to accelerate as a result of overall population growth and the increasing socioeconomic disparities between urban and rural areas (Olusanya 1972; Green 1972; Prothero 1968: 252), much attention has been devoted to the problems of urbanization, and proposals have often been put forward designed to stem the rush of rural dwellers to the towns. In an attempt to solve the urban population problems of particular areas or states, however, the equally important question of the mass movement of population from the rural area of a given state to the rural area of another or from one rural area to another within a state and the factors associated with this movement, which tends to further impoverish the area of out-migration, have been virtually neglected by planners.

Of course, rural-rural migration is not new in Nigeria, and attention has been drawn to its existence and neglect (Barbour 1965: 47–68). The volume and distance traversed has, however, considerably increased since 1930 following the establishment of civil administration spanning virtually the whole country, and the banning of human sacrifices which in the past made it very hazardous for people to venture beyond their clan territory. Today, large numbers of Ibo, Igbira, Urhobo, Hausa, and Ibibio migrants are to be found particularly in the Yoruba cocoa belt and the Benin rubber belt (Udo 1972: 1). In other words, the direction of rural-rural migration in Nigeria has by and large been north-south and east-west, the larger stream being toward the main Yoruba cocoa belt in the eastern sector of the Western State, beginning roughly from Ife Division. The emphasis here will be on migration into the farmlands of the Western State from the savannah region immediately north of the forest belt. We will examine the socioeconomic factors that act as a "push" to, as well as those that attract, the migrants. These factors have hitherto been the subject of much speculation and intelligent observation. Although these speculations and observations often contain some truth, they are not specific enough to provide a clear understanding of the process. We will also examine some aspects of Yoruba social organization which are particularly favorable to the influx of rural dwellers from other parts of the country. Finally, we will consider the question of the identity of the migrants, what land tenure rights they have, whether they are permanent or temporary settlers, their reasons for leaving their home areas, their link with the area of origin, and their contribution to the socioeconomic development of the area of settlement.

SOURCE OF DATA AND SOME CHARACTERISTICS OF THE RESPONDENTS

Exploratory investigation during the early stages of the study in 1971 revealed that migrant farmers are concentrated in the eastern quadrant of the Western State which coincides with the largest cocoa-producing area of Yorubaland. In this eastern sector, about 600 villages and hamlets almost exclusively inhabited by these migrants were discovered, the highest concentration being in Ife Division. These migrant settlements are located within short distances of the villages of the landlords.

The main survey was therefore restricted to this area, not because there are no migrant farmers elsewhere in the state, but because they are scattered over a wide area and their number in any given place is comparatively insignificant. Moreover, unlike those in the eastern sector, they invariably live with their hosts in the same communities so that locating them for interview would have been an extremely difficult task. Eight hundred and fifty-three migrant households were interviewed between July and September 1972. The preliminary data used here are drawn from this survey.

The migrant farmers are not homogeneous in terms of ethnic group or area of origin. They may be divided into three categories: (a) migrants indigenous to the Western State but from outside the survey area, (b) migrants from the neighbouring Kwara State, and (c) the rest of the migrants who are from other states in Nigeria.

Table 1 shows the relative proportions of these groups. The group of migrants from other areas of the Western State preponderate. They constitute about 70 percent of the total migrant farmers. Of the migrants

Table 1.   Place of origin of the migrants

State of origin	Number	Percent
Western State	604	70.8
Mid-West State	41	4.8
East-Central State	36	4.2
South-Eastern State	4	0.5
Kwara State	162	19.0
Benue-Plateau State	6	0.7
Total	853	100.0

from outside the Western State, however, the Kwara group is by far the largest, being 19 percent of the total or approximately two-thirds of migrants from outside the Western State. A little less than 5 percent are from the Mid-West State immediately to the east of Yorubaland and in the same vegetation zone, and the East-Central State or Iboland further east across the River Niger. The other groups — South-Eastern and Benue-Plateau States — constitute less than one percent of the total.

A breakdown of the figure for the indigenous group in Table 2 reveals

Table 2.   Migrants of Western State origin by division of origin

Division of origin	Number	Percent
Egba	7	1.2
Egbado	1	0.2
Ibadan	22	3.6
Oshun	304	50.3
Oyo	17	2.8
Akoko	38	6.3
Ekiti	63	10.4
Ondo	4	0.7
Owo	4	0.7
Ife	95	15.7
Ilesha	43	7.1
Akure	6	1.0
Total	604	100.0

that three out of every five of the migrants, as would be expected, are from the savannah belt in the extreme north of Yorubaland, where, as will be shown later, the soil is relatively poor and the climate is not suitable for the cultivation of a variety of crops. Oshun, Oyo, and Akoko Divisions of the Western State lie largely in this vegetation zone, so that if the total number of migrants from the savannah region is taken regardless of whether they originate from within or without the Western State, the overall proportion of migrants from this zone will be a little over three-fifths of the total. The migrant farmers can thus be said to be pre-dominantly from the savannah region of south-west Nigeria.

Although the migrants were engaged in various occupations prior to leaving home, most of them were farmers while the rest were largely petty traders, laborers, craftsmen, washermen, hunters, and the like (Table 3). It must not be thought, however, that those who said they were

Table 3.   The nature of the migrants' occupations before leaving home

Occupation	Number	Percent
Farming	563	66.0
Trading	65	7.6
Artisan	80	9.4
Laborer (washerman, hunter, etc.)	59	6.9
Teaching/clerical	8	0.9
None – attending school	25	2.9
No response	53	6.3
Total	853	100.0

nonfarmers before migrating were completely divorced from agriculture. The persons concerned more often than not have farms of their own on which they largely subsist and from which they may occasionally derive additional incomes. The amount of time devoted to farming is related to the type of non-agricultural occupation engaged in. A mason or road laborer, for example, may spend more of his time on his farm during peri-ods when building activities or road works are considerably reduced.

The migrants have various types of tenure rights as Table 4 shows.

Table 4.   Types of tenure rights

Types	Number of migrants	Percent
Inherited from parent	92	10.8
Acquired from family land	319	37.4
Bought from other family	61	7.1
Rented from other family	48	5.6
Pledged to me	34	4.0
Sharecropping	41	4.8
Leased to me	79	9.3
Transferred to me by other farmer	97	11.4
Various combinations of other types	82	9.6
Total	853	100.0

About 52 percent acquired rights to the land they cultivate through out-right purchase, tenancy or subtenancy, pledging, sharecropping, lease-hold, and various combinations of these. About 45 percent have temporary rights to the land they cultivate. Considering the data presented in Tables 1 and 2, the proportion in the latter category (i.e. excluding cases of outright purchase) should have been substantially higher. As, for example, 359 of the migrants are from Oshun, Oyo, and Akoko Divisions of the Western State which are clearly outside the survey area, and as 162 of them are from Kwara State, and 87 are from East-Central State as shown in Table 1, then the total number of migrants who are both from outside the survey area and outside the Western State is 608. It is, therefore, highly improbable that as many as 411 (Table 4) or 48.2 percent of the migrants inherited their land from parents or acquired it from family land.

This distortion is probably due to a misunderstanding of the question and consequent misrecording of the responses by the interviewer.[1] For example, the interviewers might have interpreted the words "acquired from family land" to mean that the migrants acquired the holdings from the family land of their landlords. If it had been understood as meaning their own family land, the responses in this category would probably have been reduced to almost nothing.

It is possible, however, that the parents of the migrants had bought the land outright from the original owners some years back so that it could have been inherited by sons or part of it could have been acquired by them; this was actually why the first two categories were included. Nevertheless, the number involved would certainly be negligible considering the system of land tenure among the Yoruba (Adegboye 1967: 340; Olusanya 1969: 30).

In fact, according to Udo (1972: 3), a widespread source of friction between migrant farmers and their hosts is the tendency for some of the migrants to claim title to the land which they have cultivated for many years. This has resulted in a new regulation in Owo, Western State, in which migrant farmers are obliged to take out short leases of rarely more than two years, after which the lease may be renewed.

It is correct to say, therefore, that the vast majority of the migrants have only temporary tenure rights to the land they cultivate and can be regarded as tenant farmers of a sort, and that they are mainly from the savannah region of southwestern Nigeria.

FACTORS CONSTITUTING A "PUSH" TO THE MIGRANTS

Southwest Nigeria, from which an overwhelming majority of the migrants originate, may be divided roughly into two vegetation or farming zones —

[1]   The question was structured.

the forest and the savannah. In the forest zone, which is well watered by heavy annual rainfall, oil palm, kolanut, cocoa (the most important export crop), and other important food crops are to be found. In the most northerly part of the region, the forest gradually thins out and the vegetation takes on the character of savannah. Here rainfall is relatively scanty and there is often an acute shortage of water, especially during the dry season (Olusanya 1969: 28). The savannah zone, therefore, tends to be much poorer than the forest zone.[2] This area (particularly Oshun Division) for several decades has exported people not only to the forest zone to the south, but also to other West African countries, especially to Ghana before the Aliens Compliance Order of 1970 forced them to return in thousands.

Further north, the savannah extends beyond the Western State into the neighboring Kwara State which forms part of an ecological zone known in Nigerian geography as the "Middle Belt" and spanning the central portion of the country from Borgu in the west to Adamawa in the east. Migrants from this area constitute about two-thirds of migrants from outside the Western State. Buchanan and Pugh (1955: 61–63), who seem to be the authors of the Middle Belt concept, contend that very low population densities are typical of most parts of the Belt. Although this view has been criticized on the grounds that the population figures on which it was based were unreliable and that the authors had at their disposal only data on divisional population densities that obscured local variations, the generalization is valid even when more adequate and recent population figures are used, since the Belt contains more extensive empty areas than any other part of Nigeria (Agboola 1968: 292–293).

The generalization is, however, subject to certain reservations. Sparseness of the population in the Belt, for example, does not apply to the whole area. Ilorin Division is a case in point. This Division of the Kwara State has a fairly dense rural population with densities varying from 200 to 400 persons per square mile (Agboola 1968: 292). So also has Kabba

---

[2]   The sharp socioeconomic contrast between communities in the savannah belt and those in the rain forest was described by Lloyd (1955: 236) as follows: "Today, one would have to go to the savannah country to the north of Oyo to find towns almost completely composed of traditional compounds. In the cocoa belt the old compounds are vanishing and being replaced by modern one- and two-storied, cement-faced residences." Also this contrast has been held responsible for what the International Labour Organization team in Western Nigeria referred to as "scholarization" or the level of primary school enrollment. According to the team, "Divisions with high cocoa production, or Divisions with large capital-forming centres have progressed." (International Labour Organisation Mission 1965: 28). These large capital-forming centers and centers of high cocoa production, incidentally, are in the forest belt.

Province which, together with Ilorin Province, constitutes Kwara State. The overall population density of Kabba Province was 117 in 1963. The Kwara State must therefore be regarded as a densely populated area within the Middle Belt in spite of the existence of areas of low density.

Added to the high density of Kwara State is the fact that this area is predominantly rural with only 18 percent of the total population living in communities with 20,000 or more inhabitants. While this proportion may appear impressive in terms of the overall degree of urbanization in Nigeria,[3] in terms of the distribution of the urban population over a land area of 28,672 square miles, the pace of urbanization can be said to have been very slow in this State. There were only nine towns in Kwara State according to the 1963 census. Two of these, Ilorin (208,546) and Offa (86,425), contained 70 percent of the total urban population of the State; within Ilorin Division itself, there were no other settlements with more than 5,000 inhabitants outside of Ilorin town and "small agricultural settlements, which give the Division some of the highest settlement densities in the area, are the predominating feature" (Agboola 1968: 292). The remaining seven towns had populations varying between 20,000 and 32,000 and these, within the Nigerian context, are invariably overwhelmingly agricultural communities. In the State as a whole, most of the few industries are concentrated in Ilorin, the capital, so that the State does not provide an adequate outlet for prospective rural-urban migrants.

The problems of the area have been further complicated by the unsuitability of most parts for large-scale agriculture and cattle raising which thrive in the savannah land in the extreme north of Nigeria. Various studies of the soils carried out in the past indicated that there is widespread occurrence of iron-pan surface underlying shallow red loams, and that the iron-pan soils come near to the top soil on the higher and middle slopes. The thickness of the iron-pan layer in the Kabba area is said to be as much as four feet (Agboola 1968: 295). While this satisfies the inhabitants' need for food crop production, it does not offer opportunities for the cultivation of export crops.

However, a more important factor which prevents the cultivation of export crops is climate. Cocoa cannot thrive here; neither can other cash crops such as kolanuts and oil palm found in abundance in the Western State, and groundnuts which grow well farther north. A case in point is the failure of repeated attempts to introduce the Allen variety of cotton into the area from 1910 to the 1930's. These experiments showed that

---

[3]　About 19 percent of Nigeria's population lives in communities with at least 20,000 people and in most of the other states the proportion is around 10 percent.

rainfall and pests are important factors in the failure of the crops. It was found that rainfall in August and after October had an adverse effect on cotton fields (Mason and Jones 1924; Golding 1925).

In the Middle Belt as a whole, the more humid conditions, the taller grasses, and woodland vegetation along the river valleys tend to offer a more favorable habitat to the tsetse fly which causes trypanosomiasis and thus makes it much more difficult to rear cattle than in the less humid climate of the northern plains where Nigeria's cattle population is concentrated.

The mass movement of farmers from the Guinea savannah to the forest zones is thus a reaction against the limited opportunities in that area. The process has become particularly pronounced since the cocoa boom of the 1950's and has led to the emergence of two categories of migrant farmers in the Western State. In the first category are farmers interested mainly in the cultivation of cocoa and in the second category are farmers from outside the forest zone who take up land for food crop production and sale to cocoa farmers both indigenous and migrant.

In addition to the Western State being the most urbanized area of Nigeria, with the implication that the demand for food crops will be high, many rural districts are short of food because of the concentration of local inhabitants on tree crop production for export. This overemphasis of the indigenous farmers on tree crop production is in turn a product of their social organization. The food situation is such that the inhabitants have to purchase up to 50 percent or more of their food requirements for the year (Udo 1972: 1).

Many of these food crop farmers are Igbiras from the Igbira Division of Kabba Province. Their hamlets (Aba Igbira), consisting of several mud huts with grass roofs, are dotted here and there in the small patches of grassland that punctuate the forest zone. Their main crop is yam which is transported in lorries to the Yoruba towns by urban middlemen or brought by travelers or local inhabitants in small quantities for direct consumption.

In many areas (notably Imesi-Lasigidi, Ile-Oluji, and Igbara Oke), the landlord almost invariably lives in the nearby town though he may have a house in a rural settlement which he visits occasionally or regularly, depending on circumstances. The migrant camps or settlements are usually named after him and he is responsible to the local authority of the area for collecting taxes from his tenants as it is not always easy for tax clerks to know their exact number or location in the bush. In other cases, the settlements, as in the case of the Igbira group, are given names denoting the origin of the migrants (Aba Ilorin, Aba Oyo, etc.). The illiterate or semi-literate among the landlords tend to live more permanently in their farm villages and can to some extent supervise the migrant farmers.

ASPECTS OF YORUBA SOCIAL ORGANIZATION

The unsuitability of the soils and climate of the Guinea savannah constitutes an important factor in the mass exodus of farmers in this area, and the forest belt immediately to the south is the destination of large numbers of these migrants because of the opportunity it offers them for planting cocoa (in particular for export) and food crops to cater to the increasing demands of the local inhabitants. That the Yoruba forest abounds with opportunities for farmers is, however, not sufficient to account for the presence and continued influx of migrant farmers.

Of course, although there is probably no area in Nigeria where such a concentration of migrant colonies is to be found as in the Yoruba area, migrants from depressed areas also find their way to other prosperous agricultural areas of southern Nigeria such as the rich farmlands of the Cross River district and areas immediately north and east of Port Harcourt in eastern Nigeria. However, the conditions governing their acceptance by the host communities in these areas are different from those in the Yoruba cocoa belt. For example, according to Udo (1972: 2), migrants are more welcome in districts where they perform duties which do not bring them into direct competition for opportunities with the indigenous people. He gives as an example the Abakaliki district in eastern Nigeria where migrant tenant rice farmers are favorably received because the indigenes attach more importance to yam cultivation than that of rice, and the swamps which the migrants cultivate are not suitable for yam and so were formerly left uncultivated.

In the Yoruba forests, in contrast, no such conditions exist and both migrant and indigenous farmers plant cocoa or any other crops they like. The only stipulated condition is that rent should be paid either in cash or in kind. This partly accounts for the influx of farmers to the area, though it does not explain why numerous colonies of migrants are to be found there, with freedom to cultivate any piece of land of high or low quality as long as they are prepared to pay for it.

Much more important, therefore, is the pattern of residence of the Yoruba, which makes prospective and long-staying migrant farmers welcome in this area, not merely as farm laborers (though a number may have intitially come in this category in order to secure much needed funds for farming implements and a few other essential articles) but largely as tenants.

The existence of large Yoruba settlements dates back some two to three hundred years (Bascom 1959: 31). The Yoruba, in other words, are traditionally town-dwellers, though they were (and a substantial proportion of them still are) urban farmers.[4]

A belt of farmlands usually surrounded the town and sometimes extended a few miles outside it. Farmers whose farms were on the outskirts of the town usually returned every day to their homes in town, while those whose farms were about a day's walk from town (probably a development of later years) usually stayed for many days, sometimes months, on their farms, returning to their "home-towns"[5] occasionally for rest and religious celebrations. This was what Lloyd (1959: 46) meant when he said:

Among the northern Yoruba all members of the town officially reside within its walls; on the blocks of farmland are hamlets. The Yoruba farmers here are commuters of degrees varying from the man who visits his farm once monthly or weekly to supervise his sons and laborers, to the poor farmer who lives in the hamlet throughout the year, returning to the town only for its annual religious festivals or for important lineage functions.

This system of dual habitation was, and is still to some extent, one of the distinguishing characteristics of the social organization of the Yoruba (Goddard 1965: 21).

The rapid pace of urbanization among the Yoruba in the past four decades, with the concomitant diversification of the towns' economy, has, however, modified significantly this pattern of residence. Today over 50 percent of the total population of the Western State live in communities with at least 20,000 inhabitants in contrast to about one fifth for Nigeria as a whole. About a quarter live in communities with at least 100,000 people. In 1952 only 38 percent of the population lived in communities with 20,000 or more people and about 20 percent in those with 100,000 or more people.

This situation has been brought about largely by the mass migration of rural dwellers to the towns on a scale probably unprecedented since the cessation of inter-tribal wars in the dying years of the last century. It would appear that in the early days of settlement, farms were within short distances of the town, so that it was unnecessary to have farm villages, and that farmers lived in town and did their farming from there. Later, however, farming had to be done much farther afield, probably as a result

[4]   This is what Kenneth Little (1960: 92) refers to as "*rus in urbe*."
[5]   The distinction between "home-town" and village (which is usually regarded as a work camp) among the Yoruba is so important that in some areas persons dying in the village are almost invariably conveyed to their ancestral compounds in the town (Olusanya 1969: 6–10).

of population growth. Since farming was almost the only way to make a living, it was imperative to live very close to the main source of livelihood, at least for short periods. Semi-permanent farm villages were therefore indispensable and farmers moved back and forth between village and town.

Today migration, particularly of youths, is more or less permanently from village to town. This is attributable to the spread of education in the Yoruba area since the introduction of free primary education in 1955 coupled with the increasingly sharp socioeconomic disparities between the urban and the rural sectors. The rural-urban drift has been facilitated by the fact that most village Yorubas belong to one town or another, and the average distance between a village and a large town is rarely more than twenty miles. In the past, poor communications made for extensive stays in the villages. Today, however, the complex network of roads which links one town with another and the numerous satellite villages with their parent towns, and the significant developments in transportation make it easy for people to move between village and town and between one town and another.

In a rural-urban migration study a few years ago, it was found that many of the inhabitants of the village Oluwatedo north-west of the Western State were not only regularly visiting their home town Oyo because of easy transportation, but were spending much more time there than in the village. In fact, some were permanently based in the town and paid only occasional visits to the farm (Olusanya 1969: 22).

Table 5.   Place of residence of landlord

Place of residence	Number	Percent
In this village	333	39.0
In another village	135	15.8
In the town	330	38.7
No response (laborer, farm inherited, etc.)	55	6.5
Total	853	100.0

This migration trend is clearly visible in Table 5 which shows the place of residence of landlords as stated by the migrants in the present study. Roughly two-fifths of the landlords lived in town, while about half either lived in the villages where the migrants were interviewed or in another village. Considering what has been said about the system of dual habitation, the latter group of landlords can hardly be regarded as permanent village dwellers, since their length of stay in the village or town depends on circumstances.

The availability of alternative modes of employment (retail trading, crafts, drumming, etc.) in the large and growing town makes protracted stays on the farm unnecessary, while the comparatively poor living conditions in the rural area make continued stay there unattractive. This situation has encouraged the mass immigration of tenant farmers from other areas and has facilitated their acceptance by the Yoruba landlords. The influx of migrant farmers is in turn tending to encourage what might be termed absentee landlordism among the forest Yoruba.

THE MIGRANTS' REASONS FOR LEAVING HOME

So far a description of the background factors that predispose the migrants to leave their home areas has been given. While it is obvious from the facts that economic considerations are very important in the decision of the rural migrants to leave home for another rural area, one frequently finds that there are other non-economic factors which contribute to the volume of emigration. This is supported by the responses shown in Tables 6 and 7.

Table 6. Which is better: life in home area or in the present place of settlement

Responses	Number	Percent
Present village/settlement	770	90.3
Home area	46	5.4
No difference	17	2.0
Don't know/no response	20	2.3
Total	853	100.0

Table 6 gives the responses of the migrants to the question as to whether or not they considered life in their home area preferable to life in their present settlement. Nine-tenths of the migrants, as would be expected, expressed a preference for life in their present area of settlement while a little less than a tenth either preferred their home area and had migrated for some reasons that are non-economic (see below) or felt that there was no difference.

In Table 7 we show the responses of the migrants to the question: Why did you not stay in your home area to do the kind of work you are doing now? They show a variety of reasons for migrating to their present settlement. A little over four-fifths of the migrants gave economic reasons in general, and about seven-tenths gave reasons that were specifically related to the unsuitability of their home areas for large-scale commercial farm-

Table 7. Migrants' reasons for not staying at home

Reasons	Number	Percent
Former work not lucrative	105	12.3
No fertile land for planting cocoa	127	14.9
Insufficient farmlands	292	34.2
Land not fertile generally	168	19.7
Family reasons	25	2.9
Change of environment	41	4.8
Not sufficient palm trees	3	0.4
No cocoa plantations in home area (produce buyer)	1	0.1
No work (laborer and mason before migrating)	13	1.5
Trouble in home area	11	1.3
No response/can't say	67	7.9
Total	853	100.0

ing. Taking the responses individually, by far the most important reason given by the migrants for leaving home is the insufficiency of farmlands: about one-third of the migrants gave this reason. Next in importance is infertility of the land in the home area generally: about one-fifth of the migrants gave this reason. Next to this is the unsuitability of the home area for cocoa in particular. All told, a little over one-third of the respondents migrated from their home areas because the land was either unsuitable for cocoa or generally infertile.

It is interesting to note the responses of those migrants who had other than economic reasons for leaving home. Almost one-tenth of them gave such reasons. Some left their homes for "family reasons" which are not specified; others left because of trouble in the area, and yet others migrated simply because they wanted a change of environment.

RELATIONSHIP OF THE MIGRANTS TO THEIR HOME AREAS

To the Yoruba, like other southern Nigerians, the home area is very important. That is where most of his kinsmen live and that is where he hopes to be buried if he happens to die unexpectedly in a "foreign" territory. He makes sure that he visits there at least once a year for the annual family reunion (Adepoju 1972: 11; Olusanya 1969: 7). In some cases, his children are sent there to live with relatives when they reach school age. He considers himself a failure in life unless he can erect a building of his own, superior in architectural design to the dwelling units in the lineage compound, or refashion the family house. Above all, his aged parents who, in conformity to tradition, must be provided for, live there. Hence his strong links with the home area and his consequent lack of a spirit of commitment to the socioeconomic development of the host area.

One clear evidence of strong attachment to the home area is the regular cash remittance home and the purposes for which it is used (Adepoju 1972: 12). Data relating to home remittance are presented in Tables 8, 9, and 10. As Table 8 shows, about 55 percent of the migrants said that they had sent money home during the past year. The proportion who said that they had sent nothing home seems unusually large, considering the responses in the other tables below. It is possible that the respondents misunderstood the words "send money home" as excluding cash taken home personally by them during home visits. This would be the case if the homes of the migrants are within short distances of their area of settlement.

As Table 9 shows, amounts varying from 1 Nigerian pound (about 3 U.S. dollars) to just over 80 Nigerian pounds (about 240 U.S. dollars) were sent home by the migrants in the year preceding the survey. About 11 percent, 19 percent and 25 percent respectively sent home sums of money ranging from £50 to over £80, £30 to over £80 and £20 to over £80. If we then include the migrants who sent home amounts between £10 and

Table 8.   Did you send money home during the past year?

Response	Number	Percent
Yes	468	54.9
No	372	43.6
No response	13	1.5
Total	853	100.0

Tabel 9.   Amount remitted home by migrants during the past year

Response	Number	Percent
Nothing	385	45.1
£1 – £9	105	12.3
£10 – £19	147	17.2
£20 – £29	55	6.5
£30 – £39	40	4.7
£40 – £49	27	3.2
£50 – £59	20	2.4
£60 – £69	20	2.4
£70 – £79	9	1.0
£80 and over	43	5.0
No response	2	0.2
Total	853	100.0

Table 10. Purposes for which money was remitted home by migrants

Responses	Number	Percent
Maintenance of relatives (parents, children, etc.)	408	87.2
Building	60	12.8
Total	468	100.0

Table 11. Migrants' intention to return home

Response	Number	Percent
Yes	500	58.6
No	333	39.0
No response	20	2.4
Total	853	100.0

£20, the proportion of migrants would increase to 45.4 percent. These proportions are significant because of what they imply about the demand on the total incomes of the migrants which, under conditions prevailing in agriculture in Nigeria, are generally small compared with non-agricultural urban incomes.

The purposes for which the remittance is made are shown in Table 10. By far the largest share of money went to the maintenance of relatives. The rest was for building.

Another evidence of the migrants' strong link with home is their intention to return home permanently at some future date (e.g. at old age). Table 11 shows that about three out of every five migrants intended to return home to settle. A large proportion, (39 percent), however, said that they had no intention of returning home. One can, however, be sure only of those who were definitely committed to returning home, since the implication of their response is that except for economic conditions in the home area, they were quite satisfied with the home situation in general. As for the other group, conditions do change and the home situation which displaced them might improve in the future, so that their attitude to their home areas might become positive.

On the other side of the coin are those indices that show a detached attitude toward the host area on the part of the migrants and so buttress their strong attachment to the home area. Two of these are inter-marriage with the women of the receiving area and ownership of buildings (as distinct from huts in the settlements) in any neighboring town. The relevant figures are shown in Tables 12 and 13. Over four-fifths of the migrants

Table 12.   Migrants' inter-marriage with the host population

Response	Number	Percent
Yes	125	14.7
No	724	84.9
No response	4	0.4
Total	853	100.0

Table 13.   Migrants' ownership of buildings in the towns around settlement

Response	Number	Percent
Yes	157	18.4
No	639	74.9
No response	57	6.7
Total	853	100.0

said they did not marry any of their wives from among the people of the area in which they were working, and three-quarters said they did not own any buildings in any of the towns around.

This strong link with home area has been a source of conflict between the migrants and the host population. One specific source of conflict, naturally, is the failure of many of the migrants to pay their taxes and rates to the host area where they earn their living. Many of them go home to pay their flat rate taxes and rates and, according to Udo

when accosted by tax agents of the district where they settle, they would readily produce their current tax and rates receipt ... In the case of the Igbira migrant farmers the practice ... was caused by the Igbira local authority which required that all migrants should pay their rates in their districts of origin. The reason for this ruling appears to be associated with the fact that the local authority was losing much of its revenue as a result of increasing migration of adult males to other parts of the country (1972: 4).

This lack of the feeling of belonging is, of course, not peculiar to the respondents in this study, but is a general characteristic of African migrants (Busia 1950; Acquah 1958: 104–105). One of the conditions attached to granting of citizenship to migrants in the Ahafo district of Ghana, for example, is that they should become fully identified with the host community by taking part in all communal projects directed at improving the locality, making monetary contributions like other citizens whenever the occasion demands it, and putting up permanent buildings in order to prove that they do not intend to send all their savings to their village of origin (Adomako-Sarfoh 1970).

CONCLUSION

There are two ways in which the mass movements of population from the savannah region to the forests of Yorubaland may be viewed. In one sense the migrants may be said to have increased the economic growth of the host territory because they pay some kind of rent to landlords in the area. They also pay (albeit grudgingly) taxes to the local authority of the area. Furthermore, the fact of their presence in large numbers underlines their indispensability to the host population who by and large have other urban interests and so could not make farming a fulltime occupation, quite apart from their continued migration to their home towns on a more permanent basis than before. About two out of every five landlords live in town and the remaining are by and large not permanent village dwellers, so that other urban activities would occupy their time while they are away from the village.

In another sense, the migrants may be regarded as exploiters. In spite of the fact that they pay rent to the landlords and taxes to the area of settlements, many malpractices have been reported whereby the share tenants, for example, falsify the quantity as well as the quality of grade of cocoa with a view to cheating the landlords. It is said that suspicious landlords often insist on being present when dried cocoa beans are being bagged and graded for marketing (Udo 1972: 3). This has been a source of constant friction between the migrants and their hosts. Moreover, a large part of the money derived from the host area is diverted to the home areas of the migrants, so that in terms of the development of the host area the direct contribution of the migrants is negligible. Perhaps this is inevitable in a country where socioeconomic disparities between political or geographical regions are very large and where the meagre resources of government are inadequate to bring about rapid overall development. It is only by this means that some kind of economic equilibrium can be brought about between regions of the country.

REFERENCES

ACQUAH, IONE
1958   *Accra survey*. London: London University.
ADEGBOYE, R. O.
1967   The need for land reform in Nigeria. *The Nigerian Journal of Economic and Social Studies* 9:339–350.

ADEPOJU, A.
1972   "Some aspects of migration and family relationships in south-west Nigeria." Seminar on Rural and Urban Family Life in West Africa, University of Ghana.

ADOMAKO-SARFOH, J.
1970   "Migrant farmers and cocoa farming in Brong-Ahafo South." First West African Regional Conference of Commonwealth Geographers, Legon, Ghana.

AGBOOLA, S. A.
1968   "Some factors of population distribution in the Middle Belt of Nigeria: the examples of northern Ilorin and Kabba," in *The population of tropical Africa*. Edited by J. C. Caldwell and C. Okonjo, 291–297. London: Longmans.

BARBOUR, K. M.
1965   Rural-rural migrations in Africa: a geographical introduction. *Cahiers de l'Institut de Science Economique Appliquée*.

BASCOM, W.
1959   Urbanism as a traditional African pattern. *Sociological Review* 7:31.

BUCHANAN, K. M., J. C. PUGH
1955   *Land and people in Nigeria*. London: London University Press.

BUSIA, K. A.
1950   *Survey of Sekondi-Takoradi*. London: Crown Agents for the Colonies.

GODDARD, S.
1965   Town-farm relationships in Yorubaland: a case study from Oyo. *Africa* 35:21.

GOLDING, F. D.
1925   *A statistical survey of the infestation of Dysdercus spp. on cotton in Nigeria*. Fourth Annual Bulletin of the Agricultural Department, Lagos.

GREEN, L.
1972   "Migration, urbanization and national development in Nigeria." Eleventh International African Seminar on Modern Migration in Western Africa, IDEP, Dakar.

INTERNATIONAL LABOUR ORGANISATION MISSION
1965   *Some trends in education in Western Region of Nigeria, 1955–1965*. Ibadan: Western Nigeria Government.

LITTLE, K.
1960   West African urbanization as a social process. *Cahiers d'Etude Africaines* 3:92.

LLOYD, P. C.
1955   The Yoruba lineage. *Africa* 3:236.
1959   The Yoruba town today. *The Sociological Review* 7:46.

MASON, T. G., G. H. JONES
1924   *A first survey of factors inhibiting the development of the cotton crop in Nigeria*. Third Annual Bulletin of the Agricultural Department, Lagos.

OLUSANYA, P. O.
1969   *Socio-economic aspects of rural-urban migration in Western Nigeria*. Ibadan: Nigerian Institute of Social and Economic Research.

1972 "Socio-economic disparities and internal migration in Nigeria: mass exodus of village dwellers to Yoruba towns." Eleventh International African Seminar on Modern Migration in Western Africa, IDEP, Dakar.

PROTHERO, R. M.
1968 "Migration in tropical Africa," in *The population of tropical Africa*. Edited by J. C. Caldwell and C. Okonjo, 250–263.

UDO, R. K.
1972 "Social relations of rural-rural migrants with host communities in southern Nigeria." Eleventh International African Seminar on Modern Migration in Western Africa, IDEP, Dakar.

Biographical Notes

John W. Adams (1929–   ) studied history as an undergraduate at Princeton and as a graduate student at Johns Hopkins before changing his field to social anthropology (Ph.D. Harvard, 1970). He has taught at Fordham University in New York City and at the University of South Carolina and was Northwest Coast Ethnologist at the Museum of Man, Ottawa. His research interests include myth and the regional organization of tribal societies. His publications include *The Gitksan Potlatch: population flux, resource ownership and reciprocity* (1973) and "Dialectics and contingency in the story of Asdiwal" (1974).

A. Bardhan was born in Comilla, Tripura (Bangla Desh) and has been a resident of India since 1948. She received her B.Sc. (Hons) and M.Sc. in Anthropology from Calcutta University. She was awarded a Junior Research fellowship (1963–1965) from the Council of Scientific and Industrial Research, Government of India for completing her Ph.D. dissertation on "Relationship of physique and menarche in Panjabi and Bengali girls." She obtained her Ph.D. from Delhi University in 1966. In the same year she received a Senior Research Fellowship from the Council of Scientific and Industrial Research, Government of India, for her project on "Socio-economic survey on schizophrenic patients of mental hospital of Delhi." In the same year she joined the National Institute of Family Planning as an anthropologist. Her special interests include research in the areas of population problems, family planning programs, population anthropology, teaching and training family planning personnel, evaluation of family planning programs, tribal demography, etc.

DINESH CHANDRA DUBEY (1927–   ) was born in India. He received his M.A. in Economics from S.D. College, Kanpur, in 1950. He did post-graduate degree work in Social Service Administration at the Tata Institute of Social Sciences, Bombay, in 1953 and received his Ph.D. in Sociology from Michigan State University in 1968. Since then he has been working in community development and rural development programs at the state and national level. He has been responsible for planning, implementing, and evaluating programs of social change for more than ten years. He joined the senior faculty of the National Institute of Family Planning, New Delhi, in 1962 where he is currently working as Head of the Social Research Division. He has conducted several studies in the field of family planning in India and has published several books and articles on community development and family planning.

KARAM ELAHI (Pakistan).   No biographical data available.

MARGARITA MARÍA ERRÁZURIZ (Chile).   No biographical data available.

GERARDO GONZALEZ (1936–   ) was born in Santiago, Chile. He studied Psychology at the Catholic University of Chile (1959–1964) and later continued his graduate studies at the University of Paris, where he received his Doctorate in Social Psychology. His dissertation was on birth control in marginal social sectors (1969). Since 1965, population, particularly population policies, has been his main field of research; he has published a number of papers published in this field. He is currently Head of the Population Policy Sector in the United Nations Latin American Demographic Center (CELADE).

JOHN GULICK (1924–   ) was born in Newton, Massachusetts. He received his B.A. (1949), M.A. (1951), and Ph.D. (1953) degrees from Harvard University. He is Professor of Anthropology at the University of North Carolina at Chapel Hill and was the first chairman of that University's Anthropology department. His numerous publications include books, chapters in books, and articles on urban anthropology and the modern cultures of the Middle East where he did field research in 1951–1952, 1961–1962, 1965, and 1970–1971.

MARGARET E. GULICK (1923–   ) was born in Fresno, California. She received her B.A. in Political Science from the University of California,

Berkeley in 1943 and is currently (1974) a graduate student in Sociology at the University of North Carolina at Chapel Hill. In 1970–1971, she was associated with John Gulick in the direction of the field research project in Isfahan, Iran, on which the article by them in this volume is based.

ALICE B. KASAKOFF (1941–   ) studied anthropology as an undergraduate at Radcliffe and as a graduate student at Harvard (Ph.D. 1970). She has done fieldwork in Peru, Tesuque Pueblo in New Mexico, and among the Gitksan Indians of British Columbia. Her research interests are currently focused on the application of geographical models to social anthropology and on demographic aspects of kinship. She has taught at Queens College, New York, and at the University of South Carolina. Her paper, "Lévi-Strauss' idea of the social unconscious," was included in *The unconscious in culture*, edited by Ino Rossi (1974).

MONI NAG (1925–   ) was born in India. He is the Chief of the Social Demography Section, International Institute for the Study of Human Reproduction and Senior Lecturer of Anthropology at Columbia University, New York. He received an M.Sc. in Statistics from Calcutta University in 1946, and M.A. and Ph.D. in Anthropology from Yale University in 1959 and 1961. He worked for the Anthropological Survey of India at Calcutta from 1948 to 1965 and has held several teaching and research positions at Columbia University since then. His special interest is in population anthropology and he is at present Chairman of the Population Commission of the International Union of Anthropological and Ethnological Sciences. Besides about fifteen articles related to population anthropology, he published a book entitled *Factors affecting fertility in nonindustrial societies: a cross-cultural study*.

AMNON ORENT (1935–   ) was born in Cologne, Germany. He emigrated to the United States in 1941. He received his B.A. from Brooklyn College (CUNY) in 1960, his M.A. in Anthropology from the University of Arizona in 1963, and his Ph.D. from the African Studies Center of Boston University in 1969. While on a research grant from the Foreign Area Fellowship Program of the Ford Foundation, 1965–1968, he did field research among the Kafa tribe of southwest Ethiopia. He has lectured at Boston University (1963–1965, 1968) and was Assistant Professor of Anthropology at the University of New Hampshire (1968–1971). He is currently a lecturer in Anthropology at Tel

Aviv University, Israel, in the School of Continuing Education in Medicine and in the Faculty of Humanities. He is also conducting research for the Ministry of Health (Division of Mental Health) in urban populations in Israel.

PHILIP O. OLUSANYA (1934–) was born in Nigeria. He received his university education in Sociology at the London School of Economics and Political Science (University of London), England. From 1965–1969 he was a Research Fellow in sociology at the Nigerian Institute of Social and Economic Research, University of Ibadan, Nigeria. Since 1969, he has been a Senior Lecturer at the University of Ife, Nigeria. His special interests include demography, urban studies, and ethnic relations.

STEVEN POLGAR (1931–) is Professor of Anthropology at the University of North Carolina, Chapel Hill. Born in Budapest, he studied anthropology at the University of Chicago and public health at Harvard. His research includes work in action anthropology with the Mesquakie Indians in Iowa, community development in West Africa, schizophrenics at Walter Reed Army Institute of Research, pregnancy and family planning in poverty areas of California and New York City, and library studies on evolution and ecology. He has been a consultant with the World Health Organization and is currently Visiting Professor at the University of Exeter in England.

STEPHEN P. REYNA (1943–) received his B.A. from Columbia College (1965), and his Ph.D. from Columbia University (1972). He has taught at the University of Ife, Nigeria (1968–1969); the College of William and Mary (1971–1973); and the University of New Hampshire (1973–present). During 1969–1971 he was director of the demographic section of the Institut National Chadian pour les sciences humaines, and from 1973–1974 worked as an anthropologist for the Lake Chad Basin Commission. His interests and publications are in cultural ecology, population studies, and social anthropology.

SUSAN C. SCRIMSHAW (1945–) grew up in Guatemala and has since worked in Bolivia, Barbados, Spanish Harlem, Ecuador, and Colombia. She received her B.A. from Barnard in 1967, an M.A. from Columbia in 1969, and a Ph.D. from Columbia in 1974. She is currently a Research Associate at Columbia University's International Institute for the Study of Human Reproduction, where she also teaches in Columbia's School of Public Health. She is a member of the ICAES Commission on Anthropological and Ethnological Factors in Population and of the Executive Board of the Society for Medical Anthropologists. Her publications have concentrated on anthropology and the delivery of health care, and on factors affecting fertility and the desire for family planning.

OLGA VIDLÁKOVÁ (1928–   ) was born in Duchcov, Czechoslovakia. She studied law at the Charles' University in Prague, where she received her Ph.D. in 1951. She is a research worker in the Institute of Landscape Ecology of the Czechoslovak Academy of Sciences and is responsible for demography and administrative law in anthropological studies. Her publications include works on law and population, population policy and environment, law and environment. She is a member of the Ruling Committee of the Czechoslovak Demographic Association and the International Union for the Scientific Study of Population (IUSSP).

BENJAMIN N. F. WHITE (1946–   ) was born in England. He studied at Oxford University (B.A. 1968) and is now at the Department of Anthropology, Columbia University, where he is writing a Ph.D. dissertation based on field research in a Javanese village in 1972–1973. His interests include anthropological demography, economic anthropology, Southeast Asian ethnography and contemporary development problems.

Index of Names

Index of Subjects